ECKERSLEY
SHAKESPEARE TRUST
WITH COMPLIMENTS

Copy nr. 115
The Library,
Meadow School for
Steiner Education,
Bruton

Number and Geometry in
Shakespeare's *Macbeth*

Number and Geometry in Shakespeare's *Macbeth*
The Flower and the Serpent

Sylvia Eckersley

Floris Books

First published in 2007 by Floris Books
© 2007 Sylvia Eckersley

Sylvia Eckersley has asserted her right under the
Copyright, Designs and Patents Act 1988
to be identified as the Author of this Work.

All rights reserved. No part of this publication may
be reproduced without the prior permission
of Floris Books, 15 Harrison Gardens, Edinburgh.
www.florisbooks.co.uk

British Library CIP Data available

ISBN 978-086315-592-5

Produced in Poland by Polskabook

Edited by Alan Thewless

Introduction by Carlotta Dyson, James Dyson
and Andrew Wolpert

Contents

Acknowledgements	9
Preface	11
Introduction	15
1. Overview	21
2. Developments of the Figure	35
The Riddle of the Nine Lines and the Seven Great Steps	
3. Scene Symmetry as Illustrated in Act I	49
4. The Counting of Prose in *Macbeth*	77
5. Play Symmetry	83
6. Act Centres and Act Symmetry	109
7. Number Rhythms	119
8. The Plot of *Macbeth* (Part 1)	133
9. The Plot of *Macbeth* (Part 2)	167
10. A Work in Progress *by Alan Thewless*	197
Additional Geometrical Attributes of the 'Figure.'	
11. Shakespeare and Wilton House	227
12. Finding and Constructing the 'Figure' for a Shakespeare Play	241
Appendices	247
Numbered First Folio Text	267
Endnotes	339
Bibliography	345

Acknowledgments

For Sylvia's lifelong work to come to expression through this volume we are especially indebted to the initiative and faithful support of Sonja Landweer and Christopher Marcus, whose vision of Sylvia's contribution to the field of Shakespearean research never faltered.

Chapter Ten is entirely my own and although its primary aim is to describe some important aspects of Sylvia's work that do not appear in the other chapters, I have also taken the opportunity to give some details of how Sylvia approached the study and analysis of a Shakespeare play. I hope this will help the reader to appreciate more fully the quality of her approach and the faculties that she employed.

I begin this chapter by giving something of an introductory background to 'the marriage of art and science' that is implicit in the idea that a Shakespeare play could contain an integral geometrical template. As this subject often occupied our conversations I hope that this contribution may be in keeping with Sylvia's wishes and her intent. The placement of this chapter towards the end of the book is justified in terms of its focus on the use and meaning of a play-figure as a universal tool towards understanding a Shakespeare play; a tool that has relevance over and beyond its unique way of incorporating play, act and scene symmetries — subjects developed in the earlier chapters.

During the latter phase to complete the book there were many who offered their help with the project and, certainly, without this help we would have made little progress. Thanks in particular are due to the staff of Park Attwood Clinic who nursed Sylvia through many difficult and painful times, and helped keep alight that spark of creativity that could so easily have faded many years before her death.

I am deeply grateful to those who previously helped Sylvia in her work, particularly Alan Stott and Veronica Cecil whose appreciation, advise and practical help kept the fires of enthusiasm alive for Sylvia. Andrew Wolpert, of Emerson College, and Dr James Dyson and Carlotta Dyson have also offered a high level of stewardship for Sylvia's work over many years, and without their warm encouragement and support Sylvia would have lost much momentum. In the same vein, I would also like to thank Don Ratcliffe and Sue Whalley for their longterm practical support. I would also like to acknowledge and thank Eric Whitehead, who made the invaluable contribution of much labour on the early computer drawings of the play 'figures,' and Janice Balaskas for the sacrifice of many hours of painstaking proof reading, and practical assistance.

I am honoured that the highly respected Renaissance scholar, Kristin Rygg, took such an interest in Sylvia's research and offered so much in the way of advice. This connection was especially appreciated because Sylvia was so deeply impressed by Kristin's book, *The Masqued Mysteries Unmasked (Pythagoreanism and Early Modern North European Music Theatre)*. I would also like to express my gratitude to the trustees of the 'Eckersley Shakespeare Trust' for their support and confidence, and hope that my contribution to this project has not fallen too short of their expectations.

Permission for the reproduction of pages from the Facsimile Edition of the First Folio (Library of Congress catalogue number 52-9272), the 'Droeshout Portrait,' the 'Address to the Great Variety of Readers' and the title page for *Macbeth* was given by Yale University Press and the Beinecke Library at Yale, possessor of the original copy.

Permission to reproduce the views of Wilton House and the portraits of the third and fourth Earls of Pembroke was kindly granted by the Earl of Pembroke and the Trustees of the Wilton House Trust, Wilton House, Salisbury, UK.

Thanks also to the Trustees of The British Museum for permission to reproduce photographs of the Gilded Brass Astrolabe and the Astronomical Compendium.

Many thanks to Michael Best and 'Internet Shakespeare Editions' for their on-line First Folio text of *Macbeth,* which was utilized as a basis for the full Numbered Text reproduced towards the rear of this volume.

Alan Thewless

Preface

In 1984 Sylvia wrote to her colleague and friend, Dr. Paul Allen: 'It could either be the perfect moment for the publication of my book — or, if the worst has happened for me, part of what I have to say may have already been said ...' At this time Sylvia had already been working on the main themes for about twenty-five years, deepening and refining her ideas. Many of the essential elements were at a stage where they could be shared and already about three chapters had been written. However, the completion of the book was increasingly hampered by Sylvia's deteriorating health; this manifested itself most dramatically in the form of rheumatoid arthritis, a condition she had suffered since the age of nineteen.

It is not completely accurate, however, to lay blame for the prolonged development of the book solely on Sylvia's ill health, there was also considerable reluctance on her part to present the work too hastily to the public. This reluctance came from a deep struggle to resolve the demands of science with those of art. Born from a long line of scientists going back to the eminent Sir Thomas Huxley, (colleague of Charles Darwin) and going through to her father, Thomas Lydwell Eckersley, who was described as one of the most brilliant research workers of the century in the field of radar development, Sylvia too manifested the scientist's clarity of intellect while also developing a great sensitivity and giftedness for the visual arts. The scientist within her was striving constantly to carry out more and more research and to delve into ever greater detail, and the artist, while striving to grasp and put into words the experience of truth and beauty, was never quite happy with the wrought work and always wanted to make a new attempt.

In the 1980s and 90s Sylvia was becoming well known, albeit within a modest circle of colleagues, for her Shakespeare research, her talks and workshops on the plays, and there was excitement, even some impatience, surrounding the expected completion of the book on *Macbeth*. Unfortunately, Sylvia was now deep into her seventies and it was becoming clearer to those closest to her that the rigours of a lifetime's struggle with illness were overwhelming all possibility of progress on the book. Sylvia's good friend, the artist Sonja Landweer, then stood firm and demanded action, and an initiative to help Sylvia finish her book began in the summer of 1999 through the strong backing of the producer and playwright, Christopher Marcus. Christopher's faithful help and enthusiastic support were to prove invaluable in the project. At this point, I was able to take a sabbatical break from teaching and become more involved, working with Sylvia on a day to day basis as her assistant. Throughout this time, and in the months that followed, there was indomitable help from Dr James Dyson, Carlotta Dyson, Jacqui Thewless, Sue Whalley and many others in virtually every sphere of need, ranging from archiving through to house moves and domestic chores; all of which were essential in keeping open the window of opportunity for Sylvia's creativity.

Sylvia's health was now so fragile that only slow progress on the book could be achieved and only through the use of a tape recorder. Miraculously, we were given just over one year to work together intensively — a period of grace created by the goodwill of all who stood around the project. Although Sylvia achieved a great deal in the course of that year, we had gone beyond the 'eleventh hour' and on Palm Sunday, April 6, 2001, Sylvia died. Now like Prospero she would give up her magical arts, and her struggles in this world, to take a new journey, in the 'bark' of the gods, back to those spheres to which she felt so attuned in this life.

It was remarkable that on the day Sylvia could work no longer on her book I received a letter from the Charity Commission granting Charitable status to the group of trustees who would safeguard her literary estate; the countless manuscripts notes and drawings that were the result of her life's dedication to Shakespearean research. It was as if Sylvia had arranged, with Pythagorean precision, that on this day the results of her life's work would pass on from her own stewardship to that of a group.

The Eckersley Shakespeare Trust was formed in October 2000 with support from the late Vivian Law (Reader in the History of Linguistic Thought at Cambridge University and Fellow of Trinity College) and Professor Robert Nigel Alexander (Glasgow Academy, St Andrew's University, Magdalen College Oxford), colleagues in whom Sylvia had found a wealth of encouragement and advice. We were also extremely grateful for the support of the late Henry Herbert, the 17th Earl of Pembroke, who was well aware, and supportive, of Sylvia's studies concerning Wilton House, his ancestral home (see Chapter 11).

Regarding the reader's embarkation on the book a warning should be given concerning the variableness of some of the chapters, particularly

PREFACE   13

Chapters V, VI and VII. These have a sketchy and complex character and were only completed as first drafts when Sylvia died. They have been included in sequence but would certainly have been worked on much further had Sylvia been with us longer. However, a persistent reader will gain a great deal from 'struggling' in sequence with those earlier chapters as they present important background material for what comes later.

With regard to the later chapters and the theme of the hidden plot, Sylvia said: 'If we imagine the play as a deep pool, the story we are familiar with can be likened to the images which play on the surface of the pool. They have great richness. Yet, of a sudden, one's gaze can start to penetrate through the surface into the life within the pool's depths.' This 'life within the pool's depths' was something that Sylvia saw in the most vivid way through the auspices of play geometry, and wished to portray accurately in this book.

It was Sylvia's great wish that her work should have practical as well as scholarly results and in this way she hoped that one day *Macbeth* could be produced on stage according to the discoveries made of the hidden plot. Indeed, this book should only be counted as truly finished when such an event actually occurs. That would be a suitable epilogue indeed.

The subtitle of this book, *The Flower and the Serpent,* was not given by Sylvia herself, but comes from the words of Lady Macbeth that so intrigued Sylvia:

> Your Face, my *Thane*, is as a Booke, where men
> May reade strange matters, to beguile the time.
> Looke like the time, beare welcome in your Eye,
> Your Hand, your Tongue: looke like th' innocent flower,
> But be the Serpent vnder't ...   (1, 4)

Sylvia saw here that the image of the flower bore resemblance to the form of the *Macbeth* play 'figure;' she likened the serpent to the 'time-stream' of the play 'figure' as it coils around to complete the form. One can also see the whole play, as presented on stage, as a beautiful flower. Under this flower resides the coiling serpent of the 'figure' which, born from the seemingly constraining realms of number and form, at first seems to bring only death to the play. When we struggle at this threshold and make the discovery that this threatening serpent faithfully serves the greater mysteries of the play, acting as guide to its deeper layers of meaning, we know that we have discovered a play of greater proportions that we ever imagined. Such is the aim of this book.

It is hoped that these efforts may only serve to honour the magnitude and universality that poured forth from William Shakespeare, whose fount of creativity is a constant source of self knowledge and illumination.

> Just as in the morning all the stars of the night pale before the light of the rising sun, so the names and enterprises of all the other writers grew dim when suddenly, out of the teeming activity of the Elizabethan Theatre, there burst upon the world the full radiance of Shakespeare's sun-star.*

Alan Thewless.
February 2007.

---

* *Shakespeare and the Awakening of Modern Consciousness* by Friedric Hiebel

Introduction

In this book, Sylvia Eckersley claims to have discovered the hidden structure in Shakespeare's *Macbeth,* which compellingly suggests — maybe even discloses — new meanings in the play. We are invited to reappraise the characters of the Thane of Cawdor, Duncan and Lady Macbeth; there is a chilling insight into the life of the child Lady Macbeth speaks of; and the circumstances of her own death are shown to be less than straightforward. An astonishing series of subplots weaving beneath the surface of the spoken lines — with far-reaching implications for interpretation and dramatization — emerges from Sylvia's structural analysis of the play, discernible in terms of scenes and acts. There may also be implications for Shakespeare's true relationship with his patron, King James I, in whose presence the play was first performed, as well as for our evaluation of the quality of the First Folio text, which is often dismissed as a repository for textual errors and misprints.

Sylvia first had intimations of symmetry after learning the text of *Macbeth* by heart, but was unable to quite pin it down in relation to any of the modern printed texts available. (Depending on the way the text is printed the number of lines will vary). When she applied arithmetic and geometry to the line numbering of the First Folio edition, Sylvia was able to identify a series of internal correspondences and symmetries in the scenes, acts and the play as a whole. The application of this method then revealed a remarkably beautiful structure, a kind of geometrical-architectural template, which she calls the 'figure,' hidden within the tapestry of the play. It was daunting both to Sylvia herself and then to almost everybody else she originally spoke to. These findings seemed at first uncanny — even bizarre — but that did not deter her from tirelessly pursuing her quest, or from subjecting other Shakespearean plays to her method of structural analysis. In every case, a specific 'figure' was to emerge, often revealing further interpretative insights.

It was to the study of *Macbeth*, however, that Sylvia devoted her time and energy most consistently, leading to the clearest revelations, at least with respect to the plot and the resulting dramatic interpretations. These revelations shed further light on the psychodynamics behind the murders, modifying traditional views of their underlying motive and challenging the reader to reappraise the often stereotyped assumption that pure ambition lay at the heart of Macbeth's demise. As a result, the workings of evil are revealed to be far more subtle and also far more comprehensible, if no less tragic.

The mathematics that is asserted in Sylvia's thesis is easily verifiable. However, it is much more of a challenge to embrace the way in which it is applied, and its wider methodological implications. Does her approach decipher a hidden code, providing a key to new dimensions of interpretation? Or is it merely a contrived technique, producing a spider's web in which the author becomes trapped by both geometric and psychological projections? Our starting point is to acknowledge the existence of a mighty, all-encompassing, all-sustaining creative source of Being. It appears to us that the creative genius of Shakespeare could only derive these universally human dramas from such an archetypal source. In the great Logos structure of a cosmos that reveals itself in every detail of observable phenomena, everything is interrelated by links that enshrine and guarantee the congruence of each single part with the greater whole, embodying alignments right down into the smallest fragment. Every detail reveals meaning; nothing is arbitrary.

It is unfashionable to imagine that the spontaneous inspiration underlying artistic creativity could ever be considered to be calculable. To subject the beauty of language and expressive idiom to dry arithmetic, or even geometry, invites the critic to suggest methodological distortion and even obsession. Artistic inspiration does not need to be shown to 'add up;' moreover, to reveal that it does so is a dangerous occupation. Sylvia's research may undoubtedly provoke the accusation of one-sidedness, but this is an inevitable risk for the isolated pioneer devoted to the rigorous pursuit of an original approach, and who remains the lonely champion of its results. Sylvia herself was ever conscious of the broadest spiritual context, nowhere more evident than in the dramatic authenticity and linguistic economy of Shakespeare's writing. The focused direction of this research bears witness to the greater picture which she cherished, and to which she remained ultimately devoted. Greater truths need not be diminished by her thesis but may even be potentially enhanced.

The aim of Sylvia's research goes far beyond the arithmetical verification of theories contained within a closed system. If what is postulated in this book is true, it is an expression of the objective dimension of number and of the precision, harmony and integrity of a work of art.

INTRODUCTION   17

While mathematics may be seen as an art as well as a science, Sylvia's calculations are not undertaken purely for their own sake. Our culture tends to consider truth, beauty and goodness as elusive, variable and subjective perceptions. The notion that they might also be amenable to objectively calculable processes seems suspect to the sceptical reasoning of the modern mind. Certainly the calculations reveal something that is much greater than arithmetic. If we awaken to the spiritual origin of the inspiration behind art, then we can recognise the universal qualities and affirm our subjective relationship to them. Moreover, we will not necessarily be surprised if these are also accessible via the objective language of mathematics. We may recall how the discovery of the 'golden mean' in architecture, as well as Pythagoras' mathematical understanding of musical tones, have enhanced our appreciation of the visual arts and music. Mathematics is the language through which the individual is able to grasp truths beyond the individual ego. Language is the medium in which the individual ego consciously realizes and expresses itself.

There are those who possess an intuitive Platonic sense for geometric structure; others might be endowed with a Pythagorean gift for conceiving such harmonies in the form of numbers. For those versed in the knowledge of the sacred geometry underlying classical architecture, art and music, it should come as no surprise that mathematics reveals and expresses at least one aspect of this universal order. And yet the notion that such numerical correspondence could be rightfully sought in the brilliant, but presumably hastily scribbled and inaccurately copied, words of an often improvising playwright four hundred years ago, seems at best unlikely and at worst frankly absurd. However, when a pioneer in this field claims to have discerned this hidden truth and resolutely perseveres with her research, the results at least deserve to be given a fair hearing, irrespective of how improbable, or even unpalatable, the assumptions underlying the methodology might seem. Are we willing to allow the phenomena to speak and to demonstrate to us that Shakespeare's mercurial, artistic energy both carries, and is carried by, archetypal cosmic form? Could it have been precisely the task of Hemming and Condell to put right, in the First Folio, the inaccuracies that had found their way into the texts of Shakespeare's plays, either through inevitable circumstance and naïve human hands or, as they themselves declared in their introduction, to ensure that:

> ...diverse stolne, and surreptitious copies, maimed,
> and deformed by the frauds and stealths of iniurious

> impostors, that expos'd them: [that] even those, are now
> offer'd to your view cur'd, and perfect in their limbes;
> and all the rest, absolute in their numbers, as he con-
> ceived them...

Sylvia Eckersley's studies span both mathematics and language. She has sought to give voice to the meaning behind Shakespeare's words that revealed itself to her through the harmonies of number and form. If the 'figure' that Eckersley has discerned bears a true relation to the cosmic archetype behind the play, then it attests to the magnitude of what flowed through Shakespeare — and to the mighty inspiration for which he was the instrument! Seen in this light, the secret of his genius does not lie in encyclopaedic knowledge or comprehensive life experience, which some regard as unavailable to a provincial glovemaker's son, but rather in his self-less capacity to serve this Logos-archetype, both in its content and structure.

In the realm of the Logos, substance and form are inseparable, constituting a unity of Being and manifestation. It is this unity that breathes through Shakespeare's creativity as a playwright, permeating his use of language and his sovereign grasp of stagecraft. We cannot be surprised that the mighty cosmic source of this art would render its earthly result nothing less than '... perfect in their limbes' ... and '... absolute in their numbers ...'. Shakespeare's genius was to be the channel through which unity could come to expression in diversity. While we cannot discount the possibility that he may sometimes have counted lines, we cannot imagine that he constructed his text intellectually. If he appeared to write on whim, this spontaneity was the expression of his intuitive attunement to the Logos content. It was through a comparable achievement that the great human story born out of the Greek temples could transcend its Mystery origins and become 'such stuff' as drama is made of. The stage the world became will become the world again; Prospero may be seen as the precursor of the next step by which the theatre is transposed back into life.

We can recognise the value of a particular field of research and the general validity of its results without necessarily having to accept every last detail of interpretation. Sylvia Eckersley died before this book was ready to be published. She would have welcomed the opportunity to engage in dialogue — to a far greater extent than her life circumstances allowed — with scholars, actors, directors, producers and lovers of

Shakespeare generally. Had this been possible, then perhaps the scope of her work would have increased still further and some of its finer details may have changed. Yet these very details are highly provocative in their own right, mutually supportive and certainly intriguing, and the scope of the work is surely more than equal to the task it sets out to accomplish.

The Trustees of Sylvia's literary legacy are greatly indebted to Alan Thewless, without whose intensive collaboration with Sylvia in the last eighteen months of her life, her long endeavour to assemble the details of her research into a coherent form suitable for publication may well not have come to fruition. We are also immensely grateful to Alan for completing the final editing and for adding Chapter 10, in which he provides precious insights into how Sylvia worked and into some of the wider implications of her unfinished research.

Sylvia had hoped that her work on *Macbeth* could serve as a model for similar research on other Shakespeare plays, taking it beyond the 'figures' which she had 'discovered' for many of them, and perhaps incorporating some of the fragments of research she herself was able to do. All this material is preserved by the Trustees of her literary legacy in the Eckersley Shakespeare Trust archive, with the intention of making it available to researchers interested in continuing this work.

As this unusual work is launched, it remains for the reader to decide for himself whether the proposed thesis deepens the Shakespearean story as such, resolves some of the apparent contradictions in *Macbeth* and enhances the dramatic content of this play. In Prospero's words from the Epilogue of Shakespeare's *The Tempest:*

> Gentle breath of yours my sails must fill,
> or else my project fails, which was to please.

Carlotta Dyson
James Dyson
Andrew Wolpert

1. Overview

At the time of the Renaissance Neo-Platonic ideas, first put forward in Italy, became widespread in Europe. The works of men such as Pico della Mirandola, Francesco Giorgi and Alberti, had a strong influence on the architects of the time, who composed their buildings according to numerical and musical harmonies. The major poets were likewise influenced, though less openly. The list of those, in whose works a numerical structure has been discerned later, includes Dante, Spenser, Milton, Chapman and Donne, as well as many others. It also includes Shakespeare, whose early poem 'Venus and Adonis' has been analyzed by Professor Alastair Fowler along the same lines.[1]

However, no study of Shakespeare's plays from the number aspect seems to have been published so far, although Professor Fowler clearly recognises Shakespeare as one of the greatest numerologists of all. Whereas much numerology is simply a matter of 'decorum' Professor Fowler claims that, in 'Venus and Adonis,' an awareness of number structure is essential to a full appreciation of the meaning.

Here, a more far-reaching claim will be made, namely that an awareness of the number structure of a Shakespeare *play* is essential to a full appreciation of its *plot*. Admittedly, this sounds both arrogant and preposterous. How can there be number structure in plays written at high speed by an actor-poet? They are too copious, too spontaneous and free — and they have no stanzas or regular paragraphs. Are we to suppose that Shakespeare counted lines?

This is indeed unthinkable — at least in any ordinary use of the word 'count' — though in fact the plays do have a kind of subterranean stanzaic structure. However, we should establish the phenomena first, and afterwards try to explain them; and the phenomena are there, in at least nine of Shakespeare's plays, for anyone to observe.[2]

Everything I claim rests essentially on one happy moment of serendipity, which followed many years of questioning and research related chiefly to scene symmetry. Sometime in the early 1950s, I was asked to take a class of school children for English Literature for one term, and the book chosen was Shakespeare's *Macbeth*. While rereading the Banqueting Scene, which we proposed to act, I was struck by two lines near the beginning of the scene (Act 3 Scene 4). The lords have just arrived and have been welcomed by Macbeth and more indirectly by Lady Macbeth, who is evidently sitting a little apart on a throne or grand chair (that is, not at the table). Macbeth says:

1190	*Macb.* Our selfe will mingle with Society,
1191	And play the humble Host:
1192	Our Hostesse keepes her State, but in best time
1193	We will require her welcome.

Lady Macbeth replies:

1194	*La.* Pronounce it for me Sir, to all our Friends,
1195	For my heart speakes, they are welcome.

At this moment the First Murderer comes in, presumably at a side door, and is not instantly observed by Macbeth. The Lords must now be bowing and smiling towards the Queen; Macbeth says:

1196	*Macb.* See they encounter thee with their harts thanks

Then he turns towards the table, where the Lords have just sat down, and continues:

1197	Both sides are euen: heere Ile sit i'th' mid'st,

As I had been recently studying Shakespeare's scene symmetry, I was struck by these two lines. They had very much the quality of a centre but, on further investigation, they were found to be nowhere near the centre of this scene; they were nearer the beginning. It struck me then that they could not be far away from the centre of the whole play; it certainly seemed like this in my edition. But if so, was it intentional? There seemed to be no way of finding an answer to this question because every editor has his own ideas about lineation, even regarding which passages are corrupt and maybe should be cut out altogether. There seemed to be very little I could do to ascertain whether those striking lines were intended by their author to mark the very centre of the play. It did not occur to me to look in the First Folio because of the reputation of that book as a carelessly edited volume and one certainly not to be

1. OVERVIEW

relied upon. It was not until many years later, when working in a public library in Essex, that I observed a handsome volume bound in greenish grey — a facsimile of Shakespeare's First Folio edited by the American scholar Charlton Hinman.[3] Idly I lifted it out and observed that it was numbered, not in terms of scenes, as usual, but in terms of whole plays. Every printed line counted as 'one' and this included all stage directions. It occurred to me to see where, on this system, those two central-sounding lines in *Macbeth* actually fell. So I counted the lines taken up by stage directions and subtracted them from the grand total. This calculation came to 2392 lines. Then I looked for the position of the two lines:

    1196   *Macb*. See they encounter thee with their harts thanks
    1197   Both sides are euen: heere Ile sit i'th' mid'st,

These fell at lines 1196 and 1197. In a play totalling 2392 (not counting stage directions) 2392 divided by 2 equals 1196. Therefore, by this method of counting they fell at the exact centre of the play! It took a little while to grasp the full significance of this; it was either coincidental or a 'one-off' and some kind of joke in this particular play; or it had implications for the printing of the First Folio which were quite extraordinary.

Before looking more closely at the text of *Macbeth* I located, with the help of Charlton Hinman's numbering system, the mathematical centre of three more plays: *Julius Caesar,* which directly precedes *Macbeth* in the Tragedy section of the First Folio, *A Midsummer Night's Dream* and *The Merchant of Venice,* both of which come in the first, or Comedy, section. The centre of *Julius Caesar* (Play-lines 1312 & 1313) falls around the middle of Act 3 Scene 1, shortly after Caesar has been murdered. The play centre falls just after the re-entry of Mark Anthony:

                  Enter Antony
                  Bru. But heere comes Antony:
                  Welcome Mark Antony.
                      Ant. (*gazing at the body of Caesar*)
                  Ant. O mighty Caesar! Dost thou lye so lowe?
Play   1312   Are all thy Conquests, Glories, Triumphes, Spoiles
Centre 1313   Shrunke to this little Measure? Fare thee well
                  I know not Gentlemen what you intend,
                  Who else must be let blood, who else is ranke:
                  If I my selfe, there is no houre so fit

>   As Caesars deaths houre; nor no Instrument
>   Of halfe that worth, as those your Swords; made rich
>   With the most Noble blood of all this World

The Play centre of *The Merchant of Venice* comes early in Act III shortly after Bassanio has arrived in Belmont, and after a brief conversation with Portia in which she tries to persuade him to stay a little while before coming to the caskets to make his choice. The central passage begins:

>   *Bass.* Let me choose,
> For as I am, I liue vpon the racke.
>   *Por.* Vpon the racke Bassanio, then confesse
> What treason there is mingled with your loue.
>   *Bass.* None but that vglie treason of mistrust.
> Which makes me feare the enioying of my loue:
> There may as well be amitie and life,
> 'Tweene snow and fire, as treason and my loue.
>   *Por.* I, but I feare you speake vpon the racke,
> Where men enforced doth speake any thing.

Play Centre { 1331 / 1332 }

>   *Bass.* Promise me life, and ile confesse the truth.
>   *Por.* Well then, confesse and liue.
>   *Bass.* Confesse and loue
> Had beene the verie sum of my confession:
> O happie torment, when my torturer
> Doth teach me answers for deliuerance:
> But let me to my fortune and the caskets.

The lines at the very centre of *The Merchant of Venice* are lines 1331 and 1332.

The total count of play-lines for *A Midsummer Night's Dream* is 2138 and at the centre of the play, in Act 3 Scene 2 (lines 1069 and 1070), we are brought to the moment when Demetrius finally gives up his vain chase of Hermia.[4]

>   *Her.* A priuiledge, neuer to see me more;
> And from thy hated presence part I: see me no more
> Whether he be dead or no. *Exit.*
>   *Dem.* There is no following her in this fierce vaine,
> Here therefore for a while I will remaine.

1. OVERVIEW

		So sorrowes heauinesse doth heauier grow:
Play	1069	For debt that bankrout slip doth sorrow owe,
Centre	1070	Which now in some slight measure it will pay,
		If for his tender here I make some stay. *Lie downe.*

What do we find when we compare the central lines of these various plays and relate them to the central lines of *Macbeth?* We straight away notice that the word 'measure' appears both in *Julius Caesar* and in *A Midsummer Night's Dream* also just after the play centre of *Macbeth* Macbeth says:

1198	... anon wee'l drinke a Measure
1199	The Table round. There's blood vpon thy face.

That is just after he has seen Banquo's murderer at the door. Mark Anthony, gazing at Caesar's murdered body, says:

	1311	*Ant.* O mighty *Caesar*! Dost thou lye so lowe?
Play	1312	Are all thy Conquests, Glories, Triumphes, Spoiles,
Centre	1313	Shrunke to this little Measure? Fare thee well.

This word 'measure' does not occur close to the centre of *The Merchant of Venice,* but there is another word indicating quantity, the word 'sum:'

1133	*Bass.* Confesse and loue
1134	Had beene the verie sum of my confession:

Again, we have the indication of an exact amount!

We observe that in two of the centres we have looked at there is a prostrate body; the dead body of Caesar, covered with a bloody cloak, and the nearly asleep one of Demetrius who has collapsed on the ground in despair. In the other two plays there is the thought of a prostrate body; in *Macbeth* the murderer appears at the door of the banqueting hall just before the two central lines and immediately we are aware of what he has just done — that is, murdered Banquo and left him lying 'With twenty trenched gashes on his head,' (Act 3 Scene 4, line 30). In *The Merchant of Venice* the talk between Bassanio and Portia has just been of the 'rack,' that instrument of torture where the victim lies down and is pulled apart to the point of agony.

We could say that at every play centre encountered so far there is either a physically present prostrate body or the thought of such a body. At three play centres, in *The Merchant of Venice, A Midsummer Night's Dream* and *Julius Caesar* there is suffering — Bassanio's agonising uncertainty, Demetrius' weary despair, Mark Anthony's controlled sorrow and rage. Only at the centre of *Macbeth* is there no obvious suffering but instead false joviality. Yet behind this mask and surfacing from his earlier words, 'O full of scorpions is my mind dear wife,' we recognise his true inner state.

Although the sample was a small one, after considering these other play centres I was left with a strong impression that although none was as explicit as the centre of *Macbeth*, they had certain properties in common, recognisable by anyone looking out for them. I felt reassured that the *Macbeth* centre was not a coincidence or a 'one-off.'

The next step was to look at the pages that preface the thirty-six printed plays in the First Folio. These early pages of prefatorial material include: poems by Ben Jonson and others; the rather strange Droeshout engraving of the poet's face and upper body; the dedication to the Pembroke brothers; 'The Address to the Great Variety of Readers;' the catalogue of the plays included in the book divided neatly into Comedies, Histories and Tragedies; and, finally, the list of principal actors in Shakespeare's plays. Was there any hint to be found here that this book was something more than it appeared to be?

Indeed there was and when I found it in 'The Address to the Great Variety of Readers' it spoke so loudly and clearly that it felt more like a statement than a hint. This address first exhorts the reader to buy the book and then goes on to regret that the author himself was not able to edit it. Finally, it pleads that the actual editors — John Heminge and Henry Condell — have spent much time in that task (in fact seven years altogether) and then makes the remarkable claim:

> ...as where (before) you were abus'd with diverse stolne, and surreptitious copies, maimed, and deformed by the frauds and stealthes of iniurious impostors, that expos'd them: even those, and now offer'd to your view cur'd, and perfect in their limbes; and all the rest, absolute in their numbers, as he conceived the.' (see Plate 2)

1. OVERVIEW

This short passage, I discovered later, is taken by scholars to mean that the metre in the printed plays is now correct, but I think that a seven-year-old might understand it better! Numbers here mean numbers in their commonest sense and the opening words of this address might warn us that a certain childish simplicity is required. 'From the most able to him that can but spell there you are numbered.' It might well have been written, 'From the most able to him that can but *count* there you are numbered.' These words are in fact an invitation to the reader to examine the numerical setting out of the text.

It is of course true that to count 'one' for each printed line of speech, regardless of how many words or syllables this contains, makes no obvious sense in relation to our understanding of prosody. It does not teach us where a whole pentameter should be regarded as complete, nor how long we should pause between two half-pentameters printed on separate lines. Above all, it does not teach us how we should regard prose, where the length of a printed line seems to be more or less arbitrary and unconnected with rhythm. One can only suppose that this primitive method of giving each line the numerical value of 'one' provides us with the 'answers' we need, like the answers in the back of an arithmetic text book, though not as yet the logical steps by which these answers are reached! For prose passages I had simply to accept a rule of thumb: 'each line of printed prose must be treated exactly like a line of printed verse.' Later I will discuss the problem of prose at more length and show how the counting of prose-lines in the First Folio can, after all, make perfect sense.

Earlier studies of scene-symmetry in *Macbeth* — together with a certain faith in the original text and the literal precision of metaphor — had already led me to suspect the presence of a new plot working like a strong undercurrent within the play. The question now was this: would an accurate mapping of the structure of this play, from the point of view of its number structure, substantiate this alternative plot?

Macbeth, a relatively short play, presents many problems to scholars. Some regard it as so compact and well-built that it could scarcely have been altered. Others believe that Act 1, Scene 2 is almost certainly interpolated or mutilated, and that the Hecate scenes are not original. Traces of a fuller treatment of the Cawdor story are suspected, and the extraordinary length of Act 4, Scene 3 is felt to be out of scale with the rest.

Carelessness, cutting, re-writing are suspected, yet the exact position of the central lines suggest that the Folio text may, after all, be undamaged. We allow ourselves to regard the oddities as intentional, and just because they are peculiar, to take them seriously as hints or clues. In fact, the structure of the play does confirm the new plot (or rather the original and implied plot, buried with deliberation and good reason), but on the way it leads us into an entirely new country.

My first attempt at gaining a sense of the structure of the play proceeded as follows. The play was mapped on graph-paper, with the scale, 1 Folio line: $1/_{10}$ inch. The map showed, in continuous linear form, the simple features of the text — act divisions, scene divisions, exits, entrances, passages of prose and (later) songs. A similar map, not quite so accurate, might have been made from a copy of the Folio text, with the double columns divided into single ones and these laid end to end. The effect of the map was to display visually proportions, which are usually experienced by the ear. But since our visual sense today is so strong, it showed many things in a striking way, which had not previously been recognised.

The centre of the play was also marked, and later the centres of all Acts and Scenes (though I was not yet sure about the structure of Acts).[5] This led to a natural use of the geometrical compass. With its point at a scene or act centre, mirrored passages might be conveniently linked by arcs of a circle, thus:

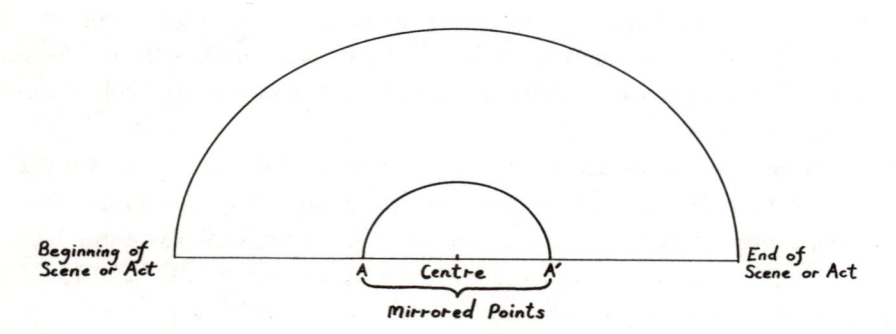

Figure I

In this way, time was expressed by a straight line and relationships by curved lines. The idea, however, of reversing this seemed at once more in tune with tradition and experience. The heavenly bodies, from which our sense of time is derived, move in curves: so I let the time-stream of the play be curved, and the relationship between mirrored passages be straight.

At once the question arose: in what manner of curve should the time-stream flow? The question was simultaneously logical, geometrical and

1. OVERVIEW

aesthetic. The curve must be continuous; a threefold symmetry must appear, qualitatively different for play, act and scene. The numbers of the play gave me enough information to construct such a figure exactly.

I was looking for a geometrical form, something like a circle, but not just a circle; like a spiral, but with its end coinciding with the beginning. The essential hint was found in Act I of *Macbeth*. This act contains seven scenes whose sum is 540, or 6 x 90 lines. In linear form the act looks like this:

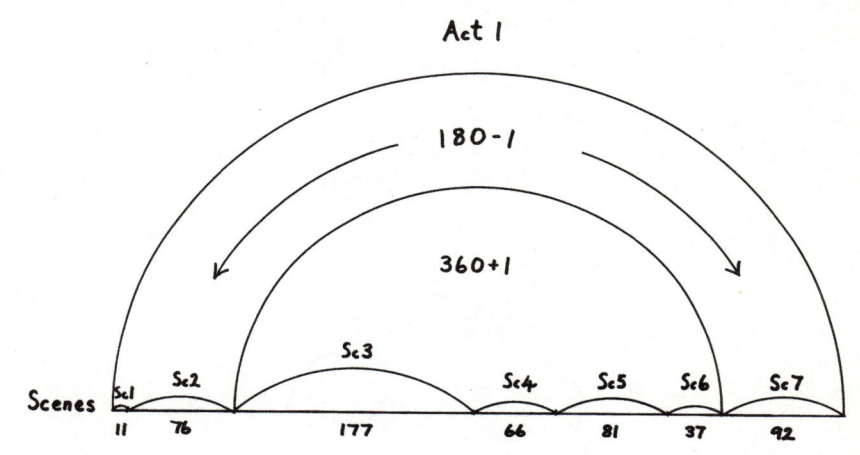

Figure 2

It may be observed that Scenes 1 and 2 are roughly balanced by Scene 7, and that Scene 3 (the long scene on the Heath) is roughly balanced by Scenes 4, 5 and 6. The centre falls near the beginning of Scene 4.

It may also be observed that the sum of the four 'inner' scenes is (360 + 1) lines, and the sum of the three 'outer' scenes (180 − 1) lines.[6] These numbers at once suggested the degrees of a circle. The curve implied here must be:

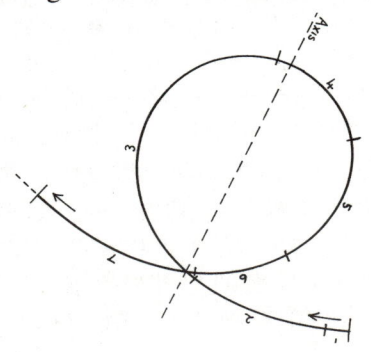

Figure 3

Aesthetically, all acts must have the same basic form. The 'wings' may differ in length from act to act, but the central circle must surely be the same. I had to imagine five such loops, dancing in a ring and then taking hands. Like this:

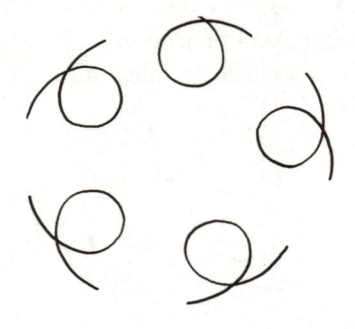

Figure 4

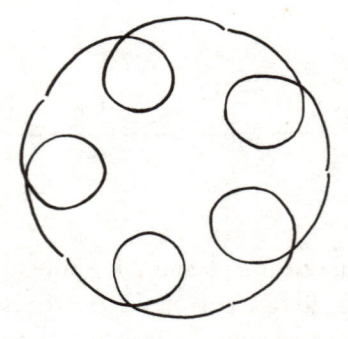

Figure 5

The numbers of the play gave me enough information to construct such a figure with exactness. We only have to subtract 360 lines in turn from each act total, add up the bits left over to make a great embracing circle and, finally, make a small but crucial amendment, to come to a total for the great circle of 600 lines. By this simple calculation we arrive at a total for the great circle of 600 lines and a ratio for the whole figure of 600:360 or 5:3. Calibration is not difficult. Anyone with elementary geometric skills and a good protractor could achieve it. The angles of act axes are determined by the lengths of the wings in the individual acts. The figure, accurately drawn on a small scale, but without detail, looks like this:

1. OVERVIEW

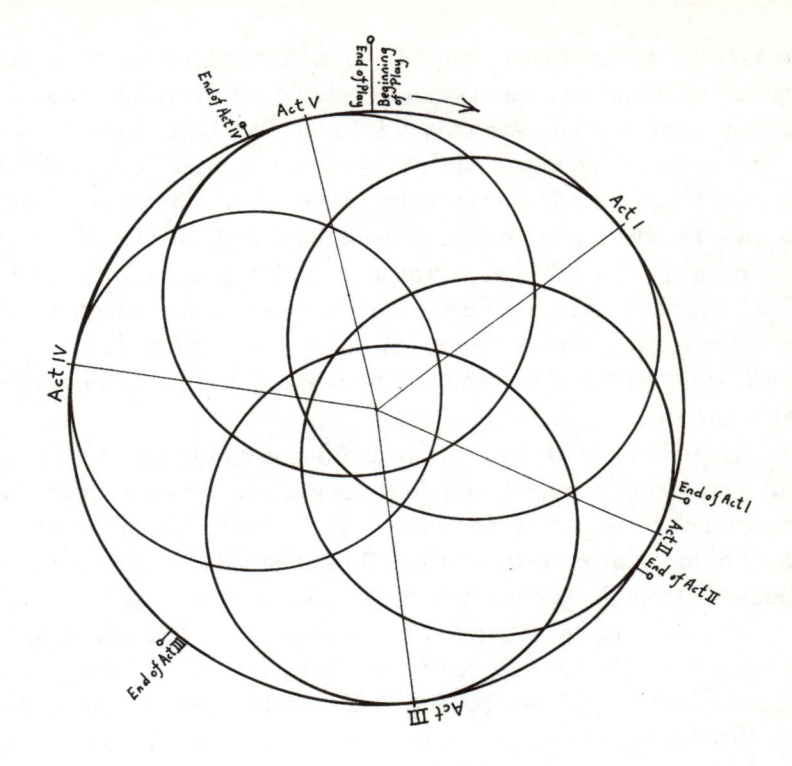

Figure 6

Once drawn it looks as solid as an astrolabe, yet we ask: is it a figment of the mind, a spider's web, an illusion? Or was this figure wrought long ago, with antique instruments, on paper, or parchment, stone or metal? Certainly the numbers were given, not invented; certainly these lightning-flash ideas seem 'given' too. Perhaps this form is rather the spiritual shape of an earthly act of creation, an archetype that caused the play to 'grow that way,' like a mathematically perfect pinecone? Let it anyway be explored, and its properties discovered.

The prime concepts of geometry that were first built into the plays are of course present: arcs or chords of circles elegantly link all symmetrical points. But the figure also has many other intriguing and meaningful geometrical properties. Are other intersections other relationships, also reflected in the action and word-stream of the play? I must confess that if they were not, this book would never have been written. In fact, the more journeys of exploration one makes, the more remote seems the possibility that chance is here the master-hand — so striking, eloquent and enchanting are the word (or sound) echoes and connections to be found, and there are, for instance, lines of intersection linking recurrent images, or leading straight from evil thought to evil deed. There are scenes (arcs) with a common centre, separate in time but overshadowing one another, where the same mood and pattern appears again, transformed. There are great concentric circles, which cut each act in two mirror-points and link all acts together, along whose pathways we find avenues of the clearest musical echoes. At one moment the figure takes on the aspect of a map of destiny, at the next an aeolian harp, at the next a table of poetic logarithms. We can play with it, but perhaps we continue too long at our peril. In the end only the right questions asked in the right mood get the right answers.

The play-figure (Figure 6) arose from the principle of symmetry, but a second principle of form, reflected in number waves, can also be discovered there. Along the circling time-stream we can inscribe the great prime-number rhythms which flow all together — now above, now below — from the beginning of the play to the end.

Some rhythms are referred to by number-jokes. The weeks, or time-rhythm waves, in 'Weary sev'nights, nine times nine,' (line 23, 1, 3) can, for instance, all be counted. Other rhythms may be pointed to by numbers alone, as surely as if they had been named. Thus my original total of the play is 2392 lines; but this does not include the songs, whose traditional length we venture to say is 5 and 4 lines respectively. If we add them, we not only perfect the figure but reach a grand total of 2401 lines (see Chapter 2). This number — the kind of number a Renaissance mathematician and magus would know as a friend — proves to be 49 x 49, or 7 x 7 x 7 x 7. It not only points to a 7 rhythm but to a 49 rhythm and a 343 rhythm.[7] These rhythms are all traceable. At line 343, for instance, (1, 5) Lady Macbeth, looking up from the letter, speaks her own words for the first time in the play:

> 343   Glamys thou art, and Cawdor, and shalt be
> 344   What thou art promis'd: ...

Each rhythm seems to speak its own message; and long rhythms like the 343 one, sign themselves at the nodes or pauses with recurring words and themes. Here we find the thought of inescapable destiny repeated, and also the words 'hand' and 'pray.' Along the path of this rhythm we meet Lady Macbeth for the last time in the play too, as she washes her hands in the midst of sleep (play line 2058 [6 x 343, or 6x7x7x7], Act 5

1. OVERVIEW

Scene 1). Shorter rhythms, which flow across the long ones, can more easily be traced by the ear alone; and their ebb and flow can also be mapped in terms of elements such as short and long vowels, end-stopped and overflowing lines, strong and weak endings, and so on.

In general, however, the study of rhythms, which grows into the study of timing, is more difficult than the study of symmetry. Yet we may live in rhythms, without always fully grasping them, and become conscious, to a greater or less degree, of the endless interplay between surging wave and symmetrical form, between life and image. Only when we 'possess' the play as a singer possesses a song — never really through detached manipulations of geometry and text — do we allow it to speak with a new voice, or rather with many new voices.

This is the law of symmetry, that one passage 'speaks' to another across a still-point centre. The effect of this law is that two dimensions give way to three; a landscape of in-between events appears. They may of course be disputed, but if the figure is accepted, if symmetry is accepted, there can be no quarrel about which passage speaks to which.

In this sense we come to something like proof — for proof belongs to the sphere of mathematics — and behold we *have* mathematics, though in a sphere where there is much else besides.

As already noted, the discovery of the *Macbeth* play-figure leads to an awareness of new elements of the plot and a full discussion of the new plot will occupy Chapters 8 and 9. Briefly, it hinges on the true character of King Duncan, whom, it is argued, Macbeth already hates when the play opens. It also provides that 'defence of the Macbeths' that history was willing to furnish (and many actors too), but which the play itself has so far steadily refused to yield.

Crucial parts of the argument are linguistic. As Hilda Hulme points out, a certain faith in original texts is the attribute of linguists rather than editors.[8] The danger has always been that, in thinking that we know what a play is about, we interpret or change the words in terms of our pre-conception. Once the conception itself is changed many words in this play take on other, often simpler, meanings and their own original printed form (as 'Barlet' instead of 'Martlet,' Act 1, Scene 6, play-line 416) makes sense.

If we ask *why* the plot we have discovered was buried we may come to at least two good answers. First, in the context in which the play was first written and performed it was politically expedient to bury it. (Banquo was only a mythical ancestor of James I of England: King Duncan was a real one.) Second, the very process of discovering the hidden plot is also the process of discovering the mystery of the figure. It was planned as a door: one of many such doors to be found throughout the plays.

The 'Figure' discovered behind *Macbeth* proves to be one variation of a basic geometrical theme. Other similar 'Figures,' but with different ratios of great to small circles, have now been constructed by the author, and always from numbers that fall into place as easily as well-trained dancers.[9] So far, the game does not fail. However, this magical kind of writing was done, or was partly done, by sheer practice. Yet somewhere in the background there might well have been a great occultist and mathematician.[10] There may have been an esoteric circle, like the Sidney circle, to which the poet belonged, and to which the esoterist and mathematician, John Dee was also connected.[11]

The implications of the figure are of course not just academic. If ever it comes to be widely accepted, it must at least slow the tide of 'Shakespeare-esque' productions, in which Shakespeare's text is dismembered, re-arranged, reduced, expanded and generally mutilated. It *ought* to lead to an entirely new concept of production, where the study of the play, which includes study of its structures, and the acting of the play, are fused into one. Then, and only then, in the white-heat of action, will the profoundest laws of prosody be understood. To this Shakespeare points through the words of Macbeth:

> Strange things I haue in head, that will to hand,
> Which must be acted, ere they may be scand.   (3, 4)

What Macbeth first has 'in head' is to consult the witches again at the pit of Acheron. He will enter a world of magic spells — as Shakespeare himself does when he writes a play, though the cauldron stirred is a cosmic one, and the meeting place a region unimaginably higher than the pit.

2. Developments of the Figure
The Riddle of the Nine Lines and the Seven Great Steps

Before venturing further into how my understanding of the nature and character of the Macbeth figure matured, it is important to look at the songs of Acts 3 and 4 which, although only featured slightly in the Folio text, are a crucial 'ingredient' in terms of the way the geometrical figure was brought to completion.

We cannot scan the lines of the play properly until we act it. When we do that we can no longer skim over those italicized words in Act 3, Scene 5: *'Sing within, come away, come away, &c.'* We have to decide who sings exactly what.

The song in this first Hecate scene, and the other song in the cauldron scene could provide our required importance between them if they were the right lengths.[1] But are they? As Hecate is taken up into the air, hauled by an engine invisible to the spectator, so we too lose the ground beneath our feet. This ground, hitherto, has been the printed Folio Text, to whose sure lines or furrows we can always return. But now we have lost security (perhaps our chiefest enemy) and find ourselves in a hiatus of speculation.

The song traditionally sung here (Act 3, scene 5, line 35) is also found in Middleton's play *The Witch* (Act 3, 3):

>   'Come away, come away
>   Hecate, Hecate, come away!
> *Hecate*: I come, I come, I come, I come,
>   With all the speed I may,
>   With all the speed I may.

This much is usually sung in *Macbeth* though the scene in *The Witch* continues:

> *Hecate*: Where's Stadlin?
> *Voice*: Here.

Hecate:	Where's Puckle?
Voice:	Here.
	And Hoppo too, and Helluvain too;
	We lack but you, we lack but you;
	Come away, make up the count.
Hecate:	I will but 'noint, and then I mount.... etc.

The lines of the traditional song in *Macbeth* are five; though the words that follow in 'The Witch' are so curiously relevant to our enquiry that we wonder if we should 'make up the count' by continuing farther and including them too. However, the *Macbeth* tradition is strong and, furthermore, other witches in the air also seem to be five: Stadlin, Puckle, Hoppo, Helluvain and Hecate. So, provisionally, we may accept tradition and take the first song in *Macbeth* to end at 'With all the speed I may!' and to consist of five lines.

The second song falls between lines 43 and 48 in Act 4, scene 1. It follows Hecates' command 'And now about the cauldron sing... etc.' (regarded by Kenneth Muir — the Shakespeare author and critic — and others, as 'manifestly spurious') and is indicated by the stage directions *'Musicke and a song' Black Spirits &c.'* Again, this song is found in *The Witch* (5, 2). The words traditionally sung in *Macbeth* are:

> Black spirits and white
> Red spirits and gray
> Mingle, mingle, mingle,
> You that mingle may!

Here we have four lines (though they can be written as two); and also a reference to four kinds of spirits: black, white, red and gray ones. If we take four to be 'meant' and add this number of lines to the five of the first song, we have nine lines altogether for our make-weight. This, however, according to our calculations, is one line too many.

Could the first song really be four lines long, with the last two or the first two intended as one? But this is a game at which we may not cheat: for somehow the rules are as important as the results, and seem indeed to have a language of their own. Here, at the songs, we are freed from the bondage of the Folio lineation: but also, just here, there are two voices pointing to the same answers. 'Five' for the first song is given by tradi-

2. DEVELOPMENTS OF THE FIGURE

tion and by the 'count' of Middleton's Witches. 'Four' for the second song is also given by tradition and by the count of spirits.

This does not necessarily imply that *The Witch* was written before *Macbeth*. We believe that it was written later as a deliberate pointer to certain hidden aspects of *Macbeth*. Let us then for the moment, accept the total of nine and see where it leads us.

The songs will expand the 'great circle' to 592 + 9, or 601 lines. They will also expand the grand total of the play from 2392 to 2401 lines: again a number that looks like a near miss, just one more than perfect roundness.

Yet the number 2401 proves in the end to go one better than 2400, not one worse. When we look for its prime factors we find that seven goes into it 343 times; again the 343 is divisible by seven, and that seven goes into it 49 times; again seven goes into this seven times. So the number two thousand four hundred and one is just such a number as the Platonists would see inscribed in gold, the magical product of $7 \times 7 \times 7 \times 7$. It will, in fact, answer our purpose very well.

Looking now at a more detailed impression of the Figure as drawn in Chapter 1, we arrive at Figure 7. Here, it can clearly be seen how the nine extra lines for the songs are included in those positions where the songs are sung. When, however, we consider the character of this Figure in relation to the play text itself, certain important questions arise, which challenge the correctness of this layout.

We have indeed closed the gap in the Great Circle and, with the overlap of one, we have indeed attained the beautiful number 2401 (7x7x7x7), but in doing so we have altered the length and structure of two acts: Act 3, where the first song occurs and Act 4, where the second song occurs.

Act 3 contains 520 lines, so its central two lines are lines 260 and 261, the last line in Scene 3 (the murder of Banquo) and the first line in Scene 4 (the Banqueting Scene, when his ghost appears). The words around this point indicate clearly an awareness of the Act centre. At the end of Scene 3 Banquo has been murdered and Fleance, his son, has just escaped. The last four lines of this scene are divided between the third, the second and the first murderer. The third murderer is the newcomer, the mystery man. The second and the first are the ones whom Macbeth briefed earlier in the act. The third murderer is the one who seems to know the terrain and the customs of the court rather well. The words here are:

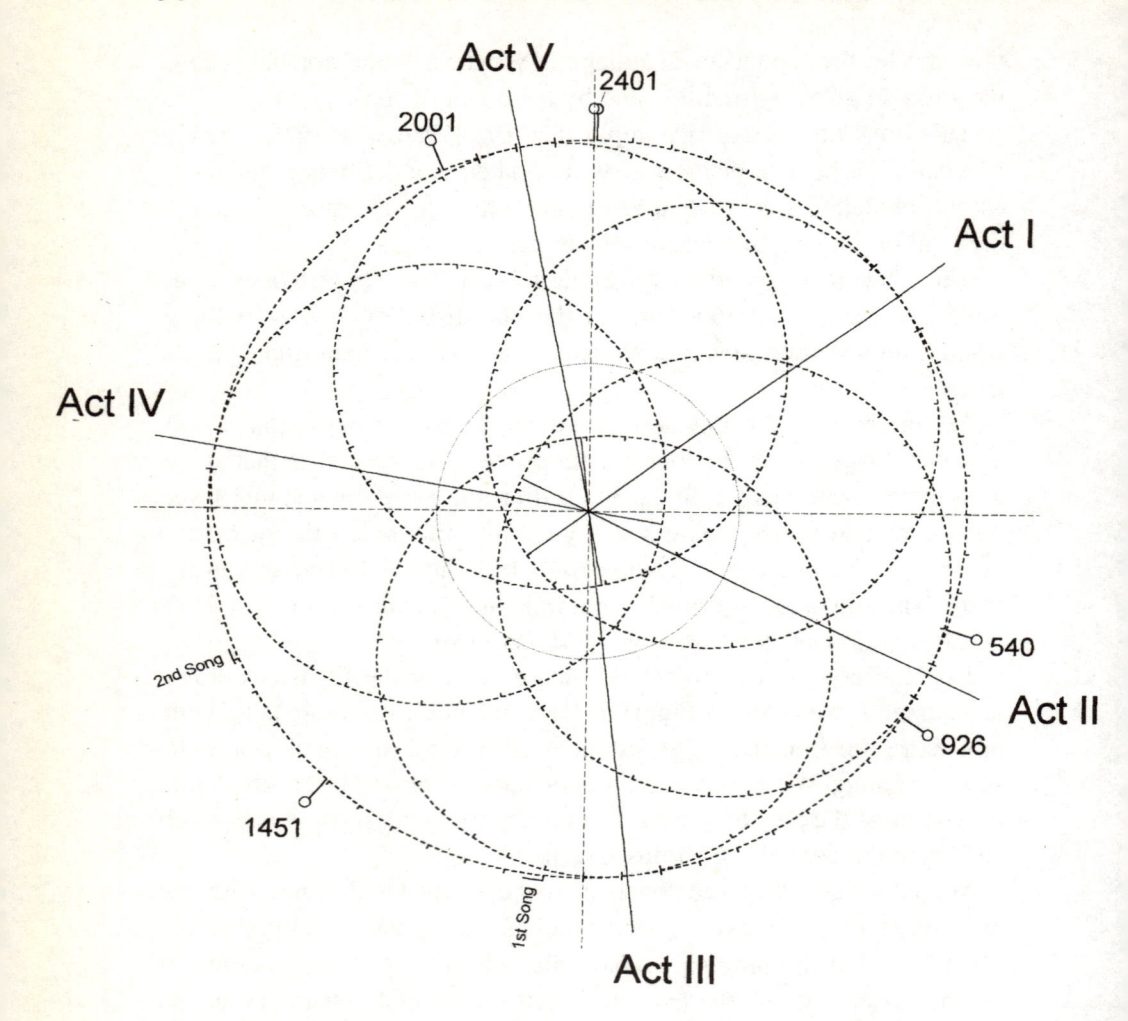

Figure 7. Macbeth (Layout 1). The gap in the great circle closed by the songs. The lines for the two songs are here inserted into the Figure in the places where the songs occur. Though this is a logical step to take in order to complete the Figure, it creates a problem in that it ruins the textual symmetry of Act III. The answer to this problem involves, firstly, a deeper uinderstanding of the play itself and then, through this a unique geometrical solution: see Layout 2.

Act	257	3. There's but one down: the son is fled
	258	2. We have lost
	259	Best half of our affair.
	260	1. Well, let's away, and say how much is done.

                                          Exeunt

2. DEVELOPMENTS OF THE FIGURE 39

The next scene, set in the banqueting hall, opens with Macbeth's words to his guests, the Lords who have just arrived:

> 261   *Macb.* You know your own degrees, sit downe:
> 262   At first and last, the hearty welcome.

'How much is done' is half of their affair, and their affair is the Act. The degrees which the Lords know are 181 degrees of the small circle, that is, the second of the two lines at its nadir.[2] In short, the division between Scenes 3 and 4 is also the division between the two halves of the Act. The words, 'sit down' follow the pattern of act centres, already noted in Chapter 1, where we find either the actual words: 'sit' or 'set,' or the idea behind them, and they also follow the pattern of the play centre, to which we come at line 10 of this scene:

> 10   *Macb.* See, they encounter thee with their heart's thanks
> 11   Both sides are even: here I'll sit i'the midst.

However, this act centre in Act 3, though clearly recognised in the text, is based on the numbers that do not include the song at the end of the Hecate scene! If we include this song in the numbering we come to a total of 525 lines in the whole Act and this would shift the Act centre to the single line, line 263: 'Our self will mingle with society.' In short it would ruin the clear symmetry of the Act.[3] We have to conclude that the extra five lines for this song: 'Come away, come away. Hecate, Hecate come away, etc.,' cannot be interpolated where the song is sung. And yet these lines, together with the four lines for the second song: 'Black spirits and white, etc.,' which comes in the cauldron scene in Act 4, are absolutely essential for the completion of the Great Circle and indeed of the whole Figure and have to come somewhere.

If the first song, sung as Hecate flies upwards, cannot be thought of as part of the ordinary text, then surely neither can the second song. Singing is not the same as speaking, and this is indicated by a brief italicized note in place of the fully set-out text. So, we are left with a problem. The songs have to be counted; they complete the Figure and they bring us to the beautiful number 2401, or 7 x 7 x 7 x 7. But, if they are not to be counted in their places where should they be counted?

Five plus four adds up to nine. Are we looking for a hint of nine extra lines, or nine line spaces, somewhere in the text? Hecate's words, spoken just before her little spirit summons her away with the first lines of the first song, give us a strong hint of where to look for those necessary nine lines. She looks up and says:

1378	Upon the corner of the moon
1379	There hangs a vap'rous drop, profound,
1380	I'll catch it ere it come to ground;
1381	And that distilled by magic slights,
1382	Shall raise such Artificial Sprights,
1383	As by the strength of their illusion,
1384	Shall draw him on to his confusion.
1385	He shall spurn Fate, scorn Death, and beare
1386	His hopes 'bove Wisdom, Grace, and Fear:
1387	And you all know, Security
1388	Is Mortals chiefest enemy.
	Music, and a song.
1389	Hark, I am call'd: my little Spirit see
1390	Sits in a foggy cloud, and stays for me.
	Sing within. Come away, come away, etc.

And the witches end the scene with:

1391	Come, let's make haste, she'll soon be
1392	Back again.

Hecate speaks of catching the magic moon-drop and then of its distillation. We are not told when or where this distillation is to take place; whether it is on or off stage, and the matter remains mysterious. This mystery may be linked with a second mystery:- What exactly is supposed to happen at the first italicized stage direction: *'Music, and a song'?* It is followed by Hecate's words, 'Hark, I am call'd,' so the song must either contain a pre-arranged signal or words similar to, 'Come away, come away.' My strong hunch, which I cannot prove, is that this mysterious interlude gives time; time for the distillation of the magic drop.

A distilled vapour may be imagined rising upwards into the air, mingling with a second plume of vapour as the second charm song is sung, and finally condensing at the pit of Acheron just before the magic sprites or apparitions make their appearance. This is the moment when Macbeth, who has conjured forth every kind of natural and human chaos, says:

2. DEVELOPMENTS OF THE FIGURE 41

      1506   Even till destruction sicken: Answer me
      1507   To what I aske you.

The witches reply,
      1508   1 Speake.
      1509   2 Demand.
      1510   3 Wee'l answer.
      1511   1 Say, if th'hadst rather heare it from our mouthes,
      1512   Or from our Masters.

Macbeth opts for the Masters themselves, 'Call 'em: let me see 'em.' Obediently the first witch commands,

      1514   1 Powre in Sowes blood, that hath eaten
      1515   Her nine Farrow: Greaze that's sweaten
      1516   From the Murderers Gibbet, throw
      1517   Into the Flame.

Finally, they all summon the procession of apparitions, that is: the Armed Head, the Bloody Child, the Child Crowned with a tree in his hand.

      1518   *All*. Come high or low:
      1519   Thy Selfe and Office deaftly show.   *Thunder*.

Here, surely, is our searched for 'nine' in the sow that hast eaten 'Her Nine Farrow,' and here surely, in 'Greaze,' is a shorthand reference to degrees! These words clearly point to the enactment of a spell. The blood of this especially unnatural sow is poured into the cauldron and fat from a murderer's gibbet is cast on the fire, which flares up.

    Immediately, the spell has its effect, strange apparitions appear and speak to Macbeth (They are often presented in the form of puppets manipulated from below). We are made aware that there is a region underneath the cavern and we suspect that the name, the 'Pit of Acheron,' applies to this region. After her brief appearance, Hecate simply vanishes from the scene, this time perhaps not upwards but downwards. This is surely the place where a chasm is made in the earth, and in the text, where hell breaks through! In short, where the effects of the songs, each of which functions as a kind of spell, unite and cause that chasm with explosive power. The words, 'mingle,

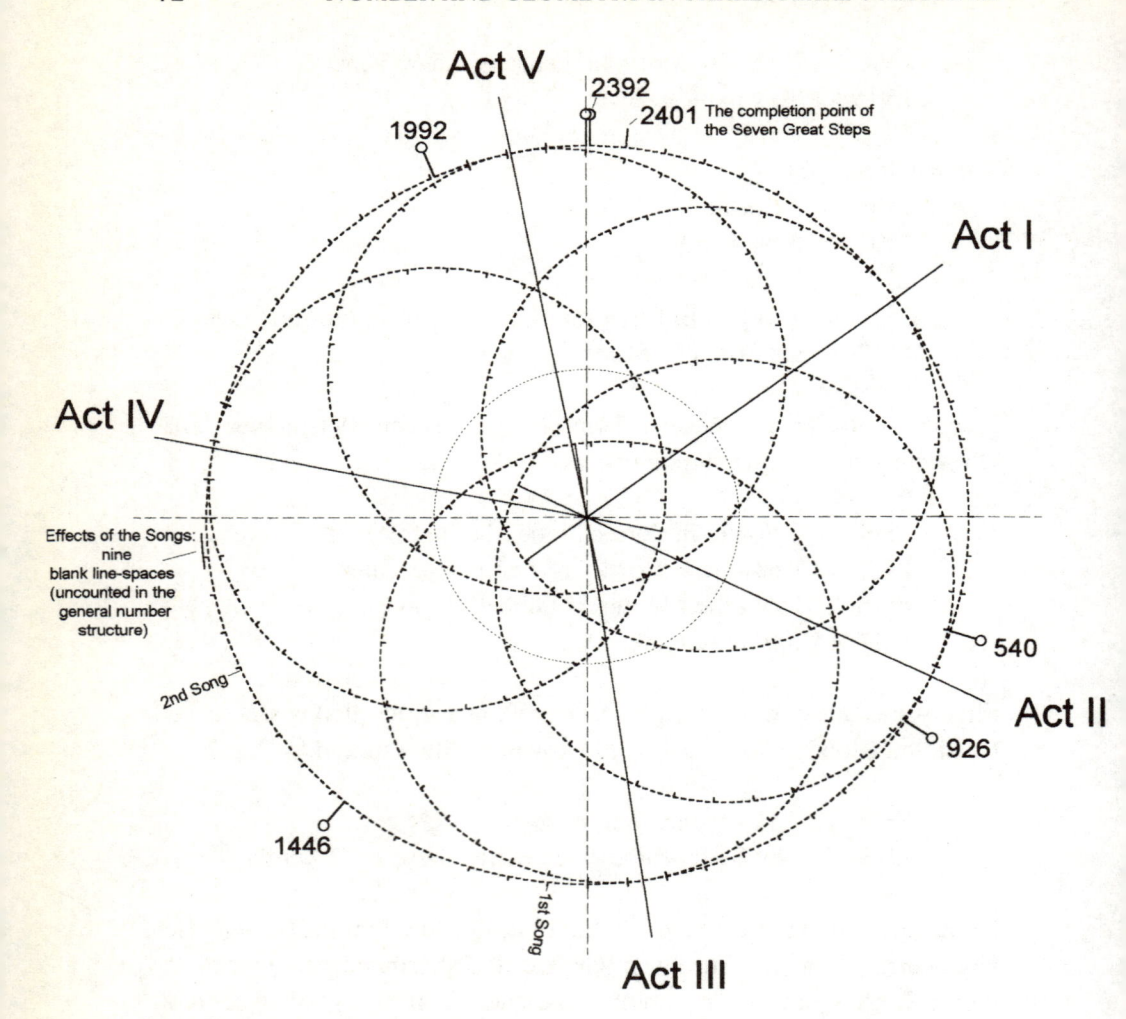

Figure 8. Macbeth (Layout 2). The crucial nine lines are 'poured; into then cauldron-like Figure, along with the sow's blood. Thus the Figure is completed and the Act Symmetries of the First Folio Text remain undisturbed in their numbering. At this point the Figure assumes the role of a Key, opening up further understanding of the play.

mingle, mingle,' in the second song could point to the stirring together of the two different kinds of liquids.

We could now say that the symmetry of Act 4 is even more distorted by the nine-line interpolation than it would have been by the original four. Yet we could also say that there are no words in this interpolation, there are only deeds, therefore the numbering of the Act remains the

2. DEVELOPMENTS OF THE FIGURE 43

same — although the way it looks geometrically is certainly changed. The essential thing about a wordless interpolation is that we simply leap over it and continue the numbers exactly as before. If this were not so, anybody who didn't understand the geometry, but did understand number structure would become lost at this point.[4]

We now redraw the Figure including the space of the nine empty lines in Act 4 (see Figure 8). Since there are 600 line spaces on the Great Circle, one line space is subtended at the centre of that circle by 0.6°, therefore nine line-spaces is represented by 5.4°. The result is that we are ahead as regards the drawing, but not as regards the numbers. To move ahead also with the numbers means to extend the count by means of an overlap on the Figure of nine lines. With this, the number structure can, therefore, now match the geometrical structure. A further outcome is, of course, the meeting of the end of the play with its beginning We can now show on this new Figure the 'black hole' for the sow's blood — and the increased overlap after we have reached the vertical.

A major play-rhythm, that of the 343 lines, 'the Seven Great Strides,' may help us to appreciate something of the fullness of this numerical and geometrical resolution.

The next step is to inscribe the Seven Great Strides — 343 lines each — on our new Figure (see Figure 9).

Since 2401 is 7 to the fourth: or 7x7x7x7, it can also be seen as 7 times 7 to the third, or 7 x 343. The number 343 first announces itself early in Act 1 Scene 5, just as Lady Macbeth ends her reading of the letter. Up to this moment we have not heard her true voice, we have heard her reading what Macbeth has written. As soon as she looks away from the letter she says,

      343   Glamys thou art, and Cawdor, and shalt be
      344   What thou art promis'd ...

In a way we meet Lady Macbeth for the first time here.

Twice 343 is 686 and this line, which brings us to the end of the second stride, falls in Act II Scene 2 shortly after the murder of King Duncan. Lady Macbeth has just snatched the daggers and taken them back to the scene of death, while Macbeth stands staring with horror at his bloody hands. The words around 686 are:

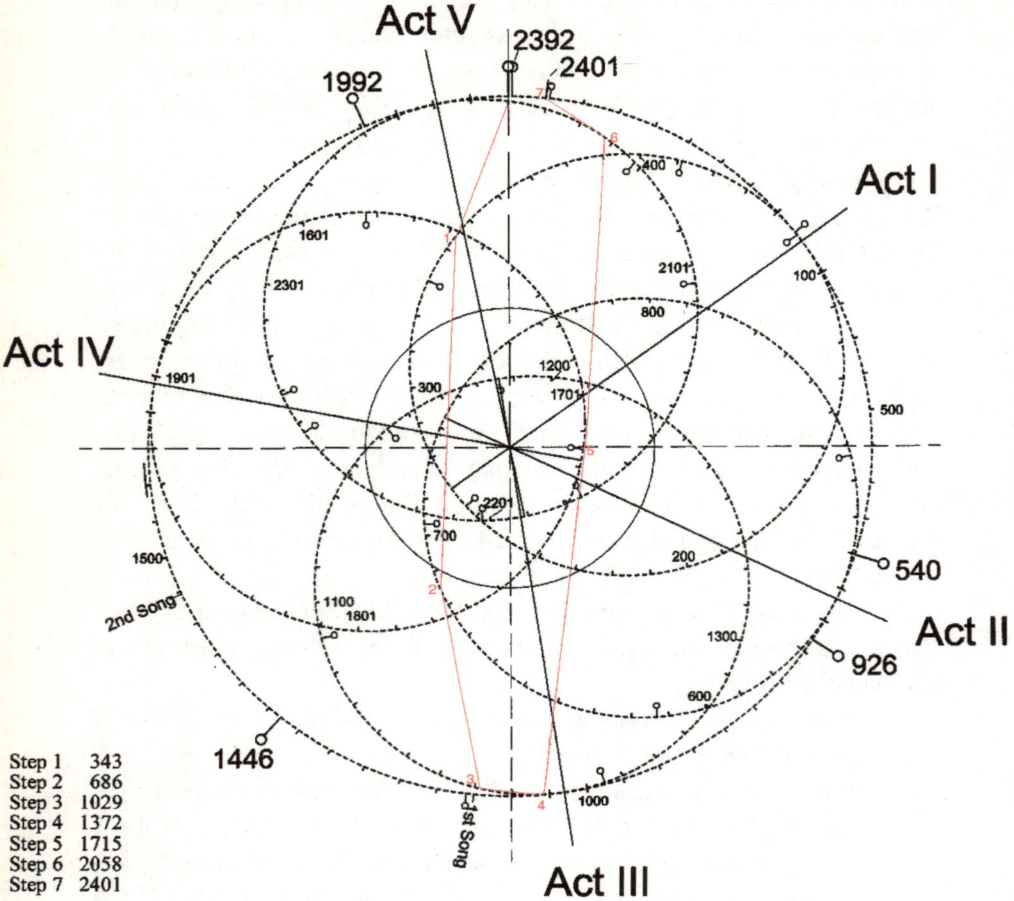
Act V
2392
2401
1992
Act I
1601
2301
2101
100
800
Act IV
1901
1200
1701
300
500
2201
700
540
200
1500
1100
1801
2nd Song
Act II
1300
926
600
1446
1000
1st Song
Act III
400
Step 1 343
Step 2 686
Step 3 1029
Step 4 1372
Step 5 1715
Step 6 2058
Step 7 2401

Figure 9 The Seven Steps of 343 lines

685 Will all great Neptunes Ocean wash this blood
686 Cleane from my Hand? no: this my Hand will rather
687 The multitudinous Seas incarnardine,
688 Making the Greene one, Red.

Line 686: 'Cleane from my Hand?' brings us to the end of the second great stride. Later, we discover that in this passage there is a major clue to the plot, but for the time being we will just observe that it is a moment

2. DEVELOPMENTS OF THE FIGURE

of high drama in which Macbeth is once again suffering the scorn of his wife while possessed of a kind of vision of the future.

3 x 343 is 1029 and this line, which brings us to the end of the third great stride, falls in Act 3 Scene 1 while Macbeth is closeted with the two stooges who will later murder Banquo. To build up his case Macbeth is pretending that it was Banquo who was to blame for their recent sufferings:

1028	Are you so Gospell'd, to pray for this good man,
1029	And for his Issue, whose heauie hand
1030	Hath bow'd you to the Graue, and begger'd
1031	Yours for euer?

The imagery he uses relates perhaps to a church, certainly to the Christian faith, perhaps his own discarded faith; and we may notice the word 'hand' again echoing that line, at 686: 'Cleane from my Hand? no: this my Hand will rather' (the end of the second great stride, 2 x 343).

4 x 343 is 1372 and now we are at the end of the fourth or central great stride and have arrived at line 17 in the Hecate scene (Act 3 Scene 5). The goddess Hecate is instructing the lesser witches:

1369	But make amends now: Get you gon,
1370	And at the pit of Acheron
1371	Meete me i'th' Morning: thither he
1372	Will come, to know his Destinie.
1373	Your Vessels, and your Spels prouide,
1374	Your Charmes, and euery thing beside;

Line 1372 seems to point to a crucial turning point in the story.

So far, the angle of every line in relation to the circle in which it belongs, has been exactly as before but in the midst of the next 343 step we come to the 'Sow's Blood' chasm and from then on the relationship of lines to Figure is slightly different; so, the next line we are looking at is still 5 x 343, that is 1715, but geometrically it falls in a slightly different place, that is nine line-spaces further on than in our original conception. Line 1715 is in fact the penultimate line in Act 4 Scene 2, that is the scene with Lady Macduff and her little boy, which ends with the entry of the murderers and the slaying of the little boy. The last lines of this scene are:

1707   What are these faces?
         Enter Murtherers.
1708   *Mur.* Where is your Husband?
1709   *Wife.* I hope in no place so vnsanctified,
1710   Where such as thou may'st finde him.
1711   *Mur.* He's a Traitor.
1712   *Son.* Thou ly'st thou shagge-ear'd Villaine.
1713   *Mur.* What you Egge?
1714   Yong fry of Treachery?
1715   *Son.* He ha's kill'd me Mother,
1716   Run away I pray you.   *Exit crying Murther.*

In the word 'pray' there is once again an echo (from the 3rd stride):

1028   Are you so Gospell'd, to pray for this good man,
1029   And for his Issue ...

And now, at the end of the sixth stride, line 2058 (6 x 343) we are in Act 5 Scene 1, that is the 'Sleepwalking' Scene. We have just heard Lady Macbeth's last words at the previous line, 2057: 'To bed, to bed, to bed.' Now, however, on the altered figure, the distance around the act circle to the vertical looks short and now we experience exactly why the overlap must extend over most of Act 1 Scene 1. If it were to reach exactly to our original ending position, the seventh stride would only be 334 lines, therefore we need nine more lines to reach the ultimate total of 2401. There seems to be only one way of finding these, we make the overlap longer thereby covering, as before, the first words in Act 1 Scene 1, 'When shall we three meet again?,' with the last words in Act 5 Scene 7, 'Whom we inuite, to see vs Crown'd at Scone.' but continuing on for nine more lines to end at line 10 of Act 1 Scene I: 'Padock calls anon:' As it is printed in the First Folio the singular line continues: 'faire is foule, and foule is faire.'[5]

In thus repeating words found at the beginning of the play we may well ask, 'What conceivable meaning can these words have now? What are the three witches doing and saying?'

With this thought we recognise something. In the First Folio printing of the first scene of *Macbeth* 'First Witch, Second Witch and Third Witch' is not written, simply 1, 2 and 3. It has been our experience, in

2. DEVELOPMENTS OF THE FIGURE

studying this play from the viewpoint of symmetry, that the same words take on different meanings according to their context and background. Why should this not be exactly what is happening here, giving us the experience that we come to the same words but that the beings who speak them have undergone a change? If we split this curious tenth line into two parts, then this leaves us asking could 'Padock calls anon' — the first part of the last line met by the overlap — be the true ending of the play?

The divisions between the seven great steps punctuate the story like signposts. At the end of the first great step we meet Lady Macbeth in her true nature for the first time. At the symmetrically corresponding position, that is at the end of the sixth step and the beginning of the seventh we, in effect, encounter her for the last time. The five inner steps move between the entry and the departure of Lady Macbeth. The end of the second step, 686, takes us to the moment when Macbeth gazes at his bloody hands and knows that he will be led ever deeper into murder. The end of the third step and beginning of the fourth, or central, step hisses with hatred for those whom he intends as his next victims, 'Are you so Gospell'd, to pray for this good man, And for his Issue.' At the end of the fourth step we encounter the voice of Hecate, a stronger power than any of the earthly witches, 'Will come to know his Destinie.'

What becomes clear when we study the relationship of Text and Figure more closely is that the 'Wayward Sonne' (play line 1366), of whom Hecate has just spoken, is not Macbeth; it is Fleance. So, we can find here, again, a symmetrical connection between the third and fourth steps. Macbeth's destiny is finally to see the procession of eight kings and to recognise that it is Banquo's progeny and not his own who will inherit the kingdom of Scotland. At the 'Pit of Acheron' (reference – play line 1370; the place where Macbeth will gaze into the cauldron) he is thrown into despair by this discovery and the upshot is that he commits murder on a scale undreamed of by the man who we first encounter as a military hero in Act 1. The fifth step ends with the murder of Macduff's little boy and all his family, 'He has killed me mother,' line 1715. After this, the sixth step takes us to our last view of Lady Macbeth,

> 2057   *Lady.*   To bed, to bed, to bed.
> 2058   *Doct.*   Will she go now to bed?
> 2059   *Gentlewoman.*   Directly.

The seventh step, which balances the first, leads us inevitably to that singular overlap. Nine lines are now added to the original one line overlap and we end at line 10 of Scene 1:

10   Padock calls anon: (faire is foule, and foule is faire,)

Later in our studies we will return to the potent questions concerning the Figure's overlap: the meeting of the end of the play with its beginning. For the present, however, one question cannot fail to impress itself upon us very strongly: 'What can it mean when at the end of the play three beings talk about a meeting with Macbeth?' Macbeth is dead; we have just seen his bloody severed head planted in the ground by Macduff on lance or pole. Is not that the end of his story?[6]

3. Scene Symmetry as Illustrated in Act I

Act 1 Scenes 1 and 2

We now turn to the beginning of Act 1, to the *'Thunder and Lightning'* that announce the three witches, and to that doubtful scene, generally thought to have been cut, or written by an alien hand, in which we first meet King Duncan and his sons, and hear news of a battle raging further south.

The first scene is very short: an eleven-line glimpse into the hellish doings that will permeate the rest of the play.

1	1. When shall we three meet againe?
2	In Thunder, Lightning, or in Raine?
3	2. When the Hurley-burley's done,
4	When the Battaile's lost, and wonne.
5	3. That will be ere the set of Sunne.
6	1. Where the place?
7	2. Vpon the Heath.
8	3. There to meet with *Macbeth*.
9	1. I come, *Gray-Malkin*.
10	*All*. *Padock* calls anon: faire is foule, and foule is faire,
11	Houer through the fogge and filthie ayre. *Exeunt*.

Its chief business is to make an appointment between the witches and Macbeth: they will meet him on the heath that same evening when the battle is over.

In the First Folio the penultimate line, line 10, is very long: '*All. Padock* calls anon: faire is foule, and foule is faire,' but most editors divide it into two, giving twelve lines to the scene. If we keep the Folio lineation, however, we have the following rhyme scheme: AABBB C DDEFF. Here, C, the 'ace' of 'Where the place?' stands by itself, and follows a clear group of five lines consisting of a couplet and a triplet. It is followed in turn by a couplet, a single line, 'I come, *Gray-Malkin*.' and another couplet, making a second five-line group having the shape which the Greeks gave to odd numbers: two symmetrical blocks with a 'one' growing up in the centre. Thus, the central position of line 6, 'Where the place?' seems clearly indicated by the rhyme structure; and the voice that asks the question is that of the first witch, the leader of the three. We also find time as well as place within the central group of three lines:

                5   3. That will be ere the set of Sunne.
                6   1. Where the place?
                7   2. Vpon the Heath.

The questions of course are not really questions, but a catechism. The second witch is not actually asked to make a decision but to confirm and remember one.

The witches meet in storm and will depart through fog, perhaps the dense rain clouds above the storm. Foul weather is evoked at the beginning and end of the scene in echoing couplets.

                1   1. When shall we three meet againe?
                2   In Thunder, Lightning, or in Raine?
and
                10   *All. Padock* calls anon: faire is foule, and foule is faire,
                11   Houer through the fogge and filthie ayre. *Exeunt.*

Thus, in the short space of Scene 1 a hint already appears of that symmetry which will unfold in later scenes.

Of Scene 2, in which we hear of Macbeth's prowess in battle, John Dover Wilson, in his introduction to the Cambridge edition of 1951, says:

> ... the sorry state of the second scene, the only blot, but a real blot on the play's perfection, is demonstrably the work of an alien hand. The scene has undoubtedly been drastically and crudely cut and may even be a centre of two or more original scenes not too carefully stitched together.

This scene does indeed make a strange impression. The verse is irregular, the sounds abrupt and harsh, the images often confused:

3, SCENE SYMMETRY

Scene 1   *King*. What bloody man is that? he can report,
      2   As seemeth by his plight, of the Reuolt
      3   The newest state.

Every line, indeed every phrase of Duncan's opening speech is cut off with a short explosive 't;' almost nothing of the music we associate with Shakespeare's verse is perceptible, and when we try to extract a clear picture of the battle from the descriptions given to the King, first by the wounded sergeant and later by the Thane of Rosse, we find it is not at all easy. However, an outline can be discerned: an attack from the west led by the rebel Macdonwald; the latter slain by Macbeth, and the attack repulsed; an attack from the east by invaders from Norway, helped in some way by the rebel Cawdor; fearful slaughter and victory at last to the loyal troops; a heap of gold extorted from the Norwegian king in exchange for permission to bury his dead.

The question at the moment must be whether there are any signs of symmetry in this scene, or none. Its main content is epic rather than dramatic; a story or reflection of events punctuated by the arrival and departure of the two messengers and by the king's exclamations of admiration, anxiety, joy and anger.

The scene falls at a first reading into the following episodes:

8 lines: Arrival of the bleeding Sergeant.
18 lines: His account of the attack from the West culminating in the death of the rebel leader Macdonwald at the hands of Macbeth. Ends 'O valiant Cousin, worthy Gentleman.' line 26.
11 lines: The Sergeant's account of the attack from the East by the Norwegian army. Ends 'Dismay'd not this, our Captaines, *Macbeth* and *Banquo*?' line 37.
11 lines: The valour of the King's captains: description of the dreadful slaughter in this second battle -- still raging when the Sergeant left. Ends 'Goe get him Surgeons,' line 48.
6 lines: Arrival of Rosse. Ends 'Whence cam'st thou, worthy *Thane*?' line 54.
12 lines: Rosse's account of the Norwegian attack. Cawdor's role mentioned (though hardly made clear), for the first time. News of the loyalist victory abruptly announced. Ends 'Great happinesse.' line 66.

5 lines: The end of the story: the King of Norway has sued for peace and been forced to pay out ten thousand dollars. Ends line 71.

5 lines: Duncan pronounces sentence of death on the Thane of Cawdor, and bids Ross tell Macbeth that he is to succeed to Cawdor's title. Ends 'What he hath lost, Noble Macbeth hath wonne,' line 76.

If we set this out as an abstract pattern, it looks like this:

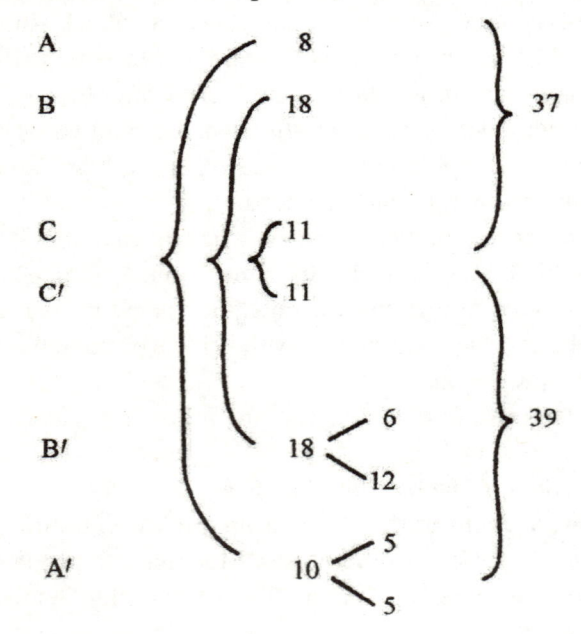

```
A           8
B          18      } 37
C          11
C'         11
                6
B'         18 <      } 39
                12
                5
A'         10 <
                5
```

Figure 10

The scene does in fact fall into two nearly equal parts, with the mathematical centre coming at the beginning of the 39 group. The central two lines — usually rearranged by editors to form one — are spoken by the sergeant:

Scene 38   Yes, as Sparrowes, Eagles;
      39   Or the Hare, the Lion:

We find here an animal image: not a little cat, but a big cat — a lion with a hare trembling before it; not a fish or a shoal of fishes, but great birds and little birds soaring and swooping in flight and attack.

Since these two central lines form a quite distinct central couplet

3, SCENE SYMMETRY

(distinct even to the eye on the folio page), the pattern may, without cheating, be re-written 37-2-37. It is true that this splits the second 11 group into 2-9, and thus spoils the shifted symmetry of the 18-11-11-18. However, if we now return to the play and re-clothe these arid numbers with the reality from which they have been drawn, we find that the mathematically central couplet is, without any doubt, the effective mirror around which the scene is structured; and that the shifted symmetry is really a kind of shadow of the basic symmetry. Let us move outwards again from this mirror surface, looking at the main paragraphs, and the more obvious correspondences.

The sergeant's account of the battle with the Norwegians straddles the centre, with the attack from the East falling before the centre, and the response to that attack falling after it. After this central part comes Rosse's account of the attack from the East; and opposed to it, before the start, the captain's account of the attack from the West. Here we find an exact balance between the described encounter between Macbeth and Macdonwald (lines 22–24) and the on-stage encounter between Rosse and King Duncan (lines 53–55).

Finally, after the climax, 'Great Happinesse.' there comes the end of the story, and the pronouncement of Cawdor's death (scene lines 67 to 76). These 10 lines stand opposite the arrival of the sergeant and the beginning of the telling of the story (8 lines and 2½ lines respectively):

Scene   9   *Cap*. Doubtfull it stood
        10   As two spent Swimmers, that doe cling together,
        11   And choake their Art: The mercilesse Macdonwald

This is the general answer to the King's question, and gives a picture of two exhausted armies struggling in the rain, and no clear outcome yet. It must be followed by a strong pause, before the teller goes back to the beginning with, 'The mercilesse Macdonwald ...' and recounts the dramatic details. By this pause prologue and epilogue are more equal, that is, the prologue becomes 10½ (8 + 2½) to balance the 10 lines of the epilogue.

The last five lines of the scene have for their subject the pronouncement of Cawdor's death:

Scene 72   *King*. No more that *Thane* of Cawdor shall deceiue
         73   Our Bosome interest: Goe pronounce his present death,

74   And with his former Title greet *Macbeth*.
75   *Rosse*. Ile see it done.
76   *King*. What he hath lost, Noble Macbeth hath wonne.
                                                    Exeunt

In them we may perhaps find a comment on the first five:

Scene 1   *King*. What bloody man is that? he can report,
      2   As seemeth by his plight, of the Reuolt
      3   The newest state.
      4   *Mal*. This is the Serieant,
      5   Who like a good and hardie Souldier fought
      6   'Gainst my Captiuitie: ....

Cawdor will soon be bloody, if beheading is the manner of his death; and the man who orders his execution, without trial or further enquiry, might even be looked on as bloody too. There is a word-echo also in the first and last lines of the scene, '*What* bloody man ...' and '*What* he hath lost....' Such echoes in the sphere of sound everywhere reinforce, or perhaps create, connections in the sphere of sense.

Moving inwards now more slowly, we listen again to the sergeant's first words, and to the lines that mirror them:

Scene 9   *Cap*. Doubtfull it stood
      10   As two spent Swimmers, that doe cling together,
      11   And choake their Art: The mercilesse Macdonwald
      12   (Worthie to be a Rebell, for to that
      13   The multiplying Villanies of Nature …
and
      64   Curbing his lauish spirit: and to conclude,
      65   The Victorie fell on vs.
      66   *King*. Great happinesse.
      67   *Rosse*. That now *Sweno*, the Norwayes King,
      68   Craues composition:

Here, '**sw**immers' is echoed in '**Sw**eno,' and the hiss of fear in 'merci**less**,' in the sigh of relief in 'happi**ness**.'

Less easy to pinpoint (though we can count the l's and v's) is the exuberant sense of movement, like high waves, in 'multiplying Villainies'

3, SCENE SYMMETRY

and 'Curbing his lauish spirit.' The turning points of the two battles, in which Macbeth shows his utmost valour, also stand in direct opposition. Here mirrored lines are:

Scene 15   Of Kernes and Gallowgrosses is supply'd,
16   And Fortune on his damned Quarry smiling,
17   Shew'd like a Rebells Whore: but all's too weake:
18   For braue *Macbeth* (well hee deserues that Name)
19   Disdayning Fortune, with his brandisht Steele,

and

58   Norway himselfe, with terrible numbers,
59   Assisted by that most disloyall Traytor,
60   The Thane of Cawdor, began a dismall Conflict,
61   Till that *Bellona's* Bridegroome, lapt in proofe,
62   Confronted him with selfe-comparisons,

Praise of Macbeth contrasts with blame of Cawdor; and the condemning voice and strong 'or' sounds in F**or**tune, 'Wh**ore**' and '**all**' are found again in 'Trai**tor**' and Thane and Caw**dor**. We also find a Roman deity named in corresponding lines (16 and 61); Fortune (Fortuna), and Bellona both seeming to look on the battle from another sphere.

The first passage continues to its dramatic climax: the moment when Macbeth slays the rebel leader, Macdonwald, severs his head from his body, and sets it up on the walls of that stronghold around which the battle must be raging. The description of Macdonwald's death (with its chorus from Duncan) falls at lines 23–26:

Scene 23   Which neu'r shooke hands, nor bad farwell to him,
24   Till he vnseam'd him from the Naue toth' Chops,
25   And fix'd his Head vpon our Battlements.
26   *King.* O valiant Cousin, worthy Gentleman.

We find it echoed in lines 51–54, which follow the entry of Rosse:

Scene 51   *Lennox.* What a haste lookes through his eyes?
52   So should he looke, that seemes to speake things strange.
53   *Rosse.* God saue the King.
54   *King.* Whence cam'st thou, worthy *Thane*?

As Rosse gallops (or marches swiftly) up to Duncan, the young Lennox stares in amazement at his face, at the violent haste in the eyes, mingled perhaps with a stranger ingredient. So too the soldiers stared up at the grisly head of Macdonwald, the eyes staring out, or closed, when Macbeth had stuck it as a trophy on the castle wall.

Within these passages (but not line-for-line) we find 'vn**seam**'d him' echoed by '**seemes** to speake ...' and '**worthy** gentleman' by '**worthy** *Thane*.' It is also difficult to escape the hint of another cross-reference. To 'unseam' someone from the nave to the chops (navel to the throat) is a very strange thing to do, as editors have pointed out. From the order of words it must involve a long upward stroke; neither a simple sword-thrust, nor the downward swing of a battle axe. Are we meant to think how strange this is, and to look for another meaning? (see Appendix 6, The Venom of the Toad).

In the central part of the scene (lines 27 to 50) we find the sunrise and storm image, with which the sergeant leads in the grim news of the Eastern attack, echoed in the first sighting of Rosse. The sergeant's words are:

Scene	27	*Cap*. As whence the Sunne 'gins his reflection,
	28	Shipwracking Stormes, and direfull Thunders:
	29	So from that Spring, whence comfort seem'd to come,
	30	Discomfort swells: Marke King of Scotland, marke,

They are mirrored by the four lines flanking the entry of Rosse and Angus:

Scene	47	*King*. So well thy words become thee, as thy wounds,
	48	They smack of Honor both: Goe get him Surgeons.
		Enter Rosse and Angus
	49	Who comes here?
	50	*Mal*. The worthy *Thane* of Rosse.

Here 'swells' is transformed into 'so well,' and the syllable 'come' in '**com**fort,' '**come**,' 'dis**com**fort,' is found again in 'be**come** thee' and 'who **comes** here?' We may even find in the arrival of the dawn, when the sun's rays are darkened by stormclouds, a parallel to the arrival of this wild-looking horseman who bears ill news, but good news behind it. Following the strong pause at 'Mark' comes the news at last of Sweno's

3, SCENE SYMMETRY

attack; and mirrored across the centre, the story of how the King's captains summoned their last reserves of strength to meet it.

These two passages, with the central couplet between them, make up 16 lines, whose end is reached when the sergeant's own strength deserts him. These central 16 lines are:

Scene	31	No sooner Iustice had, with Valour arm'd,
	32	Compell'd these skipping Kernes to trust their heeles,
	33	But the Norweyan Lord, surueying vantage,
	34	With furbusht Armes, and new supplyes of men,
	35	Began a fresh assault.
	36	*King*. Dismay'd not this our Captaines, *Macbeth* and
	37	*Banquoh*?
	38	*Cap*. Yes, as Sparrowes, Eagles;
	39	Or the Hare, the Lyon:
	40	If I say sooth, I must report they were
	41	As Cannons ouer-charg'd with double Cracks,
	42	So they doubly redoubled stroakes vpon the Foe:
	43	Except they meant to bathe in reeking Wounds,
	44	Or memorize another *Golgotha*,
	45	I cannot tell: but I am faint,
	46	My Gashes cry for helpe.

Attack and repulse stand in precise symmetrical relationship; and the hill on which the Norwegian lord stands 'surueying vantage,' with its serried banners streaming in the wind, is surely transformed across the centre into the hill of Golgotha, where the crosses stand with outstretched arms, silhouetted against a clouded sky. The picture becomes clear if we imagine narrow banners floating horizontally, or the rigid banners of mediaeval war, each one long enough to touch, or seem from afar to touch the pole that carries the next. One hill is transformed into the other; and yet the range is continuous: for at the centre we are surely still high up, in the cold sunny world of the eagle, the mountain hare (the commonest hare in Scotland) and the mountain lion.

If metaphor in Shakespeare is never idle or random, then the sergeant speaks of Golgotha, because the thought of Golgotha is in his mind; and if every play has its own unique landscape, then this unseen battle took place at a particular time of day and at a particular time of year: it is not just a shadowy fusion of the two separate battles which Holinshed describes. Was not the time of year Easter, or a little after Easter, when the images of the Passion were in the minds of everyone? If it was, then somewhere, somehow, this single hint will be corroborated.

Act 1 Scene 3

The symmetry which is found throughout the play may be illustrated first in the third scene in Act 1, the long scene on the heath where the witches meet Macbeth and Banquo on their way home from battle (see Appendix 2).

The first 38 lines of this scene form a kind of prologue, given entirely to the witches and written in rhyming tetrameters. At line 30 there comes the sound of a drum, followed at once by the ritual charm:

Scene	33	*All*. The weyward Sisters, hand in hand,
	34	Posters of the Sea and Land,
	35	Thus do go, about, about,
	36	Thrice to thine, and thrice to mine,
	37	And thrice again, to make up nine,
	38	Peace, the Charm's wound up.

Lines 39 to 81 contain the crucial meeting with the witches and the prophecies to Macbeth and Banquo. Macbeth shall be 'Thane of Glamis,' 'Thane of Cawdor' and 'King hereafter.' Banquo shall 'get Kings' but never wear the crown himself. At line 81, 'Speak, I charge you.,' the witches vanish and the two generals are left alone once more on the darkening heath, utterly amazed ('Interlude of Wonder'). Banquo, as before, is first to speak:

Scene	82	*Banq*. The Earth hath bubbles, as the Water ha's,
	83	And these are of them: whither are they vanish'd?

and a few lines later, at line 93, they hear (we imagine) the galloping of horses as the King's messengers Rosse and Angus arrive to greet them.

Lines 94-138 see the fulfilment of the second prophecy to Macbeth, and his first reactions of amazement and disbelief to that strange fulfilment: the least expected of all since Macbeth knew 'By Sinel's death'

3, SCENE SYMMETRY

that he was 'Thane of Glamis,' and knew, too, that he had a certain title to the throne. But to be Cawdor?

Scene 115   *Macb*. The *Thane* of Cawdor lives:
      116   Why do you dress me in borrowed Robes?

The message from the King fulfilling this prophecy seems to confirm the witches' supernatural powers. This part ends with a half-aside exchange between Macbeth and Banquo, who suspects they have met with 'Instruments of darkness.' Line 138 is 'Cousins, a word, I pray you.' when the four men split clearly into two groups - a three and a one.

Macbeth, now left effectively alone, utters his inmost thoughts in the dramatic convention of soliloquy:

Scene 139   *Macb*. Two Truths are told,
      140   As happy Prologues to the swelling Act
      141   Of the Imperial Theme. I thank you Gentlemen:

The pith of this section is the thought of murder, which seizes him with such power that he stands as if shaken by a tempest, with thundering heart and hair rising from his scalp. He is awakened by Banquo at line 164, 'Worthy *Macbeth*, we stay upon your leisure,' makes brief apology for his strange seizure and proposes that they all continue on their journey towards the royal camp or temporary headquarters.

This long scene, subdivided for the present in the simplest way by comings, goings and regroupings, thus falls into sub-scenes of the following lengths:

      38 lines   Witches' Prologue.
      43 lines   Prophecies.
      12 lines   Interlude of Wonder.
      45 lines   Fulfilment of Second Prophecy.
      25 lines   Soliloquy: The Vision of Murder.
      14 lines   Envoi: Macbeth takes command, etc.

On either side of the 'Interlude of Wonder' (the only moment when Macbeth and Banquo are alone on the stage), we therefore have stretches of time which are almost, but not exactly, equal (38 + 43 = 81: 45 + 25 + 14 = 84); and this interlude falls almost, but not exactly, at the centre of the scene. At the end, two groups: 25 and 14, together almost balance the 38-line witches' prologue coming at the beginning.

We could set out the grouping like this, dividing the Interlude of Wonder according to the position of the mathematically central line.

Figure 11

$$\underbrace{38 \quad 43}_{81} \quad - \quad \underbrace{7\text{-}1\text{-}4}_{} \quad - \quad \underbrace{45 \quad 39}_{84}$$

$$88 \quad - \quad 1 \quad - \quad 88$$

The pattern is imperfect but so close to a more rigid symmetry that we can hardly ignore it. By simple calculation, we have inscribed the mathematical centre into the scheme. Now let us identify this line and see whether the action and the images behind mirrored parts confirm or deny the concept of balance.

The total number of lines in the scene is 177. The odd central line must, therefore, be line 89, 'That takes the reason prisoner,' and the central group around it must be the five lines:

Scene 87   *Banq.* Were such things here, as we do speak about?
       88   Or have we eaten on the insane Root,
       89 *Scene Centre* That takes the Reason Prisoner?
       90   *Macb.* Your Children shall be Kings.
       91   *Banq.* You shall be King.

Line 89 marks the place where the theme of madness, central to the play, breaks through for the first time: and next to it comes the theme of Macbeth's envy — that Banquo has fathered children.

On the far side of this central region lies the first fulfilment of those prophecies. Ross's words. 'He bade me, from him, call thee *Thane of Cawdor*,' fall at lines 111 and 112: though Macbeth does not fully believe them until he has learnt of Cawdor's mysterious treason and downfall. Then he breathes in wonder:

Scene 126 (52-)   *Macb.* Glamis, and *Thane* of Cawdor:
       127 (51-)   The greatest is behind.

These lines, 52 and 51 lines from the end of the scene, exactly echo the witches' second two 'hails' to Macbeth, 51 and 52 lines from the begin-

3, SCENE SYMMETRY 61

ning. The first hail is echoed by, 'Do you not hope your Children shall be Kings,' (line 128).

Moving further outwards from the centre, we come to the witches' meeting with Macbeth and Banquo. Lines 40 and 41, 'What are these, So wither'd, and so wild in their attire ...?' are matched (across the scene) by lines 137 and 136, 'In deepest consequence. Cousins, a word, I pray you.' This is the moment when Macbeth is left alone by his companions. The first six lines of his soliloquy, with its sickening see-saw rhythm, echo the charm, when the sisters rotate and reverse in a circle: and the remaining part, till 'Time, and the Hour, runs through the roughest Day.' (line 163), echoes the threats of the first witch towards an unnamed sailor, beginning with the threat of storm at line 15, 'I myself have all the other,.'

The thought of murder, which grips Macbeth as a vision, is thus seen as the direct reflection of the threats or invocations uttered by the first witch; and the very beating of his heart: 'And make my seated Heart knock at my Ribs,' is found to echo the beating of the drum, 'Wrack't, as homeward he did come. *Drum within.*' We may compare the two four-line groups:

Lines Forward

Scene	29	1. Here I have a Pilot's Thumb,	
	30	Wrack't, as homeward he did come.	*Drum within.*
	31	3. A Drum, a Drum:	
	32	*Macbeth* doth come.	

Lines Back from the end

Scene	32-	If good? why do I yield to that suggestion,
	31-	Whose horrid Image doth unfix my Heire,
	30-	And make my seated Heart knock at my Ribs,
	29-	Against the use of Nature?

We may also note that the word 'Hair,' in the First Folio, is spelt 'Heire' and we may wonder whether the thought of Duncan has anything to do with Macbeth's hope of progeny.

In the final section beginning, 'Worthy *Macbeth*, we stay upon your leysure.,' Macbeth pulls himself together and thanks the King's messengers, Rosse and Angus, for their trouble. Finally he turns to Banquo and says, (we imagine *sotto voce*) that they should say no more for the present about their strange encounter with the witches. This may leave us wondering how much Banquo has said to the others already while Macbeth, alone, was experiencing his soliloquy and his vision of murder. This last section matches the beginning of the scene with the story of the 'Sailor's Wife' and the 'Chestnuts.' It also helps to confirm that the sailor and his wife are no other than Macbeth and Lady Macbeth, since there can hardly be two others in the play, one important and the other remote, who suffer from insomnia.

Act 1 Scene 4

The following three scenes, scenes 4, 5 and 6 are relatively short: in the Folio lineation they have 66, 81 and 37 lines respectively. In Scene 4, mostly set by editors in a palace at Forres, and perhaps imagined as taking place late at night, or very early in the morning, we have the first on-stage meeting between Macbeth and King Duncan. Again there is a kind of prologue, this time of 16 lines only, in which we learn of Cawdor's execution and the noble manner of his dying. After the two lines:

Scene 15 He was a Gentleman, on whom I built
16 An absolute Trust.

we have the entry of Macbeth, with Banquo, Rosse and Angus. Lines 17 to 33 enclose King Duncan's welcome to Macbeth, with the latter's stiff reply (at lines 25-31). This part ends with Duncan's words:

Scene 32 *King*. Welcome hither:
33 I haue begun to plant thee, and will labour
34 To make thee full of growing.

The King then turns to Banquo, embraces him and weeps:

Scene 40 My plenteous Ioyes,
41 Wanton in fullnesse, seeke to hide themselues
42 In drops of sorrow.

3, SCENE SYMMETRY   63

With a certain abruptness the King now addresses the assembled company to make an announcement of state: he intends to overrule the old law of succession and appoint his eldest son Malcolm - still a boy - to be his heir. This brings us to lines 48 and 49.

Scene 48   But signes of Noblenesse, like Starres, shall shine
      49   On all deseruers.

The scene ends with three short paragraphs: six lines for the theme of Duncan's visit to Inverness, ending with Macbeth's leavetaking: six lines for Macbeth's soliloquy on his way out: 'Starres hide your fires,' and five lines for a fragment of conversation between Banquo and the King, whose theme is the excellence of Macbeth. The last speaker is Duncan:

Scene 64   ... Let's after him,
      65   Whose care is gone before, to bid vs welcome:
      66   It is a peerlesse kinsman.   *Flourish. Exeunt.*

We may now tentatively set out the parts of this scene as follows:

16 lines: Prologue. Cawdor's death.
        ENTRY OF MACBETH ETC.
17 lines: Duncan's welcome to Macbeth.
9 lines: Duncan's welcome to Banquo.
7 lines: Naming of Malcolm as 'Prince of Cumberland.'
6 lines: 'From hence to Envernes.'
6 lines: 'Starres hide your fires.'
        EXIT OF MACBETH.
5 lines: Praise of Macbeth, 'Let's after him.'

The sum of the last three sections which follow the conclusion of state business is 17(6+6+5): the sum of the two previous ones is 16(9+7).

We may therefore write the scheme as follows:

$$\left.\begin{array}{r}16\\17\end{array}\right\}33$$

$$\left.\begin{array}{r}16\\17\end{array}\right\}33$$

Figure 12

The centre of the scene falls at the moment when Duncan turns from Macbeth to welcome Banquo. The four central lines are:

Scene 32 *King.* Welcome hither:
     33 I haue begun to plant thee, and will labour
     34 To make thee full of growing. Noble *Banquo*,
     35 That hast no lesse deseru'd ...

What we may first observe is simple contrast across this centre. King Duncan embraces his older general, Banquo, with the utmost simplicity and openness. He has not embraced Macbeth. Indeed the stiffness of Macbeth's answer to the King is matched by the strange obscurity and constraint of the King's first words to Macbeth: 'The sinne of my Ingratitude euen now / Was heauie on me ...' The vague promises of this speech also contrast with the very precise appointment — the accession to the throne — given later to Malcolm.

Moving outwards from the centre we find that the courage and openness of Cawdor, the traitor who dies, contrasts precisely with the secrecy, terror, and soul-darkness of Macbeth, the traitor who will bring about death. At lines 5, 6 and 7 we have:

Scene 5 *(Mal.)* Who did report, that very frankly hee
      6 Confess'd his Treasons, implor'd your Highnesse Pardon,
      7 And set forth a deepe Repentance:

At lines 60 and 61, their mirror image, we find:

    60 *(Mac.)* The Eye winke at the Hand: yet let that bee,
    61 Which the Eye feares, when it is done to see. *Exit*

These are the closing lines of the 'Stars hide your fires' soliloquy.

The King's last words to Macbeth, 'My worthy *Cawdor*,' may acquire a new dimension too. These words in which King Duncan clothes a new man so easily, even callously, in a dead man's title, fall at line 55. This is the mirror-line to line 12, 'As 'twere a carelesse Trifle;' the phrase marking the end of Malcolm's description of Cawdor's death. 'Worthy' means 'brave.' Do we find behind the words 'My worthy *Cawdor*' the image of a brave man stepping up to the block, from which a moment later that 'carelesse Trifle,' his head, will roll into the dust?

3, SCENE SYMMETRY

Finally, we may compare the centre of this scene, 'I haue begun to plant thee...' with the centre of Scene 3, 'Or haue we eaten on the insane Root...' In both there is the image of a plant with roots in the earth. One is an evil plant that drives man mad; the other ought to be a good plant, set in the earth by a good and generous King; yet its fruits are evil.

Act 1 Scene 5

At the end of Scene 4 we leave Macbeth pausing to look up at the stars before mounting his horse and riding north as fast as he can towards Inverness. At some point, either then or later, he sends a swift rider ahead to warn his wife of Duncan's imminent arrival. Scene 5 takes us to Macbeth's castle shortly before the messenger arrives, and there we meet Lady Macbeth for the first time.

It could be early in the morning. She is in the middle of reading a letter from Macbeth: one he has somehow found time to write and despatch by messenger *after* his meeting with the witches, but presumably *before* his audience with the King. In this letter Macbeth tells his wife of his extraordinary encounters on the heath on his way home from battle. The fulfilment of two prophecies gives hope for the third. The letter ends at line 12 with *'Lay it to thy heart, and farewell.'*

Now Lady Macbeth looks up from the letter and speaks her thoughts aloud:

Scene 13   Glamys thou art, and Cawdor, and shalt be
       14   What thou art promis'd ...

She is filled with elation and determination; not at all, it seems, with surprise. The stumbling block is Macbeth's kindly and generous nature, which prevents him from taking the ruthless action needed to achieve advancement. At line 29: 'To haue thee crown'd withall,' a messenger bursts into the room:

Scene 31   *Mess.* The King comes here to Night.
       32   *Lady.* Thou art mad to say it.

Lady Macbeth's words rush out before she can stop them, and the rest is a quick cover-up: 'Is not thy Master with him?'

At line 40 the messenger departs to look after his exhausted fellow — the one who has galloped ahead of Macbeth with the news — and Lady Macbeth, alone once more, begins her terrible invocation.

Scene 41   The Raven himselfe is hoarse,
      42   That croakes the fatall entrance of *Duncan*
      43   Vnder my Battlements. Come you Spirits …[1]

With 'Come you Spirits,' she invokes evil beings that will harden her heart, congeal all the flowing compassion in her body and blot out the piercing glance of heaven, that she may have strength and resolution to murder the King with her own hand that night, as opportunity offers.

This passage ends at line 57 with the words 'To cry, hold, hold,' as Macbeth himself, as exhausted perhaps as the breathless messenger, suddenly confronts her. There follow eleven lines of brief and pregnant exchanges between husband and wife. She greets him with ecstasy, then comes straight to the point:

Scene 63   *Macb*. My dearest Loue,
      64   Duncan comes here to Night.
      65   *Lady*. And when goes hence?
      66   *Macb*. To morrow, as he purposes.
      67   *Lady*. O neuer,
      68   Shall Sunne that Morrow see.

Her thought is his and his terror is visible. She gazes intently at him.

      69   Your Face, my *Thane*, is as a Booke, where men
      70   May reade strange matters, to beguile the time.

She bids dissemble when King Duncan comes, to put on a mask of innocence and welcome. She repeats, she will do it, that deed which will give masterdom 'to all our nights, and days'. Macbeth is undecided; she bids him ironically to 'Look up clear.' This is the moment of 'favour' and great opportunity when the stars (those very stars from which a moment ago she wished to hide) are luring King Duncan to his doom.

The sub-divisions of this scene may be thus summed up:

3, SCENE SYMMETRY

12 lines: Letter, news of prophecies, sudden hope.
17 lines: Lady Macbeth's soliloquy on her husband's character. She will spur him on.
   ENTRY OF MESSENGER
11 lines: News of King Duncan's arrival.
   EXIT OF MESSENGER
17 lines: Lady Macbeth's summoning of spirits to harden both heart and body, and of darkness to hide her deed.
   ENTRY OF MACBETH
11 lines: Exchange between Lady Macbeth and Macbeth. Duncan must never leave alive.
   DRAMATIC PAUSE
13 lines: The 'book' of his face, which must be disguised. They must have faith in the moment and resolution. *She* will do it.

The sum of the first three sections is 40(12+17+11); the sum of the last three is 41(17+11+13).

We may therefore write the scheme as follows:

$$28 \begin{cases} 12 \\ (17) \\ (11) \end{cases} 40$$

– scene centre, line 41, 'The Raven himselfe is hoarse,'

$$28 \begin{cases} (17) \\ (11) \\ (13) \end{cases} 41$$

Figure 13

Act 1 Scene 6

The following scene is set out of doors, against the backdrop of Inverness Castle. The air is delicious, the evening sun (we imagine) is shining and, from their hanging, mud-built nests, high up in 'every coign of vantage,' the house martins swoop, fetching food for their young. Banquo is walking, or riding, beside the King, and the scene is set for the audience by an exchange between them, which takes up the first eleven lines. As they look up to the castle battlements, perhaps Lady Macbeth looks down, and sees the royal cavalcade. She hastens downstairs, and at line eleven appears at door or gate to give the King a formal reception. Duncan sees her from a little distance:

Scene 12   *King*. See, see, our honor'd Hostesse:
13   The Loue that followes vs, sometime is our trouble,
14   Which still we thanke as Loue. Herein I teach you,
15   How you shall bid God-eyld vs for your paines,
16   And thanke vs for your trouble.

After the first line there must follow a pause, in which the King and hostess approach one another. 'Herein I teach you' seems to refer to 'The loue that follows vs;' but could also imply a gesture from the King, answering Lady Macbeth's formal obeisance.

Lines 11–23 are given to the first exchange of courtesies; then Duncan enquires abruptly for his absent host: 'Where's the Thane of Cawdor?' Clearly the King had actually tried to race Macbeth to Inverness, but ' his great Loue (sharpe as his Spurre) hath holp him / To his home before vs:' (line 28). The question is not answered, and Duncan does not press for an answer, but continues graciously, 'Faire and Noble Hostesse / We are your guest to night.' Lady Macbeth now responds with a polite, if strained, book-keeping image; 'All our seruice, / In euery point twice done, and then done double …' The King takes her hand; and together they enter the castle.

The scene has just 37 lines. We may sum up its sub-divisions thus:

11 lines : Prologue. Duncan and Banquo.
           Scene is set.
    ENTRY OF LADY MACBETH.
5 lines : Meeting between Duncan and Lady Macbeth.
7 lines : Lady Macbeth's welcoming speech.
5 lines : 'Where's the Thane of Cawdor.'
9 lines : Final courtesies.
          'Conduct me to mine Host.'

We find that Lady Macbeth's speech of welcome lies approximately, but not exactly, in the centre of the scene. Thus:
  A single line lies at the mathematical centre, 'Were poore, and single

3, SCENE SYMMETRY   69

$$\left.\begin{array}{c}11\\5\end{array}\right\}16$$

$$7\qquad 7$$

$$\left.\begin{array}{c}5\\9\end{array}\right\}14$$

Figure 14

Businesse ...' and this falls at the centre of Lady Macbeth's five-line opening clause:

Scene 17   *Lady*. All our seruice,
       18   In euery point twice done, and then done double,
   Scene
       19   Were poore, and single Businesse, to contend
       20   Against those Honors deepe, and broad,
       21   Wherewith your Maiestie loades our House:

The scene closes and opens with a few lines (4 and 3) spoken by the King. Between line 24 '*King*. Where's the Thane of Cawdor? ...' and line 33, 'Still to returne your owne,' we have first the image of a horseman (the King) following hard on the heels of another (Macbeth), whose love for his wife makes him spur on his horse; and then the image of a great household, with its provisions and coffers, where a lord and lady wait to receive the second rider and give back to him what is seen as truly his. Matching these lines in the first half of the scene are lines 5–14, with their image of the Castle and the swooping birds, leading to 'The love that follows us ...'

Love follows Duncan, attends him on his journey, as Duncan himself, an urgent horseman, has just followed Macbeth. And as the summer guest, the elegant martlett ('barlet' in the folio), enters the tiny hole in the top of his nest to find warmth and shelter there, so does Duncan enter the dark gateway into Macbeth's Castle, looking for the welcome he has always received.

At the centre of this scene there is neither bird nor plant, yet there *is* a kind of cell-like growth; the growth of a geometrical progression:

Scene 17   *Lady*. All our seruice,
       18   In euery point twice done, and then done double,

There is also, in the repetition of the words 'double' and 'trouble' (line 13) a foreshadowing of the witches' refrain in Act 4:

Pl.   1456   *All*. Double, double, toile and trouble;
      1457   Fire burne, and Cauldron bubble.

Out of the present, the nightmare future will grow, as four grows out of two, and eight grows out of four.

Act 1 Scene 7

We come now to Scene 7, 92 lines long, and the last scene in Act 1. It is later in the evening, and the great feast, taking place somewhere just off stage, has nearly ended. The folio stage directions are:

Ho-boyes.   Torches.
Enter a Sewer, and diuers Seruants with Dishes and Seruice
ouer the Stage. Then enter Macbeth.

The scene is sometimes set in the castle courtyard, which becomes the central scene in Act 2, but more often in an anteroom or passageway next to the banqueting hall. Whatever the outer setting, the inner space for this scene is Macbeth's soul, which struggles to reach a decision, almost succeeds, and then in the terrible climax is swept into reverse by a torrent too strong for it.

The first 28 lines, beginning like a knell with 'If it were done when 'tis done, then 'twere well, / it were done quickly ...' are given to Macbeth's great soliloquy, in which he weighs action and consequence. This passage is shot through with vivid yet complex imagery, which only begins to come into focus when we remember that the speaker has just been riding through the night at break-neck speed. He took the shortest route, setting his horse to leap the rushing burns, and spurring it on to lengthen his lead over the King, who gallops with his retinue so close behind that Macbeth can almost hear the thunder of hooves when he draws rein to listen. We may imagine too that daylight brings hungry men to the river banks with spear and net, hoping to catch trout for breakfast, and that Macbeth will pass them as he leaps from bank to sandy shoal, and from shoal again to bank. It is also clear from this passage that ways and means of encompassing Duncan's death have been

3, SCENE SYMMETRY

considered earlier in the evening; and that Macbeth first meant to slay the King quite openly.[2] The last sentence of this soliloquy, beginning at line 25 is broken off by the entry of Lady Macbeth, who has slipped out of the hall to search for her absent husband.

Scene 25   (Macbeth)   ... I haue no Spurre
       26   To pricke the sides of my intent, but onely
       27   Vaulting Ambition, which ore-leapes it selfe,
       28   And falles on th' other.   *Enter Lady*.
       29   How now? What Newes?

She upbraids him, but at that moment we feel he hardly hears her, as he is screwing up his courage to tell her of his decision; 'We will proceed no further in this businesse.' She listens until line 37 'Not cast aside so soone' and then turns on him with unutterable scorn.

Scene 38   *La*. Was the hope drunke,
       39   Wherein you drest your selfe?

At line 41 she gives the thrust that she knows will go home, calling into question his love for her, his courage and his manhood. Macbeth, who a few hours before was fighting with heroic prowess, is yet pierced by her words, though his answer has both dignity and nobility:

Scene 50   I dare do all that may become a man.
       51   Who dares no more is none. (usually changed to 'who dares do more ...'

But she has eloquence, logic, and demonic imagery to shatter this thought as on a rock.

Scene 52   *La*. What Beast was't then
       53   That made you breake this enterprize to me?
       54   When you durst do it, then you were a man:
       55   And to be more then what you were, you would
       56   Be so much more the man. Nor time, nor place
       57   Did then adhere, and yet you would make both:
       58   They haue made themselues, and that their fitnesse now
       59   Do's vnmake you...

Between line 52 'What Beast was't then?' and lines 63 / 64 .'..had I so sworne / As you haue done to this.' comes the climax of the scene and the disintegration of Macbeth's decision.

'If we should faile?' (line 65) implies that he has already given in; between this line and line 79, comes the consolidation of victory. Lady Macbeth outlines a scheme that will hide the deed (now a deed to be shared between husband and wife) and put the guilt on others. Macbeth is won over, and filled with admiration for her masculine courage.

In the last 13 lines, from 'Bring forth Men-Children onely' to the final rhyming couplet, we have Macbeth's decision, now written as an inescapable fate; the fate of a man who must henceforth wear a mask:

Scene 91   Away, and mock the time with fairest show,
      92   False Face must hide what the false Heart doth know.
                                                    Exeunt

We can now summarize the sub-divisions of this scene:

28 { 28 lines : Macbeth's soliloquy.
                To murder Duncan, or not to murder him?

               ENTRY OF LADY MACBETH

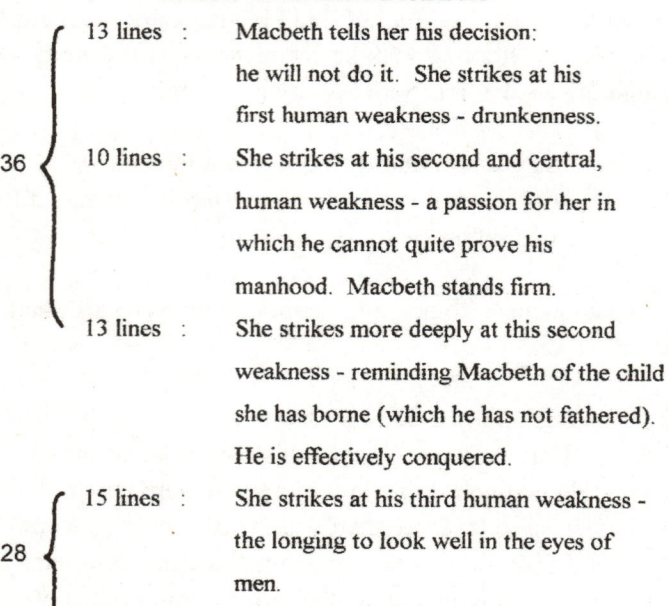

     13 lines : Macbeth tells her his decision:
                he will not do it. She strikes at his
                first human weakness - drunkenness.

36 { 10 lines : She strikes at his second and central,
                human weakness - a passion for her in
                which he cannot quite prove his
                manhood. Macbeth stands firm.

     13 lines : She strikes more deeply at this second
                weakness - reminding Macbeth of the child
                she has borne (which he has not fathered).
                He is effectively conquered.

     15 lines : She strikes at his third human weakness -
28 {   the longing to look well in the eyes of
                men.

     13 lines : Final decision: the deed will be done.

Figure 15

3, SCENE SYMMETRY

The last two groups, 15 and 13 lines, total 28, so that the symmetry of this scene is immediately apparent. The clearest dramatic pauses, falling at 'How now? What Newes?' and 'If we should fail?' mark off the two long 28-line groups at the beginning and end. In the central region lie three lesser groups (13, 10, 13) totalling 36 lines.

At the centre of the 10 group comes a half-expected image; that of a cat poised above a pool where there lurks a fish. The image crystallizes the naked accusation of cowardice and impotence that comes in the central lines:

Scene	42	...Art thou affear'd
	43	To be the same in thine owne Act, and Valour,
	44	As thou art in desire? Would'st thou haue that
Scene	⎰45	Which thou esteem'st the Ornament of Life,
Centre	⎱46	And liue a Coward in thine owne Esteeme?
	47	Letting I dare not, wait vpon I would,
	48	Like the poore Cat i'th' Addage.
	49	*Macb.* Prythee peace:
	50	I dare do all that may become a man,
	51	Who dares no more, is none.

The actual words, 'Cat i'th' Addage' follow the central two lines, but the picture of a being who longs to catch a fish, but hates the cold wetness into which it must dip its paw, is already there, crouched in Lady Macbeth's thought, at the mathematical centre of the scene.

Moving outwards from the centre we find that lines 52–56, beginning 'What Beast was't then...?' match exactly the accusation of drunkenness coming at lines 38–41.

These symmetrical groups of lines are:

Scene	38	*La.* Was the hope drunke,
	39	Wherein you drest your selfe? Hath it slept since?
	40	And wakes it now to looke so greene, and pale,
	41	At what it did so freely? From this time,

And,

41- (52)	*La.* What Beast was't then
40- (53)	That made you breake this enterprize to me?

39- (54) When you durst do it, then you were a man:
38- (55) And to be more then what you were, you would
37- (56) Be so much more the man.

Reading them, we may remember the Porter's words on the subject of drink,

Play 730   Lecherie, Sir, it prouokes, and vnprouokes: it prouokes
      731   the desire, but it takes away the performance. Therefore
      732   much Drinke may be said to be an Equiuocator with Le-
      733   cherie: (2, 3)

To be drunk, therefore, is in a very precise sense to be *not* a man. It has long been assumed that this sense was intended by Lady Macbeth. The pattern however confirms it. The irony of 'What Beast was't then?' is of course that it *was* a beast, or had much to do with one; the beast that stalks everywhere 'With *Tarquin's* rauishing sides' (play line 604) through the darkness of night.

Finally, we come to the two 28-line groups that begin and end the scene. The first, Macbeth's soliloquy, is one of the most-discussed passages in Shakespeare, and to analyse all the correspondences between it and the last 28 lines would take us beyond the scope of this chapter. Two things, however, can be at once observed: the moment of final decision mirrors the initial struggle to decide; and the troop of brave little boys that Lady Macbeth should bear in the dark night of the future — each one first an infant at the breast — matches the 'naked new-born babe' that symbolizes pity, and the sky, full of cherubim, riding on the blast that will show the truth to all mankind.

We find, too, in both passages, a suggestion of a still room, full of retorts and 'Limbecks,' where strange things are brewed; poison to be dropped in a chalice of wine or soporifics to 'convince' the senses of inconvenient guards. The same still room we imagine as that in which Lady Macbeth prepares, or pretends to prepare, her husband's drink in Act 2.

There remains a question: what of the fishing image? It lies at the centre, where the cat is the fisherman. It also comes at the beginning in 'trammel vp the Consequence, and catch / With his surcease, Successe.'[3] The blow, which should be the 'be-all and the end-all,' is like that of a spear; the halve-net should land the fish. Do we find any hint of this image reflected at the end of the scene, as we might expect? The final quatrain opens:

Scene 89   *Macb*. I am settled, and bend vp
      90   Each corporall Agent to this terrible Feat.

If Lady Macbeth is a sailor's wife, then Macbeth is in some sense a sailor and has been 'master o' the Tiger.' Sea fishing is as familiar to him as river fishing. He has lent a hand to haul in the nets, bending iron muscles to bring aboard some special catch; a huge shoal, or perhaps a shark caught by mistake.

The image fits, though as yet there is no proof. We can only say that one passage seems to speak to another, to illumine another as in a dialogue, and that if such mirrorings are found everywhere then the critical apparatus needed to interpret meaning and intention must be embedded already in Shakespeare's text.

4. The Counting of Prose in *Macbeth*

I knew when I first made the discovery about the centre of *Macbeth*, that the prose had to be counted. The reason for this was quite simple; that the centre of the play fell at the mathematical centre, which could only be calculated if you counted each printed line in the First Folio as 'one,' and this included prose, iambic pentameters, iambic tetrameters and short lines indifferently. So I knew the counting worked and it worked with other plays too, but I did not know why at that time.

The fact that prose lines cannot be counted as verse lines is, of course, what one would expect, and what everyone believes, but the curious thing is that it is quite untrue. If we count 'one' for each printed prose line, just as we do for each printed line of verse, everything else falls into place. We have therefore to start the other way about. The question is not: 'Can we count prose lines?' but, 'What can the counting of prose lines possibly mean, considering that such printed lines are arbitrary units, depending on type-size and column width, not in any way to be compared with pentameters, or other verse lines, which all have a musical shape?'

It appears that what the First Folio provides for each prose passage (or short section of one) is a total, an answer; something like the answer to a sum that we find at the back of a textbook. It does not tell us directly how the sum was done, but it helps us.

When, during a performance, the iambic measure of verse gives way to the rhythm of prose, the audience does not sit up with a jolt. The heartbeat of the play has not died under the knife. Words, breaths and syllables flow on; only the speed varies more —the heartbeat is less regular. The line of ten syllables (or eleven) is lost, but in its place there is the 'natural phrase' or 'wave' of speech, which may be quite long or quite short. In fact every writer of free verse uses such phrases, one to a line, so that we could say he is experimenting with ways of dividing up prose.

Yet the poet makes his own rules. If his poem were to be written out in the form of continuous prose and three people were asked to reconstruct the original form, their results would probably differ. Likewise, if three people attempted to subdivide a prose passage in a Shakespeare play into its main natural phrases, their results might also differ; they might have individual ideas on how any given passage should best be spoken.

One thing, though, that I believe our three people would certainly find is that it is the easiest thing in the world to make the number of natural phrases in a given passage tally precisely with the number of lines on which that passage is printed in the 1623 Folio. I say this as the result of experiment and observation. I had known for some time that the number of Folio-lines, on which each prose passage was printed, was numerically significant but I did not know why. I simply followed the rule; treat prose lines as if they are lines of verse, 'each printed line counts as one,' and all the totals will come right. How else could it be that the clear centre of *Macbeth* falls at the exact mathematical centre?

My experiment with the prose in *Macbeth* consisted in setting out each prose passage as if it were free verse in the most natural way I could, so that some lines were short and some quite long, and then counting how many lines I had used. Finally, this total was compared with the number of lines on which the original prose passage was set out (a number I was careful not to note in advance). The result was striking; either the numbers were identical or they differed only by one line, in which case it was a question of a slight rearrangement, always a simple one. This experience confirms our impression that the number of lines taken up by a passage of prose is musically significant. After reading Richard Flatter's book, *Shakespeare's Producing Hand,* which confirms my own work, I have thought that the way prose is set out is really a teaching method telling the actor how he should speak any given passage.

Of course, further research needs to be carried out; others need to check my results in *Macbeth* and yet others to look (and listen) to prose passages in other Shakespeare plays. Meanwhile, the rule of thumb remains unshaken, and as a way of trying to understand it, mine at least makes a beginning.

So supposing this correlation is basically correct; supposing the poet consciously or instinctively was counting prose in phrases according to his own rules, we still have to enquire how the printed result filled the right number of lines. It would seem to involve an extraordinary kind of fiddling about. Yet a writer can know his own writing, and also enough of particular printing, to set convenient margins before he starts; and where it is only a matter of balancing, say, three phrases within three lines (as it often is), the matter is easy enough. If some rewriting were needed, the trouble would not be not so absurd when we consider what was at stake;

4. THE COUNTING OF PROSE IN *MACBETH*

the manifold symmetries of a precisely-constructed verse-play.

In *Macbeth* there are four passages of prose, or mainly prose: the letter in Act 1 Scene 5; the Porter episode in Act 2; part of the exchange between Lady Macduff and her son in Act 4; and most of the sleepwalking scene in Act V. In the following we will render into natural phrases the first section of prose in Macbeth, (the letter in Act 1 Scene 5) showing the same number of lines as that arranged in the lines of text printed in the First Folio. Following this we will illustrate the same with the Porter's 'Hell-Gate' monologue (Act 2 Scene 3), which is the longest continuous passage of prose in the whole play, and in a sense the first true one since the letter of Act 1 is merely read by Lady Macbeth and not spontaneously spoken.

Act 1 Scene 5 *(lines of text as in First Folio)*

Enter Macbeths Wife alone with a Letter.

331 Lady. They met me in the day of successe: and I haue
332 learn'd by the perfect'st report, they haue more in them, then
333 mortall knowledge. When I burnt in desire to question them
334 further, they made themselues Ayre, into which they vanish'd.
335 Whiles I stood rapt in the wonder of it, came Missiues from
336 the King, who all-hail'd me Thane of Cawdor, by which Title
337 before, these weyward Sisters saluted me, and referr'd me to
338 the comming on of time, with haile King that shalt be. This
339 haue I thought good to deliuer thee (my dearest Partner of
340 Greatnesse) that thou might'st not loose the dues of reioycing
341 by being ignorant of what Greatnesse is promis'd thee. Lay
342 it to thy heart and farewell.

Act 1 Scene 5 *(lines rendered into natural phrases)*

Enter Macbeths Wife alone with a Letter.

331 Lady. They met me in the day of successe:
332 and I haue learn'd by the perfect'st report,
333 they haue more in them, then mortall knowledge

334	When I burnt in desire to question them further,
335	they made themselues Ayre, into which they vanish'd.
336	Whiles I stood rapt in the wonder of it,
337	came Missiues from the King, who all-hail'd me Thane of Cawdor,
338	by which Title before, these weyward Sisters saluted me,
339	and referr'd me to the comming on of time, with haile King that shalt be.
340	This haue I thought good to deliuer thee (my dearest Partner of Greatnesse)
341	that thou might'st not loose the dues of reioycing by being ignorant of what Greatnesse is promis'd thee.
342	Lay it to thy heart and farewell.

Act 2 Scene 3 (lines of text as in First Folio)

Enter a Porter.

Knocking within.

704	*Porter.* Here's a knocking indeede: if a man were
705	Porter of Hell Gate, hee should haue old turning the
706	Key. *Knock.* Knock, Knock, Knock. Who's there
707	i'th' name of *Belzebub*? Here's a Farmer, that hang'd
708	himselfe on th' expectation of Plentie: Come in time, haue
709	Napkins enow about you, here you'le sweat for't. *Knock.*
710	Knock, knock. Who's there in th' other Deuils Name?
711	Faith here's an Equiuocator, that could sweare in both
712	the Scales against eyther Scale, who committed Treason
713	enough for Gods sake, yet could not equiuocate to Hea-
714	uen: oh come in, Equiuocator. *Knock.* Knock,
715	Knock, Knock. Who's there? 'Faith here's an English
716	Taylor come hither, for stealing out of a French Hose:
717	Come in Taylor, here you may rost your Goose. *Knock.*
718	Knock, Knock. Neuer at quiet: What are you? but this
719	place is too cold for Hell. Ile Deuill-Porter it no further:
720	I had thought to haue let in some of all Professions, that
721	goe the Primrose way to th' euerlasting Bonfire. *Knock.*
722	Anon, anon, I pray you remember the Porter.

4. THE COUNTING OF PROSE IN *MACBETH*

Act 2 Scene 3 (lines rendered into natural phrases)

Enter a Porter.

Knocking within

704 *Porter.* Here's a knocking indeede:
705   if a man were Porter of Hell Gate, hee should haue old turning the Key.
706   *Knock.* Knock, Knock, Knock.
707   Who's there i'th' name of *Belzebub*?
708   Here's a Farmer, that hang'd himselfe on th' expectation of Plentie:
709   Come in time, haue Napkins enow about you, here you'le sweat for't.
710   *Knock.* Knock, knock.
711   Who's there in th' other Deuils Name?
712   Faith here's an Equiuocator,
713   that could sweare in both the Scales against eyther Scale,
714   who committed Treason enough for Gods sake, yet could not equiuocate to Heauen:
715   oh come in, Equiuocator.
716   *Knock.*Knock, Knock, Knock. Who's there?
717   Faith here's an English Taylor come hither, for stealing out of a French Hose:
718   Come in Taylor, here you may rost your Goose.
719   *Knock.* Knock, Knock. Neuer at quiet: What are you?
720   but this place is too cold for Hell. Ile Deuill-Porter it no further:
721   I had thought to haue let in some of all Professions, that goe the Primrose way to th' euerlasting Bonfire.
722   *Knock.* Anon, anon, I pray you remember the Porter.

What is interesting is that the four prose passages in *Macbeth* have a precise relationship to one another in the mathematical structure of the whole play. The passage containing the fateful letter is echoed symmetrically across the play centre by the passage in Act 5 Scene 1 where the Doctor and Gentlewoman speak of the fall into madness of Lady Macbeth.[1] The same symmetrical mirroring is also evident in the relationship of the other two prose passages: the Porter's monologue of Act 2, and the dialogue between Lady Macduff and her son in Act 4 Scene

2. In a later chapter we will study further these mirrored prose episodes, for their relationship with each other, across the play centre, is a dynamic one; not only interesting in terms of play structure but also informing a deeper understanding of the text itself.

5. Play Symmetry

The three kinds of symmetry — play, act and scene — have certain elements in common. All are mathematically exact and at the same time organic and fluid. That is, the total number of lines in any group gives an exact number with whose midway point there is no arguing; but within (or above) these fixed boundaries, balancing passages float more-or-less freely, rather as the actual words in a strict metrical line float a little freely above the felt rhythmic beat below. If their stresses coincide precisely with that of the felt beat the verse becomes a boring succession of hammer blows.

In a Shakespearean scene (or act, or play) divided by entrances, exits, regroupings, fights, changes of subject and so forth, passages that balance each other and thereby converse across the centre are always roughly equal, never exact in length.

If one were to map the play on tracing paper, fold it neatly at the centre and hold it up to the light, the natural divisions would never coincide, but always be a few lines apart. This kind of overlapping also resembles the overlapping of masonry, essential for the strong fusing of structure. And yet we come back to mathematical exactness whenever we find a single line echoing another, as not infrequently happens, for instance in the 'drumbeat' and the 'heart beat' mirror of Act 1 Scene 3.

Scene centres within an Act are marked by qualities particular to that Act.[1] Act centres also have special qualities as we have noted before where, in Macbeth, they are marked either by the word 'set' or 'sit,' or by the idea of sitting or setting (echoing the centre of the play).

In the end, conversations that arise between balancing passages, exactly balancing lines, even words, begin to shed new light on plot and character. Critical analysis is, as it were, 'built in' to the text of the plays, and this might be called the point, or 'over point,' of this astonishing hidden structure.

So far, all we know for certain about play symmetry is that the writer of the play was aware of the mathematical centre. The halfway position being so clearly marked, makes us wonder about the quarter position at line 598 (2392 ÷ 4). Looking now at this line let us see if there is any hint of an awareness of its position. The line falls in the dagger speech (2, 1) and with the next two lines reads,

> 598   Thus to mine Eyes. Now o're the one halfe World
> 599   Nature seemes dead, and wicked Dreames abuse
> 600   The Curtain'd sleepe ...

The sentence beginning 'Now o're the one halfe World,' brings to mind Macbeth standing on the summit of a hill at night, looking around him at the darkened world where everyone is asleep. To look around at one half-world implies that he is in the centre of it, and of course the centre of a half is a quarter.

Looking now at the three quarter mark of the play (line 1794) and the play mirror of the quarter mark (line 1795), we shall see whether there is any hint of an echo in word or meaning. Lines 1794 and 1795 come in Act 4 Scene 3, Malcolm has just been describing his vice of lust and Macduff responds by saying that this vice needn't prevent him from accepting the office of king. Macduff says,

> 1793 (600-)   Boundlesse intemperance
> 1794 (599-)   In Nature is a Tyranny: It hath beene
> 1795 (598-)   Th' vntimely emptying of the happy Throne,
> 1796 (597-)   And fall of many Kings.

The three quarter mark is 'In Nature is a Tyranny.' We find here no reference to the fraction ¾ but we do find a repetition of the word 'Nature,' which Shakespeare, in this play at least, and certainly this particular line, uses as a synonym for sexual activity, and we find this an extremely appropriate thought which we can now perceive pervading the earlier passage where Macbeth's words as he looks imaginatively o're the darkened world, could well include the thought of sleep after sexual fulfilment. Perhaps this thought is not only concerning people generally but, as it lives in the soul of Macbeth, relates quite specifically to certain people close to him. We know already that his thoughts are turned toward the murder of the King. Now we wonder if he bears in his thoughts some knowledge of the King's sexual activities that night. More will become clear on this theme in Chapter 8 on the hidden plot of *Macbeth*.

As it stands, in this earlier scene we are placed in the 'dagger speech' and Macbeth is steadily approaching the king's chamber. It is the hour when men sleep after fulfilment and the thought of murdering the king is quite clearly reflected in the play mirror line, 'Th' vntimely emptying of the happy Throne' (598).

5. PLAY SYMMETRY 85

Now we shall see whether the main divisions in the first half of the play are reflected across the centre in divisions, which may or may not be marked in the second half of the play.

The first clear correspondence appears when we observe the relationship between 540 lines forwards and 540 lines backwards from the end of the play. Line 540 marks the end of Act 1, and the words in the last two lines are Macbeth saying:

> 539   Away, and mock the time with fairest show,
> 540   False Face must hide what the false Heart doth know.
> *Exeunt.*

540 lines backwards (540-) from the end of the play bring us to line 1853, in Act 4 Scene 3, the very long scene in England. Macduff has just expressed despair because Malcolm has finally convinced him that he has vices which render him unfit to rule Scotland. Now the test is over, Macduff has convinced Malcolm of his sincerity and Malcolm now decides that he must tell him the truth, that the vices he pretended to were not real. So the words around the 540- division are,

> 1851 (542-)   ... but God aboue
> 1852 (541-)   Deale betweene thee and me; For euen now
> 1853 (540-)   I put my selfe to thy Direction, and
> 1854 (539-)   Vnspeake mine owne detraction. Heere abiure
> 1855 (538-)   The taints, and blames I laide vpon my selfe,
> 1856 (537-)   For strangers to my Nature. I am yet

The two lines: 'Vnspeake mine owne detraction. Heere abiure / The taints, and blames I laide vpon my selfe' mark the centre of the scene. We therefore come to the line 'unspeak mine own detraction (540-) just one line beyond the scene centre. Essentially, the end of this act (Act 1) is mirrored by the centre of a scene on the other side of the play (4, 2) and what is expressed in these positions are exact opposites. At the end of Act 1 Macbeth expresses that a mask must be worn and on the other side a mask must be taken off.

When we consider further the relationship between the first and second halves of the play we observe at once that the last act, Act 5, with 400 lines is much shorter than Act 1, which has 540 lines. Act 5 is, therefore, 140 lines shorter. This means that after line 400, Act 1 is balanced by the end of Act 4. In fact, around line 400 there is a change in Act 1. We are nearing the end of Scene 5. Lady Macbeth has just made it clear that she intends Duncan to be murdered that night and that she will do it. Macbeth has looked at her in comprehending consternation. Now, assuming that her will will be carried out she starts instructing Macbeth in how he should comport himself when the King arrives. 'O never, / Shall Sunne that Morrow see' are lines 397 and 398.' She continues 'Your Face, my *Thane*, is as a Booke, where men / May reade strange matters, to beguile the time.' These are lines 399 and 400. She goes on:

401	Looke like the time, beare welcome in your Eye,
402	Your Hand, your Tongue: looke like th' innocent flower,
403	But be the Serpent vnder't. He that's comming,
404	Must be prouided for: and you shall put
405	This Nights great Businesse into my dispatch,
406	Which shall to all our Nights, and Dayes to come,
407	Giue solely soueraigne sway, and Masterdome.
408	*Macb*. We will speake further,
409	*Lady*. Onely looke vp cleare:
410	To alter fauor, euer is to feare:
411	Leaue all the rest to me. *Exeunt*

The lines matching the end of Act 1 Scene 5 are at the end of Act 4 Scene 3. Macduff is speaking:

1982 (411-)	And Braggart with my tongue. But gentle Heauens,
1983 (410-)	Cut short all intermission: Front to Front,
1984 (409-)	Bring thou this Fiend of Scotland, and my selfe
1985 (408-)	Within my Swords length set him, if he scape
1986 (407-)	Heauen forgiue him too.
1987 (406-)	*Mal*. This time goes manly:
1988 (405-)	Come go we to the King, our Power is ready,
1989 (404-)	Our lacke is nothing but our leaue. *Macbeth*
1990 (403-)	Is ripe for shaking, and the Powres aboue
1991 (402-)	Put on their Instruments: Receiue what cheere you may,
1992 (401-)	The Night is long, that neuer findes the Day. *Exeunt*

5. PLAY SYMMETRY
87

This is the end of Act 4. It continues, line 400 back:

1993 (400-)	*Doct.* I haue too Nights watch'd with you, but can
1994 (499-)	perceiue no truth in your report. When was it shee last
1995 (498-)	walk'd?
1996 (497-)	*Gent.* Since his Maiesty went into the Field, I haue
1997 (496-)	seene her rise from her bed, throw her Night-Gown vp-
1998 (495-)	pon her ...

The repetition of the word 'night' at the end of Act 4, and beginning of Act 5 — 'The Night is long, that neuer findes the Day,' and 'I haue too Nights watch'd with you' — remind us of the repetition of the same word in this last section of Act 1 Scene 5, 'and you shall put / This Nights great Businesse into my dispatch, / Which shall to all our Nights, and Dayes to come, / Giue solely soueraigne sway, and Masterdome.'

Now we find a clear correspondence between Scenes 6 and 7 of Act 1 and the last part of Act 4 Scene 3. King Duncan and Banquo have just arrived at Inverness Castle, where the King expresses great pleasure and a sense of well-being at the whole aspect and climate:

412	*King.* This Castle hath a pleasant seat,
413	The ayre nimbly and sweetly recommends it selfe
414	Vnto our gentle sences.

Banquo draws the King's attention to the birds that are flying around the walls of the castle and which have built their mud nests in every convenient place. He describes this bird as the temple-haunting barlet but every editor assumes that this must be a misprint and substitutes the word 'martlet' for 'barlet.' It is remarkable that his language suggests a pleasant place suitable for love-making:

415	*Banq.* This Guest of Summer,
416	The Temple-haunting Barlet does approue,
417	By his loued Mansonry that the Heauens breath
418	Smells wooingly here: no Iutty frieze,
419	Buttrice, nor Coigne of Vantage, but this Bird
420	Hath made his pendant Bed, and procreant Cradle,

| 421 | Where they must breed, and haunt: I haue obseru'd |
| 422 | The ayre is delicate. *Enter Lady.* |

As Lady Macbeth enters, the love theme is immediately followed up:

Enter Lady.
423	*King.* See, see, our honor'd Hostesse:
424	The Loue that followes vs, sometime is our trouble,
425	Which still we thanke as Loue. Herein I teach you,
426	How you shall bid God-eyld vs for your paines,
427	And thanke vs for your trouble.

At this point we wonder if this imagery is deliberate and what Banquo is making of these evocative words. We perhaps begin to be aware that something could be living between the King and Lady Macbeth to which these thoughts of love-making and birth refer. We note also the strange word 'Mansonry' (that is, the craft of making a man's son) and feel once more that the Folio spelling points us in the right direction.

Duncan continues with 'Herein I teach you, / How you shall bid God-eyld vs for your paines, / And thanke vs for your trouble.' 'Herein I teach you,' could refer to the words just spoken by Duncan — 'Which still we thanke as Loue' — or they could refer to a gesture, maybe even a kiss, which has just happened on the stage. If we go so far as to read in this scene the imagery of love-making and procreation then we could say its main theme is incarnation. Suddenly, when this point becomes clear, massive implications come on its heels and our conventional interpretation of the play begins to shift. These matters will, of course, need to be looked at more closely and we will take them up shortly in our chapter on the plot. However, it is interesting for the time being to look at the contrasts expressed in the play mirror of this section of the play.

On the other side of the play Rosse is just breaking the news to Macduff that his wife and children have all been murdered and this, of course, follows the scene in which we witness the murder of one child, the little boy. Macduff is slowly taking it in; his family no longer lives on the earth, they are all excarnated souls.

1966 (427-)	*Macd.* He ha's no Children. All my pretty ones?
1967 (426-)	Did you say All? Oh Hell-Kite! All?
1968 (425-)	What, All my pretty Chickens, and their Damme

5. PLAY SYMMETRY
89

    1969 (424-)   At one fell swoope?
    1970 (423-)   *Malc.* Dispute it like a man.
    1971 (422-)   *Macd.* I shall do so:
    1972 (421-)   But I must also feele it as a man;
    1973 (420-)   I cannot but remember such things were
    1974 (419-)   That were most precious to me: Did heauen looke on,
    1975 (418-)   And would not take their part? Sinfull *Macduff,*
    1976 (417-)   They were all strooke for thee: Naught that I am,
    1977 (416-)   Not for their owne demerits, but for mine
    1978 (415-)   Fell slaughter on their soules: Heauen rest them now.

When we look at what is being expressed in these lines and compare this with the content of their earlier mirrored lines, we find a striking contrast. Lines 415 to 427 forwards express the themes of pleasure, love-making and incarnation. Lines 415- to 427- express anguish, grief and excarnation.

We look next at the end of Act 2, and for its matching passage across the play centre. At the end of Act 2 Scene 4 the old man is saying:

    925   Gods benyson go with you, and with those
    926   That would make good of bad, and Friends of Foes.

These lines are mirrored by lines 1467 and 1468, in Act 4 Scene 1, that is while the three witches are round the cauldron throwing in nasty ingredients. At line 1467 we come to the second line of their repeated chorus:

    1466 (927-)   *All.* Double, double, toyle and trouble,
    1467 (926-)   Fire burne, and Cauldron bubble.
    1468 (925-)   *3* Scale of Dragon, Tooth of Wolfe,

The earlier line, 'Gods benyson go with you,' is echoed in the first line of the following verse 'Scale of Dragon, Tooth of Wolfe.' Here we have a contrast between the benevolence of the first words and the malevolence of the mirrored words. Now the nasty ingredients contain some bits of human remains:

1472 (921-)	Liuer of Blaspheming Iew,
1473 (920-)	Gall of Goate, and Slippes of Yew,
1474 (919-)	Sliuer'd in the Moones Ecclipse:
1475 (918-)	Nose of Turke, and Tartars lips:
1476 (917-)	Finger of Birth-strangled Babe,
1477 (916-)	Ditch-deliuer'd by a Drab,

evidence, one supposes, either of past murders or of grave robbing. The earthly witches' very particular cookery is followed by, '*Enter Hecat, and the other three Witches*' (the stage directions in the First Folio) and with the words, 'O well done: I commend your paines, / And euery one shall share i'th' gaines.'

We could say that the words of blessing and good will, at the end of Act 2 are mirrored in Act 4 Scene 1 by a passage of intensified evil. We wonder, in fact, if perhaps the first two verses of the cauldron chant are merely an introduction and the powerful trouble really only begins with the third verse.

One aspect of play symmetry only lightly touched upon so far (in the chapter on the counting of prose) is the interesting way that the four prose passages are placed in precise mathematical relationship to one another on either side of the play centre. In *Macbeth* there are four passages of prose, or mainly prose: the letter in Act 1; the Porter episode in Act 2; part of the exchange between Lady Macduff and her son in Act 4; and most of the sleepwalking scene in Act 5.

The twelve-line prose letter with which Act 1 Scene 5 begins, is matched across the play centre by the lines surrounding the final exit of Lady Macbeth in Act 5 Scene 1, that is the sleepwalking scene; these enclose the words, 'To bed, to bed, to bed.' Thus our first encounter with Lady Macbeth has a direct mathematical relationship with our last, they match precisely.

Opposite: *Mirrored Text A. Act 1 Scene 5 (and Act 5 Scene 1). The left-hand column shows play-lines 331–342 in sequence. The right-hand column shows corresponding mirrored lines of text which, because they are numbered from the end of the play (dashed numbers will always indicate reverse counting), must be read from bottom to top for continuity. This arrangement shows at a glance the relationship of the mirrored lines of play text. Line 331, for example, can be seen next to its companion line (331-) which is 331 lines from the end of the play.*

5. PLAY SYMMETRY 91

324 - *Gent.* Good night good Doctor. Exeunt.
325 - I thinke, but dare not speake.
326 - My minde she ha's mated, and amaz'd my sight.
327 - And still keepe eyes vpon her: So goodnight,
328 - Remoue from her the meanes of all annoyance,
329 - God, God forgiue vs all. Looke after her,
330 - More needs she the Diuine, then the Physitian:
331 - To their deafe pillowes will discharge their Secrets:
332 - Do breed vnnaturall troubles: infected mindes
333 - *Doct.* Foule whisp'rings are abroad: vnnaturall deeds
334 - *Gent.* Directly.
335 - *Doct.* Will she go now to bed?
         Exit Lady.
336 - done, cannot be vndone. To bed, to bed, to bed.
337 - Come, come, come, come, giue me your hand: What's
338 - *Lady.* To bed, to bed: there's knocking at the gate:
339 - *Doct.* Euen so?
340 - he cannot come out on's graue.
341 - looke not so pale: I tell you yet againe Banquo's buried;
342 - *Lad.* Wash your hands, put on your Night-Gowne,
343 - dyed holily in their beds.
344 - knowne those which haue walkt in their sleep, who haue
345 - *Doct.* This disease is beyond my practise: yet I haue
346 - *Gent.* Pray God it be sir.
347 - *Doct.* Well, well, well.
348 - for the dignity of the whole body.
349 - *Gent.* I would not haue such a heart in my bosome,
350 - *Doct.* What a sigh is there? The hart is sorely charg'd.

Scena Quinta.

Enter Macbeths Wife alone with a Letter.

331 *Lady.* They met me in the day of successe: and I haue
332 learn'd by the perfect'st report, they haue more in them, then
333 mortall knowledge. When I burnt in desire to question them
334 further, they made themselues Ayre, into which they vanish'd.
335 Whiles I stood rapt in the wonder of it, came Missiues from
336 the King, who all-hail'd me Thane of Cawdor, by which Title
337 before, these weyward Sisters saluted me, and referr'd me to
338 the comming on of time, with haile King that shalt be. This
339 haue I thought good to deliuer thee (my dearest Partner of
340 *Greatnesse) that thou might*'st not loose the dues of reioycing
341 by being ignorant of what Greatnesse is promis'd thee. Lay
342 it to thy heart and farewell.

The first line of the letter, 'They met me in the day of success,' is matched by words spoken by the doctor: 'To their deafe pillowes will discharge their Secrets.' From here we must go backwards to the line 'Wash your hands, put on your Night-Gowne, looke not so pale,' to come to the line that corresponds with the last line of the letter, 'Lay it to thy heart and farewell.' We see that the first three lines of the letter correspond, in reverse order, with the first three lines of regular verse spoken by the doctor: 'Foule whisp'rings are abroad: vnnaturall deeds / Do breed vnnaturall troubles, infected mindes / To their deafe pillowes will discharge their Secrets.' Lines 4 and 5 of the letter are echoed in lines that hover between verse and prose, 'Will she go now to bed?' *Gentlewoman*: 'Directly' (though the iambic rhythm is strong). Finally, at line 6, we come to Lady Macbeth's last words in the play: 'What's done cannot be vndone. To bed, to bed, to bed.' Now the prose of the letter is fully matched by the prose of the sleepwalking scene in Lady Macbeth's two last utterances, divided by the doctor's words, 'Even so.'[2]

If we continue reciting the words of Act 1 Scene 5, as we move backwards through Act V Scene 1, we arrive at the beginning of that chiefly prose scene, 'I haue too Nights watch'd with you ...' At this point we are 11 lines away from the end of Act 1 Scene 5 just as the theme is changing from implied murder to the look on Macbeth's face. The last line is, 'May read strange matters to beguile the time.'

To sum up, the two whole scenes virtually mirror each other across the play centre, but the prose of the letter is only mirrored in seven lines of prose in Act 5 Scene 1, otherwise verse balances prose. This is understandable in terms of Bradley's dictum that prose tends to be used when consciousness is somewhat deranged.[3] On the other hand, the fact that these two scenes virtually balance one another is also understandable because the evil, which is planted in the earlier scene, comes to fruition in the later one.

The way that the Porter episode is balanced across the play centre by the entire exchange between Lady Macduff and her son also yields much to careful study. This exchange begins in verse moves to prose around the scene centre, returns to a verse couplet spoken by Lady Macduff, and ends with the theme of treachery by taking the two kinds of rhythm and mixing them up in a singular third kind of speech. The Porter-episode, on the other hand, is entirely in prose, except for the couplet spoken by Macduff when the Porter at last lets him in, and possibly the Porter's first reply. Macduff's words: 'Was it so late, friend, ere you went to Bed, That you doe lye so late?' are echoed line for line in his wife's: 'Thou speak'st withall thy wit, and yet I'faith with

## 5. PLAY SYMMETRY	93

703 I would thou could'st. *Exeunt*

Scena Tertia

Enter a Porter.

Knocking within.

704 *Porter* Here's a knocking indeede: if a man were
705 Porter of Hell Gate, hee should haue old turning the
706 Key. Knock, Knock, Knock, Knock. Who's there
707 i'th' name of Belzebub? Here's a Farmer, that hang'd
708 himselfe on th' expectation of Plentie: Come in time, haue
709 Napkins enow about you, here you'le sweat for't. Knock.
710 Knock, knock. Who's there in th' other Deuils Name?
711 Faith here's an Equiuocator, that could sweare in both
712 the Scales against eyther Scale, who committed Treason
713 enough for Gods sake, yet could not equiuocate to Hea-
714 uen: oh come in, Equiuocator. Knock. Knock,
715 Knock, Knock. Who's there? 'Faith here's an English
716 Taylor come hither, for stealing out of a French Hose:
717 Come in Taylor, here you may rost your Goose. Knock.
718 Knock, Knock. Neuer at quiet: What are you? but this
719 place is too cold for Hell. Ile Deuill-Porter it no further:
720 I had thought to haue let in some of all Professions, that
721 goe the Primrose way to th' euerlasting Bonfire. Knock.
722 Anon, anon, I pray you remember the Porter.

Enter a Messenger.

703- *Wife.* Poore pratler, how thou talk'st?

704- haue a new Father.
705- would not, it were a good signe, that I should quickely
706- *Son.* If he were dead, youl'd weepe for him: if you
707- But how wilt thou do for a Father?
708- *Wife.* Now God helpe thee, poore Monkie:
709- and hang vp them.
710- are Lyars and Swearers enow, to beate the honest men,
711- *Son.* Then the Liars and Swearers are Fools: for there
712- *Wife.* Why, the honest men.
713- *Son* Who must hang them?
714- *Wife.* Euery one.
715- *Son.* And must they all be hang'd, that swear and lye?
716- And must be hang'd.
717- *Wife.* Euery one that do's so, is a Traitor,
718- *Son.* And be all Traitors, that do so.
719- *Wife.* Why one that sweares, and lyes.
720- *Son.* What is a Traitor?
721- *Wife.* I, that he was.
722- *Son.* Was my Father a Traitor, Mother?

Figure 16. Mirrored text B. Showing mirrored play-lines of Act 2 Scene 3, in left-hand column (read downwards) and those of Act 4, Scene 2 (read upwards for continuity).

Enter Macduff, and Lennox

723- *Macd.* Was it so late, friend, ere you went to Bed,
724- That you doe lye so late?
725- *Port.* Faith Sir, we were carowsing till the second Cock:
726- And Drinke, Sir, is a great prouoker of three things.
727- *Macd.* What three things does Drinke especially
728- prouoke?
729- *Port.* Marry, Sir, Nose-painting, Sleepe, and Vrine.
730- Lecherie, Sir, it prouokes, and vnprouokes: it prouokes
731- the desire, but it takes away the performance. Therefore
732- much Drinke may be said to be an Equiuocator with Le-
733- cherie: it makes him, and it marres him; it sets him on,
734- and it takes him off; it perswades him, and dis-heartens
735- him; makes him stand too, and not stand too: in conclu-
736- sion, equiuocates him in a sleepe, and giuing him the Lye,
737- leaues him.
738- *Macd.* I beleeue, Drinke gaue thee the Lye last Night.
739- *Port.* That it did, Sir, i'the very Throat on me: but I
740- requited him for his Lye, and (I thinke) being too strong
741- for him, though he tooke vp my Legges sometime, yet I
742- made a Shift to cast him.

723- And yet I'faith with wit enough for thee.
724- *Wife.* Thou speak'st withall thy wit,
725- *Son.* Then you'l by 'em to sell againe.
726- *Wife.* Why I can buy me twenty at any Market.
727- *Son.* Nay how will you do for a Husband?
728- How wilt thou do for a Father?
729- *Wife.* Yes, he is dead:
730- My Father is not dead for all your saying.
731- Poore Birds they are not set for:
732- *Son.* Why should I Mother?
733- The Pitfall, nor the Gin.
734- Thou'dst neuer Feare the Net, nor Lime,
735- *Wife.* Poore Bird,
736- *Son.* With what I get I meane, and so do they.
737- *Wife.* What with Wormes, and Flyes?
738- *Son.* As Birds do Mother.
739- And what will you do now? How will you liue?
740- *Wife.* Sirra, your Fathers dead,
741- I take my leaue at once. *Exit Rosse.*
742- It would be my disgrace, and your discomfort.

Enter Macbeth.

743- *Macd.* Is thy Master stirring?

743- *Rosse.* I am so much a Foole, should I stay longer

Figure 17

5. PLAY SYMMETRY 95

wit enough for thee,' the first being play-lines 723/4 (counting forwards) and the second being play-lines 723/4 (counting backwards from the end of the play). What certainly appears most interesting is that both couplets mark a division of themes and both are verse-interpolations in areas of prose.play).

The Porter's 'Hell-Gate' monologue is the longest continuous passage of prose in the whole play and, in a sense, the first true one, since the letter in Act 1 Scene 5 is merely read by Lady Macbeth, not spontaneously spoken. It is matched by dialogue, by speech-waves varying in length from one to three lines of text, where prose rhythms move back several times to iambic ones.

Apart from the mathematical relationship, the balanced positioning of these episodes in the play symmetry, between the Porter's 'Hell-Gate' monologue and the touching dialogue between Lady Macduff and her son, we find that these parts are also strongly linked by theme, especially the Hell-Gate monologue and the innocent questioning of the child:

1671	722-	*Son*. Was my Father a Traitor, Mother?
1672	721-	*Wife*. I, that he was.
1673	720-	*Son*. What is a Traitor?
1674	719-	*Wife*. Why one that sweares, and lyes.
1675	718-	*Son*. And be all Traitors, that do so.
1676	717-	*Wife*. Euery one that do's so, is a Traitor,
1677	716-	And must be hang'd.
1678	715-	*Son*. And must they all be hang'd, that swear and lye?
1679	714-	*Wife*. Euery one.
1680	713-	*Son*. Who must hang them?
1681	712-	*Wife*. Why, the honest men.
1682	711-	*Son*. Then the Liars and Swearers are Fools: for there
1683	710-	are Lyars and Swearers enow, to beate the honest men,
1684	709-	and hang vp them.

In both we find the idea of treachery and of swearing and of hanging and in both a kind of knowledge of men but uttered in contrasting voices: the thick voice of evil and the high clear voice of goodness and innocence. These two 19-line passages are also clearly framed; the earlier one by Macbeth's words (in the previous scene), 'I would thou could'st!' (703) and by Macduff's couplet: 'Was it so late, friend, ere you went to Bed,

That you doe lye so late?' (723 and 724), and the later one by Lady Macduff's words, 'Poore pratler how thou talk'st!' (703-) and 'Thou speak'st withall thy wit.' (724-). It is hard to believe that there is any accident in the matching of these two passages. But if there is no accident what are we being told?

At this point there is perhaps the danger of taking too much for granted with regard to perceptions and conclusions, which are deemed noteworthy. I must, therefore, say a little about the practical aspects, the habits, of working in the way here described, so that with patience and good will the 'substance' of what is here being spoken of may be experienced and, hopefully, accepted. This may in any case be a good moment to recapitulate what these habits are, and to express again the conviction that unless one has acquired them, certain kinds of study are virtually impossible and can only lead to frustration.

The first of these habits is that of memorizing; turning the printed word into something inwardly heard and known. The second is listening to the sounds of syllables at least as closely as one listens to sense. The third perhaps is getting used to reading backwards or up the page, line by line, as easily as one reads downwards.[4]

The memorizing habit is essential if one works alone. If one passage is known by heart, then it is possible to recite it to oneself while following the other passage backwards line for line. If two are studying the play together then this process is in a way easier; it is simply a question of a forwards reading of one passage set against a backward reading of the other.

At this point someone will ask but why should you expect such a close and curious relationship between passages that may be far apart spatially in the text and, by ordinary standards, unconnected in theme? Here the answer has to be: I expect it is because again and again I find it, and because it becomes increasingly clear that the poet had faculties almost beyond our imagination, after which we can only limp. Of course, every Shakespeare actor undergoes such training, but only to a certain extent. He learns his part, but rarely much more.

Moving away now from the prose passages we will return once more to the start of our journey, the axis of symmetry for the whole play, and study the lines of Act 3 as they gather around it.

From the simplest point of view the balance between what precedes the play centre and what follows after it is very clear. Before that centre there comes the murder of Banquo and the escape of Fleance, and after that centre comes the report of the murder and the escape, and then the

5. PLAY SYMMETRY

vision of Banquo's ghost. The murder itself is preceded by Macbeth's fears, suspicions and plottings, and the vision of the ghost is followed by a terrible reckless intention to plunge even deeper into blood should that be necessary. However, across the play centre, within this whole central area, there are some very precise sound and sense echoes, which we will note.

The two-line play centre itself, from which this journey of discovery began, falls at scene-lines 10 and 11 in Act 3 Scene 4. Ten lines back from a point between the two central lines we come to line 1 of Scene 4, and between lines 11 and 14 back, we arrive at the last four lines of the previous scene (Scene 3). These are:

14 (1183)   3. There's but one downe: the Sonne is fled.
13 (1184)   2. We haue lost
12 (1185)   Best halfe of our Affaire.
11 (1186)   1. Well, let's away, and say how much is done.

Eleven lines forward from the midpoint we come to:

11 (1186-)   *Mur.* Most Royall Sir
12 (1185-)   *Fleans* is scap'd.
13 (1184-)   *Macb.* Then comes my Fit againe:
14 (1183-)   I had else beene perfect;

Line 12 forwards is, *'Fleans* is scap'd.' Line 12 backwards is, 'Best halfe of our Affaire.' Their affair — that is the instructions they have been given — is to murder two people, the father, Banquo and the son, Fleance. One half of this instruction has not been fulfilled, therefore the 'Best halfe of our Affaire' is Fleance. It is elegant that these words are matched by *'Fleans* is scap'd.'

A little earlier we come to lines 19, 20 and 21 lines back from the central point:

21 (1176)   *Ban.* It will be Rayne to Night.
20 (1177)   1. Let it come downe.
19 (1178)   *Ban.* O, Trecherie!
             (Flye good *Fleans* ...)

And lines 19–21 forward from the centre we come to:

19 (1178-)   *Mur.* I, my good Lord: safe in a ditch he bides,
20 (1177-)   With twenty trenched gashes on his head;
21 (1176-)   The least a Death to Nature.

In 'twenty trenched gashes' we hear the echo of 'O, Trecherie!' though the chime is not exact (one is twenty lines forward and the other is nineteen lines back) yet the treachery is of course the stabbing, which must coincide with 'Let it come downe,' and this is exactly twenty lines back from the play midpoint.

At 43 lines back from the play centre we come to line 1 of Scene 3, 'But who did bid thee ioyne with vs?' At 42 and 43 lines forward from the play centre, (1238, 1239) at its last line of the column, we come to: 'Pleas't your Highnesse / To grace vs with your Royall Company?' Both lines have to do with the joining of one person to an assembled group. Five lines later we come to Lennox's words, 'What is't that moues your Highnesse?' which must surely mark the moment when Macbeth is first aware of the ghost. And three lines further, at lines play-lines 1247 and 1248, he speaks to the ghost directly:

> 1247 Thou canst not say I did it: neuer shake
> 1248 Thy goary lockes at me.

These words are balanced across the play centre by:
> 1248- And with thy bloodie and inuisible Hand
> 1247- Cancell and teare to pieces that great Bond,
> 1246- Which keepes me pale ...

The strong echo of the syllable 'Cans/c' is hardly one that can be missed, and each of these two lines is accompanied by an image of blood ('And with thy *bloodie* and inuisible Hand' and 'neuer shake / Thy *goary* lockes at me'). We could even say that it is just the attempt to cancel this 'indissoluable bond' (an oath sworn in blood?) that has the power to make the ghost visible to Macbeth!

The lines that match the first vision of the ghost are 'Good things of Day begin to droope, and drowse,' which express perfectly that shift in consciousness that must surely go with spiritual vision. At lines 1260, 1261, we come to Lady Macbeth's furiously hissed whisper:

> 1260 This is the Ayre-drawne-Dagger which you said
> 1261 Led you to Duncan. O, these flawes and starts

At the corresponding lines, 1260 and 1261 back, we come to:

> 1261- *Macb.* O, full of Scorpions is my Minde, deare Wife:
> 1260- Thou know'st, that Banquo and his Fleans liues.

5. PLAY SYMMETRY

The repetition of 'O' expresses a certain amazed indignation; Macbeth's in relation to his own experiences; Lady Macbeth's in relation to her husband's behaviour which she is unable to understand.

At lines 1270, 1271 and 1272, Macbeth is again addressing the ghost, in horror:

>   1270   If Charnell houses, and our Graues must send
>   1271   Those that we bury, backe; our Monuments
>   1272   Shall be the Mawes of Kytes.

This is balanced across the play centre by lines 1270, 1271 and 1272 back from the end of the play, at a place where Lady Macbeth is saying to Macbeth:

>   1272-   *Lady*. Come on:
>   1271-   Gentle my Lord, sleeke o're your rugged Lookes,
>   1270-   Be bright and Iouiall among your Guests to Night.

In fact this matches the moment when he is the very opposite of bright and jovial. It is interesting that these two passages lie at the centre of their respective scenes, though these are of very different lengths.

The ghost fades at 'Mawes of Kytes,' but returns after line 1291, 'Then Ile sit downe: Giue me some Wine, fill full.' Once again Macbeth is not instantly aware of it and only cries out at line 1297, 'Auant, & quit my sight, let the earth hide thee.' These words are matched across the play centre by line 1297 back, spoken by Lady Macbeth, 'Nought's had, all's spent. Where our desire is got without content.' Horror is matched by deep depression and at the recognition that simple murder does not solve anything. We observe here also the 'or' vowel chime between 'Auant' and 'Nought's had.'

At lines 1301, 1302, 1303, Lady Macbeth again tries to cover up her husband's extraordinary behaviour:

>   1301   Thinke of this good Peeres
>   1302   But as a thing of Custome: 'Tis no other,
>   1303   Onely it spoyles the pleasure of the time.

Immediately Macbeth addresses the ghost again, 'What man dare, I dare,' and this line matches the penultimate line in Act 3 Scene 1, 'Banquo, thy Soules flight, / If it finde Heauen, must finde it out to Night.' The contrast between this terrible and solemn thought and Lady Macbeth's words is great.

The remaining part of the banqueting scene to line 1355, is now matched by the last part of Macbeth's consultation with the men who will murder Banquo. Macbeth's terrified challenge to the ghost matches his final instructions to the murderers and when Lady Macbeth, also terrified that he might reveal too much, dismisses the Lords, her words, 'A kinde goodnight to all.,' followed by, exit Lords, which fall at line 1330 are now matched at line 1330 back by, 'With bare-fac'd power sweepe him from my sight.' Again we have the same idea — getting rid of somebody, or some people. (See mirrored text C opposite.)

Macbeth's final words in this scene, in which he expresses a reckless determination to plunge even deeper into blood are matched by his earlier speech to the murderers, making it absolutely explicit what it is he wants them to do.

In the same scene, at line 1342, we come to, 'There's not a <u>one</u> of them but in his house / I keepe a Seruant Feed.' At lines 1342- and 1343-, earlier, we come to '2. *Murth*. I am <u>one</u>, my Liege, / Whom the vile Blowes and Buffets of the World / Hath so incens'd, that I am recklesse what I doe,.' 'One' is only a little word but it often seems to be in almost insignificant turns of phrase that we find a direct chime.

We note that the end of this same scene does not match any earlier obvious break. In fact, it is not until a few lines early in the Hecate Scene, that we come to words that match and echo a break in Scene 1. Hecate is furious with the other witches because up till then they have been ignoring her,

> 1357 *Hec*. Haue I not reason (Beldams) as you are?
> 1358 Sawcy, and ouer-bold, how did you dare
> 1359 To Trade, and Trafficke with Macbeth,
> 1360 In Riddles, and Affaires of death;
> 1361 And I the Mistris of your Charmes,
> 1362 The close contriuer of all harmes,
> 1363 Was neuer call'd to beare my part,

In the mirrored (earlier) passage Macbeth has said, in effect, 'Banquo has hurt you in all these ways, now what are you going to do about it?' The first murderer replies,

5. PLAY SYMMETRY

Scena Secunda.

1303	Onely it spoyles the pleasure of the time.	1303-	If it finde Heauen, must finde it out to Night. *Exeunt.*
1304	*Macb.* What man dare, I dare:	1304-	It is concluded: *Banquo,* thy Soules flight,
1305	Approach thou like the rugged Russian Beare,	1305-	*Macb.* Ile call vpon you straight: abide within,
1306	The arm'd Rhinoceros, or th' Hircan Tiger,	1306-	*Murth.* We are resolu'd, my Lord.
1307	Take any shape but that, and my firme Nerues	1307-	Ile come to you anon.
1308	Shall neuer tremble. Or be aliue againe,	1308-	Of that darke houre: resolue your selues apart,
1309	And dare me to the Desart with thy Sword:	1309-	Then is his Fathers, must embrace the fate
1310	If trembling I inhabit then, protest mee	1310-	Whose absence is no lesse materiall to me,
1311	The Baby of a Girle. Hence horrible shadow,	1311-	Fleans, his Sonne, that keepes him companie,
1312	Vnreall mock'ry hence. Why so, being gone	1312-	To leaue no Rubs nor Botches in the Worke:
1313	I am a man againe: pray you sit still.	1313-	That I require a clearenesse; and with him,
1314	*La.* You haue displac'd the mirth,	1314-	And something from the Pallace: alwayes thought,
1315	Broke the good meeting, with most admir'd disorder.	1315-	The moment on't, for't must be done to Night,
1316	*Macb.* Can such things be,	1316-	Acquaint you with the perfect Spy o'th' time,
1317	And ouercome vs like a Summers Clowd,	1317-	I will aduise you where to plant your selues,
1318	Without our speciall wonder? You make me strange	1318-	Within this houre, at most,
1319	Euen to the disposition that I owe,	1319-	*Macb.* Your Spirits shine through you.
1320	When now I thinke you can behold such sights,	1320-	1. *Murth.* Though our Liues
1321	And keepe the naturall Rubie of your Cheekes,	1321-	Performe what you command vs.
1322	When mine is blanch'd with feare.	1322-	2. *Murth.* We shall, my Lord,
1323	*Rosse.* What sights, my Lord?	1323-	For sundry weightie Reasons.
1324	*La.* I pray you speake not: he growes worse & worse	1324-	Masking the Businesse from the common Eye,
1325	Question enrages him: at once, goodnight.	1325-	That I to your assistance doe make loue,
1326	Stand not vpon the order of your going,	1326-	Who I my selfe struck downe: and thence it is,
1327	But go at once.	1327-	Whose loues I may not drop, but wayle his fall,
1328	*Len.* Good night, and better health	1328-	For certaine friends that are both his, and mine,
1329	Attend his Maiesty.	1329-	And bid my will auouch it; yet I must not,
1330	*La.* A kinde goodnight to all. *Exit Lords.*	1330-	With bare-fac'd power sweepe him from my sight,
1331	*Macb.* It will haue blood they say:	1331-	Against my neer'st of Life: and though I could
1332	Blood will haue Blood:	1332-	That euery minute of his being, thrusts
1333	Stones haue beene knowne to moue, & Trees to speake:	1333-	*Macb.* So is he mine: and in such bloody distance,
1334	Augures, and vnderstood Relations, haue	1334-	*Murth.* True, my Lord.
1335	By Maggot Pyes, & Choughes, & Rookes brought forth	1335-	*Macb.* Both of you know *Banquo* was your Enemie.
1336	The secret'st man of Blood. What is the night?	1336-	To mend it, or be rid on't.
1337	*La.* Almost at oddes with morning, which is which.	1337-	That I would set my Life on any Chance,
1338	*Macb.* How say'st thou that *Macduff* denies his person	1338-	So wearie with Disasters, tugg'd with Fortune,
1339	At our great bidding.	1339-	1. *Murth.* And I another,
1340	*La.* Did you send to him Sir?	1340-	To spight the World.
1341	*Macb.* I heare it by the way: But I will send:	1341-	Hath so incens'd, that I am recklesse what I doe,
1342	There's not a one of them but in his house	1342-	Whom the vile Blowes and Buffets of the World
1343	I keepe a Seruant Feed. I will to morrow	1343-	2. *Murth.* I am one, my Liege,
1344	(And betimes I will) to the weyard Sisters.	1344-	Which in his Death were perfect.
1345	More shall they speake: for now I am bent to know	1345-	Who weare our Health but sickly in his Life,
1346	By the worst meanes, the worst, for mine owne good,	1346-	Grapples you to the heart; and loue of vs,
1347	All causes shall giue way. I am in blood	1347-	Whose execution takes your Enemie off,
1348	Stept in so farre, that should I wade no more,	1348-	And I will put that Businesse in your Bosomes,
1349	Returning were as tedious as go ore:	1349-	Not i'th' worst ranke of Manhood, say't,
1350	Strange things I haue in head, that will to hand,	1350-	Now, if you haue a station in the file,
1351	Which must be acted, ere they may be scand.	1351-	That writes them all alike: and so of men.
1352	*La.* You lacke the season of all Natures, sleepe.	1352-	Particular addition, from the Bill,
1353	*Macb.* Come, wee'l to sleepe: My strange & self-abuse	1353-	Hath in him clos'd: whereby he does receiue
1354	Is the initiate feare, that wants hard vse:	1354-	According to the gift, which bounteous Nature
1355	We are yet but yong indeed. *Exeunt.*	1355-	The House-keeper, the Hunter, euery one

Scena Quinta.

Figure 18 Mirrored text C. Showing mirrored play-lines of Act 3. the left-hand column shows ply-lines 1303–1355 (read downwards) and the right-hand column shows the mirrored play-lines (read upwards for continuity)

1361- We are men, my Liege.
1360- *Macb*. I, in the Catalogue ye goe for men,
1359- As Hounds, and Greyhounds, Mungrels, Spaniels, Curres,

In the field of Dogs he is clearly on firm ground, 'I, in the Catalogue ye goe for men,' line 1360 back, matches line 1361 forwards, '(*Hec*.) And I the Mistris of your Charmes.' A moment earlier, line 1357 back, 'All by the Name of Dogges,' matches '(*Hec*.) Haue I not reason (Beldams) as you are?' She calls them names: 'Beldames' which might be thought of as the names of Dogs.

Finally, the end of the Hecate scene (3, 5) matches the last lines of the end of Macbeth's murderous soliloquy about Banquo. Lines 1392 and 1391 back are, '(*Macb*.) Onely for them, and mine eternall Iewell / Giuen to the common Enemie of Man,' Which matches, 1391f 'Come, let's make hast, shee'l soone be / Backe againe. *Exeunt*.' Hecate is painted by Shakespeare as the very embodiment of evil, that is, 'the common Enemie of Man.'

At lines 1374 and 1374 back we observe a clear coincidence, 1374, 'Your Charmes, and euery thing beside;' 1374 back, *Macb*. 'And all things else, that might.' 'Everything else' gives the same sense in both sentences.

Moving outwards still further from the centre we come to Act 3 Scene 6, which is the last scene in the act. We meet Lennox and a lord in secret conference, but it is a transformed Lennox, no longer the innocent young man who describes the wildness of the night to Macbeth and then accompanies him as they go to the king's chamber. It is a disillusioned Lennox now full of suspicion about the murder of the king and also the murder of Banquo. The first part of the scene matches Macbeth's soliloquy as he rehearses to himself why it is he fears Banquo so much while the servant goes to fetch the murderers. After Macbeth's extaordinary behaviour at the banquet Lennox has become suspicious both in respect of the murders of Duncan and Banquo, and his suspicion may be taken to represent a more widespread general suspicion.

1393 *Lennox*. My former Speeches,
1394 Haue but hit your Thoughts
1395 Which can interpret farther: Onely I say
1396 Things haue bin strangely borne. The gracious Duncan

5. PLAY SYMMETRY

> 1397 Was pittied of Macbeth: marry he was dead:
> 1398 And the right valiant Banquo walk'd too late,
> 1399 Whom you may say (if't please you) Fleans kill'd,
> 1400 For Fleans fled: Men must not walke too late.
> 1401 Who cannot want the thought, how monstrous
> 1402 It was for Malcolme, and for Donalbane
> 1403 To kill their gracious Father? Damned Fact,
> 1404 How it did greeue Macbeth?

Lennox judges these murders from the outside and guesses their cause. This passage matches Macbeth's soliloquy on Banquo in the first half of the play (1404- to 1393-).

Scaena Sexta.

Enter Lenox, and another Lord.

1393	*Lenox.* My former Speeches,	1393-	Put Rancours in the Vessell of my Peace
1394	Haue but hit your Thoughts	1394-	For them, the gracious *Duncan* haue I murther'd,
1395	Which can interpret farther: Onely I say	1395-	For Banquo's Issue haue I fil'd my Minde,
1396	Things haue bin strangely borne. The gracious *Duncan*	1396-	No Sonne of mine succeeding: if't be so,
1397	Was pittied of *Macbeth*: marry he was dead:	1397-	Thence to be wrencht with an vnlineall Hand,
1398	And the right valiant *Banquo* walk'd too late,	1398-	And put a barren Scepter in my Gripe,
1399	Whom you may say (if't please you) *Fleans* kill'd,	1399-	Vpon my Head they plac'd a fruitlesse Crowne,
1400	For *Fleans* fled: Men must not walke too late.	1400-	They hayl'd him Father to a Line of Kings.
1401	Who cannot want the thought, how monstrous	1401-	And bad them speake to him. Then Prophet-like,
1402	It was for *Malcolme*, and for *Donalbane*	1402-	When first they put the Name of King vpon me,
1403	To kill their gracious Father? Damned Fact,	1403-	*Mark Anthonies* was by *Caesar*. He chid the Sisters,
1404	How it did greeue *Macbeth*? Did he not straight	1404-	My Genius is rebuk'd, as it is said

Figure 19. Mirrored Text D. Showing mirrored play-lines in Act 3. the left-hand column shows play-lines 1393–1404 (read downwards) and the right-hand column shows the mirrored play-lines (read upwards for continuity).

There the same murders are being looked at from the point of view of the murderer, from within, and are followed by the thoughts of regret that the issue has not been more positive.

In this mirrored passage words 'gracious Duncan' come close to each other but not exactly at the same line. At line 1396 Lennox's words are: 'Things haue bin strangely borne. The *gracious Duncan* / Was pittied of Macbeth ...' At line 1394 backwards, we come to: 'For them, the *gracious Duncan* haue I murther'd, / For Banquo's Issue haue I fil'd my Minde, / No Sonne of mine succeeding ...'

We see also the interesting mirrored references to Fleance, one reference being an obvious fabric of lies, and the other relating to true results inscribed in images of destiny.

> 1398 And the right valiant *Banquo* walk'd too late,
> 1399 Whom you may say (if't please you) *Fleans* kill'd,
> 1400 For *Fleans* fled …

and its mirror:

> 1400- They hayl'd him Father to a Line of Kings.
> 1399- Vpon my Head they plac'd a fruitlesse Crowne,
> 1398- And put a barren Scepter in my Gripe,

At the end of Lennox's speech he touches upon Macduff's disgrace, and to the Lord he says, 'Sir, can you tell / Where he bestowes himselfe?' (1416, 1417). This matches Macbeth's words earlier to the servant. 'Sirrha, a word with you: Attend those men / Our pleasure?' (1417-, 1416-). The question is the same, 'Where are they?' or 'Where is he?' In Lennox's speech two people are also named in italics, Malcolm and Donalbane, and this naming comes within one line. A little later in this scene we note the echoing of the word 'Night' in line 1428, 'Giue to our Tables meate, sleepe to our *Nights*:' and in line 1428 back, 'Adieu, till you returne at *Night*.' These are Macbeth's last words to Banquo.

We continue outwards as far as the end of Scene 6, which is also the end of the Act. Moving backwards however in the other direction we do not quite come to the beginning of the Act. Twenty lines of Scene 1 have already passed by and we encounter Macbeth in conversation with Banquo. The last line of Scene 6 is, '*Lord*. Ile send my Prayers with him.' and this is matched across the play centre by Macbeth's words, 'Ride you this afternoone?' (see Figure 20, Mirrored Text E), an enquiry that sounds innocent but which of course is not: 'Prayers' would in deed have been appropriate!

Shortly before this, in Scene 6, we hear about the messenger sent by Macbeth to Macduff to request his presence at the feast, or possibly to ask why he did not come.

It sounds as if the Lord who reports it was an eyewitness to this conversation and I think we have to imagine that the Lord is a neighbour of Macduff's, and is able to provide direct information from that quarter. In any case this conversation helps to illustrate the fears, which both the

5. PLAY SYMMETRY 105

1434	Len. Sent he to *Macduffe*?	1434-	*Macb*. We heare our bloody Cozens are bestow'd
1435	*Lord*. He did: and with an absolute Sir, not I	1435-	*Ban*. My Lord, I will not.
1436	The clowdy Messenger turnes me his backe,	1436-	*Macb*. Faile not our Feast.
1437	And hums; as who should say, you'l rue the time	1437-	For a darke houre, or twaine.
1438	That clogges me with this Answer.	1438-	I must become a borrower of the Night,
1439	*Lennox*. And that well might	1439-	'Twixt this, and Supper. Goe not my Horse the better,
1440	Aduise him to a Caution, t' hold what distance	1440-	*Ban*. As farre, my Lord, as will fill vp the time
1441	His wisedome can prouide. Some holy Angell	1441-	Is't farre you ride?
1442	Flye to the Court of England, and vnfold	1442-	In this dayes Councell: but wee'le take to morrow.
1443	His Message ere he come, that a swift blessing	1443-	(Which still hath been both graue, and prosperous)
1444	May soone returne to this our suffering Country,	1444-	*Macb*. We should haue else desir'd your good aduice
1445	Vnder a hand accurs'd.	1445-	*Ban*. I, my good Lord.
1446	*Lord*. Ile send my Prayers with him. *Exeunt*	1446-	*Macb*. Ride you this afternoone?

Figure 20. Mirrored Text E. Act 3. Play-lines 1434–1466 (read downwards) and their mirrored companion lines numbered from the end of the play (read upwards for continuity).

Lord and Lennox feel on behalf of Macduff's safety. Matching these words across the play centre comes the earlier passage between Banquo and Macbeth:

1439-	Twixt this, and Supper. Goe not my Horse the better,
1438-	I must become a borrower of the Night,
1437-	For a darke houre, or twaine.
1436-	*Macb*. Faile not our Feast.
1435-	*Ban*. My Lord, I will not.

These words, 'My Lord, I will not,' balance exactly the line across the play centre, *Lord*. 'He did: and with an absolute Sir, not I. 'My Lord, I will not' chimes with 'Sir, not I.' Here, we have another example of almost the same words balancing each other, but with a different meaning, where the main opposition is between our fears for Banquo's safety, and the fear of the Lord and Lennox on behalf of Macduff's safety. Other word-echoes in this region come at lines 1428 forwards and backwards.

Having now moved as far as Act 4 on the far side, and Act 2 on the nearside, it becomes irresistible to check at least one more thing before concluding this chapter: what is the play mirror of the moment when Macbeth murders King Duncan? The deed is done early in Act 2 Scene 2 and we know it takes place at some point whilst Lady Macbeth is speaking the first nine nines of this scene, beginning:

614	That which hath made thê drunk, hath made me bold:
615	What hath quench'd them, hath giuen me fire.
616	Hearke, peace: it was the Owle that shriek'd,
617	The fatall Bell-man, which giues the stern'st good-night.
618	He is about it, the Doores are open:
619	And the surfeted Groomes doe mock their charge
620	With Snores. I haue drugg'd their Possets,
621	That Death and Nature doe contend about them,
622	Whether they liue, or dye

Was it that moment when the owl shrieked or was it the next moment when she says:

618	He is about it, the Doores are open:
619	And the surfeted Groomes doe mock their charge
620	With Snores ...

Lady Macbeth seems to know exactly what is going on in the King's chamber but, like her, we guess at the precise moment of the stabbing.

Lady Macbeth's nine lines are play-lines 614 to 622. We calculate the corresponding position on the far side of the play by subtracting these numbers from the play total, 2392, and then adding one to this answer. This brings us to lines 1779, 1771, (614- to 622- in our reverse counting from the end of the play), that is a passage in Act 4 Scene 3, which takes place in England. It is a moment when Malcolm is testing the sincerity of Macduff by accusing himself of vices that he does not possess. Line 1769 (624-) onwards:

1769 (624-)	...yet my poore Country
1770 (623-)	Shall haue more vices then it had before,
1771 (622-)	More suffer, and more sundry wayes then euer,
1772 (621-)	By him that shall succeede.
1773 (620-)	*Macd.* What should he be?
1774 (619-)	*Mal.* It is my selfe I meane: in whom I know
1775 (618-)	All the particulars of Vice so grafted,
1776 (617-)	That when they shall be open'd, blacke Macbeth

5. PLAY SYMMETRY

    1777 (616-)   Will seeme as pure as Snow, and the poore State
    1778 (615-)   Esteeme him as a Lambe, being compar'd
    1779 (614-)   With my confinelesse harmes.

Macduff then denies that there can be anyone worse than Macbeth. When we come to the plot this particular example of play symmetry will help us to affirm that Macbeth had a motive for murdering King Duncan, which almost, but not quite, exonerates him from committing the most terrible crime in this the first of his murders. We note the echo of the word 'open.' 'He is about it, the Doores are *open*' (618).

    619-   *Mal*. It is my selfe I meane: in whom I know
    618-(1775) All the particulars of Vice so grafted,
    617-   That when they shall be <u>open'd</u>, blacke Macbeth
    616-   Will seeme as pure as Snow, and the poore State

We may take Malcolm's words as nothing more than fantasy, or we may also see them as expressing the kernel of truth.

6. Act Centres and Act Symmetry

We touched upon the subject of symmetry in Acts 3 and 4 in Chapter 2, concerning the songs in *Macbeth*. There we noted the main elements of symmetrical balance as we explored the riddle of the nine song lines and their positioning within the geometrical 'Figure.' In this chapter we will take a broader look at elements of symmetry within all the acts.

While studying the nature of prose in *Macbeth*, I looked again at the act centre of Act 2, which is embedded in the prose of the porter's second monologue, on the effect of drink on lechery. From the entry of Macduff and Lennox at the top of the second column (page 137 Folio) to the first line of the central couplet ('-cherie; It makes him and it marres him' etc.) there are eleven lines. From the second line of the central couplet ('and it takes him off...') to 'Our knocking ha's awak'd him: here he comes' are also eleven lines. The central two lines of the Act, therefore, lie exactly in the centre of the exchange between Macduff and the porter — an exchange in prose framed by two lines of verse at the beginning and two at the end. Visually the solid block of printing at the top of the column is broken by the gap for the entry of Macbeth. If we cut out the verse that frames the prose, and shrink our view to 9 + 9 lines, beginning Porter: 'Faith Sir ...' and ending 'made a Shift to cast him,' then we are looking at three blocks of printing, symmetrically arranged around the act centre with the largest group in the middle.

In this act at least the eye can 'see' a framed act centre. If the same

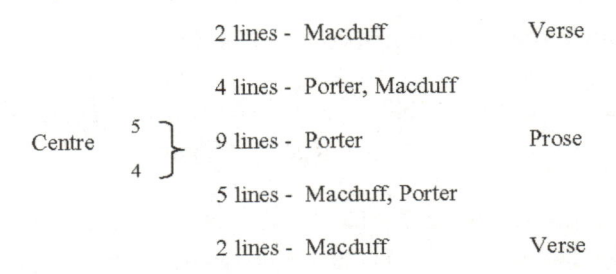

		2 lines - Macduff	Verse
		4 lines - Porter, Macduff	
Centre	5 }	9 lines - Porter	Prose
	4	5 lines - Macduff, Porter	
		2 lines - Macduff	Verse

Figure 21

> *Enter Macduff, and Lenox.*
>
> *Macd.* Was it so late, friend, ere you went to Bed,
> That you doe lye so late?
> *Port.* Faith Sir, we were carowsing till the second Cock:
> And Drinke, Sir, is a great prouoker of three things.
> *Macd.* What three things does Drinke especially
> prouoke?
> *Port.* Marry, Sir, Nose-painting, Sleepe, and Vrine.
> Lecherie, Sir, it prouokes, and vnprouokes: it prouokes
> the desire, but it takes away the performance. Therefore
> much Drinke may be said to be an Equiuocator with Le-
> cherie: it makes him, and it marres him; it sets him on,
> and it takes him off; it perswades him, and dis-heartens
> him; makes him stand too, and not stand too: in conclu-
> sion, equiuocates him in a sleepe, and giuing him the Lye,
> leaues him.
> *Macd.* I beleeue, Drinke gaue thee the Lye last Night.
> *Port.* That it did, Sir, i'the very Throat on me: but I
> requited him for his Lye, and (I thinke) being too strong
> for him, though he tooke vp my Legges sometime, yet I
> made a Shift to cast him.
> *Enter Macbeth.*

| Act Centre

Figure 22. Centre of Act 2.

were true of all the acts it would point to great consciousness in the sighting (and numbering) of prose lines in Act 2.

This led to a re-investigation of the *printing* of the other act centres.

Act I centre, page 133 (Folio)

The central two lines fall at lines 6 and 7 of Scene 4:

Act   270   Confess'd his Treasons, implor'd your Highnesse Pardon,
      271   And set forth a deepe Repentance:

Here, the central symmetrical block is very clear, and its position similar to the central block in Act II. It begins with the beginning of the scene, and ends with the end of Malcolm's speech: 'As 'twere a carelesse Trifle.'

6. ACT CENTRES AND ACT SYMMETRY   111

Scena Quarta.

*Flourish. Enter King, Lenox, Malcolme,
Donalbane, and Attendants.*

King. Is execution done on *Cawdor*?
Or not those in Commission yet return'd?
 Mal. My Liege, they are not yet come back.
But I haue spoke with one that saw him die:
Who did report, that very frankly hee
Confess'd his Treasons, implor'd your Highnesse Pardon, | Act
And set forth a deepe Repentance: | Centre
Nothing in his Life became him,
Like the leauing it. Hee dy'de,
As one that had beene studied in his death,
To throw away the dearest thing he ow'd,
As 'twere a carelesse Trifle.
 King. There's no Art,
To finde the Mindes construction in the Face:
He was a Gentleman, on whom I built
An absolute Trust.
 Enter Macbeth, Banquo, Rosse, and Angus.

Figure 23. Centre of Act 1.

The eye can pick out the central two lines by the exceptional length of the first one, ending in 'Highnesse Pardon.'

Act 3 centre, page 141 (Folio)

Here the central two lines bestride the division between Scenes 3 and 4. In the printing, the first of these two lies at the bottom of the left-hand column, and the second lies at the top of the right-hand column: (see Figure 24).

Just before the First Murderer speaks the Second Murderer says:

Act 258 We have lost'
    259 Best halfe of our Affaire.

referring to the escape of Banquo's son, Fleance. So the First Murderer's

The Tragedie of Macbeth. 141

Lady. But in them, Natures Coppie's not eterne.
Macb. There's comfort yet, they are assaileable,
Then be thou iocund: ere the Bat hath flowne
His Cloyster'd flight, ere to black *Heccats* summons
The shard-borne Beetle, with his drowsie hums,
Hath rung Nights yawning Peale,
There shall be done a deed of dreadfull note.
Lady. What's to be done?
Macb. Be innocent of the knowledge, dearest Chuck,
Till thou applaud the deed: Come, seeling Night,
Skarfe vp the tender Eye of pittifull Day,
And with thy bloodie and inuisible Hand
Cancell and teare to pieces that great Bond,
Which keepes me pale. Light thickens,
And the Crow makes Wing toth' Rookie Wood:
Good things of Day begin to droope, and drowse,
Whiles Nights black Agents to their Prey's doe rowse.
Thou maruell'st at my words: but hold thee still,
Things bad begun, make strong themselues by ill:
So prythee goe with me.   *Exeunt.*

Scena Tertia.

Enter three Murtherers.

1. But who did bid thee ioyne with vs?
3. *Macbeth.*
2. He needes not our mistrust, since he deliuers
Our Offices, and what we haue to doe,
To the direction iust.
1. Then stand with vs:
The West yet glimmers with some streakes of Day.
Now spurres the lated Traueller apace,
To gayne the timely Inne, end neere approches
The subiect of our Watch.
3. Hearke, I heare Horses.
Banquo within. Giue vs a Light there, hoa.
2. Then 'tis hee:
The rest, that are within the note of expectation,
Alreadie are i'th' Court.
1. His Horses goe about.
3. Almost a mile: but he does vsually,
So all men doe, from hence toth' Pallace Gate
Make it their Walke.

Enter Banquo and Fleans, with a Torch.

2. A Light, a Light.
3. 'Tis hee.
1. Stand too't.
Ban. It will be Rayne to Night.
1. Let it come downe.
Ban. O, Trecherie!
Flye good *Fleans*, flye flye flye,
Thou may'st reuenge. O Slaue.
3. Who did strike out the Light?
1. Was't not the way?
3. There's but one downe: the Sonne is fled.
2. We haue lost?
Best halfe of our Affaire.
1. Well, let's away, and say how much is done.   *Exeunt.*

Scena Quarta.

Banquet prepar'd. Enter Macbeth, Lady, Rosse, Lenox, Lords, and Attendants.

Macb. You know your owne degrees, sit downe:
At first and last, the hearty welcome.
Lords. Thankes to your Maiesty.
Macb. Our selfe will mingle with Society,
And play the humble Host:
Our Hostesse keepes her State, but in best time
We will require her welcome.
La. Pronounce it for me Sir, to all our Friends,
For my heart speakes, they are welcome.
Enter first Murtherer.
Macb. See they encounter thee with their harts thanks
Both sides are euen: heere Ile sit i'th'mid'st,
Be large in mirth, anon wee'l drinke a Measure
The Table round. There's blood vpon thy face.
Mur. 'Tis *Banquo's* then.
Macb. 'Tis better thee without, then he within.
Is he dispatch'd?
Mur. My Lord his throat is cut, that I did for him.
Mac. Thou art the best o'th'Cut-throats,
Yet hee's good that did the like for *Fleans*:
If thou did'st it, thou art the Non-pareill.
Mur. Most Royall Sir
Fleans is scap'd.
Macb. Then comes my Fit againe:
I had else beene perfect;
Whole as the Marble, founded as the Rocke,
As broad, and generall, as the casing Ayre:
But now I am cabin'd, crib'd, confin'd, bound in
To sawcy doubts, and feares. But *Banquo's* safe?
Mur. I, my good Lord: safe in a ditch he bides,
With twenty trenched gashes on his head;
The least a Death to Nature.
Macb. Thankes for that:
There the growne Serpent lyes, the worme that's fled
Hath Nature that in time will Venom breed,
No teeth for th'present. Get thee gone, to morrow
Wee'l heare our selues againe.   *Exit Murderer.*
Lady. My Royall Lord,
You do not giue the Cheere, the Feast is sold
That is not often vouch'd, while 'tis a making:
'Tis giuen, with welcome: to feede were best at home:
From thence, the sawce to meate is Ceremony,
Meeting were bare without it.

Enter the Ghost of Banquo, and sits in Macbeths place.

Macb. Sweet Remembrancer:
Now good digestion waite on Appetite,
And health on both.
Lenox. May't please your Highnesse sit.
Macb. Here had we now our Countries Honor, roof'd,
Were the grac'd person of our *Banquo* present:
Who, may I rather challenge for vnkindnesse,
Then pitty for Mischance.
Rosse. His absence (Sir)
Layes blame vpon his promise. Pleas't your Highnesse
To grace vs with your Royall Company?
          Mcab.

Figure 24. Centre of Act 3

6. ACT CENTRES AND ACT SYMMETRY 113

words, 'How much Is done' indicate that half is done, and this is the mid-point of the act. The degrees that Macbeth speaks of in the next line also refer to the degrees of the act circle which, at the division between the two scenes, are 180.

The block around the act centre is here divided into two parts: nine lines from 'You know you own degrees ...' to the space for '*Enter First Murderer*,' and nine lines back from 'Well, let's away and say how much is done.' to Banquo: 'O, Trecherie!' the moment he is stabbed. The shape of these two blocks is, again, clear to the eye. We note that the word 'sit' occurs at this act centre in Macbeth's words, 'You know your own Degrees, sit downe' which is nearly but not quite identical with the word 'set' at the centre of Act 1, 'Set forth a deep Repentance,' and the 'set' at the centre of Act 2, 'sets him on and takes him off.' A moment later we come to the centre of the play, 'Here I'll sit i'th midst.'

Act 4 centres, pages 145, 146 (Folio)

Act 4 is anomalous. In the first part of the Act there comes the witches' spell beginning with '1 Powre in Sowes blood, that hath eaten / Her nine Farrow.' It is here that the nine lines for the songs have to be inserted. This leaves us with the question: Should these lines be numbered, which would alter the entire numeration of the rest of the play, or should they be blank? In the end, as we discussed in Chapter 2, they prove to be blank, which leaves the rest of the numbering as it was.

The first thing that is affected is the angle of the axis of the act, but of course the first 'wing' is now nine lines longer in appearance than the second. So we have two different kinds of centre. On the one hand there is the simple numerical centre, and since the total is still 546 lines, this centre must fall between lines 273 and 274. If, however, we add nine for the gap, the total becomes 555, and for this number the centre is logically 555 divided by 2, which is the single line 278. However, we have to remember that from 'The sow's blood' onwards in this case we are adding nine. So to find 278 we must subtract nine and look for this number in our numbered play.

The simple numerical centre

This falls at lines 273 and 274. We are in Scene 3, the long scene in England, which begins with the encounter between young Malcolm, who fled there some time before, and Macduff who has just arrived. The central act-lines are lines 3 and 4 in this scene, but we give the first 6 lines in order to make sense. These are:

Act	271	*Mal.* Let vs seeke out some desolate shade, & there
	272	Weepe our sad bosomes empty.
	273	*Macd.* Let us rather
	274	Hold fast the mortall Sword: and like good men,
	275	Bestride our downfall Birthdome: each new Morne,
	276	New Widdowes howle, new Orphans cry, new sorowes
	277	(Strike heaven on the face, that it resounds)

<blockquote>

Scæna Tertia.

Enter Malcolme and Macduffe.

Act Centre

Mal. Let vs seeke out some desolate shade, & there
Weepe our sad bosomes empty.
Macd. Let vs rather
Hold fast the mortall Sword : and like good men,
Bestride our downfall Birthdome : each new Morne,
New Widdowes howle, new Orphans cry, new sorowes
Strike heauen on the face, that it resounds
As if it felt with Scotland, and yell'd out
Like Syllable of Dolour.
Mal. What I beleeue, Ile waile ;

</blockquote>

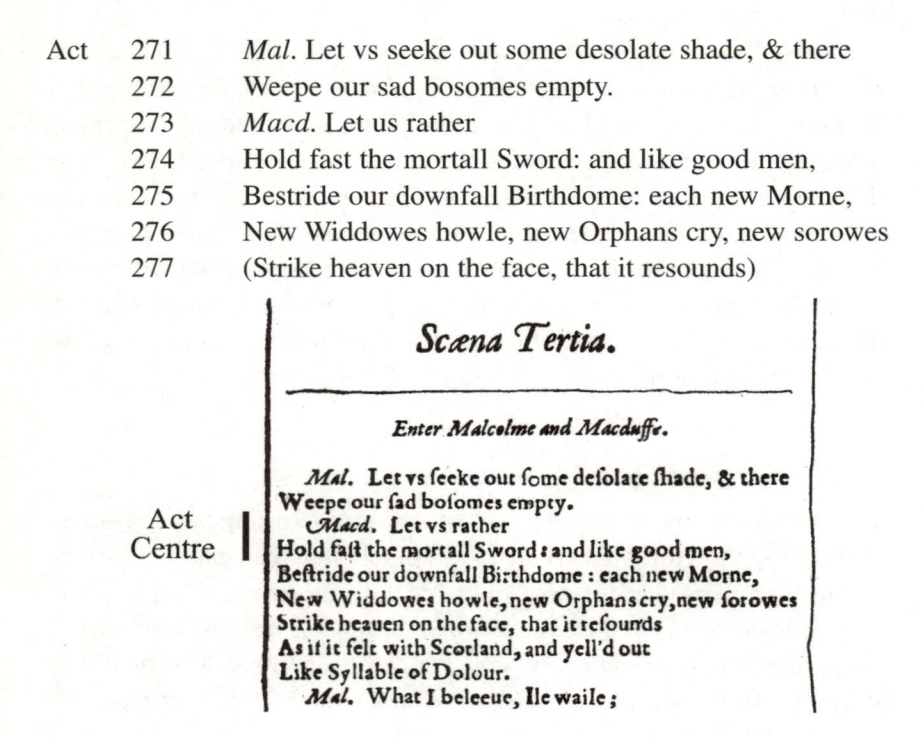

Fig 25. Centre of Act 4

Visually, the act centre is marked by diminishing lines to the short line, 'Let vs rather,' and then slightly increasing average lines, which leaves a big gap on the right. This position indicates the central end of the act axis, and immediately we see how the phrase 'Mortall Sword' encloses the meaning, among others, that here is the sharp line of the axis.

When we ask ourselves whether there is any hint of the 'sit,' 'set' idea, that we found at the centre of Acts 1, 2 and 3, we realize that to seek out some desolate shade, and there cry ones heart out, must inevitably involve the act of sitting. We may also notice the word 'sad,' not in the central two lines, but one line early. 'Sit,' 'set,' 'sad:' Is this part of a sequence? A look at the dictionary also tells us that the word 'bestride' has two meanings. It can mean 'march across,' but it can also mean 'sit or stand across' as in bestriding a fallen friend to protect him, or bestrid-

6. ACT CENTRES AND ACT SYMMETRY   115

ing a horse. In this context it could have both meanings, as when they go into battle Malcolm and Macduff will surely be on horseback. Their horses and their armies will *bestride* Scotland. So in this central block the sitting idea is also strong.

We now look for what I call 'out riders' (symmetrical correspondences). Where there is a centre of any kind it always seems possible to discover identical words at identical distances on either side of that centre. These we do find in the present case.

Act	267	*Mur*. What you Egge?	
	268	Yong fry of Treachery?	
	269	*Son*. He ha's kill'd me Mother,	
	270	Run away I pray you.	*Exit crying Murther.*

Scena Tertia.

Enter Malcolme and Macduffe.

	271	*Mal*. Let vs seeke out some desolate shade, & there
	272	Weepe our sad bosomes empty.
Act IV Centre	273	*Macb*. Let us rather
	274	Hold fast the mortall Sword: and like good men,
	275	Bestride our downfall Birthdome: ...
	276	New Widdowes howle, new Orphans cry, new sorowes
	277	Strike heauen on the face, that it resounds
	278	As if it felt with Scotland, and yell'd out
	279	Like Syllable of Dolour.
	280	*Mal*. What I beleeue, Ile waile;

Figure 26. Centre of Act 4.

At line 280 (7 lines forward from the act centre) we come to Malcolm's words, 'What I beleeue Ile waile.' At line 267 (7 lines back from the Act Centre) we come to the Murderer's words, '*What* you Egge?' If we count fifteen lines forwards from the Act Centre (Act line 288) we come to Malcolm's words, 'To offer *vp* a weake, poore innocent Lambe'(see numbered text), and if we count fifteen lines backwards from the Act

Centre we come to the words of Macduff's wife, 'Do I put *vp* that womanly defence.' If we count 27 lines forwards from the Act Centre (Act line 300) we come to Malcolm's words, 'Where I did finde my *doubts*.' And if we count 27 lines backwards, we come to the words of the messenger who warns Lady Macduff, 'I *doubt* some danger do's approach you neerely.'

Although there is a great gap of space between the royal palace in London and Macduff's castle in Fife, and probably some gap of time, too, it is as if Malcolm and Macduff are subconsciously aware of the terrible event which has just befallen Macduff's family. Malcolm's doubts concerning the trustworthiness of Macduff seem to echo the messenger's fear and suspicion that some dreadful danger threatens Macduff's wife.

Act 5 centre, page 149 (Folio)

Act 5 is exactly 400 lines long. Its centre therefore falls on lines 200 and 201. These come just after the centre of Scene 4, where we encounter the united Scottish and English armies, who have just arrived at Burnham Wood. Malcolm commands the soldiers to chop off branches from the trees so that they can disguise the marching army. There is also a discussion about Macbeth and how he plans to resist any siege, as well as about how many of his army are deserting. The two central lines are:

Act	200	Both more and lesse haue giuen him the Reuolt,
	201	And none serue with him, but constrained things,
		(Whose hearts are absent too.)

These lines fall close to the bottom of the right-hand column on page 149 and opposite a space in the left-hand column. They also fall just two lines later than the scene centre, the single line, 'Tis his maine hope.'

It is interesting that we find the word 'setting' here, not at the act centre but within the three lines at the centre of the Scene. So that in fact we have found it in three situations, at the centre of the play, at the centre of some acts and at the centre of a scene. Here it gives a picture of a besieging army encircling a castle, and this idea is carried on into the picture that we find at the centre of the act, which is of men escaping from that castle towards the encircling enemy, and of others impatiently held within its walls, possibly sitting about and longing to get away.

We now apply the test of 'out-riders.' Can we find words on either

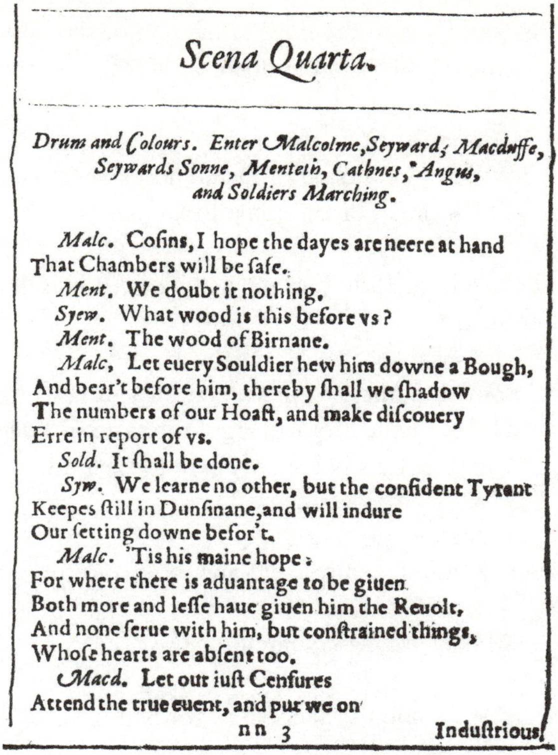

6. ACT CENTRES AND ACT SYMMETRY   117

> *Scena Quarta.*
>
> *Drum and Colours. Enter Malcolme, Seyward, Macduffe, Seywards Sonne, Menteth, Cathnes, Angus, and Soldiers Marching.*
>
> *Malc.* Cosins, I hope the dayes are neere at hand
> That Chambers will be safe.
> *Ment.* We doubt it nothing.
> *Syew.* What wood is this before vs?
> *Ment.* The wood of Birnane.
> *Malc.* Let euery Souldier hew him downe a Bough,
> And bear't before him, thereby shall we shadow
> The numbers of our Hoast, and make discouery
> Erre in report of vs.
> *Sold.* It shall be done.
> *Syw.* We learne no other, but the confident Tyrant
> Keepes still in Dunsinane, and will indure
> Our setting downe befor't.
> *Malc.* 'Tis his maine hope: | Act
> For where there is aduantage to be giuen | Centre
> Both more and lesse haue giuen him the Reuolt,
> And none serue with him, but constrained things,
> Whose hearts are absent too.
> *Macd.* Let our iust Censures
> Attend the true euent, and put we on
>   nn 3   *Industrious*

Figure 27. Centre of Act 5

side of this act centre that balance each other; or possibly corresponding ideas?

Act   210   But certaine issue, stroakes must arbitrate,
         211   Towards which, aduance the warre.   *Exeunt marching*

Counting ten and eleven lines back from the act centre, we come to Malcolm's words:

Act   211-   *Malc.* Let euery Souldier hew him downe a Bough,
         210-   And bear't before him, thereby shall we shadow

Here two kinds of strokes balance each other. Old Siward at the end of the scene is talking about those strokes of the sword needed to overcome an enemy. Malcolm, earlier on, is probably also speaking of strokes of the sword, but ones which will be used in cutting off branches. Moving further outwards, we come to the lines at the end of the previous scene. Macbeth is giving instructions to the doctor, his last words are:

Act 180   *Macb*. Bring it after me:
    181   I will not be affraid of Death and Bane,
    182   Till Birnane Forrest come to Dunsinane.

These are lines 21, 20 and 19 before the act centre. Lines 19, 20 and 21 after the Act Centre are:

Act 182-   *Sey*. It is the cry of women, my good Lord.
    181-   *Macb*. I haue almost forgot the taste of Feares:
    180-   The time ha's beene, my sences would have cool'd.

The theme of both passages is fear.
   At line 22 back from the centre we come to the doctor's words,

Act 179   Makes vs *heare* something.

At line 22 forward we come to Macbeth's words:

Act 222   To *heare* a Night-shrieke, and my Fell of haire.

The theme of both lines is hearing.
   At line 27 before the centre we come to Macbeth's words:

Act 174   I would applaud thee to the very Eccho,
175   That should applaud againe ...

At line 27 forward we come to Seyton's words:

Act 227   The Queen (My Lord) is dead.

This line is indeed an echo of the earlier one. If we simply listen to it we hear the same sound, 'Would applaud,' 'Queen, (My lord).' The relationship between Macbeth's instructions to the doctor and the report of the Queen's death are discussed in detail in the chapter on the death of the Queen. Here it is enough to say that this relationship is very close and highly significant, illustrated and emphasized by the balancing of words around the act centre.

7. Number Rhythms

The 'Wearie Seu'nights'

There is one particular rhythm in the play to which our attention seems to be drawn deliberately. At the beginning of Act 1 Scene 3 the first witch utters a curse against a sailor whose wife has evidently insulted her sometime previously. The curse is rather specific; he will it seems be buffeted by winds from all quarters of the compass. He will be 'drained dry.' He will suffer from continuous insomnia. Men will come to fear and dread him, and all this misery will continue for exactly eighty-one weeks.

91	1. A Saylors Wife had Chestnuts in her Lappe,
92	And mouncht, & mouncht, and mouncht:
93	Giue me, quoth I.
94	Aroynt thee, Witch, the rumpe-fed Ronyon cryes.
95	Her Husband's to Aleppo gone, Master o'th' Tiger:
96	But in a Syue Ile thither sayle,
97	And like a Rat without a tayle,
98	Ile doe, Ile doe, and Ile doe.
99	2. Ile giue thee a Winde.
100	1. Th'art kinde.
101	3. And I another.
102	1. I my selfe haue all the other,
103	And the very Ports they blow,
104	All the Quarters that they know,
105	I'th' Ship-mans Card.
106	Ile dreyne him drie as Hay:
107	Sleepe shall neyther Night nor Day
108	Hang vpon his Pent-house Lid:
109	He shall liue a man forbid:
110	Wearie Seu'nights, nine times nine,
111	Shall he dwindle, peake, and pine:
112	Though his Barke cannot be lost,
113	Yet it shall be Tempest-tost.

We have established in Chapter 3 that the sailor in question and his wife are no other than Macbeth and Lady Macbeth, but now we will take a closer look at the specific time rhythm mentioned in the curse. In a play where measure is beginning to show itself as all important, this information is suggestive. Could 'sev'night' be translated as a certain number, a certain number of lines in the printed First Folio? If so, how many?

The ordinary meaning of 'Seu'night' is, of course, one week. So eighty-one 'seven nights' should be just over twenty months. In this study, however, we will investigate how the word 'Seu'night' has meaning when we consider it to represent 'seventeen' nights. Today we say a 'fortnight,' not meaning four nights but fourteen nights. It therefore seems to be possible that 'Seu'night' does not only mean seven nights but could also mean 'Seventeen nights.' Also, at this point let us observe that 'sev'night' reminds us too of the word 'sonnet.'[1]

If we are going to count in seventeens, the first question is where should they begin? Should the first line of the prediction, 'Wearie Seu'nights, nine times nine,' be called line one of the first seventeen? If so, where do we arrive at seventeen? In fact, if we call 'Wearie Seu'nights, nine times nine,' 'line one' then line seventeen is the first line spoken by Macbeth on stage: 'So foule and faire a day I haue not seene.'[2] And the words, 'haue not seene,' may be called a near anagram, or perhaps a sound anagram, of seventeen; literally they would spell 'sahvonteene.'[3]

The end of the second seventeen corresponds with Banquo's words spoken to the witches following the three predictions to Macbeth. The actual line is 'Which outwardly ye shew? My Noble Partner,' and continues 'You greet with present Grace ...'

The third seventeen ends after the witches' predictions to Banquo, at the beginning of Macbeth's vain attempt to question them. The last line of this seventeen is, 'By Sinells death, I know I am *Thane* of Glamis.'

The first line of the fourth seventeen is, 'But how, of Cawdor? the *Thane* of Cawdor liues.' The fourth seventeen includes the main part of Macbeth's questioning and the main part of the 'Interlude of Wonder' when Macbeth and Banquo find themselves alone and astonished on the heath. The last line of this seventeen contains Macbeth's envious words, 'Your Children shall be Kings.'

The fifth seventeen includes the sudden arrival of Ross and Angus out of the blue with news of the King's pleasure at all he has heard of Macbeth's prowess on the battlefield and this part ends with the line, 'To giue thee from our Royall Master thanks,' spoken by Angus.

7. NUMBER RHYTHMS

The sixth seventeen includes the announcement that Macbeth has become Thane of Cawdor, and it ends with the line, 'But Treasons Capitall, confess'd, and prou'd,' which continues, 'Haue ouerthrowne him.'

The seventh seventeen includes Macbeth's final taking in of the fact that the witches' second prediction has come true with Banquo's warning of its dangerous possible consequences. It ends where Banquo has just taken the two messengers aside leaving Macbeth alone for his perilous soliloquy. This seventeen group ends 'Of the Imperiall Theame. I thanke you Gentlemen.'

The eighth seventeen is taken up with the main part of that soliloquy and ends as he wakes out of it with the words, 'Without my stirre.' By now we are beginning to suspect that each seventeen corresponds with a particular event, but this must be checked.

The ninth seventeen includes Macbeth's final return to normality with his apology to the messengers. It ends two lines from the end of the scene with Banquo's words to Macbeth, 'Very gladly.' We note that the ninth seventeen virtually coincides with a natural break in the action, and this makes us wonder whether the same is true of other multiples of nine.

Since the ninth seventeen almost coincides with the end of Scene 3, where there is a natural break, we feel justified in continuing to count in seventeens and look especially at 18 x 17, 27 x 17, 36 x 17, 45 x 17, 54 x 17, 63 x 17, 72 x 17 and finally 81 x 17. The twelfth seventeen, which just covers the centre of Scene 4, is also noteworthy for the words of the last line are, 'From hence to Enverness,' which provides another of what we have called, sound anagrams ('to Enverness' = 'severntoen').

We now pursue the great 153 line steps each representing, we suspect, nine 'Seu'nights.' At the end of 18 x 17 (line 415) we come to line 4 of Act 1 Scene 6, which is the scene in which Duncan and Banquo arrive with others at Inverness castle. The line reads, '*Banq.* This Guest of Summer,' continuing: 'The Temple-haunting Barlet does approue.'[4] 'This Guest of Summer' can mean the child which we first encountered as being suckled by Lady Macbeth as well as, of course, as the bird which builds its nest under the castle eaves. 'The Temple-haunting Barlet does approue' is, in fact, line 416 and 416 is 4 x 104 which is a significant and interesting number. Play-line 104 (Act 1) coincides with scene-line 17 early in Act 1 Scene 3 — 'All the Quarters that they know' — which describes how winds are blowing from all directions of the compass in the great storm that is threatening. 104 goes exactly 23 times into the grand total of the play (2392). The numbers suggest that we have reached a certain stage in a long journey.

At the end of 27 x 17 (line 568) come Macbeth's words to Banquo, near the beginning of Act 2 Scene 1. He is in effect repeating what he has already said to Banquo previously at the end of Act 1 Scene 3 — that is, 'We won't talk about this now, we'll talk about it later.' Only this time Macbeth is obviously lying. Banquo has just said:

> 565   I dreamt last Night of the three weyward Sisters:
> 566   To you they haue shew'd some truth.

To which Macbeth replies:

> 567   *Macb*. I thinke not of them:
> 568   Yet when we can entreat an houre to serue,
> 569   We would spend it in some words vpon that Businesse,
> 570   If you would graunt the time.

It is clearly untrue that Macbeth does not think of his encounter with the witches; his letter to Lady Macbeth (1, 5) is enough to disprove this. In effect Macbeth is just putting Banquo off and in doing so is distancing him as a friend.

At the end of 36 x 17 (line 721) we come to the Porter's words, near the end of his sleepy soliloquy just before Macduff and Lennox are let in at the 'South Entry;' the actual words of this line are, 'goe the Primrose way to th' euerlasting Bonfire.' Followed by, '*Knock*.'

> 720   I had thought to haue let in some of all Professions, that
> 721   goe the Primrose way to th' euerlasting Bonfire. *Knock*.
> 722   Anon, anon, I pray you remember the Porter.

The implication, as before, is that a journey is being travelled and that we have reached a certain stage on this journey. Ten lines further on we come to the Porter's words to Macduff and Lennox on the subject of 'Le- / cherie' and we may note this split word as it has significance in relation to the hidden child (see Chapter 9).

Three of the professions 'that goe the Primrose way to th' euerlasting Bonfire' are clearly descriptions of Macbeth, starting with the 'Farmer,

7. NUMBER RHYTHMS
123

that hang'd / himselfe on th' expectation of Plentie' — that is, murdered the King instead of waiting for Fate to bring about his demise. Next, at 'Le- / cherie' we come I believe to a hidden reference to the killing of Lady Macbeth's child, foreseen in, 'Making the Greene one, Red.' 'Sets him on, / and it takes him off' is suggestive; to take someone off is a way of saying, to take someone's life. At 'goe the Primrose way to th' euerlasting Bonfire' Macbeth is moving towards the murder of the child, a deed which will surely bring him close to 'th' euerlasting Bonfire.'

At the end of 45 x 17 (line 874) we come to the first line in Act 2 Scene 4, spoken by the Old man to Ross, 'Threescore and ten I can remember well,' which may remind us of the Porter's words, 'I pray you remember the Porter.' What we must remember is that the 'Wearie Seu'nights' do not begin until line 110 of the play therefore to any calculation relating to those 'Seu'nights' we must always add 109.

The end of 54 x 17 (6 x 9 x 17 [line 1027]) brings us to where Macbeth is speaking to the two men who he hopes will murder Banquo for him. The words here are: 'In your nature, that you can let this goe?'

>   1026   Doe you finde your patience so predominant,
>   1027   In your nature, that you can let this goe?
>   1028   Are you so Gospell'd, to pray for this good man,

He is lying about Banquo who he pretends has harmed the two men, the potential murderers, in the past. So, this is the preparation for the murder of Banquo.

At the end of 63 x 17 (7 x 9 x 17 [line 1180]) the words are, spoken by Banquo, 'Thou may'st reuenge. O Slaue!' This is the last line that Banquo speaks and corresponds with his murder.

At the end of 72 x 17 (8 x 9 x 17 [line 1333]) we come to Macbeth's words near the end of the Banqueting Scene, 'Stones haue beene knowne to moue, & Trees to speake.' After the murder of the man who was once his close friend Macbeth falls into a state of fear and superstition.

Finally, at the end of the eighty-first seventeen (line 1486 & 9 x 9 x 17) we come to Hecate's words, 'And euery one shall share i'th' gaines.'[5]

>   1485   *Hec*. O well done: I commend your paines,
>   1486   And euery one shall share i'th' gaines:

Hecate's words are interesting when we remember the first Witch's words when she utters the curse, 'Wearie Seu'nights, nine times nine, / Shall he dwindle, peake, and pine' (If it is true that 'a's were pronounced more like 'i's then 'paines' would have been pronounced more like 'pines'). At every ninth 'Seu'night' Macbeth dwindles a little more as he distances himself further from Banquo and now he is about to encounter those apparitions which Hecate herself initiated when she distilled the drop, 'Vpon the Corner of the Moone.' In commanding the second song, she must know that it will be caught up in the distillation process just as the first song, *'Come away, come away'* was caught up.

So Hecate has reappeared just in time to commend the witches for bringing about Macbeth's descent into sin and misery. A moment later, the two distilled songs join forces to create a gap into the depths of hell, a place below, that is the 'Pit of Acheron,' out of which the apparitions appear to tempt and confuse Macbeth. (See Figure 28 for beginning and end of 'Wearie Sev'nights'). Through the completion of the rhythmic curse, the 'Wearie Seu'nights, nine times nine,' a new stage has been reached; the power of the First Witch's curse has run out and it appears that it is now the power of Hecate that takes over, although in fact she herself seems to vanish mysteriously from the scene as the second song is sung. Our impression is that in some way she is directing proceedings from somewhere below the stage, where the visible events take place. Now the soul of Macbeth, which the First Witch did not have power to shipwreck utterly, will be tempted to commit the worst crime yet.

The Ninety-Two Rhythm and Square Numbers

The 'Wearie Seu'nights' point to one among several rhythms, which can be traced within this play. The very structure of the first play-line total, 2392 lines, leads us to another one. 2392 may be seen as two pairs of numbers: 23 and 92. We may observe that 23 is one of the factors of the whole (2392) and further, that 23 goes exactly four times into 92. It follows, therefore, that it goes exactly 104 times into the first total, and since 104 is eight times 13 we have come to the complete set of factors: 23, 8 and 13. We may start to look first for the sequence of 92s running throughout the play and see if they have any qualities in common (see Appendix 4).

In Act 1 the sequence is: lines 92, 184, 276, 368 and 460. 92 is indeed a dramatic line; we are close to the beginning of Scene 3 in Act 1 and the first witch is just starting to tell the story of the Sailor's Wife. The line

7. NUMBER RHYTHMS 125

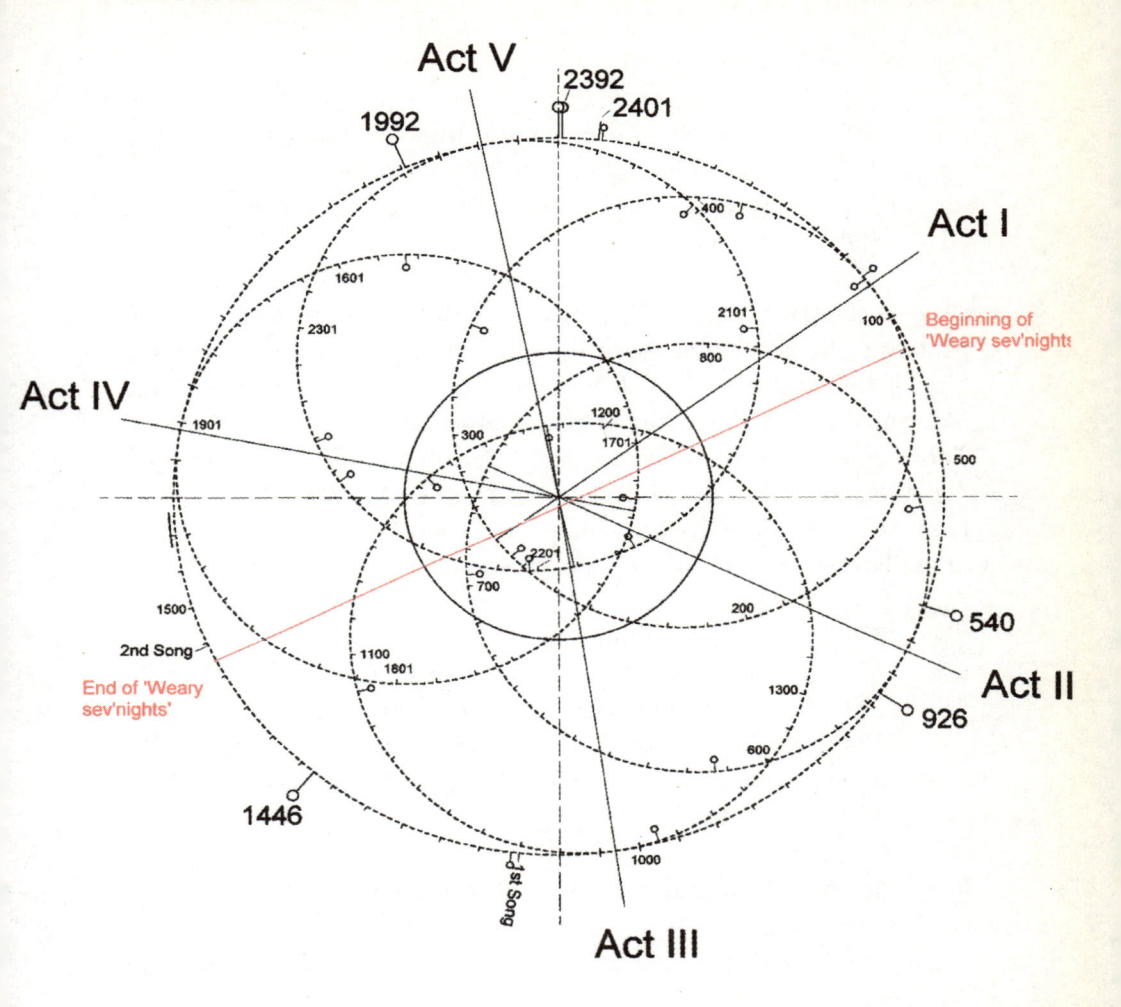

Figure 28. Beginning and End of 'Wearie Sev'nights'

is, 'And mouncht, & mouncht, and mouncht.'

At line 184, Ross is just beginning to describe the King's pleasure at hearing about *Macbeth*s' prowess on the battlefield: 'His Wonders and his Prayses doe contend.'

Line 276 includes those lines where Malcolm is telling his father about the noble manner of the Thane of Cawdor's dying, 'To throw away the dearest thing he ow'd, / As 'twere a carelesse Trifle.' (275f).

The action around line 368 concerns the delivery, in haste, of a message to Lady Macbeth.

> 365 *Mess.* So please you, it is true: our *Thane* is comming:
> 366 One of my fellowes had the speed of him;
> 367 Who almost dead for breath, had scarcely more
> 368 Then would make vp his Message.

There is the sense of great urgency here for Macbeth's messenger is left panting for breath in the courtyard while the castle messenger relieves him of his charge and quickly conveys the news to the Lady. Lady Macbeth then bids him return to his exhausted fellow and look after him. This man had ridden even faster than Macbeth himself to bring news of the immanent arrival of the King to Inverness castle. When he has gone, Lady Macbeth returns to her soliloquy only now she is thinking not only of her husband's character but of that of the King.

> 371 The Rauen himselfe is hoarse,
> 372 That croakes the fatall entrance of *Duncan*
> 373 Vnder my Battlements. Come you Spirits,
> 374 That tend on mortall thoughts, vnsex me here,
> 375 And fill me from the Crowne to the Toe, top-full
> 376 Of direst Crueltie ...

It is to defend herself against the King that she summons spirits to undo her feminine aspect.

Line 460 brings us to the place where Macbeth is just entering into the arguments against the murder of King Duncan, 'Commends th' Ingredience of our poyson'd Challice / To our owne lips. Hee's heere in double trust' (459 & 460).

We already seem to discern a sequence of stories related to the ninety-two rhythm and we also observe the repetition of certain sounds. First the 'ow' or 'un' sound in 'And m**ou**ncht, & m**ou**ncht, and m**ou**ncht:' (92). 'His W**on**ders and his Prayses doe contend' (184). 'To thr**ow** away the dearest thing he **ow**'d,' (275). Finally, at 460, 'To our **ow**ne lips.' The vowel is repeated at 275, 'the dearest thing he **ow**'d' and less emphatically, at 367, 'Who **al**most dead for breath.'

We also notice a repetition of the word 'give:' '**Giue** me, quoth I' (line 93) and '**Giue** him tending' (line 369), and also a repetition of words containing the syllable, '**end**:' 'His Wonders and his Prayses doe con-

7. NUMBER RHYTHMS 127

tend' (184); 'Giue him ten**d**ing' (369); also, 'Comm**end**s th' Ingredience of our poyson'd Challice' (459).

There is often a suggestion of the image of a head or a face, with the mouth especially strong: 'And mouncht, & mouncht, and mouncht.' In the words 'His Wonders and his Prayses doe contend' we see the King speaking. At 'As 'twere a carelesse Trifle,' we come to the picture of Cawdor's head which he threw away with such carelessness. 'To our owne lips,' brings us the picture of drinking.

In Act 2, the sounds and images continue — '... who's there? / *Macb*. A Fri**end**.' (553, 554) — which has the same **end** sound. Early in Act 2 we come to the beginning of the story of Duncan's contentment in bed and again we encounter the 'giue' word, 'That Nature **giues** way to in repose, / **Giue** me my Sword: who's there?' (552f). The 'ow' or 'un' sound seems to have disappeared but when we turn to the thirteenth 92, that is the centre of the play, we find it again, '*Macb*. See they enco**un**ter thee with their harts thanks / Both sides are euen: heere Ile sit i'th' mid'st,' (1196f). We also encounter it again at the ninth 92, '**Ou**t-run the pawser, Reason Here lay *Duncan*,' (829); also at the tenth 92, (921) '*Macd*. No C**o**sin, Ile to Fife,' and finally, at the twelfth 92, 'Should be with**ou**t regard: what's d**o**ne, is d**o**ne' (1105). We have the impression that the key words change as the play flows on and then, at 23 times 92 (2116) we are suddenly arrested by a new sound,

2115 The minde I sway by, and the heart I beare,
2116 Shall neuer sagge with doubt, nor shake with feare.

'Doubt' repeats the 'ow' sound but, 'shake with feare' (Shake-speare) does this mean anything?

23 times 92 is 23 x 23 x 4, and 23 x 23 x 4 is (23 x 2)² which is to say: 46². At this point in the 'Figure' the time stream of Act V is just crossing the axis of Act I, which points like a spear upwards and to the right (see Figure 29). 2116 is a 'Square Number,' such a number as the writer of this play found significant. It may also remind us of a well-known finding in Psalm 46 of the King James Bible. At 46 words from the beginning of the psalm we come to the word 'shake' and 46 words in from the end takes us to the word 'speare.' Both situations look like a signature.[6] Then we remember that the extended play (2401 lines) ends with another square number, 49². So perhaps we have to think of a sequence of square numbers with, 'Shall neuer sagge with doubt, nor

128　　　NUMBER AND GEOMETRY IN SHAKESPEARE'S *MACBETH*

Figure 29. 'shake with feare'

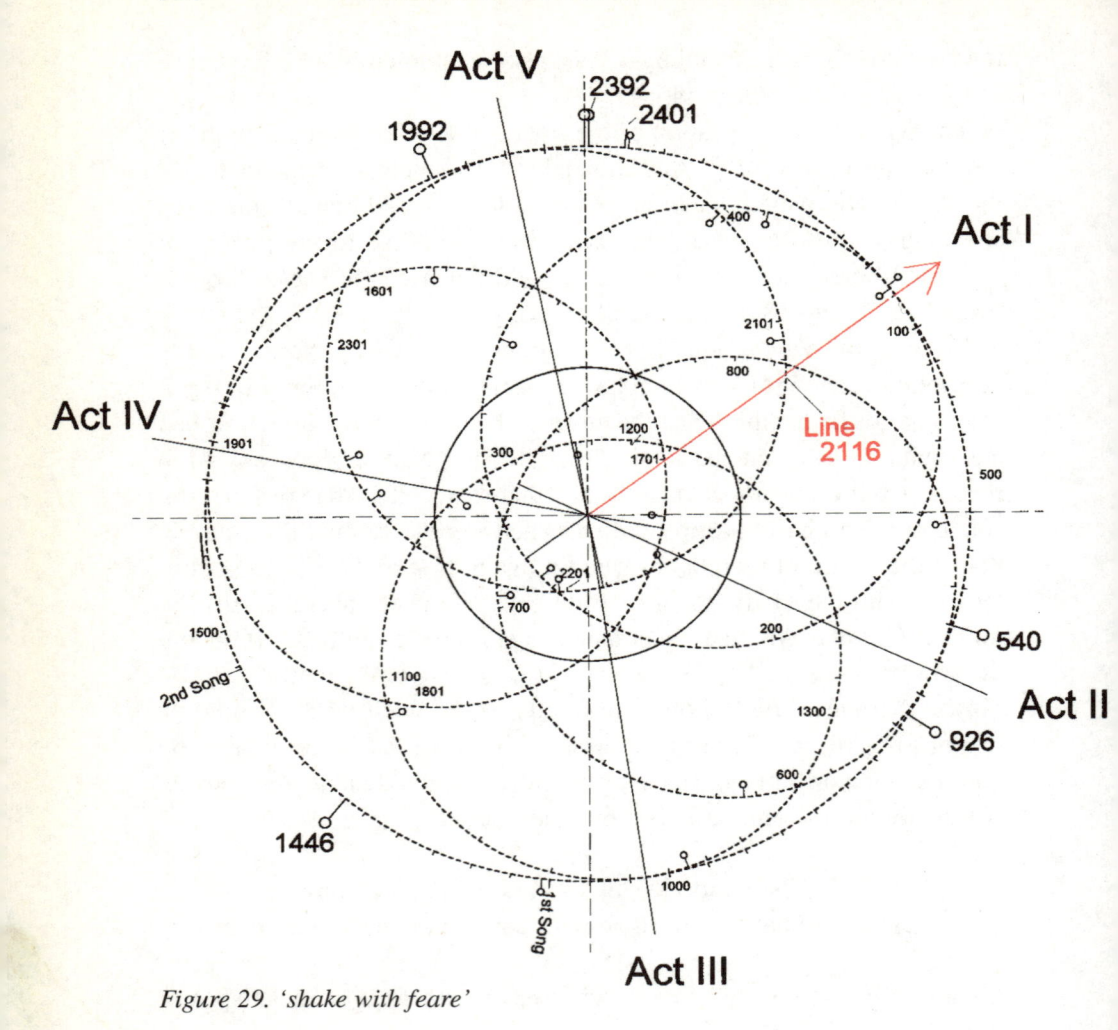

shake with feare,' coming at the crossing place between that sequence and the 92 sequence.

　　Looking now at the sequence of square numbers just after the central section of the play we come to 35^2, that is line 1225. Lady Macbeth is just reproaching her husband because he is failing in his duties as a host; she says:

　　　　1223　　*Lady*. My Royall Lord,
　　　　1224　　You do not giue the Cheere, the Feast is sold
　　　　1225　　That is not often vouch'd, while 'tis a making:

This last line (1225) is 35^2. Lady Macbeth seems to be saying: we must

7. NUMBER RHYTHMS 129

be reminded on the way of the goals we are approaching. The numerical 'Feast' within the play is certainly 'vouch'd' at this line for 35^2 is also 25 x 49, that is the product of two square numbers. This takes us a further step for we can see that now there is a special delight in the quality of square numbers, and square numbers within square numbers. We are drawn now to look at another similar configuration of square numbers, this time secreted within play line 1764, namely 42^2 or 36 x 49 (6 x 6) x (7 x 7). We are here within Scene 3 of Act IV. Malcolm is just agreeing with Macduff about the wretched state of Scotland:

> 1762   I thinke our Country sinkes beneath the yoake,
> 1763   It weepes, it bleeds, and each new day a gash
> 1764   Is added to her wounds. ...

Again we have a picture of a continuing state of affairs. We can perhaps even see these gashes as strong pencil marks inscribed at intervals on the text of the play.

Since discovering that the twenty-third 92 has brought us to a square number and also to the utterance of what seems to be Shakespeare's name we are drawn now to look at 23^2, since 23 is a simple factor of the small play-total (2392). 23^2, or line 529, is very close to the end of Act 1. Macbeth has just been won over by his wife:

> 528   *Macb*. Bring forth Men-Children onely:
> 529   For thy vndaunted Mettle should compose
> 530   Nothing but Males.

Line 529 speaks of the elements that go to make up a human being much as if they were metallic elements that go to make up an alloy such as brass. It is interesting that one of those elements in Lady Macbeth's case is her skill at deceit and this is what has won Macbeth over and what he so greatly admires. The scene ends with his words,

> 539   Away, and mock the time with fairest show,
> 540   False Face must hide what the false Heart doth know.

And it is interesting that at line 46^2, to which we have compared this line, Macbeth makes a boast which is instantly shown to be untrue for the words, 'Shall neuer sagge with doubt, nor shake with feare' do not disguise the fact that when the messenger arrives to give news of the English force Macbeth is clearly inwardly terrified.

Among the square numbers that lead up to 46^2, and finally to 49^2, we find certain ones that are suggestive of reading a book. Line 256 (16^2) falls close to the end of Act 1 Scene 3 and Macbeth is just thanking the King's two messengers:

    255   Kinde Gentlemen, your paines are registred,
    256   Where euery day I turne the Leafe,
    257   To reade them.

Line 400 (20^2) is close to the end of Act 1 Scene 5:

    399   Your Face, my *Thane*, is as a Booke, where men
    400   May reade strange matters, to beguile the time.

If we obey the injunction of line 256 and 'turne the Leafe' until we reach the play-mirror of this line, we come to a single word; this is at line 33 of Act 5 Scene 3. The word is, 'Seyton,' which though it can be pronounced in different ways, nevertheless brings to mind the name, 'Satan.' This follows shortly after that significant line from which our search for square numbers began: 'Shall neuer sagge with doubt, nor shake with feare.' Seyton himself seems to enter very promptly when Macbeth calls him, almost as if he were standing just outside the door, and there follows that three-sided conversation between Macbeth, the Doctor and Seyton. The Doctor, who entered the room with Macbeth, is first subjected to probing questions by him and finally given succinct instructions, 'Come sir, dispatch.,' 'Pull't off I say,' which is usually taken to apply to Macbeth's armour but can so easily apply to the circumstances surrounding the death of Lady Macbeth (see Chapter 9). We can well believe that Seyton is an aspect of the Devil, which has at this very moment entered into the heart and soul of Macbeth, who then makes the evil suggestion that the Doctor should end the life of his wife.

Going back to the original line, 256 (16^2), it is noteworthy to see that there is an interesting echo with the Seyton episode, for straight after line 256 we come to the place where, inwardly, Macbeth can no longer speak

7. NUMBER RHYTHMS 131

the truth to his friend.

> 258   Let vs toward the King: thinke vpon
> 259   What hath chanc'd: and at more time,
> 260   The Interim hauing weigh'd it, let vs speake
> 261   Our free Hearts each to other.

Macbeth is here masking his troubled thoughts and for the first time succumbing to those powers of evil which will not only separate him from his friend, but also lead him eventually to plot his murder.

8. The Plot of *Macbeth* (Part 1)

The Thane of Cawdor

The only known version of *Macbeth*, that of the 1623 Folio, is generally believed to be shortened and probably corrupt. This belief is based on three main arguments: the strangeness and irregularity of the second scene in the play; the contradictions of the Cawdor story; and the difference of style between the Hecate scenes in Acts 3 and 4, and the earlier witch scenes in Act 1.

The second scene in Act 1, in which a bleeding captain brings news of the battle in Fife to King Duncan, has already been discussed from the point of view of structure. Its surprising symmetry leads us to suspect that it is not after all interpolated or corrupt. However strange the language, we have reason to hope that, in the end, it will make complete sense. It is in this scene that we hear the first fragment of the Cawdor story. As the act unfolds the contradictions in that story become so flagrant that it is easy to believe that the longer version of it was once carelessly shortened or changed. Yet, once again, structure makes us pause. The act is one, and its form, we have seen, is tight and perfect. If we do not assume a fixed plot in advance perhaps those fragments, too, will make sense in the end.

We experienced the word 'Cawdor' as a foreboding sound. It is croaked nineteen times through Act 1, and then no more. By Scene 6, when King Duncan arrives at Inverness Castle, Cawdor and Macbeth are one.

We first hear this name from Ross, who has ridden in haste from the field of battle to give the news of victory to the king. Cawdor, we learn, is a Scottish traitor who has given help to Sweno, the invading King of Norway. Sweno's men, and the loyalist Scottish troops have been engaged in heavy fighting, during which Macbeth (Bellona's bridegroom) seems to have met Cawdor face-to-face. In the end Duncan's army has won the day. These are Ross's words:

69	Norway himselfe, with terrible numbers,
70	Assisted by that most disloyall Traytor,

71	The Thane of Cawdor, began a dismall Conflict,
72	Till that Bellona's Bridegroome, lapt in proofe,
73	Confronted him with selfe-comparisons,
74	Point against Point, rebellious Arme 'gainst Arme,
75	Curbing his lauish spirit: and to conclude,
76	The Victorie fell on vs.

Perhaps Ross felt it was time to get to the point and tell the King the good news. Certainly the account of the fighting ends abruptly, and nothing at all is said then or later of how Cawdor was captured. That he was there, in the midst of the fray, perhaps even in personal combat with Macbeth seems, however, to be directly implied.

The second time that we hear Cawdor's name is at the end of this scene, when King Duncan decrees his death:

83	*King.* No more that Thane of Cawdor shall deceiue
84	Our Bosome interest: Goe pronounce his present death,
85	And with his former Title greet Macbeth

Duncan simply assumes that Cawdor has been, or will easily be, captured.

The third time we hear this name, it comes as a prophecy from the mouth of the second witch:

137	1. All haile Macbeth, haile to thee Thane of Glamis.
138	2. All haile Macbeth, haile to thee Thane of Cawdor.
139	3. All haile Macbeth, that shalt be King hereafter.

These words, uttered at dusk on a lonely heath, astound Macbeth, but a few moments later he comes to himself:

159	*Macb.* Stay you imperfect Speakers, tell me more:
160	By Sinells death, I know I am Thane of Glamis,
161	But how, of Cawdor? the Thane of Cawdor liues
162	A prosperous Gentleman: And to be King,
163	Stands not within the prospect of beleefe,
164	No more then to be Cawdor.

It seems that Macbeth saw Cawdor alive and unhurt when the fighting was over. Yet 'prosperous gentleman' is an odd phrase more appropri-

8. THE PLOT OF *MACBETH* (PART 1)

ate to a laird at home with his acres around him than to a panting foe armed with a shield and sword. And if Macbeth knew that Cawdor was a leading rebel, why is he surprised that he should have lost his title? Logically he must know him for a gentleman who has incurred the king's displeasure; one, indeed, who has not prospered.

The 'ore' sound blows through this passage like a breath of wonder itself. Macbeth utters the name Cawdor no less than three times in the space of four lines and then again a fourth time; the seventh in the Act sounding after the witches have vanished:

> 178   *Banq.* You shall be King.
> 179   *Macb.* And Thane of Cawdor too: went it not so?
> 180   *Banq.* To th' selfe-same tune and words: who's here?

It is Ross who is there, accompanied by Angus, and it is Ross (after a flowery preamble) who utters the name of Cawdor for the eighth time:

> 198   He bad me, from him, call thee Thane of Cawdor:
> 199   In which addition, haile most worthy Thane,
> 200   For it is thine.

Within moments, the prophecy has been fulfilled. Again it is Banquo who first finds words:

> 201   *Banq.* What, can the Deuill speake true?

And again Macbeth insists, half stupidly:

> 202   *Macb.* The Thane of Cawdor liues: (the ninth echo)

And now he goes on with growing anger and misgiving:

> 203   Why doe you dresse me in borrowed Robes?

Macbeth knows that Cawdor was alive, a few hours since; not only alive, but well; and he has a sensation that is perhaps familiar to him, of being shoved too quickly into another man's shoes, made to act a part in which he is not at home. Ross says not a word to clarify matters. He leaves Angus to answer Macbeth and Angus flounders. He only knows what he has been told; that the Thane of Cawdor has confessed to treason:

> 207 Whether he was combin'd with those of Norway,
> 208 Or did lyne the Rebell with hidden helpe,
> 209 And vantage; or that with both he labour'd
> 210 In his Countreyes wracke, I know not:
> 211 But Treasons Capitall, confess'd, and prou'd,
> 212 Haue ouerthrowne him.

Angus' uncertainty is as strange as Ross's silence: since they have been riding beside each other for some time and Ross, who first gave the news of Cawdor's treason to King Duncan, might have been expected to know more details.

But the outcome of events is not uncertain, and the dramatic pause here must be a long one. At last Macbeth takes it in. The man he knew is doomed, and the title 'Cawdor' has become his own. And moments later he is rapt in a dream of the future:

> 213 *Macb.* Glamys, and *Thane* of Cawdor:
> 214 The greatest is behinde ...

Soon Macbeth, left alone by the others, will be caught up in the vision of murdering Duncan. The moment has passed when Angus, and the audience, might have learned more from the man who ought best to know about Cawdor's mysterious role. But it is here, in the encounter with Angus and Ross that the great contradiction is focused.

Macbeth has certainly met Cawdor recently. 'The Thane of Cawdor lives!' is spoken twice and with the conviction of direct experience. Ross says that it was on the battlefield that he met him, yet of this encounter Macbeth never speaks a word. He seems, indeed, to know nothing about it and neither does anyone else, since no one can furnish Angus with anything better than rumour.

The thirteenth sounding of Cawdor brings us the news of his death. In the opening lines of the next scene, King Duncan asks his son:

> 265 *King.* Is execution done on *Cawdor*?
> 266 Are not those in Commission yet return'd?

There follow young Malcolm's famous words:

> 267 *Mal.* My Liege, they are not yet come back.

268		But I haue spoke with one that saw him die:
269		Who did report, that very frankly hee
270		Confess'd his Treasons, implor'd your Highnesse Pardon,
271		And set forth a deepe Repentance:
272		Nothing in his Life became him,
273		Like the leauing it …

The Thane of Cawdor's stands closer to us now than ever before. Yet still there is something wrong; the phrases are off-key. Why 'implor'd your Highness pardon?' Does not a man at the point of death care more for the pardon of God than for that of an earthly King? Though Cawdor may have wished to make peace with all men before he died, he must have had a reason for supporting a rebellion against Duncan. And the latter's victory and harsh cruelty in condemning him to death without trial, were hardly calculated to touch his heart. One can confess something in a spirit of bravado as well as a spirit of regret. In fact, these words of Malcolm's are not merely odd they are wholly ambiguous. Their alternative meaning, once we have seen it, fits as well, if not better.

Suppose it is God's pardon that Cawdor is concerned about. Suppose Duncan has indeed been unjust to him, and suppose we interpret 'set forth' in its more natural meaning of 'set out,' 'propose,' 'suggest?' Then Cawdor is saying: 'I confess my treasons frankly (that is because they were justified): and I implore God to pardon the man who now condemns me to death without trial. Let him repent, though, of this deed and of others, before it is too late.' In the Folio printing there is no sign of the genitive in 'Your Highnesse pardon.' It can just as well be pardon for your Highness; and 'Implore' addressed to God, takes on a more exact and original sense.

If Duncan is guilty, he may feel stricken with guilt. What is the first thing he says after Malcolm has reported Cawdor's dying words?

281		O worthyest Cousin,
282		The sinne of my Ingratitude euen now
283		Was heauie on me.

These words are spoken, of course to Macbeth, who has just arrived, and are taken to express in gracious hyperbole Duncan's sense of debt to his brave captain. Yet this need not end their meaning. Thoughts overlap, and context is all important; 'even now' wakens to sudden precision, when we take it to mean not some time before this scene opened, but literally 'even now,' that is, a moment ago.

The importance of this moment is also confirmed by structure.

Act 270   Confess'd his Treasons, implor'd your Highnesse Pardon,
     271   And set forth a deepe Repentance:

The lines have the act numbers 270 and 271. Since Act 1 is 540 lines long, this couplet lies at its exact centre. Geometrically it has no mirror, and therefore must mirror itself. If it is Duncan who has wronged Cawdor, rather than Cawdor who has wronged Duncan, then the whole story wears a different aspect. Perhaps there is good reason why the evidence against Cawdor is so thin.

The Character of Ross

It is Ross, and Ross alone, who says that Cawdor was present on the battlefield. He announces it loudly, in public, to the King; and later it is he who carries both the order for Cawdor's execution and the news of his inheritance to Macbeth. Ross has for some time been under suspicion as a character darker than he at first seems. He has even been cast as the third murderer who joins the other two at the last moment to dispatch Banquo and Fleance. Roman Polanski, in his film of *Macbeth*, makes Ross dark throughout. However, our only direct evidence about him comes from his manner of speech, and his speech is eloquent (he clearly has a useful knowledge of court customs), and reveals him first as an actor, a storyteller next, and as a man who undergoes profound change.

Ross is with the King's party when Duncan arrives at Inverness, but we do not meet him again directly until the end of Act 2. Then in Scene 4 he confirms a story so tall that the audience is surely expected to disbelieve it. This scene (2, 4) must be set somewhere outside the walls of Inverness Castle. Duncan lies murdered within and the sky is darkened by an eclipse. Ross and an older man, taking the role of a Greek chorus, have been exchanging news of portents.

     889   *Rosse*. And Duncans Horses,
     890   (A thing most strange, and certaine)
     891   Beauteous, and swift, the Minions of their Race,

8. THE PLOT OF *MACBETH* (PART 1)

892	Turn'd wilde in nature, broke their stalls, flong out,
893	Contending 'gainst Obedience, as they would
894	Make Warre with Mankinde.
895	*Old man*. 'Tis said, they eate each other.
896	*Rosse*. They did so:
897	To th' amazement of mine eyes that look'd vpon't.

If Ross's eyes had looked upon it, why did he not recount the best bit of the story himself? It seems more likely that he is just piqued at having told a tale to one who knew it already, and determined not to be outdone.

But perhaps the most striking thing about Ross is the way he changes from Act 4 onwards. In Acts 1, 2 and 3, the phrases he uses are flamboyant, bombastic, turgid or sycophantic. Again and again it is Ross's words that tangle us up, and make us say that Shakespeare could never have written them.

72	Till that Bellona's Bridegroome, lapt in proofe,
73	Confronted him with selfe-comparisons,
74	Point against Point, rebellious Arme 'gainst Arme,
75	Curbing his lauish spirit ... (1, 2)
188	Nothing afeard of what thy selfe didst make
189	Strange Images of death, as thick as Tale
190	Can post with post ... (1, 3)[1]
880	... by th' Clock 'tis Day,
881	And yet darke Night strangles the trauailing Lampe: (2, 4)

Ross's first words in the banqueting scene (spoken just after the ghost of Banquo has glided in unseen) are precisely calculated to please the King:

1237	*Rosse*. His absence (Sir)
1238	Layes blame vpon his promise. Pleas't your Highnesse
1239	To grace vs with your Royall Company? (3, 4)

But in the scene with Lady Macduff and her son in Act 4, we find in Ross's speech a new note of sincerity and even of beauty:

> 1641   ... yet know not what we feare,
> 1642   But floate vpon a wilde and violent Sea
> 1643   Each way, and moue ...   (4, 2)

He is talking to a cousin now, of course, a near friend, but the old man was no courtier. With him Ross could surely have been his more natural self but that has got lost, in the habit of hyperbole.

Later in Act 4, when he brings the news of tragedy to Macduff, we feel that Ross has been purged, as the audience too should be purged, by pity and horror. He cannot bear to break the news, but stirring Macduff to action first, almost lets the news break itself:

> 1935   *Rosse.* Would I could answer
> 1936   This comfort with the like. But I haue words
> 1937   That would be howl'd out in the desert ayre,
> 1938   Where hearing should not latch them.   (4, 3)

It seems that the change in Ross is noticed earlier by Malcolm:

> 1895   My countryman: but yet I know him not.   (4, 3)

And that something once stood between them:

> 1897   ... Good God betimes remoue
> 1898   The meanes that makes vs Strangers.   (4, 3)

It is in Act 4 that the tide of the play turns; and the change in Ross is part of that turning. In Act 5 we do not find him numbered in Malcolm's army, we first find him on the field of battle at the very end. It is he who tells old Siward of his son's death and who praises the boy's courage in simple words.

> 2349   *Rosse.* Your son my Lord, ha's paid a souldiers debt,
> 2350   He onely liu'd but till he was a man,
> 2351   The which no sooner had his Prowesse confirm'd
> 2352   In the vnshrinking station where he fought,
> 2353   But like a man he dy'de.   (5, 7)

We may contrast this with his own airy rhetoric at the beginning of the play.

72	Till that Bellona's Bridegroome, lapt in proofe,	
73	Confronted him with selfe-comparisons,	
74	Point against Point, rebellious Arme 'gainst Arme,	
75	Curbing his lauish spirit: and to conclude	(1, 2)

One sounds like an eyewitness report, the other, like a fabrication.

Earlier, it was claimed that structure sheds light on plot. The corollary is that ideas on plot — even wild and seemingly absurd ones — may be tested by structure, and will either find rejection or confirmation. We have already noted the curious ambiguity that lies at the mathematical centre of Act 1: 'Confess'd his Treasons, implor'd your Highnesse Pardon, / And set forth a deepe Repentance.' First, this sheds doubt on Duncan's condemnation of the Thane of Cawdor. Next, it sheds doubt on the character of Duncan, and finally, it sheds doubt on Ross, who begins to appear as the tool of King Duncan. Ross, and Ross alone, reports that the Thane of Cawdor was present on the battlefield.

Though Ross has described loudly how Macbeth encountered the King of Norway who was 'Assisted by that most disloyall Traytor, / The Thane of Cawdor,' Macbeth himself seems to have a different memory of the Thane. One hardly describes a foe, encountered on the field of battle, 'A prosperous Gentleman'! The phrase rather conjures up a man living comfortably at home on his own broad acres, and when Ross finally names Macbeth as the new Thane of Cawdor, Macbeth is astonished and repeats, 'The Thane of Cawdor liues,' and immediately links the name with the idea of borrowed clothes, 'Why doe you dresse me in borrowed Robes?'

We seem to be led to a glimpse of a different scenario, of Macbeth and Banquo tramping home from battle in filthy war-torn garments, now soaked with rain, calling in at a friend's house on the way and being kindly lent new dry clothes to continue on their journey. Is it possible that the Thane of Cawdor was never on the battlefield at all? That the King, for some reason wants him out of the way? That Ross is, indeed, the King's tool and the whole story is a plant? It would certainly make sense, and fit the character of Ross as we first perceived.

If, behind the fragmentary story of Cawdor, there lies the concept of a 'frame-up,' in which Ross acts as the King's agent, then behind the innocent, white-haired figure of Duncan, there must lie a more complex character than we have so far apprehended. Let us then first scrutinize the evidence in the play from which we have deduced that character, and then see if structure can illuminate it further.

The Character of Duncan

The historical Duncan of Holinshed is younger than Shakespeare's. He is also a feeble ruler, which makes sense of the rebellion at the beginning of the play (1, 2. Lines 11, 12 etc). Muir suggests that Shakespeare made his Duncan 'old and holy' so that he might act as a foil to Macbeth. We now look again at the references to Duncan in the play to see if they can shed any further light on the character that Shakespeare meant him to have.

To bear witness that he was old we have Lady Macbeth's words, 'yet who would have thought the old man to have had so much blood in him?' (5, 1) Our impression that he was holy also comes chiefly from what is said about him, and is really a complex of impressions.

As the arguments against murder crowd upon him (1, 7) Macbeth foresees that Duncan's virtues, 'Will pleade like Angels, Trumpet-tongu'd' after his death. Later, early in Act 3 when different inner arguments persuade him to a second murder (that of Banquo), he says, 'for him the gracious Duncan have I murdered.' and we recognise 'gracious' as the standard epithet in references to Duncan.

In Act 4, when Malcolm invents vices for himself as a test of Macduff's loyalty, the latter defends the young man's parents with bitter indignation:

1836	Since that the truest Issue of thy Throne
1837	By his owne Interdiction stands accust,
1838	And do's blaspheme his breed? Thy Royall Father
1839	Was a most Sainted-King: the Queene that bore thee,
1840	Oftner vpon her knees, then on her feet,
1841	Dy'de euery day she liu'd ... (4, 3)

Earlier (Act 2) it is Macduff who cries 'O horror, horror, horror' when he finds Duncan lying murdered in his bed, and he makes us feel then that this killing is more terrible than most.

777	Most sacrilegious Murther hath broke ope
778	The Lords anoynted Temple, and stole thence
779	The Life o'th' Building. (2, 3)

Whether it is the office of King that made the murder a special sacrilege or rather the personality of this particular King, we do not know, but certainly the words 'virtues,' 'gracious,' 'sainted,' all build up to an impression of natural goodness, and that Duncan was loved we have the evidence of his own words in Act 1, Scene 6:

The Loue that followes vs, sometime is our trouble

However, we are looking at Duncan now with a new suspicion: and in fact, if we examine these passages more closely they begin to appear as double-edged as Malcolm's report of Cawdor's death. If Cawdor's last words imply guilt on the part of the King, rather than repentance on the part of the man he has condemned, then a whole new scenario opens up. Why is it that it is Ross alone who knows anything about the presence of Cawdor on the battlefield? Either the others were unobservant or Ross, for some reason, is lying. If he is lying then surely it is the King who wants him to lie. Once more, we come to the thought that the whole story must be a 'plant.'

A concordance or etymological dictionary makes it clear that at least one common meaning of 'gracious' was 'charming,' 'good-looking:' something closer in sense to graceful than to 'filled with grace.' It also shows that 'sainted' is by no means equivalent to 'saintly.' We see that the word bears a passive sense (as indeed its form suggests), of objects 'made holy,' of people 'regarded as a saint' (not necessarily with justification). In the context of Macduff's indignation it almost seems to mean 'prayed for,' since he goes on at once to speak of Duncan's wife who spends many hours on her knees in prayer.[2] If the link is a causal one then the words of the play are not incompatible with the idea that King Duncan was a charming, handsome man, who needed to be prayed for — or at least, on whose account his wife was often in prayer. We may remember King Duncan's words to Lady Macbeth as he arrives at Inverness Castle, 'Herein I teach you, / How you shall bid God-eyld vs for your paines, And thanke vs for your trouble.' He is evidently a man who thinks it proper that others should pray for him.

Macbeth believed that Duncan's virtues would plead against 'the deep damnation of his taking off.' Because he is murdered he will die unshriven, but holy men can take death as it comes, with an easy conscience. That Duncan risks damnation through sudden death is an argument against his unsullied holiness. In fact, Macbeth was so deeply aware of this risk that it is the theme of his last words before he commits murder:

> 611   I goe, and it is done: the Bell inuites me.
> 612   Heare it not, Duncan, for it is a Knell,
> 613   That summons thee to Heauen, or to Hell. *Exit.* (2,2)

The fate of his soul is uncertain; it hangs in the balance.

The 'sainted-king' passage spoken by Macduff comes as the despairing climax to Malcolm's strange self-accusation in Act 4 Scene 3; that long scene set in England, which most editors regard as tedious. Malcolm tests the sincerity of Macduff by painting sins he has never committed, and never intends to commit. It all seems curiously far-fetched. Is all this designed as a chorus, intended to give a sense of time passing and to sound a note of suspicion, which conveys the all-pervading mistrust that spreads outwards from Scotland? How can it profit us, in the context of the whole play, to be given this abstract portrait of royal lust and avarice, as well as a list of counterbalancing virtues?

The theme returns; virtue and vice in balance. We come to the classical image of justice with her scales; and, perhaps, to another human portrait, which is not abstract after all. Ideas as detailed as Malcolm's usually come from somewhere. Shakespeare, we know, took many of them from Holinshed. But is Malcolm supposed to have drawn them from history too? Or could he have taken them more directly from life?

The King he knew best was his father. Could these, we ask, be *Duncan's* vices, and *Duncan's* virtues, that suggest themselves so promptly and copiously to the boy? Could this be the real man behind the figure that we have known for centuries but not recognised? The virtues come last; a concise list of twelve, proper to a successful head of state.

> 1820   *Mal.* But I haue none. The King-becoming Graces,
> 1821   As Iustice, Verity, Temp'rance, Stablenesse,
> 1822   Bounty, Perseuerance, Mercy, Lowlinesse,
> 1823   Deuotion, Patience, Courage, Fortitude,
> 1824   I haue no rellish of them ...

8. THE PLOT OF *MACBETH* (PART 1)

The vices — only two (as opposed to Holinshed's three) — come first and are described vividly and at length:

1786	... But there's no bottome, none
1787	In my Voluptuousnesse: Your Wiues, your Daughters,
1788	Your Matrons, and your Maides, could not fill vp
1789	The Cesterne of my Lust, and my Desire
1790	All continent Impediments would ore-beare
1791	That did oppose my will ...

And:

1804	*Mal.* With this, there growes
1805	In my most ill-composd Affection, such
1806	A stanchlesse Auarice, that were I King,
1807	I should cut off the Nobles for their Lands,
1808	Desire his Iewels, and this others House,
1809	And my more-hauing, would be as a Sawce
1810	To make me hunger more, that I should forge
1811	Quarrels vniust against the Good and Loyall,
1812	Destroying them for wealth.

It is as if a heap of rank herbs were balanced by a small pile of gold coins, but of course we rush to defend Duncan. The very thought seems like blasphemy. Then, we remember that Macduff has already defended him and taken the thought as implied.

1836	Since that the truest Issue of thy Throne
1837	By his owne Interdiction stands accust,
1838	And do's blaspheme his breed? Thy Royall Father
1839	Was a most Sainted-King ...

It seems that Macduff knows exactly what Malcolm is saying: in effect, 'I have inherited my father's vices.' But Macduff is one who sees the best in men, who does not wish to credit rumour; and besides, even if there were truth in Malcolm's portrait, he is shocked that a son should speak ill of a dead parent. For us, however, the question must be quite simple and open: does the language of symmetry elsewhere in the play confirm or deny this thought?

Let us listen again to Macbeth's words as he weighs the pros and cons of murder in Act 1 Scene 7:

464	Besides, this *Duncane*
465	Hath borne his Faculties so meeke; hath bin
466	So cleere in his great Office, that his Vertues
467	Will pleade like Angels, Trumpet-tongu'd against
468	The deepe damnation of his taking off:

Was he a gifted man, modest about his abilities, discreet in exercising his royal powers? Or was he modest and discreet about his sexual abilities but in other ways a good and efficient King? Both meanings can be there at once. If the second is intended then Macbeth is saying, not everyone knows of his private vices, but all know of his public virtues. Therefore, the memory of his virtues will live and the common people will mourn him and condemn the one who slays him.

In Act 3 Scene 2 Macbeth, tormented now by suspicion and sick with sleeplessness, envies the dead Duncan:

1116	*Duncane* is in his Graue:
1117	After Lifes fitfull Feuer, he sleepes well,
1118	Treason ha's done his worst: nor Steele, nor Poyson,
1119	Mallice domestique, forraine Leuie, nothing,
1120	Can touch him further.

Our impression is of many and continuing threats against Duncan's life. 'Fitful fever' could, after all, be the description of a particular life, and not just of the general human condition. Again, of course, it can well be both: the particular that illustrates the general is the precise province of poetry.

Recalling once again Duncan's words in Act 1 Scene 6:

424	The Loue that followes vs, sometime is our trouble,
425	Which still we thanke as Loue. Herein I teach you,
426	How you shall bid God-eyld vs for your paines,
427	And thanke vs for your trouble.

we look more closely at the theme of prayer linked to Duncan. He is greeting Lady Macbeth and asking her to intercede with God that he may reward Duncan for causing her pains. To be loved may sometimes be inconvenient, but still we should be grateful because love is love.

It is not entirely clear whether King Duncan is using a self-satisfied

8. THE PLOT OF *MACBETH* (PART 1)

royal 'we' at first, or whether he is speaking of mankind (or womankind) in general. In view of the 'I' in 'Herein I teach you,' the latter seems more likely. Either way, the King clearly has a strong sense that he is bestowing a royal favour, and has bestowed such favours in the past. Here 'pains' has of course at least two meanings: 'trouble' (of the sort that a woman takes to make her house ready for a guest) and 'suffering,' particularly physical suffering, as in the pains of labour.

The thought here is complex and so far removed from twentieth-century attitudes that it is, perhaps, hard to take seriously. But, in short, Duncan asks his hostess to pray for him, and this can only strengthen the thought that his wife — who spent so many hours on her knees each day — may also have prayed for her husband, and not just for mankind in general.

The Sainted-King passage is part of Macduff's indignant and sorrowful outburst:

1833 (560-)	Fit to gouern? No not to liue. O Nation miserable!
1834	With an vntitled Tyrant, bloody Sceptred,
1835	When shalt thou see thy wholsome dayes againe?
1836	Since that the truest Issue of thy Throne
1837	By his owne Interdiction stands accust,
1838	And do's blaspheme his breed? Thy Royall Father
1839	Was a most Sainted-King: the Queene that bore thee,
1840	Oftner vpon her knees, then on her feet,
1841	Dy'de euery day she liu'd. Fare thee well,
1842	These Euils thou repeat'st vpon thy selfe,
1843	Hath banish'd me from Scotland. O my Brest,
1844 (549-)	Thy hope ends heere.

Counting back from the end of the play these twelve lines are play-lines 560- to 549-, and they therefore mirror lines 549 to 560, counting forwards from the beginning of the play. We are taken back to Act 2 Scene 1, to the dark courtyard where Banquo and Fleance see the flare of a torch and confront Macbeth with his servant.

549	A heauie Summons lyes like Lead vpon me,
550	And yet I would not sleepe:
551	Mercifull Powers, restraine in me the cursed thoughts
552	That Nature giues way to in repose.

148   NUMBER AND GEOMETRY IN SHAKESPEARE'S *MACBETH*

Enter Macbeth, and a Seruant with a Torch.

553   Giue me my Sword: who's there?
554   *Macb*. A Friend.
555   *Banq*. What Sir, not yet at rest? the King's a bed.
556   He hath beene in vnusuall Pleasure,
557   And sent forth great Largesse to your Offices.
558   This Diamond he greetes your Wife withall,[3]
559   By the name of most kind Hostesse,
560   And shut vp in measurelesse content.

Except for the words 'A friend,' Banquo speaks throughout.

Between these two passages, one in Act 2 and the other in Act 4, there are many correspondences in thought, feeling, and verbal music. Macduff's despair echoes Banquo's heaviness, and the prayers of the kneeling Queen match his prayer to 'Merciful powers.' Our thought seems to find confirmation when we re-read Banquo's words and find the sequence: oppression, heaviness, thoughts of lust ('nature') pleasure, bed, drowsy contentment — surely the very pattern of sexual desire and fulfilment. But the most striking correspondence falls at lines 554-557, counting forwards and backwards from the end of the play. Counting forwards, the lines are:

554   *Macb*. A Friend.
555   *Banq*. What Sir, not yet at rest? the King's a bed.
556   He hath beene in vnusuall Pleasure,
557   And sent forth great Largesse to your Offices.

Counting backwards they are:

557- (1836)   Since that the truest Issue of thy Throne
556-   By his owne Interdiction stands accust,
555-   And do's blaspheme his breed? Thy Royall Father
554- (1839)   Was a most Sainted-King: the Queene that bore thee …

The strong musical echoes, that awaken matching thoughts, fall sometimes within a mirrored line or two; sometimes they are line for line. Thus 'the King's a bed.' falls at line 555. At lines 555- and 554- we find 'Thy Royall father / Was a most Sainted-King:' 'And sent fo**rth** great larg**esse** to your **Off**icers' (557) is echoed by 'Since that the truest issue of thy **Thr**one' (557-), and in both we can hear strong 's' and 'thr' sounds and the 'of' syllable. Both speak too of an issue, or sending forth, and we may remember how often ideas of gold (the largesse) and of seduction are linked by Shakespeare.[4] If the faculties, which King Duncan bore so meekly, were indeed sexual faculties, then the conversation between these two passages becomes rather eloquent, even if the exact situation in Act 2 Scene 1 is not immediately clear. Obviously the King has experienced unusual pleasure because he has just been enjoying meat and drink at an unusually splendid feast; and obviously too the distribution of 'Largesse' is to be understood literally. Why not? The King could afford public generosity precisely because of other, less public, economies. However, Shakespeare's words have a way of meaning at least two things at once, which leaves one wondering whether the speaker of those words — here Banquo — is supposed to be aware of alternative or extra meanings which the reader can easily pick up. This question in relation to Banquo has occurred before, specifically in Act I Scene 6, as he draws the King's attention to the little birds swooping around the mud-built nests seen in every nook and cranny of the castle walls. Does Banquo know he has said 'Barlet' instead of 'Martlet' and 'Mansonry' *(the craft of making a man's son)* instead of 'Masonry?' We cannot immediately be sure, yet these 'misprints' can still speak to us, the readers.

Looking once again at the earlier passage, line 559 'By the name of most kind Hostesse,' is echoed by line 559-, 'With an vntitled Tyrant, bloody Sceptred,' and both speak of names, or lack of true names — one for the feminine principle, the other for the masculine. 'And shut vp in measurelesse content.' finds its echo in the first line of the second passage, Macduff's indignant, 'No not to liue. O Nation miserable!' And hearing these two lines and noting the 'sh' sounds in na<u>t</u>ion and mea<u>s</u>ureless, we think of measureless misery, and suddenly conceive an earlier indignation, this time against King Duncan. Is he fit to govern? No, not to live! Therefore Macbeth will slay him.

It is, surely, only Duncan's apparently cast-iron alibi that has kept these thoughts stifled for so many centuries. For not only do they give purpose to the long, tedious scene in England, they also illuminate image, action and motive throughout the play. They tell us in what ways Duncan has wronged both Cawdor and Macbeth; why there is a rebellion going on in the first act; and why Lady Macbeth takes it for granted that it is she who will dispatch the King:

385   That my keene Knife see not the Wound it makes,
386   Nor Heauen peepe through the Blanket of the darke,
387   To cry, hold, hold.

The image is of a blanket without holes, so that no light can shine through, just as no star can be seen through thick cloud or fog. The metaphor demands that the knife be under the blanket.

We have come to the plain thought that Duncan has been the lover of Lady Macbeth in the past, and would expect her to entertain him as before whenever he made a royal visit to Inverness Castle. This is perhaps not a brand new thought, but is likely to have been confined to burlesque.

Is not such arcane evidence overruled by much stronger objections? For what dramatic purpose could it serve for the very hinge of a plot to be hidden? If Shakespeare meant King Duncan to be the seducer of his cousin's wife — a link no more extraordinary than a thousand others in fable or history — why did he not make the matter clear and open so that all could follow it and enjoy the play to the full?

To this we suggested answers earlier, which might be summed up as a counter-question: what has ever been the point of burying treasure and laying a trail of clues? Is it not that in following the clues certain faculties are awakened, so that in the end the treasure is not just found but won? Before new discoveries are made, we seem to do very well without them. The familiar plot of *Macbeth* with its gentle King Duncan has stood the test of four centuries, yet it has also presented nearly insuperable problems to directors and chief protagonists. Many actresses playing Lady Macbeth have been torn between a natural sympathy for the character they portray and the verdict of the intellect, which paints her as a cruel monster. The hidden plot, which we have attempted to indicate, solves the greatest of these problems.

At the centre of the play there now stands not a weak man spurred on by a fiend-like wife to commit a deed for which he has little stomach, but a far more moving, dramatic, terrible and comprehensible situation. For Macbeth, hatred rather than ambition, becomes the prime motive; although ambition is there. For Lady Macbeth, it is surely the need to rid herself of an incubus that is wrecking her marriage.

She is not a fiend by nature, but summons fiend-like qualities to do what has to be done. At last her role becomes playable; so too does that of Macbeth. The witches' words, 'That shalt be King hereafter,' play on a passion in him much deeper and stronger than sluggish ambition. In fact, as soon as we are free of the old Duncan stereotype, the good old man, white-haired and pious, whom many scholars never seem to question, ideas and possibilities begin to crowd upon us at every page.

Avarice, also a Vice of Duncan

By putting two thoughts together, the thought of lust and the thought of the King, we come to the child. But before we ask 'What became of the child?' we must return to Malcolm's second pretended vice; the vice of avarice. If we cannot attach this too to his murdered father without special pleading, our whole argument must fail.

The great colour strokes of the play are gold, blood red and raven black. The glitter of gold, explicit and implicit, runs strongly through the first two acts, beginning with the sunrise in Act 1 Scene 2: '*Cap*. As whence the Sunne 'gins his reflection' (line 38), and touching Sweno's bright ('Ten thousand') dollars (line 82), the circlet that should crown Macbeth ('the Golden Round') (line 357), and in Scene 7 the 'Golden Opinions' he has won (line 483). Later it sinks into red, in the faces of the grooms gilded with blood, and in that same golden blood lying like threads of lace on Duncan's skin. Finally, in the last scene of Act 2 (line 880), the primary gold of the sun is eclipsed by black '... byth' Clock 'tis Day, / And yet darke Night strangles the trauailing Lampe.' We sense that all that gold symbolizes of spiritual and worldly wealth is of central importance to the chief protagonists of the play; it lies close to the heart.

A greyer thread, expressed in such words as 'pay,' 'account,' 'addition,' 'whole,' 'audit,' is interwoven with the shining one, reminding us of the purely monetary aspect of gold. The word 'pay' is linked with Macbeth. The first thought we observe, in the minds of two people who meet him after the battle is that he ought to be paid.

193	*Ang*. Wee are sent,	
194	To giue thee from our Royall Master thanks,	
195	Onely to harrold thee into his sight,	
196	Not pay thee.	(1, 3)
285	*Duncan*. ... Would thou hadst lesse deseru'd,	
286	That the proportion both of thanks, and payment,	

287	Might haue beene mine: onely I haue left to say,
288	More is thy due, then more then all can pay. (1, 4)

There is no evidence, in fact, that Macbeth is ever paid. He is given a new title and the forfeited lands of another, but not any money. The themes of 'accounting' and 'auditing' belongs rather to Lady Macbeth:

441	*La*. Your Seruants euer,
442	Haue theirs, themselues, and what is theirs in compt,
443	To make their Audit at your Highnesse pleasure,
444	Still to returne your owne. (1, 6)

Later to Macbeth:

488	*La*. ... And wakes it now to looke so greene, and pale,
489	At what it did so freely? From this time,
490	Such I account thy loue. (1, 7)

Even love might, it seems, be entered into the great ledgers of Inverness, by a lady as skilled in the art of addition as she is in the art of distillation. Did Angus know perhaps that money was of special importance to the Macbeths? Would Duncan have paid his younger captain, given time? Or did he think the Thanedom of Cawdor enough, and secretly not mean to pay him, either from feudal concepts, shortage of cash, or a certain reluctance?

The immediate evidence is that Duncan had money and was generous with it. We learn from Banquo of the great largesse sent out to the offices of Inverness Castle while Macbeth was absent from a banquet. This must be taken literally as well as in the sense suggested earlier. Only now we are left to wonder how this great largesse compared with the sum of money that was Macbeth's rightful due. It could have been no more, but multiplied to the eye in little coins, much less: in short, a temporising measure. We are reminded suddenly of another largesse distributed only a day or so earlier, and of Duncan's curious reaction — or rather non-reaction — to the news of it. In his speech to the King (2, 1) Ross first accuses Cawdor of treachery and then abruptly announces the victory. After Duncan's out breathing of joy: 'Great happiness!' Ross continues:

78	*Rosse*. That now *Sweno*, the Norwayes King,
79	Craues composition:

8. THE PLOT OF *MACBETH* (PART 1)

> 80   Nor would we deigne him buriall of his men,
> 81   Till he disbursed, at Saint *Colmes* ynch,
> 82   Ten thousand Dollars, to our generall vse.

But the king only replies:

> 83   *King.* No more that *Thane* of Cawdor shall deceiue
> 84   Our Bosome interest: Goe pronounce his present death,
> 85   And with his former Title greet *Macbeth.*

It sounds as if Ross expected a reaction to the news of the dollars but got none; as if the King's mind is so fixed on the treachery of Cawdor that he is deaf to all else.

Yet there could be another explanation; the two thoughts could be joined so that the heap of golden coins somehow reminds the King of Cawdor. And Duncan's reaction to the news of the dollars could be one of anger instead of joy, precisely because they were disbursed or dispersed for general use instead of being handed over to the royal treasurer. This anger would then be fused as white heat with his anger against the man on whom (in matters good or ill) he placed an absolute trust. The phrase 'deceiue / Our Bosome interest,' may remind us of Antonio and Shylock discussing the bond, and the practice of usury; again, money is felt to lie as close to the heart as love or hate.

Later, at Inverness, the King is undoubtedly angry with his host for failing to welcome him at the castle gate and then for leaving the banquet early. May not his own disbursal of largesse be a kind of revenge for that earlier disbursal forced on Sweno (even if not directly by Macbeth) on the island of Inchcolm. The coins, we may be sure, will never be entered in the columns of those ledgers. And if our guess is right that Duncan was indeed reluctant to give Macbeth what he was strictly owed, then such a show of generosity would be as good a way as any of putting off the evil day of payment.

Macduff takes avarice to be a more serious vice than lust; his reply also accords with our interpretation.

> 1813   *Macd.* This Auarice
> 1814   stickes deeper: growes with more pernicious roote
> 1815   Then Summer-seeming Lust: and it hath bin
> 1816   The Sword of our slaine Kings: yet do not feare,

    1817   Scotland hath Foysons, to fill vp your will
    1818   Of your meere Owne. All these are portable,
    1819   With other Graces weigh'd.

Macduff at once admits that the avarice of Scotland's Kings has sometimes led to their murder. He says nothing of Duncan, but 'Sword of our slaine Kings' with its sorrowful, meditative tone can only match one image in the mind of the man who actually discovered the dead body of a particular King, with bloodstained daggers laid near.

Macduff also regards Malcolm as the proper owner of Scotland's 'Foysons;' this again is a feudal idea and we take Macduff to mean that since Malcolm ought to be King, all the natural wealth of his country — all beasts of the chase, all fish and foul, all grain and fruit — ought to be his. But if, a little while back, a greater part of Scotland's foysons had already been converted by Malcolm's father into gold and jewels, for 'all these are portable,' it may refer not just to vices, but to valuables; there may literally be a portable treasure in chests and coffers that Malcolm ought to inherit — diamonds brought for gold ('graces' weighed against cash) would represent the lightest and easiest form of carried wealth, especially handy for a King whose way of life was largely peripatetic.

We begin to discern in Duncan both avarice and generosity, linked and balanced as they often are in life. But to move from speculation to firmer ground we must look again at play structure. We found that 'the kings abed' in Act 2 was mirrored strikingly by 'the Sainted King' in Act 4. Macduff's impassioned defence of Malcolm's father comes as the climax to the long antiphonal passage on lust and avarice. Now we wonder, may these two precise word-pictures not also find significant comments across the play centre?

The theme of lust — Malcolm's description and Macduff's reply — falls between reverse play lines 607- and 590-, and therefore mirrors forward play lines 590 to 607. This brings us to the second part of Macbeth's soliloquy in the courtyard:

    590   As this which now I draw.
    591   Thou marshall'st me the way that I was going,
    592   And such an Instrument I was to vse.
    593   Mine Eyes are made the fooles o'th' other Sences,
    594   Or else worth all the rest: I see thee still;

8. THE PLOT OF *MACBETH* (PART 1)

```
595    And on thy Blade, and Dudgeon, Gouts of Blood,
596    Which was not so before. There's no such thing:
597    It is the bloody Businesse, which informes
598    Thus to mine Eyes. Now o're the one halfe World
599    Nature seemes dead, and wicked Dreames abuse
600    The Curtain'd sleepe: Witchcraft celebrates
601    Pale *Heccats* Offrings: and wither'd Murther,
602    Alarum'd by his Centinell, the Wolfe,
603    Whose howle's his Watch, thus with his stealthy pace,
604    With *Tarquins* rauishing sides, towards his designe
605    Moues like a Ghost. Thou sowre and firme-set Earth
606    Heare not my steps, which they may walke, for feare
607    Thy very stones prate of my where-about,
```

A tangible knife is slipped from its scabbard, and a moment later drops of blood appear on the visionary one. Then the phantom vanishes, and Macbeth's thoughts float onwards to the sleeping world. He thinks of curtained beds, of evil dreams and of the witches who celebrate pale Hecat's offerings. Then he hears the howl of a wolf and, seeing himself almost from outside, moves stealthily towards the deed of murder, as Tarquin moved towards the deed of rape. We especially note the First Folio words:

With *Tarquins* rauishing sides, towards his designe (sides, not strides)
Moues like a Ghost.

This gives a theme of ravening desire and rape. The correspondence with the passage on lust is so clear that we move quickly on (that is backwards) to find the lines that match the theme of avarice. The lines are 576 to 589:

```
576    My Bosome franchis'd, and Allegeance cleare,
577    I shall be counsail'd.
578      *Macb.* Good repose the while.
579      *Banq.* Thankes Sir: the like to you.    Exit Banquo.
580      *Macb.* Goe bid thy Mistresse, when my drinke is ready,
581    She strike vpon the Bell. Get thee to bed.    Exit.
582    Is this a Dagger, which I see before me,
```

583	The Handle toward my Hand? Come, let me clutch thee:
584	I haue thee not, and yet I see thee still.
585	Art thou not fatall Vision, sensible
586	To feeling, as to sight? or art thou but
587	A Dagger of the Minde, a false Creation,
588	Proceeding from the heat-oppressed Braine?
589	I see thee yet ...

Now we have arrived at the 'goodnight's' that leave Macbeth alone and the moment when he first sees the air-drawn dagger. Here is no tale of a miser counting moneybags; and yet to see something, a jewelled handle, to reach out and not be able to grasp it, is not this, after all, the primary gesture of avarice? We even speak of a 'grasping miser;' and 'cut-off,' implies that an instrument as is forged out of steel, as Macduff recognised.

We have moved backwards from just before the murder of Duncan to just before 'is this the dagger?' Further back we came to 'the kings abed.' Further on we come to the beginning of the next scene (2, 2), to the murder itself. To look for the play mirror of this, the first great climax of the play, is an irresistible next step. But before taking it we should briefly considered two general points.

First, if the mirrors of some passages are significant and those of others are not, how can we ever tell which coincidences are intentional? Or are we beginning to assume the incredible, a line for line significant matching right through the play?

To this we can only reply at present that we are exploring; and this argument is part of the exploration. What we find are loud echoes in certain passages, more muted ones in others, and, in yet others, nothing at all that we can recognise. Within the loud echoes there is an astonishing chiming of actual words or sounds, matching line-for-line, or flowing a line or two apart. These summon us to acute attention. A craftsman-like insertion of such passages is not impossible, but, however they arise, we suspect that the tangible evidence of sound and word-echoes points straight to intentional (or anyway significant) thought-echoes, perhaps in proportional intensity.

The second question is this: the louder and clearer a bell, the further it reverberates. How can we trust such reverberations? The thoughts, we find, begin to multiply, so that setting out, for instance, on a search for avarice in Duncan, we arrive at Macbeth seeing a vision of the dagger, at Macbeth making the grasping gesture in the air. It is Macbeth too

8. THE PLOT OF *MACBETH* (PART 1)

who sees himself as Tarquin — not Duncan — who lies there sleeping in bed. Can the vices of the King also be those of his murderer? Yes, surely, because they are the vices of all men; but we must also believe Lady Macbeth: 'What thou would'st highly, / That would'st thou holily:' What lives in Macbeth as he moves 'like a ghost' across the courtyard is perhaps more shadow than first cause. Vices are infectious; we fear most in the others what is latent in ourselves. We also imitate, as an artist does, the gesture of that which wholly absorbs us.

But let us come now to the moment of the murder itself, and find the mirror of this moment across the play centre. The deed falls at the beginning of Act 2, scene 2. With Lady Macbeth we listen, tense, for sounds and signs. For even as she speaks the dagger is plunged into Duncan's heart.

614	*La.*	That which hath made thê drunk, hath made me bold:
615		What hath quench'd them, hath giuen me fire.
616		Hearke, peace: it was the Owle that shriek'd,
617		The fatall Bell-man, which giues the stern'st good-night.
618		He is about it, the Doores are open:
619		And the surfeted Groomes doe mock their charge
620		With Snores.

Was it the screech of the owl that she heard, or a different cry? Which ever it was, 'goodnight,' we know, has been said to Duncan, and the doors of the body are open now for the spirit to fly out.

The mirror passage to these lines must fall between reverse play lines 620- and 614-. We are brought, we find, to the very beginning of Malcolm's self accusation:

620-	*Macd.*	What should he be?
619-	*Mal.*	It is my selfe I meane: in whom I know
618-		All the particulars of Vice so grafted,
617-		That when they shall be open'd, blacke *Macbeth*
616-		Will seeme as pure as Snow, and the poore State
615-		Esteeme him as a Lambe, being compar'd
614-		With my confinelesse harmes.

For Malcolm, read 'Malcolm's father;' for the comparison, match Duncan and Macbeth.

It is Duncan who will be opened as if by a kind of second murder, and whose blackness will one day be laid bare. Then Macbeth's guilt will almost look like innocence, and we shall see him as a lamb brought to slaughter. We notice the strong chiming of 'Doores are open,' and 'when they shall be open'd,' which points the finger of intention, saying 'this man was guilty first, and this one second.'

We also notice the word 'grafted' used by Malcolm to describe vices that were never his. Shakespeare uses the word 'grafted' elsewhere when speaking of the stream of human inheritance, (as in *Henry IV Part II,* 3. 2. 'And noble stock was grafted with Crab-tree slip').

Perhaps Malcolm thinks here of his mother's line as being the true stock, and of Duncan as the outsider, the 'crab-tree slip,' whose vices might easily have been inherited by his son, if that son had not reacted against them instead. Malcolm was, in fact, a young puritan 'as yet unknown to woman'. His prototype could well have been the latter Malcolm, called 'Malcolm the maiden', who made avowal of chastity in youth, and died at twenty-three with the vow unbroken.[5]

Now we are directly aware of how Macbeth moves across the courtyard through the shadows of avarice and lust on his way to do murder. These two vices, matched by the two daggers, are the reasons why Duncan must be got rid of: one hears (for Macbeth) chiefly a personal reason, the other — however closely it may have touched him — remains chiefly a public or national one.

The public reason, we note, comes first in time, as if to emphasize that it was the first consideration, and the grounds originate for a public assassination. 'This avarice sticks deeper;' to execute innocent men in order to grab their possessions is, after all, the worst crime in the eyes of God than to seduce their wives or daughters. A man that dies unshriven with such crimes on his conscience may well be summoned, not to heaven, but to hell. But the public hero in the end opts for secrecy. He dares not risk the backlash. He fears too much that Duncan's virtues (and he has virtues), shining more brightly after death as virtues always do, will 'plead like angels trumpet-tongued' and lead perhaps to yet another rebellion.

Relationship between Duncan and Lady Macbeth

We meet Lady Macbeth for the first time in the second half of Act 1 (1, 5). She is reading a letter from her husband, evidently written in some snatched moment on his journey north after his encounter with the three

8. THE PLOT OF *MACBETH* (PART 1) 159

witches and the astonishing fulfilment of the Cawdor prophecy (This snatched moment, we surmise, must have been *before* the King's two captains are ushered into the royal presence, perhaps while they are allowed a few hours early morning rest). The letter that Lady Macbeth reads aloud seems to cause her no surprise, only to strengthen her inner resolution. She muses in the gentle, upright, aspects of her husband's nature and concludes that it is up to her to inspire him with the will to achieve a goal that is so nearly within his grasp. In the midst of these musings a breathless messenger arrives:

361	*Mess*. The King comes here to Night.	
362	*Lady*. Thou'rt mad to say it.	
363	Is not thy Master with him? who, wer't so,	
364	Would haue inform'd for preparation.	
365	*Mess*. So please you, it is true: our *Thane* is comming:	
366	One of my fellowes had the speed of him;	
367	Who almost dead for breath, had scarcely more	
368	Then would make vp his Message.	
369	*Lady*. Giue him tending,	
370	He brings great newes,	*Exit Messenger*.
371	The Rauen himselfe is hoarse,	
372	That croakes the fatall entrance of Duncan	
373	Vnder my Battlements. Come you Spirits,	
374	That tend on mortall thoughts, vnsex me here,	

The thought of King Duncan is followed instantly by the thought of sexuality. The phrase, 'The fatall entrance of *Duncan* Vnder my Battlements,' gives a direct picture of the sexual act. When the King himself arrives at Inverness (1, 6) and Lady Macbeth comes out to greet him. Duncan says (to Banquo): 'See, see, our honor'd Hostesse.' He continues, now speaking mainly to Lady Macbeth, 'The Loue that followes vs, sometime is our trouble, / Which still we thanke as Loue.' He sees Lady Macbeth and the first thing he speaks of is love.

At the end of the play, the mad queen, walking in her sleep, remembers the night of Duncan's murder:

2030	...what need we feare? who knowes
2031	it, when none can call our powre to accompt: yet who

>   2032   would haue thought the olde man to haue had so much
>   2033   blood in him.

Who indeed would have thought it? Duncan seemed weak and old. But when we turn to the play mirror of this last passage, we find the thought at once confirmed, for we are back where we were a moment since in Act 1 Scene 5, with the messenger arriving. Here are balancing lines, set in a twelve line context:

>   371-   *Lad*. Yet heere's a spot.
>   370-   *Doct*. Heark, she speaks, I will set downe what comes
>   369-   from her, to satisfie my remembrance the more strongly.
>   368-   *La*. Out damned spot: out I say. One: Two: Why
>   367-   then 'tis time to doo't: Hell is murky. Fye, my Lord, fie,
>   366-   a Souldier, and affear'd? what need we feare? who knowes
>   365-   it, when none can call our powre to accompt: yet who
>   364-   would haue thought the olde man to haue had so much
>   363-   blood in him.
>   362-   *Doct*. Do you marke that?
>   361-   *Lad*. The Thane of Fife, had a wife: where is she now?
>   360-   What will these hands ne're be cleane? No more o'that

And the play mirror lines:

>   360   What is your tidings?
>   361   *Mess*. The King comes here to Night.
>   362   *Lady*. Thou'rt mad to say it.
>   363   Is not thy Master with him? who, wer't so,
>   364   Would haue inform'd for preparation.
>   365   *Mess*. So please you, it is true: our Thane is comming:
>   366   One of my fellowes had the speed of him;
>   367   Who almost dead for breath, had scarcely more
>   368   Then would make vp his Message.
>   369   *Lady*. Giue him tending,
>   370   He brings great newes, *Exit Messenger*.
>   371   The Rauen himselfe is hoarse,

Again, the links of sound and sense are so many and so striking that it is hard to believe that chance alone is the power we must call to account.

8. THE PLOT OF *MACBETH* (PART 1)

We note:

360	**What** is your tidings?
360-	**What** will these hands
362	*Lady*. Thou'rt mad to say it.
362-	*Doct*. Do you marke that?
363	Is not thy Master with <u>him</u>?
363-	blood in <u>him</u>.
363/364	...**who**...**Would haue** inform'd
364-/365-	...**who would have** thought
365	... **our** Thane is **comm**ing:
365-	... **our** powre to a**ccomp**t:
371	The Rauen ... is **h**oarse,
371-	Yet **h**eere's a spot.

At lines 362, 362 -, there is no word or syllable-echo; and yet we feel that these lines do match each other: each short and pregnant; each with its first stress on a monosyllable starting with 'm;' and each pointing to something else just said ('it,' 'that'), pointing to the ageing king who comes before nightfall and whose life-blood soon pours forth. This time, two passages already brought together by simple reason stand in exact symmetrical relationship; and again each seems to interpret the other.

As it transpires, it is Macbeth who murders Duncan, but Lady Macbeth first meant to, and rereading Scene 5 we understand why. To dispatch a lover is both easier and harder than to dispatch a stranger, or even a familiar acquaintance. The summoning of spirits, to harden the heart and the body, we must surely take to be literal, not metaphorical, and to involve a penetration and alteration of the entire being:

373	... Come you Spirits,
374	That tend on mortall thoughts, vnsex me here,
375	And fill me from the Crowne to the Toe, top-full
376	Of direst Crueltie: make thick my blood,
377	Stop vp th' accesse, and passage to Remorse,

378	That no compunctious visitings of Nature
379	Shake my fell purpose, nor keepe peace betweene
380	Th' effect, and hit. Come to my Womans Brests,
381	And take my Milke for Gall, you murth'ring Ministers
382	Where-euer, in your sightlesse substances,
383	You wait on Natures Mischiefe. Come thick Night,

These words always seemed oddly careless for a pen as precise as Shakespeare's in all natural scientific detail. She must (we supposed) be remembering a child born to that first husband of whom we hear in Holinshed, a child suckled a few years back, or she is thinking of the future, of the children she will bear one day to Macbeth. But now we are shaken into the present. Surely the child is there, in that very room, or the one next-door, and has been suckled and laid down to rest but a moment since, for if Lady Macbeth has a lover it is no longer strange that she should have a child, even though we know, of Macbeth, that he has no children.[6]

The second reference to a baby still being breast-fed comes in the last scene of Act 1:

507	I haue giuen Sucke, and know
508	How tender 'tis to loue the Babe that milkes me,

This too, becomes quite simple and direct, and the cruel thought that follows:

509	I would, while it was smyling in my Face,
510	Haue pluckt my Nipple from his Bonelesse Gummes,
511	And dasht the Braines out,

becomes even more terrible as the images of first and second child references coalesce. If his wife's lover is also the father of her newborn child, we must see Macbeth as a man not simply filled with hatred, but actually in torment from the outset of the play. We do in fact find that images of babies and children are torn from him again and again at moments of great stress; something many critics have noted but explained at a purely intellectual level.

Filled with fear and amazement when the witches vanish he utters the words, 'Your Children shall be Kings,' as if this meant more to him

8. THE PLOT OF *MACBETH* (PART 1) 163

than all other promises in heaven or earth. Overthrown by his wife's resolution, near the end of Scene 7, he cries, 'Bring forth Men-Children onely:' and earlier in the same scene, swayed, while he was alone, by the opposite argument:

> 469 And Pitty, like a naked New-borne-Babe,
> 470 Striding the blast, or Heauens Cherubin, hors'd
> 471 Vpon the sightlesse Curriors of the Ayre,
> 472 Shall blow the horrid deed in euery eye,
> 473 That teares shall drowne the winde.

The tears that drown the wind seem to be not only shed by the people of Scotland when they hear that King Duncan is slain, but by Macbeth himself as he gallops on horseback to reach Inverness ahead of the King. Much later in Act 3, as he stands terrified before the ghost of Banquo, the child theme breaks out again:

> 1310 If trembling I inhabit then, protest mee
> 1311 The Baby of a Girle.[7]

If the baby Macbeth is thinking of is the one his wife was suckling in Act 1, then 'Girle' has implications. Could Lady Macbeth have been still unwed when the King seduced her? Banquo was the man whom Macbeth came to fear because he was the one who knew. This appears in Act 1 Scene 6, in a passage that we have already noted as it reveals the direct links between Duncan and the theme of procreation:

> 416 The Temple-haunting Barlet does approue,
> 417 By his loued Mansonry, that the Heauens breath
> 418 Smells wooingly here: no Iutty frieze,
> 419 Buttrice, nor Coigne of Vantage, but this Bird
> 420 Hath made his pendant Bed, and procreant Cradle,
> 421 Where they must breed, and haunt: I haue obseru'd
> 422 The ayre is delicate.   *Enter Lady.*

As he arrives with the King at Inverness castle, Banquo points to the hanging mud nests of the house martins, and into five haunting lines crowd the words cradle, breed, wooingly, Barlet and Mansonry.

The temple here is the temple of the human body, haunted by the incarnating soul before it flies right in as the swooping house martins at last fly into their nests. Banquo not only knows, but also knows that Duncan knows that he knows; and he speaks at once in terms that are not just flattery, of the highest and most positive aspect of a recent hidden drama. Meanwhile, the importance of this passage seems to be confirmed when we discover its act-mirror:

Act	421-	*All*. The weyward Sisters, hand in hand,
	420-	Posters of the Sea and Land,
	419-	Thus doe goe, about, about,
	418-	Thrice to thine, and thrice to mine,
	417-	And thrice againe, to make vp nine.
Act	416-	Peace, the Charme's wound vp.

The delightful house martins, diving and soaring in the sunshine, are mirrored by the 'posters of the sea and land;' ill-omened witches circling through the dusk. Everything has another side; daytime beauty is shadowed by night-time evil; the delicate air that plays round Inverness castle lures the new guest into thickest night, where he will meet his end. If the child exists it is integral to the plot of the entire play — a plot stirred by the witches from the very beginning. We have to ask, do they know of the child?

When we studied the symmetrical structure of Act 1 Scene 3, we concluded that the sailor who had gone to Aleppo must be one with Macbeth. Early in Act 1 Scene 3 we encounter the three witches for the second time in the play. They have just met on the heath, as arranged, to lie in wait for Macbeth on his way home from battle. They know that his route will take him past the king's camp or temporary headquarters, where the loyalist captains will have to report, and this makes it easy for the witches to choose a good place where they can surprise Macbeth and Banquo as darkness falls. Perhaps they emerge from behind a rock, seeming to materialize out of wind and pouring rain.

They seem to have come from different directions of the compass. The first witch asks the second where she has been. She replies, 'Killing swine.' Then the third witch asks the first, and the latter, full of rage, embarks on a story so veiled in jargon that we may take it at first to be but a little side-shoot to the main story. The witch's tale begins with a sailor's wife munching chestnuts, which she refuses to share with her visitor, and ends with a long curse uttered not against the sailor's wife but against the sailor, the innocent husband, a deed which seems at first to be oddly unfair.

Thunder. Enter the three Witches.

88	1. Where hast thou beene, Sister?
89	2. Killing Swine.
90	3. Sister, where thou?
91	1. A Saylors Wife had Chestnuts in her Lappe,
92	And mouncht, & mouncht, and mouncht:
93	Giue me, quoth I.
94	Aroynt thee, Witch, the rumpe-fed Ronyon cryes.
95	Her Husband's to Aleppo gone, Master o'th' Tiger:
96	But in a Syue Ile thither sayle,
97	And like a Rat without a tayle,
98	Ile doe, Ile doe, and Ile doe

We are looking into the future, so the story has to remain unfinished; nor do we understand it entirely, since the witch is addressing the ears of the other two sisters, not those of the prying world.

The witch later goes on to predict that the sailor will suffer for eighty-one weeks (nine-times-nine Seu'nights), that he will not actually drown, but will have a very bad time. Then she produces a nasty limp and bloody piece of flesh (a pilot's thumb, torn off, it seems, during torture on his way home), and we hear the sound of an approaching drum, '3. A Drumme, a Drumme: / *Macbeth* doth come.' The witches know exactly what the drum means. They enter into a circular dance, swaying to and fro, this way and that, and then the King's captains, Macbeth and Banquo march on to the darkening scene.

In the story of 'Rapunzel,' one of the traditional tales told by the Brothers Grimm, the first sign that the rich man's wife is with child is her greedy longing for radishes. Here too there is a witch who comes to ask for something from a married woman, and what she asks for is the unborn child, which the mother does not dare refuse.

Is not the greed for chestnuts, felt by the sailor's wife, also the familiar greed of pregnancy? And is not 'give me that chestnut,' the same as, 'give me that child?' The child, still wrapped in the smooth sheath of the womb, draws life from the placenta, whose rays are like those of the sun, or (were they green) like shining prickles; and witches, according to tradition, need to procure children, with whose fat they anoint themselves before they fly. This theme is touched on later in the play, in the cauldron scene:

> 1476   Finger of Birth-strangled Babe,
> 1477   Ditch-deliuer'd by a Drab,

If the words 'Give me, quoth I' relate to a child demanded of Lady Macbeth, then the first witch must have journeyed to Inverness and back some time before the beginning of Act I Scene 3. This would confirm an old tradition that Lady Macbeth had dealings with the witches even before Macbeth did, and sit well with the strong sense of airy movement in the opening tetrameters of the heath scene; for when a witch journeys swiftly she flies through the air. The witches' prologue is divided from the charm (when they all dance in a ring) by the beating of the drum that heralds Macbeth — the drum that is echoed across the scene centre by the knocking of his heart.

The thumb (in country jargon) is Tom Thumb, at once little man and phallus. We wonder now whether it is not this image, even more than that of murder, that will 'unfix the heir' (so it is spelt) of Macbeth: the thumb that is the usurper at Inverness, that in one deed wracks both the rightful thumb and the rightful inheritor.

The words of the first witch also point to the child being only just born when Macbeth reaches home, since at the time of her fruitless visit to Inverness it was still in the womb. The question for reader, or listener, now becomes, 'But if there is indeed a little baby at the beginning of this story, what becomes of it? Why do we hear no more about it?' In fact, we do, but of this in the next chapter.

9. The Plot of *Macbeth* (Part 2)

The Theme of the Child

If it were not for the complete absence of all reference to Lady Macbeth's baby in the later part of the play, we would surely conclude from her own words in Act 1 (Scenes 5 and 7) that when Macbeth returns home from battle she is suckling a little baby there and then. I shall argue that if we read the subtext expressed in the exact relationships of the play we shall find this lost child and discover also in what way he met his end.

Act 2 Scene 2 begins with the murder of King Duncan and continues, '*Macb*. Me thought I heard a voyce cry, Sleep no more:' and Macbeth's hypnotized gazing at his bloody hands. Then it dips down into the Porter episode and, after Lennox's description of the unruly night, comes to a climax with Macduff's, 'O horror, horror, horror,'

As he gazes at his bloody hands, while Lady Macbeth, full of scorn, carries the daggers back to the scene of death, Macbeth is overwhelmed by the feeling that nothing in the world can wash away his guilt; nothing will restore his innocence. This passage ends with the famous lines:

686	... no: this my Hand will rather
687	The multitudinous Seas incarnardine,
688	Making the Greene one, Red.

Editors disagree about the correct phrasing of this last line. The First Folio, which is our sole authority for the text of *Macbeth*, puts the comma after 'one,' producing the line: 'Making the Greene one, Red,' and it is true that something feels not quite right about this; 'Multitudinous Seas incarnardine,' is a far flung picture of many seas. 'Green one' is singular, not plural. What: Green sea! Not the Blue one or the Black one? In fact the Green one sounds more like the name of a Being than the description of a particular sea and if we let imagination spring from the whole paragraph, rather than from the last few lines only, we realize that this phrase occurs in a very particular context: 'Will all great Neptunes Ocean wash this blood / Cleane from my Hand?' We are without doubt in the sphere of classical mythology, and in this sphere, that of Neptune (or Poseidon),

Hecate, Zeus and so on, the 'Green one' can only designate one being, and that is the semi-divine Glaucos, the 'Sea-green,' of whom many different stories are told. One of these stories recounted by Apollodorus in his 'Library of Greek Mythology' is striking in this context because it is the story of a lost child who is found, and also the story of an extraordinary creature that is threefold in its nature.

Apollodorus' story is set in Crete at the time of King Minos who, although he is one of the three great sons of Zeus by Europa, rules as an earthly king. Minos is married to Pasiphae, also of divine origin and they have a son called Glaucos, which means 'The Sea-green.' Glaucos is therefore a being that is halfway between the human and the divine. In Apollodorus the story continues:

'Now Glaucos, when he was still a young child, fell into a jar of honey while he was chasing a mouse, and was drowned. After his disappearance, Minos conducted a thorough search and consulted diviners about how he could find him. The Curetes told him that in his herds he had a three-coloured cow, and that the person who could suggest the best image to describe its colours would also be able to return his son to him alive. When the diviners were assembled, Polyidos, son of Coiranos, compared the cow's colouring to a blackberry, and when he was made to search for the child, he discovered him by a certain kind of divination. Minos declared, however, that he wanted him back alive, and Polyidos was shut in with the dead body. When he was at his wit's end, he saw a snake approach the body, and fearing that he himself would be killed if any harm came to the body he threw a stone at the snake and killed it. But then another snake appeared, and seeing that the first one was dead, it went off and then came back again carrying a herb, which it applied to the whole body of its fellow. No sooner was the herb applied than the first snake came back to life. Viewing all this with wonderment, Polyidos applied the same herb to the body of Glaucos and brought him back to life. Minos had now recovered his son, but all the same, he would not allow Polyidos to depart to Argos until he had taught Glaucos the art of divination. So, under compulsion, Polyidos taught him, but as Polyidos was sailing off, he told Glaucos to spit into his mouth, and when Glaucos did so, he forgot all knowledge of divination. As regards the descendants of Europa, this is where we must call a halt.'[1]

Another shorter story is told about a certain Glaucos, in Boeotia, on the mainland. Here the boy Glaucos is not a prince, but a fisherman who eats a certain magical plant, which has the capacity to bestow immortality. As soon as he eats it he leaps up into the air and plunges into the sea where he is transformed into a god. The story is recounted by Ovid in his book *Metamorphosis,* and we here take it up as Glaucos is looking down upon his catch of fish who, taken from their native element are expiring on the grass at his feet.

> My scaly prize, in order all display'd,
> By number on the greensward there I lay'd,
> My captives whom or in my nets I took,
> Or hung unwary on my wily hook.
> Strange to behold! yet what avails a lye?
> I saw 'em bite the grass, as I sate by;
> Then sudden darting o'er the verdant plain,
> They spread their finns, as in their native main:
> I paus'd, with wonder struck, while all my prey
> Left their new master, and regain'd the sea.
> Amaz'd, within my secret self I sought,
> What God, what herb the miracle had wrought:
> But sure no herbs have pow'r like this, I cry'd;
> And strait I pluck'd some neighb'ring herbs, and try'd.
> Scarce had I bit, and prov'd the wond'rous taste,
> When strong convulsions shook my troubled breast;
> I felt my heart grow fond of something strange,
> And my whole Nature lab'ring with a change.
> Restless I grew, and ev'ry place forsook,
> And still upon the seas I bent my look.
> Farewel for ever! farewel, land! I said;
> And plung'd amidst the waves my sinking head.
> The gentle pow'rs, who that low empire keep,
> Receiv'd me as a brother of the deep;
> To *Tethys,* and to *Ocean* old, they pray
> To purge my mortal earthy parts away.[2]

These stories have certain elements in common: in both there is a magical plant but in one story the plant bestows life and in the other it bestows immortality. There is also the theme of plunging into a liquid; in one story it is the sea and the other it is a vat of honey. Perhaps they are aspects of the same story but, as yet, we cannot be sure. For the moment the story about the princely son of King Minos seems the most significant in relation to the play of *Macbeth* for both play and legend refer to a child who vanishes and, in both, something that has a mysterious threefold quality, leads to the discovery of this lost child. Polyides, the soothsayer, compares the lost cow, or calf, to the blackberry because the fruit of the blackberry, at the beginning of its life, is greenish white, then it turns red and finally black, just as the calf does (the cow is tricoloured from the beginning). The threefold aspects of *Macbeth* — that is, scene-symmetry, act-symmetry and play-symmetry — are that on which the 'Figure' is directly based, and through which we discover many things.

However, when we think again of Macbeth's final words as he gazes at his bloody hands, '... no: this my Hand will rather / The multitudinous Seas incarnardine, / Making the Greene one, Red,' we have to ask, what exactly is he saying? Is this a threat, or is it a premonition? My own impression is that these words are uttered in a spirit of fatalism, and that the idea of murdering the child originally arose in Macbeth when Lady Macbeth said:

509	I would, while it was smyling in my Face,
510	Haue pluckt my Nipple from his Bonelesse Gummes,
511	And dasht the Braines out, had I so sworne
512	As you haue done to this.

After 'Making the Greene one, Red,' which presumably she has not heard, Lady Macbeth returns and takes immediate charge of her trembling husband. Her scorn has not diminished, 'My Hands are of your colour: but I shame / To weare a Heart so white.' As the knocking increases she commands him to go back with her to their bedroom, wash his hands and put on his nightgown so that if they are woken it will look as if they have just been in bed. Macbeth's final words in this scene are more like uttered thoughts and are probably not meant for her ears:

700	*Macb*. To know my deed,	*Knocke.*
701	'Twere best not know my selfe.	
702	Wake *Duncan* with thy knocking:	
703	I would thou could'st.	*Exeunt.*

In most productions in the past it has been taken for granted that at this point Macbeth obeys his wife and follows her; it has sometimes even been acted that Lady Macbeth drags him along, but the word '*Exeunt*' does not precisely imply that wife and husband leave together. In the play, the scene switches and at Scene 3 we are suddenly plunged into another world. It is partly the world of the Porter's imagination, that is, he is inside the gate to hell and partly the real world of the sleepy, drunken Porter gradually waking up in his lodge behind the gate. He imagines that he is letting in three candidates for hell — an irrational farmer, an 'equivocator' and a tailor, who has arrived there for 'stealing out of a French hose' — all of whom, when we think about it, reveal themselves as aspects of Macbeth. Finally the Porter struggles up and opens the gate, at last, to two early morning arrivals; that is, Macduff and his young companion, Lennox. When asked why he has overslept the Porter explains that he was up carousing the night before until the small hours, and then he launches into an exposition of the effects of drink on the human being. These are first threefold; drink is a cause of 'nosepainting, sleep and urine.' There follows a fourth effect which works in two ways, both as encouragement and discouragement, and this is lechery. At the end of this episode, which takes up, altogether, 39 lines of prose, Macbeth appears again, evidently with washed hands and suitable garments. After a brief exchange he volunteers to take Macduff to the King who had evidently arranged to greet him first thing in the morning.

The tension mounts as Lennox describes the wild night they have all just experienced and then Macduff breaks into the scene again with, 'O horror, horror, horror.' We usually assume, of course, that during the Porter episode Macbeth has followed his wife back to their bedroom and that both have washed their hands in a convenient basin and changed into night-clothes, although it is true Macbeth is sometimes played as wearing a dressing gown when he returns. However, we have no direct evidence that this is indeed what is supposed to have happened and when we further consider how often Shakespeare's crucial scenes take place off stage we are left with what might be called 'the principle of simultaneity;' that is, the reflection in a visible scene of events taking place in an invisible scene. This may lead us to scrutinise in minute detail the visible text and its precise setting out.

The second part of the Porter episode, when the Porter is talking to Macduff and to Lennox, is interesting anyway because it exactly covers the centre of Act 2. The central lines of the act are:

> Act II
> Centre
>
> *Macd.* What three things does Drinke especially prouoke?
>
> *Port.* Marry, Sir, Nose-painting, Sleepe, and Vrine. Lecherie, Sir, it prouokes, and vnprouokes : it prouokes the desire, but it takes away the performance. Therefore much Drinke may be said to be an Equiuocator with Le-cherie: it makes him, and it marres him; it sets him on, and it takes him off; it perswades him, and dis-heartens him; makes him stand too, and not stand too : in conclu-sion, equiuocates him in a sleepe, and giuing him the Lye, leaues him.
>
> *Macd.* I beleeue, Drinke gaue thee the Lye last Night.
>
> *Port.* That it did, Sir, i'the very Throat on me : but I

Figure 30

Act	191	...Therefore
	192	much Drinke may be said to be an Equiuocator with Le-
	193	cherie: it makes him, and it marres him; it sets him on,
	194	and it takes him off; it perswades him, and dis-heartens
	195	him; makes him stand too, and not stand too: in conclu-
	196	sion, equiuocates him in a sleepe, and giuing him the Lye,
	197	leaues him.

In the four central lines, two words balance each other 'Le-cherie,' which is written with a hyphen, and 'conclu-sion,' which is also written with a hyphen. It may then occur to us that, 'Le-cherie' has a distinctly French sound. This hint of French words has occurred previously in the play, Act 1 Scene 6 at 'Barlet' — compare the French 'Barralet,' meaning a little measuring drum — and only just before when we hear from the Porter of a tailor stealing out of a French hose. Now 'Le-cherie' becomes 'the darling.' The second line here, '..it makes him, and it marres him,' is set out with more spaces than the previous line and we can see, therefore, from the printing point of view it was not strictly necessary to divide the word lechery at this point. The whole line could just as easily have ended on 'with' and there would have been room for 'lecherie' on the next line. So, dare we ask what this 'darling' is doing in the middle of the Porter's speech? In the context of earlier questions and problems I think we have to.

Not long before, gazing at his bloody hands, Macbeth vowed to,

9. THE PLOT OF *MACBETH* (PART 2)

'make the Green one, Red,' or perhaps just saw in a somnambulistic way that he would, 'make the 'Green one, Red,' that is, after murdering Duncan, he meant to murder someone else. This someone else can only mean the child, the little baby who vanishes in the course of the play, who Macbeth it seems both fears and hates from the very beginning. Lady Macbeth says to him that she has given suck but she doesn't say, 'come and see my new baby' and nor does he suggest it perhaps because what *she* has suggested is a violent, murderous deed. We begin to realize that every word she utters, especially those uttered in scorn, stand to him like granite signposts determining all future action.

As the play text dips down into bawdy a space of time is opened up during which we are left guessing as to the precise actions of the chief protagonists. Certain shadowy suggestions have already been made concerning the undercroft in Inverness Castle; Lady Macbeth has already accused her husband of drunkenness:

486	*La*. Was the hope drunke,
487	Wherein you drest your selfe? Hath it slept since?
488	And wakes it now to looke so greene, and pale,
489	At what it did so freely?

Habitual drunkeness implies a cellar where wine is kept and that there was such a cellar is evident from the carousing on the night of Duncan's murder. We have also gathered that Lady Macbeth used a little room somewhere as a distillery. She knows the art of lacing pleasant drink with drugs. We know that she plans to drug the King and his two chamberlains in preparation for the murder. She also uses phrases that relate to the apparatus of distillation:

516	... when Duncan is asleepe,
517	(Whereto the rather shall his dayes hard Iourney
518	Soundly inuite him) his two Chamberlaines
519	Will I with Wine, and Wassell, so conuince,
520	That Memorie, the Warder of the Braine,
521	Shall be a Fume, and the Receit of Reason
522	A Lymbeck onely: [3] (1, 7)

This little room where the lady of the house is free to prepare drugs and even poisons is not likely to have been a public room; it is more likely to have been a room hidden underground close to the wine cellar. One thing that is clear from the text is that when Macbeth returns to the murder scene he is fortified by drink. A moment earlier he has refused to carry the daggers back at the behest of his wife, 'I am afraid, to thinke what I haue done: / Looke on't againe, I dare not.' Quite soon, however, he dares. He also speaks in a loose, overdramatic way in sharp contrast to his earlier, monosyllabic condition (in the soliloquy about the Green one he is surely just uttering his inmost thoughts). In the words he uses after the discovery of the murder we also hear words suggesting strongly that he has just been in a wine cellar:

808	All is but Toyes: Renowne and Grace is dead,
809	The Wine of Life is drawne, and the meere Lees
810	Is left this Vault, to brag of.

A moment later his speech becomes wild and careless:

827	Th' expedition of my violent Loue
828	Out-run the pawser, Reason. Here lay *Duncan*,
829	His Siluer skinne, lac'd with His Golden Blood,
830	And his gash'd Stabs, look'd like a Breach in Nature,
831	For Ruines wastfull entrance: there the Murtherers,
832	Steep'd in the Colours of their Trade; their Daggers
833	Vnmannerly breech'd with gore: who could refraine,
834	That had a heart to loue; and in that heart,
835	Courage, to make's loue knowne?

Surely, in these final words, he is gazing at his wife, and in the words 'Th' expedition of my violent Loue,' she would have known that he was speaking about another love (as would other listeners), one does not love a King with 'Violent Loue' but, at best, with a steady loyalty. But when he insists that by murdering the two chamberlains he is making his love for the King known his story becomes wildly improbable. How can he make his love known to a King who is dead? At 'Courage, to make's loue knowne?' he must be gazing intensely at his wife. He has now done what she has seemed to ask him to do. At that point she cries out 'Helpe me hence, hoa.' It is interesting that earlier actresses always assumed that she was putting on a faint to distract people from what Macbeth was saying. The tendency more recently is to experience the speaking of the words as relating to an actual faint. I suspect that as Macbeth was speaking, or just before, she came to realize what he had done and where he had been, and it was partly to distract attention away from him, and partly because she was overwhelmed by tears and sorrow. In fact there is no indication in the First Folio text that she either faints or pretends to faint at the words, 'Helpe me hence, hoa,' and if, as seems likely, she finally recognises that there has been a fourth murder (second in time), that of her own child by Duncan, a reaction of tears rather than fainting seems to make the best sense. This moment: 'Helpe me hence, hoa.' is in fact the act-mirror to Macbeth's earlier words as he stumbles away from Duncan's chamber: 'I haue done the deed.' These words are now appropriate in a different sense. The whispered exchange that follows between the King's two sons is suggestive and, I believe, provides another example of simultaneity. After the first 'Looke to the Lady,' while Lady Macbeth interprets her actions as she sees fit, Donalbaine persuades his brother to say nothing but to escape there and then. He says '... Let's away, / Our Teares are not yet brew'd.' Malcolm replies, 'Nor our strong Sorrow / Vpon the foot of Motion.' In the interim the two young men have surely been gazing at Lady Macbeth, who has made a dramatic interruption in the proceedings. As they gaze they speak of tears. If we change the emphasis to, '*Our* Teares are not yet brew'd. / *Mal*. Nor *our* strong Sorrow / Vpon the foot of Motion,' this relates what they are saying directly to what they are looking at.

The words, 'Looke to the Lady,' are uttered twice; first by Macduff at play-line 837 and again by Banquo at play-line 846. We can only guess at what has happened to make Banquo repeat the call. Had Macbeth hoped to please his wife and not cause a flood of tears? After the first '*Lady*. Helpe me hence, hoa' he is silent until 'Let's briefly put on manly readinesse, / And meet i'th' Hall together.'

In any case, we can no longer avoid the question, where did Macbeth find the baby? It must be somewhere in the course of his alternative route back to the courtyard. A route along which he drank wine, and then finally washed his hands and put on something to disguise the fact that he is dressed: any old coverall gown would do and why should there not be one hanging in the distillery? But, is it conceivable that the baby was indeed kept underground? Was Lady Macbeth hiding it away from her potentially violent husband? At this point we may remember the conversation between Banquo and his son Fleance, early in Act 2 Scene 1:

541	*Banq.* How goes the Night, Boy?
542	*Fleance.* The Moone is downe: I haue not heard the
543	Clock.
544	*Banq.* And she goes downe at Twelue.
545	*Fleance.* I take't, 'tis later, Sir.

We are looking at signs in the heavens and at the human artifacts that tell us the time of night or day. It is at least two hours before two o'clock, the time scheduled for the murder of Duncan, but: 'she goes downe at Twelue.' and 'I haue not heard the / Clock.' can also make us think of a beautiful young woman descending to the cellar of a castle and a child called Glaucos (the sound of the word is quite close to that of 'Clock') crying for his regular meal.

To our picture of a wine cellar and a little room nearby with a fire, and perhaps a butt of water and apparatus such as lymbecks, rather like an alchemist's den, we must add that of another little room or space where a cot could be secretly hidden. This little room or space is now visited regularly by Lady Macbeth, who realizes at once — when she knows that Macbeth has been to the cellar — that he has also been close to the child. It seems that there is an alternative reason why Lady Macbeth cries 'Helpe me hence, hoa,' when she does. On the one hand she recognises that following the murder of the King, her husband, fortified with alcohol, has become, 'murder happy!' It was evidently nothing to slay the two chamberlains, so it could have been 'nothing' either to slay the child when the effects of drink were first active. On the other hand her husband is talking wildly and dangerously and must somehow be stopped.

What then of the child who was hidden away in the 'undercroft' not far from the wine cellar? The words spoken by Macduff earlier in this scene make a horrible suggestion. When Lady Macbeth arrives on the scene and asks what is going on Macduff replies, at first:

795	*Macd.* O gentle Lady,
796	'Tis not for you to heare what I can speake:
797	The repetition in a Womans eare,
798	Would murther as it fell.

To the reader this may convey the image of a body being hurled through a window onto rocks below. To Lady Macbeth it may bring the same

9. THE PLOT OF *MACBETH* (PART 2)   177

picture, in a conscious or an unconscious way. Later, when Macbeth attempts to explain to Macduff why he has just slain the King's two chamberlains he uses vivid phrases that could betray to Lady Macbeth that he is speaking not of two more murders but of three. Exactly what happens between the two utterances of, 'Looke to the Lady,' we can only guess, but I believe the words whispered by the two brothers shed light on this. It would appear that nobody ever did help Lady Macbeth hence, perhaps because she appeared to recover, and then was overwhelmed once more by sobbing.

To sum up, after murdering the King and looking in horror at his bloody hands Macbeth is profoundly aware that his innocence is for ever lost and the next step has to follow. When Lady Macbeth urges him to follow her to their bedroom and get himself cleaned up he disobeys (for the second time) and instead of going upwards, he descends. His first action is to visit the vault of the wine cellar and drink copiously from a barrel of wine, and thus fortified he continues on his way. There is water down there and at some point he washes his hands, but surely after he has seized the child by the legs, so that like the crossed daggers it is, 'Vnmannerly breech'd with gore,' and hurled it through an aperture to the rocks below. As the knocking finally ceases he has to change fast into something that looks like night attire.

As in Act 1, there are two central lines to Act 2 (act-lines 29f) and like Act I they are ambiguous:

	much Drinke may be said to be an Equiuocator with Le-
293	cherie: it makes him, and it marres him; it sets him on,
294	and it takes him off; it perswades him, and dis-heartens
	him; makes him stand too, and not stand too: in conclu-

'Takes him off' has two meanings the second of which is 'murders him.' When we think of 'Le-cherie' again these lines strongly suggest the moment when the child is slain in the manner so vividly painted by Lady Macbeth (Act 1, Scene 7).

509	I would, while it was smyling in my Face,
510	Haue pluckt my Nipple from his Bonelesse Gummes,
511	And dasht the Braines out, had I so sworne
512	As you haue done to this.

The child is hurled through a window or aperture to the rocks below where it is smashed to death. As the Porter stops speaking Macbeth returns to the stage. When he greets Macduff and Macduff indicates his early morning appointment with the King, Macbeth actually volunteers to accompany him to the royal chamber, knowing full well that a far worse deed than the murder of Duncan has been committed!

Later, when Macduff returns, half speechless with shock and Macbeth launches into his passionate speech painfully explaining why he instantly slew the two chamberlains, Lady Macbeth realizes through the peculiar imagery of his words and the intensity of his gaze upon her that her husband has also slain the child. As we have previously indicated, this is a moment when indeed intervention is politic; I believe it coincides with a moment of uncontrollable distress. Lady Macbeth is not fainting, she is weeping and she wishes to hide this weeping both from her husband and from the others. A simulated faint is therefore the answer. The King's two sons, Malcolm and Donalbaine speak together between the first and the second, 'Looke to the Lady!' Given the emphasis which we have previously remarked upon ('*Our* Teares are not yet brew'd. / *Mal.* Nor *our* strong Sorrow / Vpon the foot of Motion'), their words lend support to the idea that Lady Macbeth is weeping rather than fainting.

The scene-mirror line to the second 'Looke to the Lady!' is also suggestive. The Porter is still speaking: '... it prouokes / the desire, but it takes away the performance.' Perhaps she cannot pretend any longer quite so easily. If, as we have surmised, Lady Macbeth evinces shock and deep sorrow at Macbeth's revelation rather than any sort of pleasure at his love-inspired action, then we may expect a reaction of silence from Macbeth, which indeed we find.

Later, in Act 3 Scene 2, just before the murder of Banquo, Lady Macbeth says heavily, 'things without all remedie / Should be without regard: what's done, is done.' and we sense that it is of *this deed* and not of the murder of Duncan that she is speaking. We have already spoken of the earlier line that balances the moment of the first 'Looke to the Lady!' across the act; it is: '*Macb.* I haue done the deed,' only this time she is aware that a different deed has been done.

But what of the child? Where exactly is this baby in Act 1 Scene 5, when Lady Macbeth is summoning spirits out of the air to unsex her and turn the wholesome milk in her breasts to bitter gall? And later, in Scene 7, when she attributes her husband's decision not to murder the King that night to fear and sheer lack of will?

Imagination struggles to crystallize the scenario. Did she fear that Macbeth might harm the illegitimate child? Was it being deliberately hidden away and, if so, would a little space in the cellars have been a convenient spot? She would have to go down there anyway for the mixing of opiates, but might it not be dark, damp and unhealthy for a newborn child? In the Greek story, which lies behind an essential part of this story, the child, Glaucos, is found in a cellar, drowned in honey. We need not necessarily think of this room, or the cellar of Inverness Castle, as being located in the depths of the earth. If Inverness Castle was built on a rocky eminence, sloping away at one side, rooms that were below the level of the courtyard would not have to be lightless and damp, and window access to the outside world could well overlook a precipice beneath. All this can, of course, be dismissed as wild speculation, but then the question about the existence and whereabouts of the child will remain entirely unanswered. Why does Shakespeare imply twice in Act 1 that there is a baby nearby that Lady Macbeth is suckling? Are these implications accidental; the product of mere carelessness? If not, why are implications, so crucial to Macbeth's imagination, not followed up later in the play? What happens to the child?

When we inscribe the relationships between the four significant moments just quoted in Act 2 into the Figure of *Macbeth*, what emerges is rather striking. The line balancing the first 'Looke to the Lady!' namely, 'I haue done the deed,' has already been mentioned. So now we need to look at the second 'Looke to the Lady!' spoken by Banquo. It falls at act-line 306. Its mirrored line in the act (act-line 306-) takes us to the beginning of Scene 2 where Lady Macbeth is listening acutely to the sounds emerging from the royal chamber. The line is, 'That Death and Nature doe contend about them.' If we ask ourselves exactly what this line means the answer is not quite so simple. If Macbeth is in Duncan's room, stabbing Duncan while his chamberlains are in a state of drugged sleep, it would clearly be a disaster for Macbeth if they were to wake up, and he might well respond to this event by murdering the chamberlains as well. But why should 'Nature' plead for their lives?

As previously mentioned, in this play the word 'Nature' is frequently, but not invariably, used as a synonym for sexual activity. We see that a little earlier Lady Macbeth would have had the ideal opportunity for murdering the King since she would have been in bed with him (hence 'Nor Heauen peepe through the Blanket of the darke, / To cry, hold, hold'). At some point in the story she looked upon the face of Duncan, realized that he reminded her of her father and was unable to commit the deed. Though when exactly Macbeth learnt this we do not know. It seems, in any case, that 'Nature' must have been close to the chamberlains first and 'Death' second — if not simultaneously — as in a true contending. That is unless the word 'Nature' is used in a quite different sense at this moment. But to return to the act-mirror aspect of these words we can ask the following question: have, 'Death and Nature' *contended about the child?* Yes, perhaps. If we conceive of Macbeth representing 'Death' and Lady Macbeth 'Nature.'

Earlier, we have discussed briefly the nature and point of a play that turns out to be a kind of antique 'Who done it.' Could a live audience get anything at all from more or less subtle hints in a text? Perhaps not more than subliminal suggestions. But does the widely held view, that a Shakespeare play is only realized in the acting, bear closer scrutiny? The words in the address to the great variety of readers (First Folio Preface) are rather surprising: not 'Watch him again and again' or 'Hear him again and again' but *'Read him again and again.'* A director who had done just that, especially if he had used a numbered text, might well be in a position to direct the play (or film) in such a way that the hidden plot became apparent. This could be an exciting project, but until, and unless this happens I think that only scholars with a Pythagorean bent will be able to detect it.

There is one aspect of the story that could be cited as disproving the alternative plot. By the end of Act 2 Scene 2 Macbeth clearly regrets the murder of Duncan: 'Wake *Duncan* with thy knocking: / I would thou could'st.' So how, after that, can he go straight on to murder the child? My impression is that this alternation of deed and regret is fundamental to Macbeth's character; but also the thought of slaying the child has been suggested to him so many times in advance that he could no longer resist it. First, the strong suggestion comes with Lady Macbeth's words:

> 509   I would, while it was smyling in my Face,
> 510   Haue pluckt my Nipple from his Bonelesse Gummes,
> 511   And dasht the Braines out, had I so sworne
> 512   As you haue done to this.

The second comes when he hears the mysterious voice cry:

9. THE PLOT OF *MACBETH* (PART 2)

> 656 *Macb*. Me thought I heard a voyce cry, Sleep no more:
> 657 Macbeth does murther Sleepe, the innocent Sleepe,
> 658 Sleepe that knits vp the rauel'd Sleeue of Care,

What sleep could be more innocent than that of a newborn baby? And the association of images — knitting and care — reinforces the impression. Later, when Lady Macbeth has snatched the daggers from her husband, she says:

> 677 ... the sleeping, and the dead,
> 678 Are but as Pictures: 'tis the Eye of Child-hood,
> 679 That feares a painted Deuill.

These words can hardly fail to evoke in Macbeth the picture of himself, the painted devil, striking terror into the heart of a particular child. Finally, the phrase, 'A little Water cleares vs of this deed.' must remind him of his wife's earlier admonition, 'Goe get some Water, / And wash this filthie Witnesse from your Hand.' The filthy witness is of course the blood, but it could also be that which witnesses his wife's infidelity — the apparently premature child. It is these words that Lady Macbeth has spoken in scorn that most deeply impress him; her ill opinion is more than he can bear.

It would have been extremely interesting to research the remains of Macbeth's castle at Inverness. Sadly, little appears to remain of it. Only one thing is clear, the castle in which the murder of Duncan is described as taking place is not the same as the one now described as Inverness Castle. It lay on a high ridge overlooking the River Ness and the Moray Firth, not far from the present Old Castle Road.[4] In any case, it is always perilous to confuse play reality with historical reality, especially when the play is primarily a drama, not a 'history' play.

The Death of Lady Macbeth

When a part changes, so must the whole. We have found the hidden lover, the hidden child, the hidden main spring. Looked at in the light of structure (and this time we will begin with structure) the end of the story changes too.

At the centre of Act 5 is Scene 4, whose backcloth is Birnham Wood.

The scene is short, only 27 lines, but the words are accompanied by a kind of choric action; the hewing down of boughs by the Scots and English soldiers. It ends with the soldiers marching off into imagined darkness, bearing the life of the ruined forest umbrella-like above them.

The scene is flanked by two longer scenes, Scenes 3 and 5, both set within the walls of Dunsinane Castle. Scene 3 (70 lines) contains the sighting of the English force, Macbeth's exchange with the doctor, and the armour business with Seyton, which punctuates this exchange. Scene 5 (55 lines) first brings the news of the Queen's death, and, later, to balance it, the news that Birnham Wood is moving. It ends 'arm, arm, and out.' Throughout both scenes there is a violent fluctuation of mood; crazy confidence, weakness, cruelty, numb despair and reckless action.

The two scenes stand in opposition, reflecting one another across the act-centre (see Figure 31), although the first part of Scene 3, the episode of the white-faced messenger, is not in geometrical opposition to Scene 5, but in fact, precisely opposes Scene 6. We may, therefore, expect a closer inner connection between Scene 3, on the one hand, and Scenes 5 and 6 on the other.

The stage direction: *'A crying within our women,'* falls between lines 7 and 8 of Scene 5. It is the moment, surely, not when the Queen dies, but when she is found dead, else a messenger would have said, 'My lord, the Queen is dying.' Or 'the Queen is very sick.' But Seyton's words are 'the Queen, my lord, is dead!'

Our strong impression, difficult at first to justify, is that she has been found dead in bed at dawn, or just before dawn. It comes, perhaps, from the contrast between the darkness of the forest and Malcolm words 'Cosins, I hope the dayes are neere at hand' (Scene 4), and the bright openness of 'Hang out our Banners,' which must shine in the sun, as the sun itself first shines.

If we suppose this timing, we must further suppose that the Queen died during the night — the very night of the cutting down of Birnham Wood — and then we may recognise this hewing down of green branches, and the floating away of those branches from the trunks that they once clothed as the perfect image of death; at least of death as it was conceived in Shakespeare's day. Macduff could not say of Duncan's murder, 'and stole thence / The Life o'th' Building,' unless life (not spirit) was not thought of as a separate entity, a mantle which belongs to us while we breathe.

What we find here is a most elegant example of simultaneous action, of a scene presented on the stage that coincides with, and metaphorically

9. THE PLOT OF *MACBETH* (PART 2)

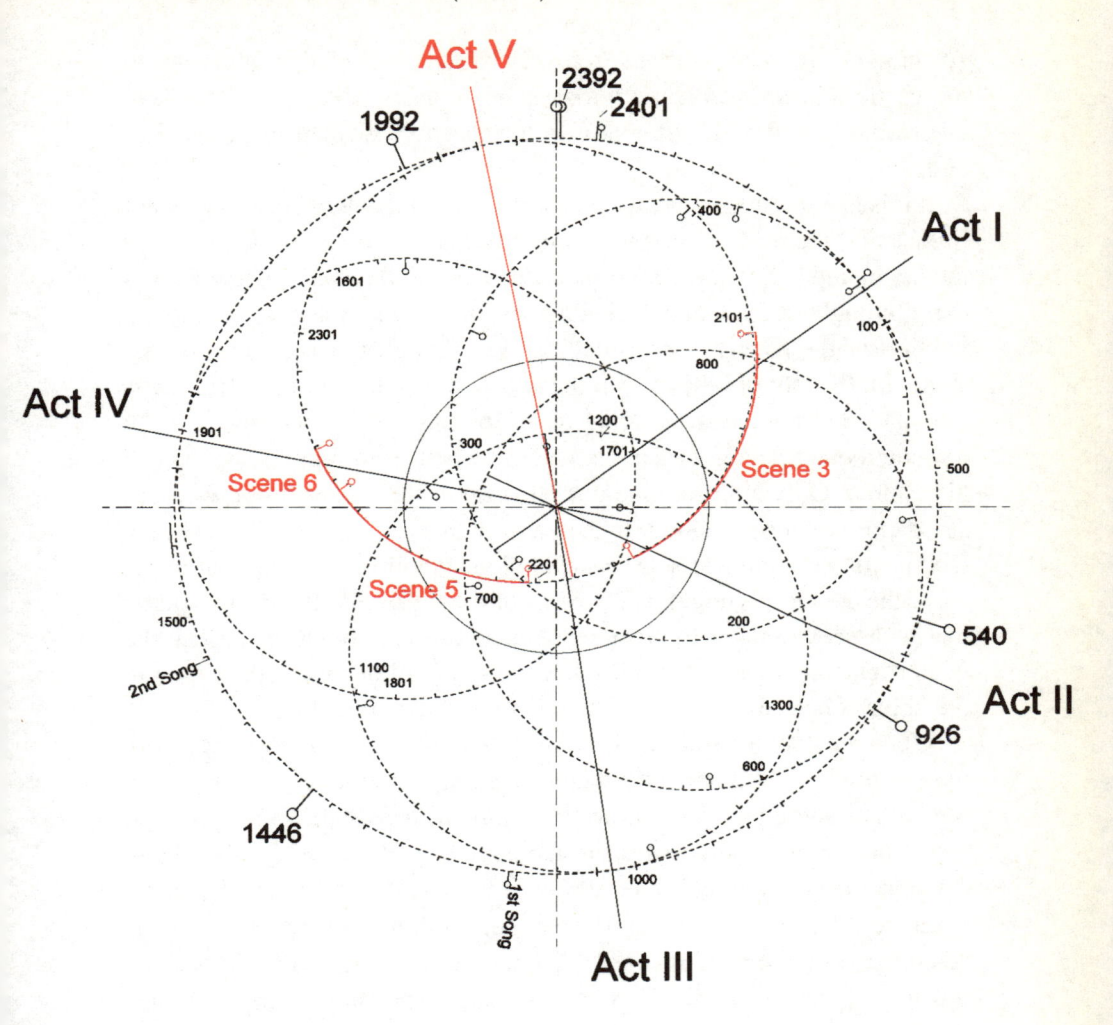

Figure 31. Comparison of Act 5 Scene 3 with Act 5 Scenes 5 and 6.

describes, another action going on elsewhere. The branches of the forest do not wither and die of their own accord; axes and knives hack them off, wielded by the hands of men. So too, we suspect, the Queen did not die a natural death, nor took her own life; it was taken off by order, as the boughs, by order, were hewn down. A first hint of confirmation comes in those same opening words:

    2177   *Malc.* Cosins, I hope the dayes are neere at hand
    2178   That Chambers will be safe.

At that very moment perhaps, a royal chamber, lit by a candle, high in the castle that looms on the horizon, is so unsafe that a murderer can enter quietly and administer poison to the crazy woman lying there in bed.

If this is not pure fantasy we will find other hints elsewhere. We do not in fact find them in the previous scene, Scene 3. The stage directions at the beginning are *'Enter Macbeth, Doctor and Attendants.'* The doctor is there throughout the scene. He witnesses the King's hysterical outburst to the messenger, listens in to his half-suicidal thoughts, observes his obsession with the talk of others; with the whispers, the hatred, the accusations that surround him. But the King does not speak to the Doctor until he has summoned Seyton thrice, learned the worst from him and demanded his armour. Only after the line does he turn to the darker figure who has stood close by him all along. In the passage that follows Macbeth asks the Doctor for three things: a 'sweet Obliuious Antidote,' to be given to his wife (the doctor has none); a diagnosis of the ills of Scotland; and a purge that will 'scowre these English hence.' The last is in effect rhetorical: the doctor must be a wise man indeed, more so in politics and tactics than in medicine if he can offer good council at this stage of affairs.

When the doctor admits he is helpless to cure mental disease, Macbeth reacts with rage: 'Throw Physicke to the Dogs, Ile none of it.' By now, Seyton is standing by with his armour, 'giue me my Staffe: / *Seyton*, send out.' But Macbeth's final words to the doctor, on the purging of his land, are punctuated by three more abrupt commands: 'Come sir, dispatch.,' 'Pull't off I say,' and 'bring it after me.' The armour business can be acted in diverse ways. However it is done, it seems that Macbeth's nervous impatience and contradictory commands chiefly serve to symbolize his desperate inner state. With the traditional interpretation of events, which sees the conversation with the Doctor and a brief one with Seyton as separate in sense though interwoven in time, there is nothing obviously wrong. Yet we could point to the continuity of thought flow across the phrase 'Pull't off I say,' which is almost too unbroken for the implied stage business, for surely the unstrapping and taking off of the armour must take a little time? It can be argued of course that Seyton is quietly removing helmet, breastplate and grieves, piecemeal, while conversation continues:

2168   *Macb*....What Rubarb, Cyme, or what Purgatiue drugge
2169   Would scowre these English hence: hear'st y of them?

> 2170   Doct. I my good Lord: your Royall Preparation
> 2171   Makes vs heare something.

But it can also be argued that this 'something' that we are meant to hear is something else. For a quite different interpretation to this passage suggests itself the moment we wonder whether the Queen's death may not also be Macbeth's last and most logical murder. 'Come sir, dispatch' and 'Pull't off I say' are not subtly veiled hints; they are simply commands in vernacular speech. We *dispatch* an enemy, a villain or a sick dog; and we *pull off* a coup, a deed. There is no denying that Macbeth could also be saying 'Finish her off; get on with it.' The question is, did Shakespeare mean it that way?

We turn again to the structure: and structure seems to give an unhesitating answer.

Macbeth tells the doctor that if he could purge his land to health he would earn his continuing gratitude:

> Act   174   I would applaud thee to the very Eccho,
>   175   That should applaud againe.

'I would applaud thee' falls at line 174. What line in Scene 5, we ask, reflects this line? It is   'Sey. The Queene (my Lord) is dead' (Act line 174-).

The 'laud' in 'applaud' is indeed echoed in the 'lord' of 'my lord,' (though modern ears, dulled by spelling, may not instantly catch it). The report of the Queen's death, in short, echoes precisely what we already believe to be a direct hint, given to the man best placed to administer poison.

In this 'applaud' there is also a simple echo of a much earlier moment. In Act 3 Scene 2 Macbeth hints to his wife that Banquo may soon be dispatched. He says:

> 1142   Be innocent of the knowledge, dearest Chuck,
> 1143   Till thou applaud the deed ...

From Macbeth, it seems, applauding has to do with despatching.

Close to the strong echo of 'would applaud' and 'Queene (my Lord)' falls another. When Macbeth asks the doctor if he has heard of the English force, his words (already quoted) fall between Act-lines 177 and 180.

Act 177   .... hear'st y of them?
     178   *Doct.* I my good Lord: your Royall Preparation
     179   Makes vs heare something.
     180   *Macb.* Bring it after me:

This passage is mirrored in act-lines 180- to 177-, lines which come early in Scene 5, just after the *'Cry of women.'* They are:

Act 180-   The time ha's beene, my sences would haue cool'd
     179-   To heare a Night-shrieke, and my Fell of haire
     178-   Would at a dismall Treatise rowze, and stirre
     177-   As life were in't.

'Hear' is echoed to the very line (179 and 179-). Indeed, there is a kind of double-echo — 'Hear'st - hear' and 'hear - hair' — and through it we learn precisely what the something *is* that Macbeth's preparation makes us hear: it is a night shriek. Without the hints to the Doctor the deed would not have been done, and the night shriek, which may be that cry of women, or an earlier shriek, would not have been heard. In these lines the second meaning not only overrides the first but also shows it up as absurd and unnecessary. How should the Doctor *not* hear of the English? He was present when the whey-faced messenger arrived and stuttered out in terror, 'The English Force, so please you.'

We find, in fact, that in Scene 5 the echoes of Scene 3 are almost continuous, and seem to resound with two messages: the leaves of the forest and the life of the Queen are one; and the death of the Queen and Macbeth's words to the Doctor are also one. '*Macb.* She should haue dy'de heereafter' acquires the simplest possible interpretation; 'she should have died, yes, but I meant it to be later.' It remains that moment when all feeling in him has died too.

Here are a few of the more striking echoes (moving now from the later scene each time to the earlier one).

Act 182-   *Sey.* It is the cry of women, my good Lord.
     181-   *Macb.* I haue almost forgot the taste of Feares: (Scene 5)

This mirrors:

9. THE PLOT OF *MACBETH* (PART 2)

Act 181 I will not be affraid of Death and Bane,
      182 Till Birnane Forrest come to Dunsinane.   (Scene 3)

'Fears' and 'afraid' fall in the same line (181- and 181); and the coming of the Forest is echoed in the cry of the women who discover that Lady Macbeth is dead. The later lines (in Scene 5):

Act 177- ...I haue supt full with horrors,
      176- Direnesse familiar to my slaughterous thoughts
      175- Cannot once start me.

mirror the earlier ones (in Scene 3):
Act 175 ...Pull't off I say,
      176 What Rubarb, Cyme, or what Purgatiue drugge
      177 Would scowre these English hence: (Scene 3)

The thought of the purgative drug matches the 'slaughterous thoughts' and the supping of horrors. The suggestion is instantly of poison; that possible alternative which for Macbeth (and his wife) earlier accompanied the thought of steel.

Act 157- *Macb.* Well, say sir.
      156- *Mes.* As I did stand my watch vpon the Hill
      155- I look'd toward Byrnane, and anon me thought
      154- The Wood began to moue.   (Scene 5)

Again, this mirrors:
Act 154 Hang those that talke of Feare. Giue me mine Armor:
      155 How do's your Patient, Doctor?
      156 *Doct.* Not so sicke my Lord,
      157 As she is troubled with thicke-comming Fancies (Scene 3)

'Hang those that talke of Feare' echoes words that are most fearful to Macbeth — 'The Wood began to moue' (Act-lines 154- and 154). The 'an' of 'began' rings with the 'ang' of 'hang.'

'How do's your Patient, Doctor?' Macbeth's first enquiry about his wife is reflected exactly in the Watchman's first report of the moving wood; 'I look'd toward Byrnane ...' (Act-lines 155 and 155-). We note the sound echo of 'Doctor' and 'look'd to.'

Scenes 3 and 5, taken together, point not only to the manner of Lady Macbeth's death, but also to the reason *why* she had to be quickly despatched.

In both scenes, Macbeth is obsessed with talking and hearing, as any man might be who has crimes to hide and a partner-in-crime who has started to babble in her sleep. She could hardly do anything worse to him. She must somehow be shut up.

Macbeth suspects rumour and hatred in every whispered word. Behind his back are curses, not loud, but deep; and in his presence 'Mouth-honor, breath / Which the poore heart would faine deny, and dare not.' To Seyton he cries 'Hang those that talke of Feare,' and to the messenger in Scene 5: 'Thou com'st to vse thy Tongue: thy Story quickly.' A moment earlier, at the centre of the scene, come those words that half deceive us by their very universality.

Act	237	... It is a Tale
	238	Told by an Ideot, full of sound and fury
	239	Signifying nothing.

That they fall at a centre cannot surprise us; nor that they balance the earlier words:

Act	239-	Raze out the written troubles of the Braine,
	238-	And with some sweet Obliuious Antidote
	237-	Cleanse the stufft bosome,

Both concern nothingness; but one with deleting evidence, the other with making light of it. The Queen was not only walking and talking in her sleep but was also writing things down:

1996	*Gent*. Since his Maiesty went into the Field, I haue
1997	seene her rise from her bed, throw her Night-Gown vp-
1998	pon her, vnlocke her Closset, take foorth paper, folde it,
1999	write vpon't, read it, afterwards Seale it, and againe re-
2000	turne to bed;

We cannot doubt that Macbeth would be as anxious to destroy those sealed missives as the waiting-woman was curious to unseal and read them. Nor can we doubt that he would be driven to make some comment

9. THE PLOT OF *MACBETH* (PART 2)

on the things his wife had been heard to say. Today, his words would be 'She's crazy. All that stuff about spots and blood doesn't mean a thing.' In a Renaissance play, they were:

>   2229   ... It is a Tale
>   2230   Told by an Ideot, full of sound and fury
>   2231   Signifying nothing.

It was of course too late to shut anyone up. With each bloody death — Duncan, Banquo, the wife and entire family of Macduff — suspicion drew nearer to certainty. By Act 5 Macbeth is branded as a murderer in the eyes of Scotland, but he is now beyond the reach of ordinary reason. The Queen is talking; night after night she is re-living the moments that he most longs to bury. It is more than he can endure.

In the perspective of the whole play we may see the death of the Queen not only as the last in a long series of silencings, but also as the final step on Macbeth's path of ever-increasing loneliness. The gifted man who might have had troops of friends has earlier murdered the closest of them.

>   1146   Cancell and teare to pieces that great Bond,
>   1147   Which keepes me pale.

This is surely no mere figure of speech. Banquo and he could once speak their 'free hearts each to other.' After the murder of Duncan, he can no longer communicate with Banquo; after the murder of Banquo, he can no longer communicate with any friend at all. There is only his wife.

What happened in the end to *that* communication? '*Lad*. The Thane of Fife, had a wife: where is she now?' Is this not the memory of a reproach, of many reproaches, from one who knows her husband to be a child-and-woman killer? From one who has learnt to fear him and probably to hate him?

When in the end she goes mad, Macbeth could say 'I, too, had a wife. Where is she now?' His central motive, his tormenting and driving love, has dissolved into nothingness, into idiocy.

>   Act 138   I haue liu'd long enough: my way of life
>   139   Is falne into the Seare, the yellow Leafe,

	140	And that which should accompany Old-Age,
	141	As Honor, Loue, Obedience, Troopes of Friends,
	142	I must not looke to haue:

A King might look for honour, love and obedience in all his subjects but a man, through the very marriage service, looks for these things especially in his wife. It is because she is so close to him — or should be so close to him — that Macbeth's death-wish for himself and his death-wish for his wife are almost one. The ambiguity that runs through this central part of the last act depends on this identity; to die, to kill, to deal gashes or to fall on one's sword. It scarcely makes any odds.

In both Scenes 3 and 5, Macbeth reveals that he is almost ready to die by his own hand. 'I haue liu'd long enough' he says in Scene 3, and at the end of Scene 5, 'I 'ginne to be a-weary of the Sun.' Again, we are hardly surprised to find that these moments stand opposite one another in relation to the act centre. Later, near the end of the battle, the thought of suicide is immediate and explicit:

Act	314	Why should I play the Roman Foole, and dye
	315	On mine owne sword?

He is ready to die, and his wife's sickness and his own sickness are so close that they can be spoken of in exactly the same words:

Act	160	Can'st thou not Minister to a minde diseas'd,
	161	Plucke from the Memory a rooted Sorrow,
	162	Raze out the written troubles of the Braine,
	163	And with some sweet Obliuious Antidote
	164	Cleanse the stufft bosome, of that perillous stuffe

It is at once the cry for help of a man in extremis ('*Seyton*, I am sick at hart,') and the cynical overture to a satanic proposition. Yet even in that proposition there is perhaps a drop of the kindness that puts a cat or a bird out of its misery. He specifies, 'some sweet Obliuious Antidote.' It should not hurt: it should be a drug such as hemlock, that death may be a peaceful floating away.

Before the decisive hint can be given though, Macbeth has to put on his armour literally and symbolically; and if, 'Pull't off I say,' is

9. THE PLOT OF *MACBETH* (PART 2) 191

not shouted impatiently to Seyton, but spoken with sinister significance and *sotto voce* to the Doctor, it must follow that the armour stays on.

We remember Macbeth's words in the prologue to Banquo's murder: 'And make our Faces Vizards to our Hearts, / Disguising what they are.' (lines 1129-1130). In this later, and much briefer, prologue to murder the evil motive in Macbeth's heart must be disguised yet more completely. The visor blots out his human identity, and the breastplate protects him from any shaft of pity. He is no longer a man, but a suit of steel. Sometimes an actor can remain as uncommitted to one of two meanings as the silent script itself. But here the new meaning surely drives out the old. At, '*Seyton*, send out:' or, at the latest, at 'Come sir, dispatch.' Seyton must leave the room. Without doing so, indeed, he can hardly obey the King's orders. Now Macbeth is free to speak to the Doctor with no eavesdroppers. He speaks softly, then perhaps more loudly for the general ear.

Act	176	What Rubarb, Cyme, or what Purgatiue drugge
	177	Would scowre these English hence: hear'st y of them?

The Doctor's answer tells Macbeth that he *has* heard, and fully understood:

Act	178	*Doct.* I my good Lord: your Royall Preparation
	179	Makes vs heare something.

The matter almost concluded, Macbeth gets up to go:

Act	180	*Macb.* Bring it after me:
	181	I will not be affraid of Death and Bane,
	182	Till Birnane Forrest come to Dunsinane.

He is *not* speaking to Seyton and saying 'Bring my armour after me.' He is still speaking to the Doctor, and himself. He is saying: 'I may need it too. I'm not afraid of dying either, or of poison. When you have prepared that drug, bring a draught of it to me too, that I may have it at hand. That 'bane' means poison in certain contexts is confirmed by the line in *Measure for Measure:*

Like rats that ravin up their proper bane (1, 2)

The Doctor has not dared to refuse. The dismay of his last couplet is understandable:

Act   183   *Doct.* Were I from Dunsinane away, and cleere,
            184   Profit againe should hardly draw me heere.   *Exeunt*

One doubt perhaps cannot be resolved. When was the drug meant to be taken to Macbeth, sooner or later? The Doctor does not know. It seems he obeys first instructions first, prepares a draught, and (surely with the connivance of the waiting-women) administers it that night to the Queen. But '*Macb.* She should haue dy'de heereafter;' sounds almost as if this was an error in timing, or perhaps Macbeth has found a scapegoat for conscience, and persuades himself that his words were taken up wrongly. It wasn't his fault; he could say it was the Doctor's fault, the fault of an over-zealous fool that misunderstood him. All of them are fools — the Doctor, the Queen who drove him to lose his 'eternal jewel' and then lost her own wits — above all, he, Macbeth the King, is himself a fool, whose day will soon become a yesterday of dusty death. 'Out, out, breefe Candle,' is Janus-headed; it looks back to a candle just blown out, and forward to another that will be snuffed out before the day is ended.

    Can we know any more of the Doctor and the waiting-woman? The Doctor was not the court physician. He came to the castle from outside, lured by 'profit.' We imagine that he was offered a large sum of gold. Yet how was he chosen? He had to be a man of certain qualities to suit the King's purpose. Have we any evidence that he was a man capable of crime?

    We meet him only twice. Firstly, when the King speaks to him in Scene 3, and earlier, in Scene 1, when he stands watch with the waiting-woman in a passage or anteroom outside the bedchamber of Lady Macbeth. They exchange whispers. They listen avidly to the sleeptalking Queen, and then whisper briefly again after she has returned to bed. In the first pentameters of the scene, the doctor says:

       2060   *Doct.* Foule whisp'rings are abroad: vnnaturall deeds
       2061   Do breed vnnaturall troubles: infected mindes
       2062   To their deafe pillowes will discharge their Secrets:
       2063   More needs she the Diuine, then the Physitian:
       2064   God, God forgiue vs all. Looke after her,

9. THE PLOT OF *MACBETH* (PART 2)

Are not these the words of a man conscious of sin? All men are sinners and he needs forgiveness too. They could even be the words of a man to whom a crime has recently been suggested.

Of the waiting-woman we know that she refused to tell the doctor what she had heard the queen say on previous nights:

> 2004 ... what (at any time) haue you heard
> 2005 her say?
> 2006 *Gent.* That Sir, which I will not report after her.
> 2007 *Doct.* You may to me, and 'tis most meet you should.
> 2008 *Gent.* Neither to you, nor any one, hauing no witnesse
> 2009 to confirme my speech.   *Enter Lady, with a Taper.*

We also know that the doctor instructs her to see that no harm comes to the queen; and to watch her, '... keepe eyes vpon her.' Yet something in this waiting-woman's speech is wholly familiar. Have we not met them again and again, those pious gossips who say 'I'm not going to tell any tales' and then, having whetted your appetite, lead you straight to the evidence? The waiting-woman may be an exception to the rule that we are all sinners, or she may not. We have only words to go by. If she is not an exception then she too will not have the courage to oppose a royal command; and when the doctor comes at night with his draught prepared he will need her assistance. Unforewarned she might call for help. For the administration of the drug by more than one person there is a small piece of evidence; the evidence that is also needed to throw light on what may look like the very judgement of Shakespeare himself.

At the end of the play, when the fighting is over, Malcolm makes a speech to the newly-named earls who stand around him. Action is promised for the righting of wrongs; exiles will be brought home and the 'cruell Ministers' of the dead king and queen will be identified, and presumably brought to justice. In parenthesis, he quotes the rumour about the queen's suicide; the sentence goes on and on like those sentences in law that must be unambiguous, yet still it finds no verb. That doesn't come till the last sentence. We quote in full:

> 2381   ... What's more to do,
> 2382   Which would be planted newly with the time,
> 2383   As calling home our exil'd Friends abroad,

2384	That fled the Snares of watchfull Tyranny,
2385	Producing forth the cruell Ministers
2386	Of this dead Butcher, and his Fiend-like Queene;
2387	Who (as 'tis thought) by selfe and violent hands,
2388	Tooke off her life. This, and what need full else
2389	That call's vpon vs, by the Grace of Grace,
2390	We will performe in measure, time, and place:
2391	So thankes to all at once, and to each one,
2392	Whom we inuite, to see vs Crown'd at Scone.

Flourish.   Exeunt Omnes.

A relative pronoun should refer back to the last noun in the sentence, spoken or written. So, 'Fiend-like Queene; / Who (as 'tis thought) by selfe and violent hands, / Tooke off her life.' seems clear enough, although we may wonder why it isn't 'took her own life.' But if grammar is no more than a frail human attempt to summarize actual usage then the 'who' in that non-sentence has, in reality, three nouns to choose from; the fiend-like queen, the dead butcher, or the cruel ministers. 'Butcher' and 'Queen' go together in one phrase, but 'cruel ministers' stand apart and have structural pride of place; it is the object of producing forth, whereas the king and queen are only part of the descriptive phrase qualifying 'cruel ministers.' We submit that it makes perfect sense for the 'who' to refer back to 'cruell Ministers.' We could also say if this refers right back to 'calling home' and 'producing forth' why should not 'who' refer back to the ministers?

The cruel ministers of Macbeth and his wife are, of course, not only the doctor and waiting-woman who administer the drug, but also the witches and the beings who attend the witches, as well as Seyton — alias Satan — who puts slanderous thoughts into the heart of Macbeth.

A word that echoes through the play provides its own key. We must think at once of:

380	... Come to my Womans Brests,
381	And take my Milke for Gall, you murth'ring Ministers,

This passage falls at lines 380 and 381 and we can look with interest at the great echo or reflection across the play. It falls at lines 380- and 381- early in Act 5, Scene 1.

381-   *Doct*. How came she by that light?
380-   *Gent*. Why it stood by her: she ha's light by her con-
379-   tinually, 'tis her command.

This reflection brings us straight back to the doctor and the gentlewoman and the moment when the queen has just entered. The light is her life, which she would not lose, and how came she by it? It seems to carry a doctor's indignation; 'How dangerous, what is she doing with a light?' 'Out, out, breefe Candle' — Macbeth's instructions are in fact as exact as his precautions.

10. A Work in Progress, Additional Geometrical Attributes of the 'Figure'

Alan Thewless

I was asked to write this chapter because of the special circumstances life afforded me in working closely with Sylvia during the last years of her life. As her colleague and assistant during the time when the book was being formed and committed to text, we talked at length about the subject matter; the finer points of creating the 'figure' for a Shakespeare play and the implications of her work as a new and challenging approach to Shakespeare, his plays and his creative genius. Latterly, she mainly wrote her book through the medium of a tape recorder for she suffered, for the most part of her life (from the age of 19 through to the time of her death at 79), from the debilitating effects of rheumatoid arthritis. In her later years she could only write with the greatest difficulty and needed continual assistance.

The inclusion of the present chapter aims to describe important elements of background both to the study as a whole and to the unique way that Sylvia approached the study and analysis of a Shakespeare play. It was also apparent that there were some details of the work that Sylvia had often talked about but had never put down in writing, in particular the subject of the use and meaning of a play-figure as a universal tool towards the understanding of a Shakespeare play; a tool having relevance over and beyond its unique way of incorporating play, act and scene symmetries. This especially needed to be described but only after the development of the initial chapters dealing with symmetry and plot.

In terms of background to the study as a whole, I felt it important to spend some moments looking at the relationship of artistic creation with the worlds of number and form, exploring notably the Pythagorean influence as it weaves its way from antiquity through to classical and renaissance times, creating a backdrop for Shakespeare's work (subjects that deeply interested Sylvia that often occupied our conversations). Yet the primary aim of this chapter will be to describe the use of the play-figure as a tool of research whose geometrical attributes extend further than those encapsulating the three-fold symmetry, which Sylvia has described in the previous chapters. I will try to show some of the ways in which Sylvia appreciated and used the 'figure' as a geometrical touchstone which, through the beauty of its many forms and relationships, could introduce or affirm aspects of a Shakespeare play not at first apparent. As I work towards this main aim I will not be able to resist the temptation to be anecdotal here and there and also to draw in other matters which describe Sylvia's contribution as 'work in progress' rather that a final statement — something Sylvia was quite clear about.

> I don't want to minimise the criticisms and questions
> which people will have. I must make it clear that certain
> things need more research and there are questions here
> and there but I also want to express the experience of how,
> dealing in detail with a whole number of plays, one gradu-
> ally is learning a kind of language, and how one learns
> more and more.

It was clear at an early stage that some chapters of this book were not going to be straightforward ones to write; not only was it evident that Sylvia's interest and enthusiasm ran somewhat ahead of the ordered presentation of text but, to a high degree, the subject matter itself was hard pressed to be expressed in the written word. For instance, we had many amusing and testing moments in trying to approach the comparison of symmetrical play-lines in such a way that the reader would have a chance of appreciating the subject Sylvia was trying to outline. The reader will, I am sure, have struggled with the parallel texts that attempt to give a working sense of the way sections of play text relate to one another across play, act or scene centres. On one side, we have the text going forward in time and next to it the symmetrical partner, going backwards in time; that is with the lines formatted backwards, going *up* the page! (See Mirrored Text A. Figure 16). aim was to try and bring something that came naturally to Sylvia — namely the meditative process of inner apprehension and comparison — into an outer portrayal, and eventually on to the written page. But this was not without its trials.

Sometimes, by way of experimentation, we would read mirrored sections of the play together. One person reading a line of the forward moving text and the other reading its mirrored line in backward moving text (thus reading up the page) and so on, through the relevant sections.

As we read large sections of text in this way, carefully comparing the mirrored lines, the process of simply reading a page of text from top to bottom became a gratifying and welcome experience! For Sylvia these mirrored play-lines could be experienced with remarkable richness; they could be pictured, felt, heard and it seemed almost as if they could be 'tasted' next to each other, for this was how Sylvia experienced a Shakespeare play. A deeply meditative inner listening was involved, combined with an unfaltering and complete memory of the play, line by line from beginning to end. It must be emphasized that this complete memory of *Macbeth* gave Sylvia a unique basis for delving into its wisdom in a most extraordinary and fruitful way. For those who met Sylvia during her lectures or workshops, this intimate familiarity with a Shakespearean play was a striking keynote; regarding *Macbeth* it was nothing less than astonishing.

Biographically it is interesting to look again at the way in which this strong relationship with *Macbeth* began. Surprisingly, it was not through the acting profession, with its rigour of learning lines, but rather within the discipline of teaching English literature. The challenge was of introducing and bringing alive the 'pearls' of Shakespeare to a group of rowdy teenage boys in the Midlands.[1] For Sylvia's future studies, it was a remarkable moment of destiny when she chose the 'Banqueting Scene' in *Macbeth* as the part that the boys should study and perhaps, if they were up to it, present as a little performance. In the event, all manner of difficulties arose as the boys grappled with the unfamiliar language of the text. Furthermore, as Sylvia read, matters were not made any easier by the inevitable transition of attention from lads to text. There was only one answer and that was for Sylvia to learn the scene by heart and thus be able to deliver its lines with maximum eye contact on the sanguine listeners, and with the full effect of delivery. This approach, apart from succeeding in its initial pedagogical goal, also set something of a precedent; for it was during this episode of learning by heart that the possible geometrical significance of those crucial lines — 'Both sides are even, / Here I sit i'the midst' — first appeared intriguing to Sylvia.

After her teaching stint finished, the fascination for these play lines and the momentum of penetrating the whole play intensified. First of all it was scene symmetry (a phenomenon already studied by Sylvia in connection with Shakespeare's *Merchant of Venice),* which was of interest. Later it became the investigation of play and act symmetry, a development made possible by Sylvia discovering the extraordinary significance of the layout of text in the First Folio of 1623.

Quite naturally, the process of committing text to memory always accompanied the study of symmetrical play lines, and gradually the whole text began to live so completely in Sylvia's inner life of imagination that it assumed the character of inner architecture. Not only did the play live in time, it also came alive as a spatial entity. It was my experience, and that of others who studied alongside her, that this way of appreciating a Shakespeare play became for her a 'faculty.' She could *see* how one part of the form of the play related to other parts, within a whole. It is not going too far to say that Sylvia inhabited *Macbeth*, lived within it, as one can live within the architectural space of a building.

It was clear that there would be particular challenges in rendering such experience into the written word; translating things pictured into things described. It was also evident that some of the aspects of Sylvia's book would make strenuous demands on the reader, for the challenge in the reading would be to glean from the written word the experience of standing pictorially and imaginatively within the 'architecture' of the play.

This phenomenon of experiencing a work of art that lives in time, as something which may also be glimpsed spatially, as a kind of tableau, an all-at-once comprehension, is not unique. Perhaps we are looking at a gift similar to that possessed by Mozart, one that enabled him to take hold of a whole piece of music in his imagination prior to it being rendered into the stream of time and written down. At the time he was working on the opera, *Don Giovanni* he wrote:

> In my imagination, I don't hear the passage of the work, one thing following the other, but I do have the whole thing in a block, to put it in such terms. That is a delight. The invention, the elaboration, all this for me is like a magnificent and grandiose dream, but when I come to superintend the whole thus assembled – that is the best moment. How is it that I don't forget it like a dream? It is perhaps the greatest gift for which I have to thank the Creator!

Naturally, we are led from here to thoughts concerning the creativity of

10. A WORK IN PROGRESS

Shakespeare himself and the question: how is it that the playwright could create such beautiful works and at the same time incorporate the demands of a threefold symmetry; play symmetry, act symmetry and scene symmetry? Furthermore, we can't ignore the opening up of further challenging implications and questions that bear upon the very nature of creative intelligence and creative genius. What really is the nature of these geometrical picture forms which embrace a *Macbeth* or *Hamlet?* Are they devised solely by human artifice, by the human mind? And the 'music' that Mozart perceived in its completeness, how did it appear to him?

To see a work of art against the backdrop of a geometrical aesthetic is something we can well appreciate; it is certainly not merely a fanciful idea. Nature herself is companioned invariably by her handmaidens — Geometry and Mathematics. We need only look at the many examples of golden section spirals found in the natural world, so strikingly evident in the chambered nautilus shell and the arrangement of florets in the head of a sunflower. The complex and far-reaching wisdom embodied in the field of geometry of the 'Mandelbrot Set' — whose astonishing forms were discoered by Benoit Mandelbrot in 1980 — or the simple beauty of the snowflake's form may fill us with awe and fascination. It seems that these 'handmaidens' are present in all that bears the quality of beauty and completeness, in all that feels 'right.' When the artist discovers in the act of creating that the thing fashioned seems 'meant to be there,' like a creation of Nature, Geometry and Number are not far distant. Their presence can be characterized as faithful companions rather than forced guests! This was openly attested to in the teachings of the ancient philosophers:

> Numbers are the source of form and energy in the world.
> They are dynamic and active even among themselves ...
> almost human in their capacity of mutual influence.
> Theon of Smyrna

When Plato wrote 'All is arranged according to number,' he was drawing upon insight that had its source in a far more ancient teaching, as was Heraclitus when, in those beautiful words, 'Man is the measure of all things,' he saw the mystery and stature of Man within the context of the great world; the macrocosm. An ancient Egyptian inscription shows how the divinity of number was revered. The words are uttered by the ibis-headed god of reckoning, Thoth:

> I am the One which transforms into Two
> I am the Two which transforms into Four
> I am the Four which transforms into Eight
> After all this, I am One.

The incorporation of number/geometrical wisdom within the great architectural works of mankind is of course well known. When we look to ancient Greek civilization, we know that the Parthenon incorporated the harmonious proportion of the golden section. The Parthenon was dedicated in 438 BC and served subsequently as a model for later Greek constructions. Going back to an earlier time, however, one can also see how the Great Pyramid of Giza is a treasure house of geometrical wisdom; a perfect embodiment on the earth, of the divine as it was witnessed in geometrical law. Among the many geometrical attributes of the Great Pyramid we can mention two examples. The first, that the square of the height has an area precisely equal to that of each of the faces. The second, that the golden section (1.618) is found when we look at the height of each face (that is, from base centre to apex), in relation to that of half the base. Finally, when we consider that the five regular solids, the Platonic solids, were revered as far back as the Neolithic times (as shown by the discovery of these solids within stone circles in Aberdeenshire, Scotland), and that complex vesica-based designs formed the ground plans of so many of the stone circles (the so called 'flattened circles') found in the British Isles, we cannot but sense that we stand before a great and far reaching mystery when we consider the relationship that has long existed between human artistic/religious endeavour and the world of Geometry and Number.

In looking at the art of Shakespeare, through Sylvia's discovery of the geometrical structure of *Macbeth*, we have at the centre of our gaze primarily the literary and dramatic arts of the Renaissance. We shall, however, be able to draw more closely to these arts only by attempting first of all to appreciate the major traditions of the past that have worked with, and revered, the mysteries of Rhythm and Number. These traditions form important elements of background for the creative impulses of Shakespeare's time.

> Not without cause is it said that all things, which consist
> of contraries, are conjoined and composed by a certain

> harmony. For harmony is the joining together of several
> things and the consent of contraries.   Boethius

It is fascinating to study the way in which consciousness of Geometrical/Number wisdom has changed and developed through the ages; to see how it has been embedded within artists' work, and how this consciousness has itself featured at the great turning points in the development of mankind.

In Kristin Rygg's recent book, *The Masqued Mysteries Unmasked (Pythagoreanism and Early Modern North European Music Theatre),* the author shows how the 'Mysteries' of Geometry, Number and Music welled up and fructified the cultures of past ages. She gives a beautiful description of the life and teaching of Pythagorus, and of the nature of Pythagorean wisdom as it filtered through as a guiding impulse in that great turning point in scientific and cultural life, which we call the Renaissance.

> What was it, then, that met the Renaissance in the shape of Pythagoreanism? For the modern human being of the 20th century Pythagoras is known primarily as a mathematician (in the modern sense of the word); for the more illumined perhaps also as the founder of numerology and musicology and the originator of the concept 'philosopher.'
>
> Our own rational way of thinking has perhaps prevented us from seeing the obvious, i.e. that the Pythagorean school first and foremost was a mystery school, with the initiation of each human being as the purpose of its structures, learning and activities. The ultimate aim of initiation was to promote the pilgrimage of mankind, enabling the human race eventually to regain its rightful access to the divine realm. Every pursuit was secondary to that end, but also designed to accomplish it ...[2]

It is fascinating to consider why certain great personalities of the Renaissance felt such a deep interest and connection with the Platonists and Pythagoreans. For instance, Marsilio Ficino (born 1433) was tremendously influential in developing a culture for these schools of learning in mainland Europe. Under the patronage of the powerful Cosimo de Medici, Ficino made the first translation into a European language of the complete works of Plato. In 1462, he was also head of the Platonic Academy of Florence. It was within this academy that the teachings of Pythagorus were re-awakened, as they had been awakened previously in the teachings of Plato's original Athenian academy. It was as if there lived in Ficino a deep wish to restore a Golden Age for humanity, where the arts were permeated with the light of the divine mysteries, enhanced and taken further through the advent of Christianity.

> Our century, like a golden age, restored to light the liberal arts that were nearly extinct: grammar, poetry, painting, sculpture, architecture, music, the ancient performance of song with the Orphic Lyre, and all that in Florence.
> Marsilio Ficino[3]

In England there were also those inspired by the golden age of the divine mysteries, but the cultivation of their renaissance needed to take place more cautiously, more secretly. The main reason for this was that cultural and religious life in these Isles was watched closely, one could even say 'policed,' by officers of a strong Puritan faction within English politics. Those suspected of heresy were interrogated; mysterious deaths were commonplace.

At the beginning of the seventeenth century, however, came a most remarkable development. Between 1605 and 1631, one inspired individual, Ben Jonson (1572–1637), he was in charge of the development of music theatre in England; the Elizabethan and Jacobean Court Masque. His close colleague, the architect and designer Inigo Jones, was resposible for designing the scenery, costumes, stage machinery and so on, for Ben Jonson's creations. Jonson had a close affinity, and dedication, to Pythagoreanism and, as Kristin Rygg demonstrates, there was certainly a strong impulse on his part to incorporate these mysteries into the contemporary form of the Court Masque. When we come to Shakespeare, therefore, it is of great interest to consider if these affinities were also present, as well as to see the extent to which Number and Geometry were represented in his impulses of creativity.

Looking once more at the prefatorial material of the First Folio we can return to those remarkable lines in the 'Address to the Great Variety of Readers' :

10. A WORK IN PROGRESS

> ... as where (before) you were abus'd with diverse
> stolne, and surreptitious copies, maimed, and deformed
> by the frauds and stealthes of iniurious impostors, that
> expos'd them: even those, and now offer'd to your view
> cur'd, and perfect in their limbes; and all the rest, abso-
> lute in their numbers, as he conceived thé.

Of course the significance of these words not only bears reference to Shakespeare's fount of creativity, but also lets us know that there were others who, with painstaking dedication, wished to make sure that the text of the plays was handed down to us in perfect numerical structure. The production of the First Folio of 1623 was a tremendous task needing the efforts of skilled artisans who carried a common aim. Is it not going too far to propose that this common aim had a Pythagorean signature, one might even say a Rosicrucian signature — something which Sylvia always considered very seriously, as we shall see at the end of this chapter. However, the 'Address to the Great Variety of Readers' is not the only reference which may be of interest to us, for when we read the poem by Ben Jonson, 'To the memory of my beloved, the Author,' also in the preface to the 1623 First Folio, we come upon a direct reference to the wellspring out of which the true poet creates:

> ... *Thy Art,*
> *My gentle Shakespeare, must enjoy a part;*
> *For though the Poets matter, Nature be,*
> *His Art doth give the fashion. And, that he,*
> *Who casts to write a living line, must sweat,*
> *(Such as thine are) and strike the second heat*
> *Upon the Muses anvile : turne the same,*
> *(And himselfe with it) that he thinkes to frame;*
> *Or for the lawrell, he may gaine a scorne,*
> *For a good Poet's made, as well as borne.*
> *And such wert thou ...*

These intriguing lines capture the essence of true poetic creativity. In one direction the poet may turn to Nature and find therein the 'sub-stance' to be worked upon and transformed; the 'raw material' of the alchemist. However, his art, as fashioner, requires something more in order that the living line may be cast. For this, he must, '*strike the second heat / Upon the Muses anvile'* and in the process, *'turne the same, / (And himselfe with it) that he thinkes to frame.'* Surely this is the process of transformation, wherein the inner life of the questing poet (or artist / alchemist) begins to become 'transparent' for the inspired creative powers; that is, the 'Divine Wedding' of the alchemists. Here the inner questing of the poet *meets with the intelligences that speak the Divine into the 'living line.'* It is interesting to note that this activity involves 'turning.' Here, therefore, we have Ben Jonson describing Shakespeare's striking of the second heat of creativity as a process of 'turning' and, of course, we may note that this is also the very movement so beautifully embraced by the 'play-figures.' Sylvia was convinced that there was much to be uncovered by investigating all the prefatorial material of the First Folio: the Address, Droushout picture and poems by Ben Jonson and others.

Sylvia was intrigued by the images and references to the play-figure, which could be discerned in the text of the First Folio. For instance, in *Macbeth* Act 1 Scene 5, we have Lady Macbeth advising her husband and evoking for him a most powerful image concerning how he should bear himself to the world, while at the same time masking the intent that is worming through his soul.

> Your Face, my *Thane*, is as a Booke, where men
> May reade strange matters, to beguile the time.
> Looke like the time, beare welcome in your Eye,
> Your Hand, your Tongue: looke like th' innocent flower,
> But be the Serpent vnder't...   (1, 4)

In the words, 'Look like the innocent flower, but be the serpent under it,' Sylvia perceived an image impression of the 'figure,' which she described in the following way: 'This is a lovely picture of the figure actually: the whole shape looks like the flower but the serpent under it is the 'time-stream,' which goes on and on, coiled like a serpent.'

She was also sure that the word 'feast,' used so frequently in *Macbeth* often referred to the figure as the receptacle of numerical abundance,

> *Lady.* My Royall Lord,
> You do not giue the Cheere, the Feast is sold
> That is not often vouch'd, while 'tis a making:[4]   (3, 4)

10. A WORK IN PROGRESS

And she felt that the following description in *Hamlet* was also a poignant reference to the figure for that play:

> *Ros.* The single
> and peculiar life is bound
> With all the strength and armour of the minde,
> To keepe it self from noyance: but much more,
> That Spirit, vpon whose spirit depends and rests
> The liues of many, the cease of maiestie
> Dies not alone; but like a Gulfe doth draw
> What's neere it, with it. It is a massie wheele
> Fixt on the somnet of the highest Mount,
> To whose huge Spoakes, ten thousand lesser things
> Are mortiz'd and adioyn'd ...
>
> *Hamlet* (3, 3)

At this point we should now turn to the main theme of the chapter and investigate some of the geometrical attributes of the figure not described elsewhere in this book. These will further our understanding of how it is possible to extend our use of the figure beyond its more obvious application with regard to play, act and scene symmetry. For if the figure of a play is indeed truthfully, and accurately, drawn it should represent in all its forms the nature of the play of which it is the basis.

Sylvia used each play figure as a tool of research for gaining clues about the nature of the Shakespeare play in question, and for affirming and supporting the interpretation. To give an initial impression of this, we will look first of all at a small project that she undertook as part of her investigation into the existence and fate of Lady Macbeth's child (see Chapter 9). In essence, it is an investigation of act and scene symmetry within Act 2 of *Macbeth* but the interconnectedness of act and scene symmetry is so synchronised that this synchronicity itself is a focus of delight and interest.

In Figure 32, A shows symmetry in Act 2 Scene 2. Line 17 reads: '*Macb.* I haue done the deed:.' Scene line 17- reads 'The multitudinous Seas incarnadine,'

> 19-   Will all great Neptunes Ocean wash this blood
> 18-   Cleane from my Hand? no: this my Hand will rather

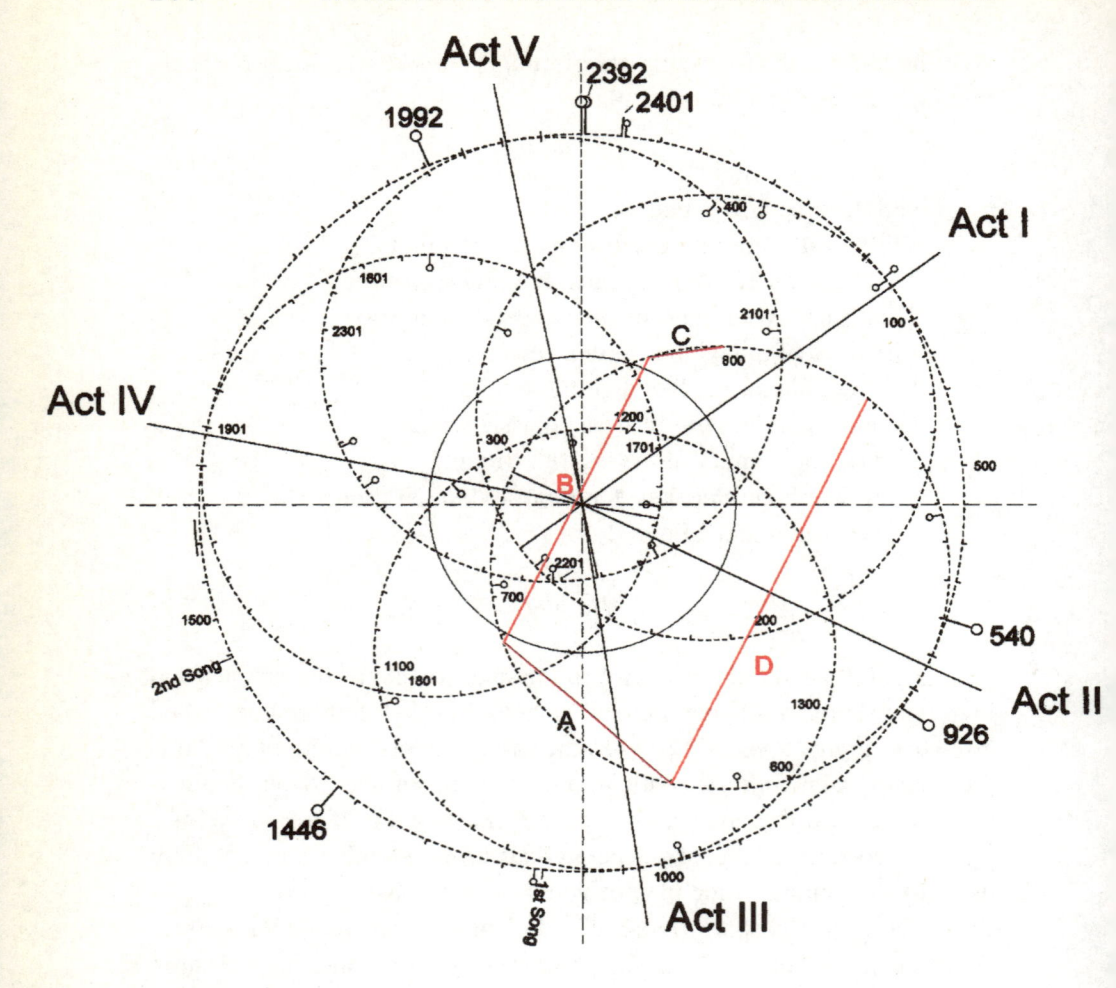

Figure 32 (Mirrors to the child)

                17-   The multitudinous Seas incarnardine,
(act line 148)   16-   Making the Greene one, Red.

There is a link between these mirrored lines which can reinforce the impression that Macbeth has slain the child, the 'Green one.' (see Chapter 9).

'B' connects with 'A' (one line difference) at act-line 148 and we see this mirrored in the act by act-line 148-. We are, therefore, given a con-

10. A WORK IN PROGRESS

nection between the line, 'Making the Greene one, Red,' and a new line, 'The Life o'th Building,'

> 150- Most sacrilegious Murther hath broke ope
> 149- The Lords anoynted Temple, and stole thence
> 148- The Life o'th' Building.

Here Macduff is announcing a death but we do not definitely know whose; it could be an announcement of the child's death just as well as that of the king's!

'C,' through scene symmetry of Scene 3, links the line, 'The Life o'th Building' (scene line 95-) with line 95, 'Would murther as it fell:'

> 92   *Macd*. O gentle Lady,
> 93   'Tis' not for you to heare what I can speake:
> 94   The repetition in a Womans eare,
> 95   Would murther as it fell.

'D' reveals the mirrored connection of line 297: 'Looke to the Lady' (this is the point where Sylvia is sure that Lady Macbeth falters because it dawns on her that Macbeth has slain her child as well as Duncan) with line 297-: '*Macb*. I haue done the deed.'

Sylvia's own description of these interconnections is as follows:

> The connections of all the references to the child in Act 2 are related to one another in a most charming way. Every single one that I looked up, where it seemed there was evidence of the child, related to another one. I more or less went round looking up all of what I thought were the significant points. I started firstly where Macbeth is saying, 'I haue done the deed' as he staggers down the steps and this becomes relevant to both deeds later on. And that is directly related to 'this my Hand will rather / The multitudinous Seas incarnardine,/ Making the Greene one, Red.' (In fact it is one line behind). 'Making the Greene one, Red,' is symmetrical across the Act to that moment when Macduff has just come in crying 'O Horror, Horror, Horror,' and goes on, 'Most sacrilegious Murther hath broke ope / The Lords anoynted Temple, and stole thence /

The Life o'th' Building.' 'The Life o'th' Building' matches 'Making the Greene one, Red,' and, of course, everything they say at that point is completely ambiguous; it's just the announcement of a murder. But when Lennox says, 'Meane you his Maiestie?' he never answers; he actually says, 'Approch the Chamber, and destroy your sight / With a new *Gorgon*.' and everything he has said before that could just as well apply to the child. Then the next thing is that Lady Macbeth says 'What's the Businesse?' and Macduff says, 'O gentle Lady, / Tis not for you to heare what I can speake: / The repetition in a Womans eare, / Would murther as it fell.' To me this has always been a picture of the child being hurled downwards onto the rocks.

While working on the prose in *Macbeth,* but looking particularly at the relationship of the prose in Act 1 Scene 5 with the prose in Act 5 Scene 1, Sylvia recounted an interesting observation. What she had to say described a phenomenon she had experienced before in working with play 'figures,' and which she called 'proximity.' This is where play lines, as they run close to each other on the 'figure,' take up some similar qualities, words and themes. She drew my attention to the paths of Act 1 Scene 5 and Act 5 Scene 1 on the figure and the way they run close to each other, converge and then cross. Here the themes, as touched upon in the chapter on play symmetry, are very closely linked. Act 1 Scene 5. opens with Lady Macbeth reading the letter sent by her husband, announcing the imminent arrival of King Duncan to their castle. It continues with that galvanising of murderous intent towards Duncan, which reaches its peak in the terrifying invocation of evil. There is such desperation in Lady Macbeth regarding the destruction of Duncan that she is willing to put aside all access to her womanly compassion and humanity and become the tool of 'murth'ring Ministers.' Yet when we read Sylvia's exposition on this we know why, and may begin to feel a sympathetic understanding. Towards the end of the scene Macbeth arrives and becomes party to Lady Macbeth's intent with nodding approval.

Act 5 Scene 1 is the 'Sleepwalking Scene.' Mostly in prose, it gives us the last opportunity of seeing Lady Macbeth; now a 'vacated' being drifting in a sea of fragmentary memories too horrific to apprehend in their entirety. She appears to us now as the wasted tool of those same powers which she invoked in Act 1 Scene 5, at the play-mirror. The reciprocal relationship between these sections of the play — Act 1 Scene V and Act 5 Scene 1 — has been touched upon in Chapter 5, but it is interesting to see this relationship of cause and effect also borne out by the 'proximity' of curves on the 'figure.'

A second illustration of 'proximity' quoted by Sylvia appears later, where lines 507-512, (Act 1) move close to lines 867-873 (Act 2). Sylvia described the relationship of these sections in the following way:

> In this region is the place where Lady Macbeth says,
> > I haue giuen Sucke, and know
> > How tender 'tis to loue the Babe that milkes me,
> > I would, while it was smyling in my Face,
> > Haue pluckt my Nipple from his Bonelesse Gummes,
> > And dasht the Braines out, had I so sworne
> > As you haue done to this.
>
> Act 2 (863-873), is where the two sons of Duncan are just about to flee and one of them says: 'The near in blood, the nearer bloody'(line 867) and it never occurred to me before that there seems to be a connection between this horrible implication of Lady Macbeth and this idea: the 'near in blood.' The 'near in blood' are indeed half brothers to the child Glaucos, so it could be a perfectly relevant comment. This is another example of the proximity of the curve.' (See Figure 33)

These are the only references Sylvia made to me about the phenomenon of 'proximity,' but they give us a further clue as to how she investigated the 'figure,' questioned it for its life and meaning, and used it to affirm and reinforce ideas regarding the text.

Looking at all the prose sections in *Macbeth*, Sylvia suggested that we might outline on the figure where they are placed, to see how they relate visually one to the other. When we looked at the result, it appealed enormously in its beauty; the forms appearing like an eloquent sketch of a dance sequence, where the first two prose sections move upwards from left to right, and the second two sections gesture in the same direction but this time downwards. Here we are looking at movement in time that is now stilled and mapped out spatially (see Figure 34).

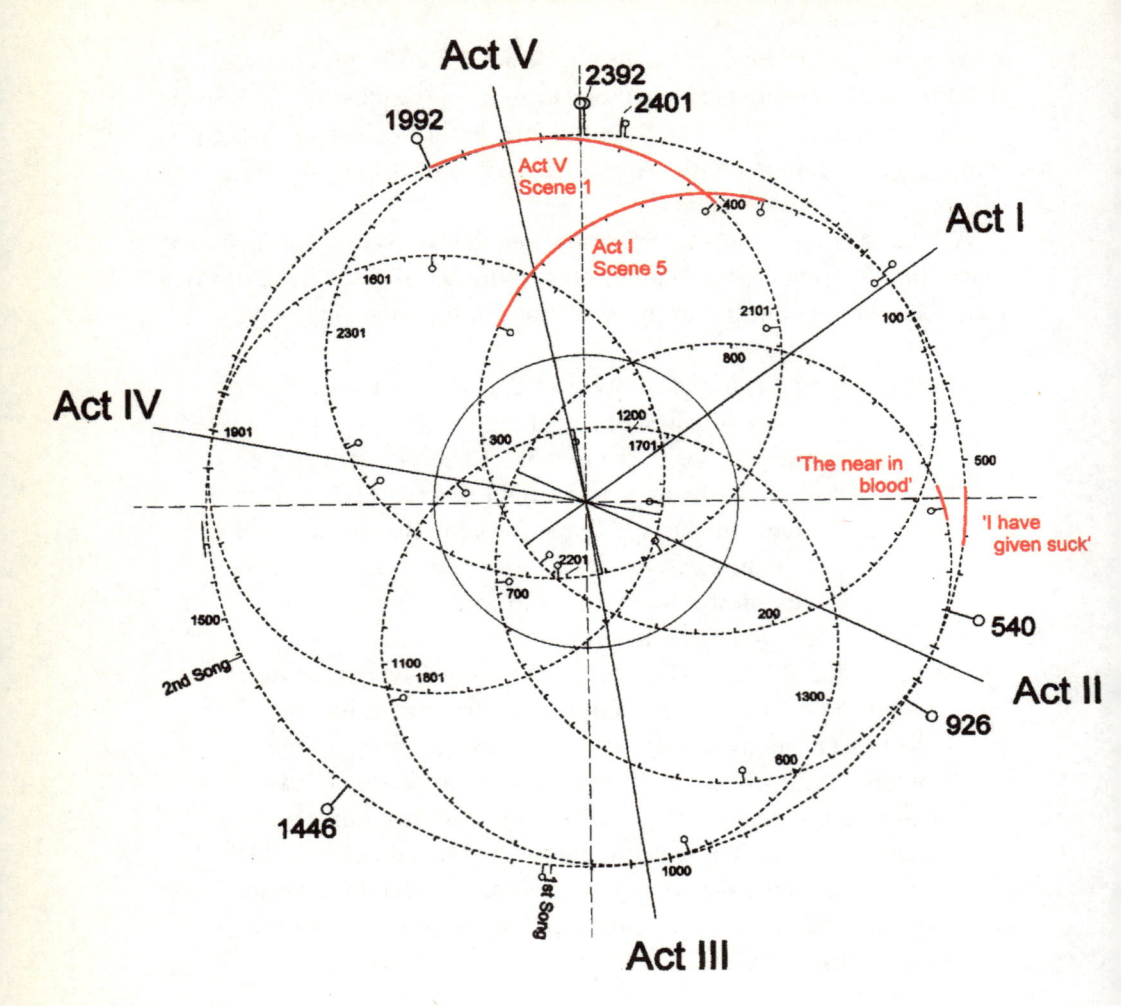

212 NUMBER AND GEOMETRY IN SHAKESPEARE'S *MACBETH*

Figure 33. Examples of 'Proximity'

A discovery, which Sylvia made a long while ago, was that if you draw a line from the point on the figure — where the first witch is making her curse: 'Sleepe shall neyther Night nor Day / Hang vpon his Pent-house Lid' (Act 1, scene 3, line 107) — and extend it so that it passes through the geometrical centre of Act 2 and meets the Act 2 circle once again on the far side, it reaches the place where the first effect of this curse is actually taking effect:

10. A WORK IN PROGRESS   213

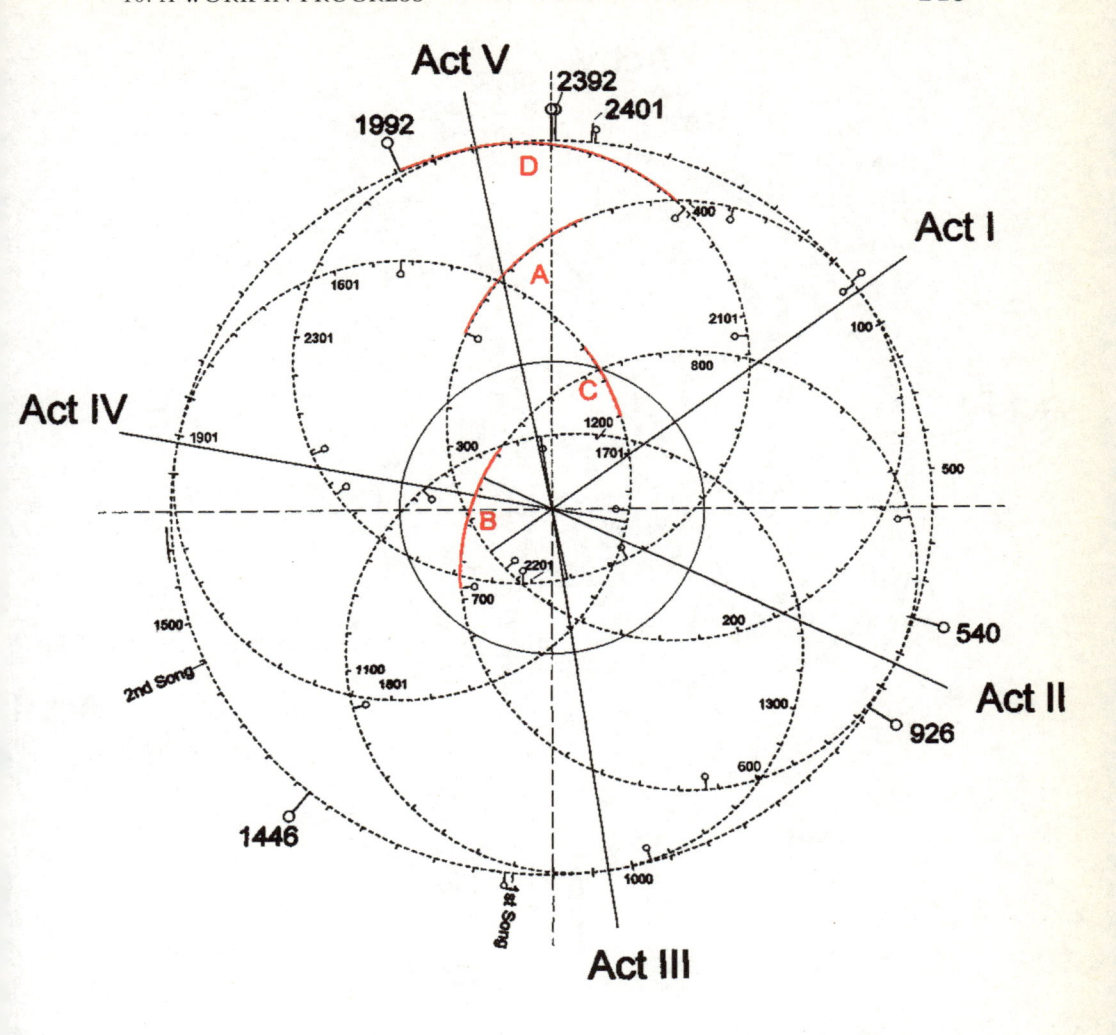

Figure 34. The arrangement of Prose in Macbeth. **A** *Reading of the letter.*
B *Porter's speech.* **C** *Lady Macduff with her son.* **D** *Sleep-walking episode.*

    656   *Macb.* Me thought I heard a voyce cry, Sleep no more:
    657   Macbeth does murther Sleepe, the innocent Sleepe,
    658   Sleepe that knits vp the rauel'd Sleeue of Care,
    659   The death of each dayes Life, sore Labors Bath,
    660   Balme of hurt Mindes, great Natures second Course,
    661   Chiefe nourisher in Life's Feast.

(See Figure 35)

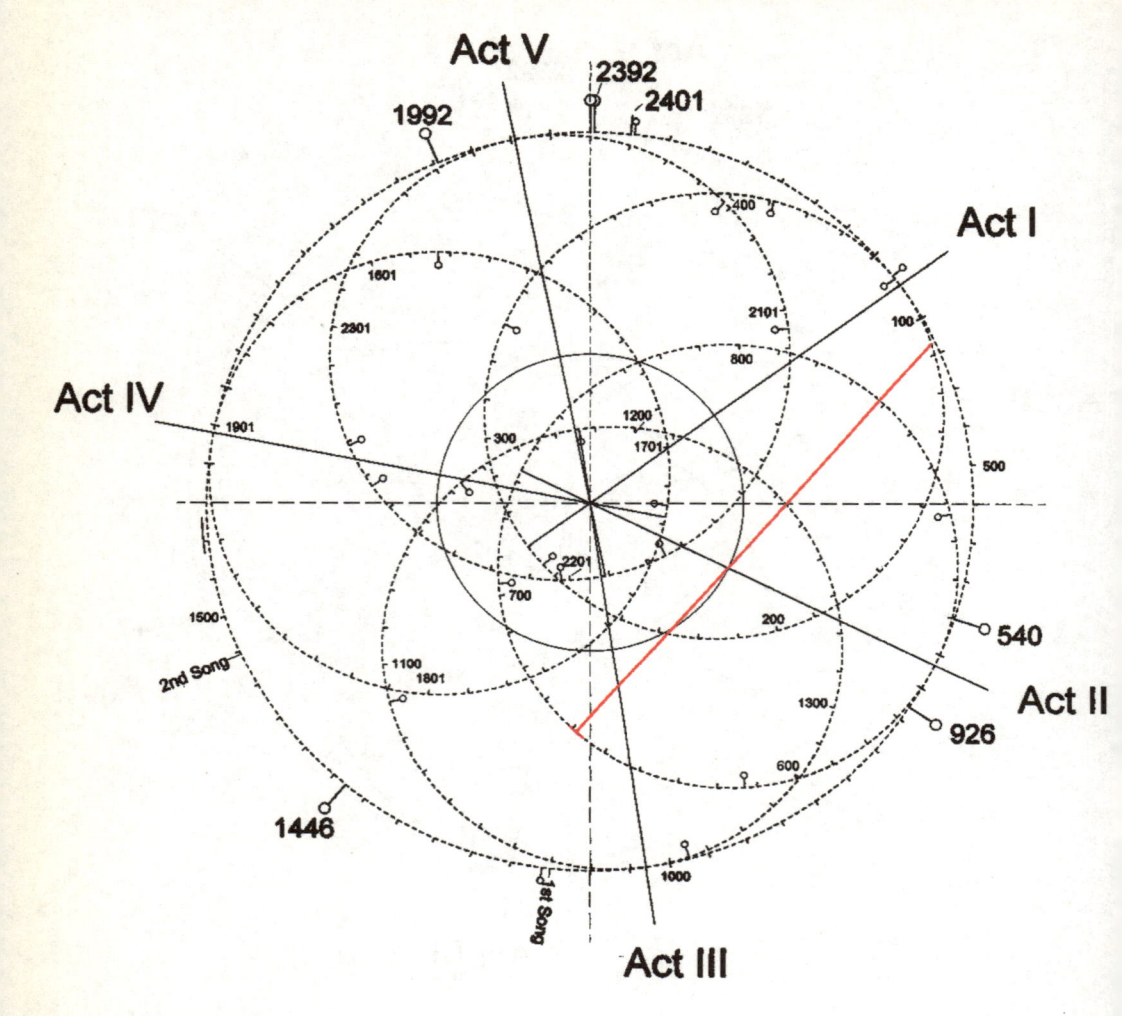

Figure 35.

A second observation of Sylvia's originates at line 397: *Lady*. O neuer, / (Shall Sunne that Morrow see.) This is the position where Lady Macbeth first reveals to Macbeth the purposeful intent towards Duncan's murder. When we extend a line from 397 and take it once more through the centre of Act 2's circle so that it meets the circle, we are again surprised to discover the nature of the section of the play to which it points (see Figure 36).

      614   *La*. That which hath made thê drunk, hath made me bold:
      615   What hath quench'd them, hath giuen me fire.

10. A WORK IN PROGRESS

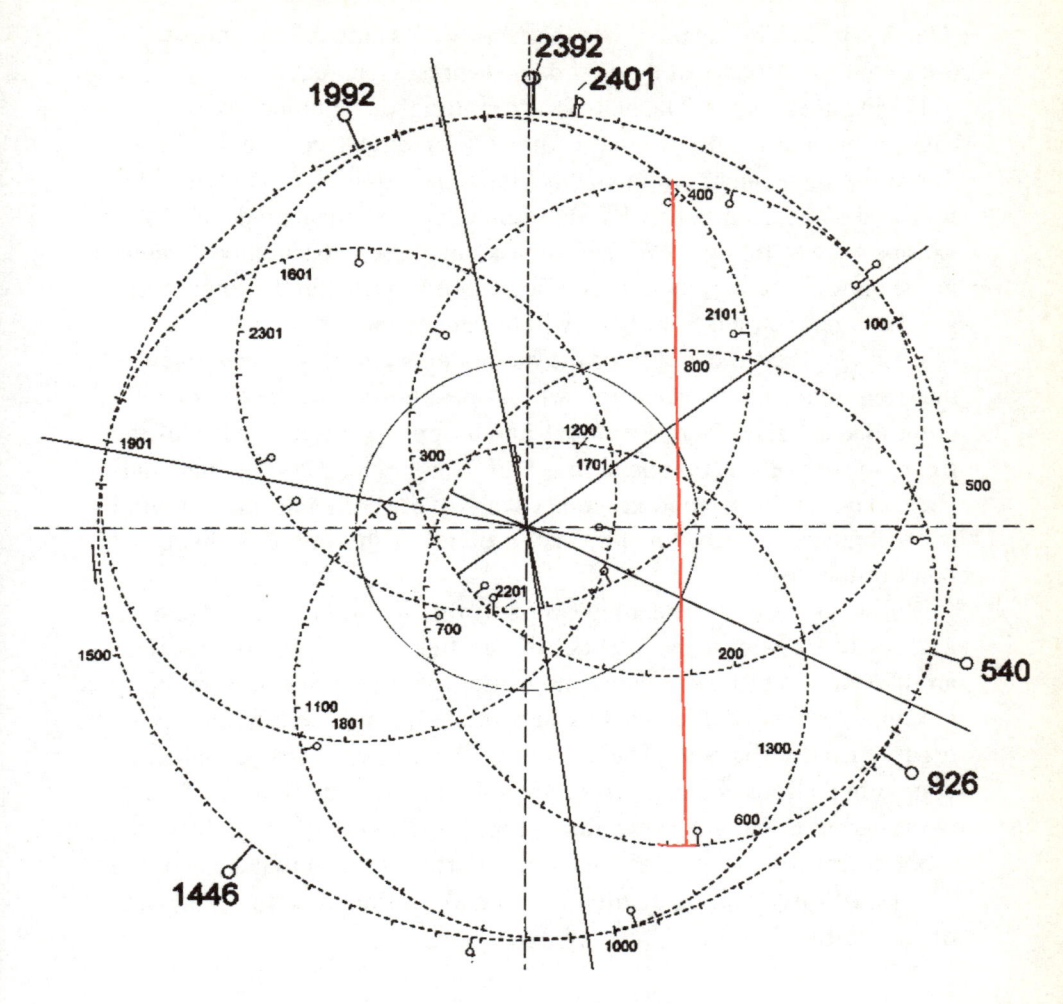

Figure 36

616	Hearke, peace: it was the Owle that shriek'd,
617	The fatall Bell-man, which giues the stern'st good-night.
618	He is about it, the Doores are open:
619	And the surfeted Groomes doe mock their charge
620	With Snores. I haue drugg'd their Possets,
621	That Death and Nature doe contend about them,
622	Whether they liue, or dye.

This is the very section of the play in which Macbeth is committing the murder, the destruction of King Duncan. The line that is intersected is

'Hearke, peace: it was the Owle that shriek'd,' which one discerns to be the actual moment when the first dagger thrust is made.

During these lines Macbeth is committing the murder his wife so eagerly desired. Thus, we see a direct geometrical connection in the figure between intent and actuality; the expression of a powerful idea followed by an exact result. Sylvia's remarks in reference to these observations were as follows: 'We have to ask, are these two situations unique in the play, or are they examples of a general law (that in the figure there will be a geometrical link) from will to later event?'

Coming close to the core of the human mystery of *Macbeth*, we can question another important geometrical position — the 'nadir' or low-point of the figure. Here a vertical line dropped from the centre of the figure meets the great circle at line 1380 (see Figure 37). The line reads 'Ile catch it ere it come to ground.' Clearly we see the marriage of word and geometrical form, for the very 'ground' of the figure is this exact point of the nadir.

But what about the meaning? What is this section of the play pointing out to us within the 'dance' of the figure? A study of the lines around this point proves most interesting. In Act 3 Scene 5 an angry Hecate is rebuking the witches and preparing to use her own powers to ensnare Macbeth. The section is charged with sexual innuendo containing strong images of procreational, seminal powers. Hecate is preparing to catch 'a vap'rous drop, profound,' as it falls from the moon towards the centre of the earth. Shortly, she will make use of the essense of this drop, its distillation, to make a final assault on the soul of Macbeth:

1378	Vpon the Corner of the Moone
1379	There hangs a vap'rous drop, profound,
1380	Ile catch it ere it come to ground;
1381	And that distill'd by Magicke slights,
1382	Shall raise such Artificiall Sprights,
1383	As by the strength of their illusion,
1384	Shall draw him on to his Confusion.
1385	He shall spurne Fate, scorne Death, and beare
1386	His hopes 'boue Wisedome, Grace, and Feare:
1387	And you all know, Security
1388	Is Mortals cheefest Enemie.

Musicke, and a Song.

10. A WORK IN PROGRESS

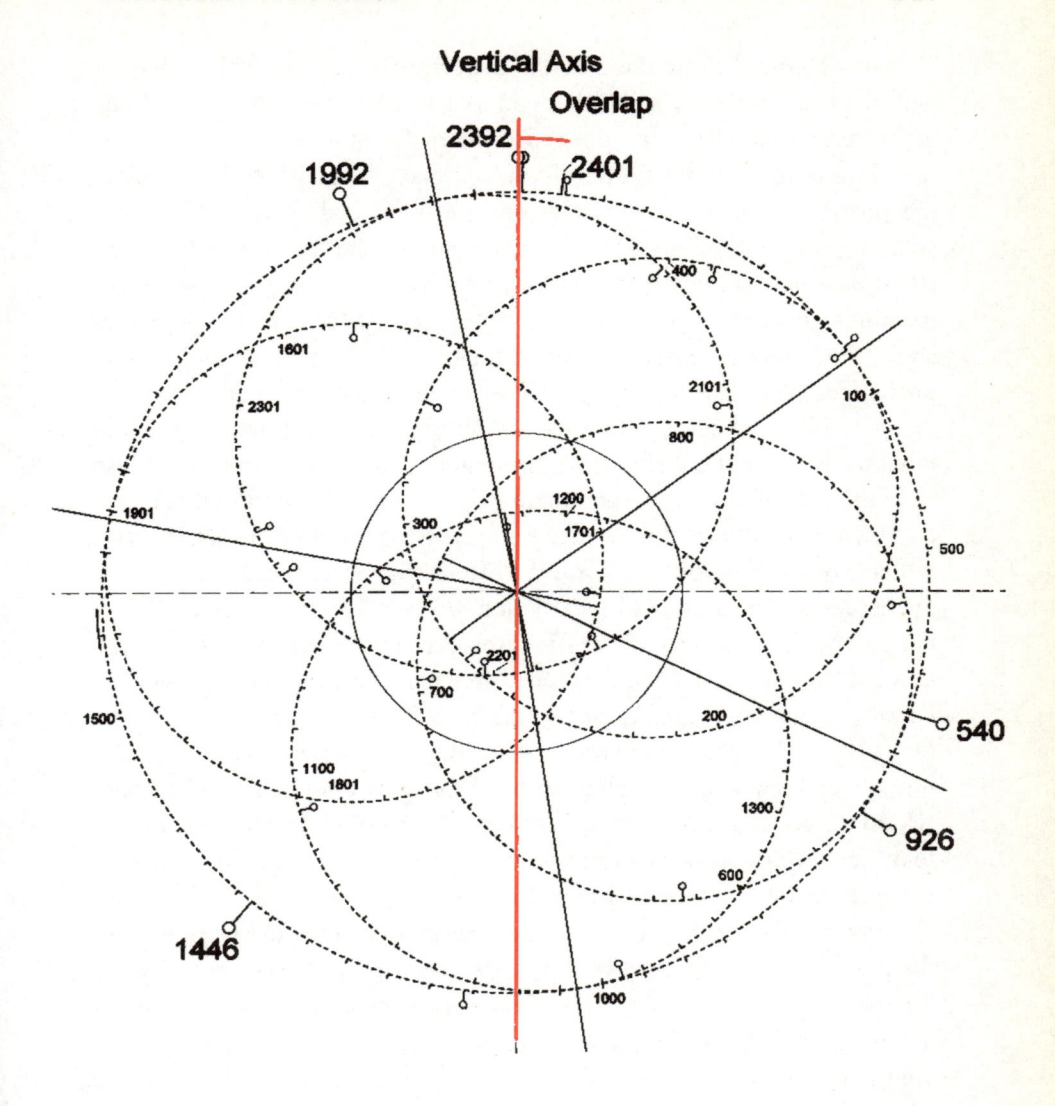

Figure 37. The vertical axis and overlap in the Macbeth 'figure.'

1389	Hearke, I am call'd: my little Spirit see
1390	Sits in Foggy cloud, and stayes for me.
	Sing within. Come away, come away, &c.
1391	1 Come, let's make hast, shee'l soone be
1392	Backe againe. *Exeunt.*

This link in space, from the moon to the centre of the earth, along whose path the profound drop will fall, is an axis often referred to in traditions of esoteric cosmology in connection with the human being's maturation as a citizen of the Earth. Upon this axis, a human being acquires the possibility of achieving self-consciousness and 'egohood.' Yet, in standing fully within all that this axis signifies, the meeting with a centre of destruction, with evil, cannot be avoided; indeed it is a necessary meeting. This rendezvous with our own potential for evil brings us into a realm of great insight and risk; who can venture this path and remain unchanged? Yet, by engaging with the challenges of this path, this axis, the possibility of human freedom is wrested, and ultimately the path towards free moral development. Intimately connected with this we also have the role of sexual maturation and sexual potency. Within this manifold dynamic we are able to discern aspects of the field of action upon which *Macbeth* unfolds. In *Macbeth* it seems we are looking at some of the deepest mysteries of incarnation post 'fall from Paradise.' This, I am sure, is why, against all expectations, at the end of the play we can still identify with Macbeth; we can, perhaps, even forgive him. Harold Bloom, in his book, *Shakespeare, the Invention of the Human,* goes so far as to say 'The universal reaction to Macbeth is that we identify with him, or at least with his imagination.'[5] Later, Bloom goes further still: 'Hamlet's inwardness is an abyss; Lear's sufferings finally seem more than human; Macbeth is all too human. Despite Macbeth's violence, he is much closer to us than Hamlet and Lear.'[6]

Opposite the figure's nadir, at the very top, appears the beginning of the play. Let us remember, however, that the figure shows an overlap at this point — the beginning now becomes the end and the end becomes a new beginning. Looking closely at the significance of this overlap we are once more led towards the core of meaning, but now as the soul of Macbeth 'hovers' over the events at the end of the play, how is it being received, what is its new beginning? Sylvia said of this:

> There are a number of references in the play to the destiny of the human soul. As he creeps like Tarquin towards the murder of Duncan, Macbeth hears the bell and he says, 'Hear it not Duncan for it is a knell that summons thee to Heaven or to Hell.' Later, when he is about to have his friend Banquo murdered he says, 'Banquo, thy soul's flight, If it find heaven, must find it out tonight.' So it is

impossible not to wonder what Shakespeare thought of the destiny of Macbeth's own soul. At the beginning of the play we encounter Macbeth as a man of brave deeds. It is also clear from Lady Macbeth's words that his natural ambition is curbed by piety; that he does not want to murder Duncan. This man becomes transformed in the course of the play into a kind of murdering monster; his deeds culminate in the slaying of the entire Macduff family. Has Shakespeare consigned him to hell? Do we find any hint about this? I think we find it just here in this singular final overlap.

Early poems refer to the place where the soul first arrives after death as 'Whinney-moor,' a kind of waste place with pricking gorse bushes. In the words of Scene 1, there are three beings who intend to encounter Macbeth on a heath. In the opening scene of the play the First Witch is not asking the other two for information, she is conducting a catechism; do they know the plan by heart? Have they got it clear what they have to do? A catechism has echoes of church ritual; of matters essential for the soul's salvation. It is, in fact, not difficult to imagine that this first scene is transformed into the last scene and that the three beings — the 1, 2 and 3 of the witches — become other beings, Angelic beings, perhaps, who encounter the soul of Macbeth after death. I have not been able to enter deeply into this conception, but the scene does feel like an experience in Purgatory rather than in the traditional Hell, and if we ask whether Macbeth, in traditional seventeenth-century terms, deserved that traditional Hell, I think the answer has to be no!

Sylvia was also intrigued by the idea that, after the death of Macbeth, in our imagination the three witches become the three Harpies, the storm goddesses — Aiello ('Howler'), Celaeno ('Screamer') and Ocypete ('Swift') — renowned for their role in 'snatching' away the soul of the newly-dead so that they may commence their sojourn in the afterlife. As an enhancement of the play's beginning this also suits the dynamic elemental atmosphere, the thunder, lightning and pouring rain, which we encountered there:

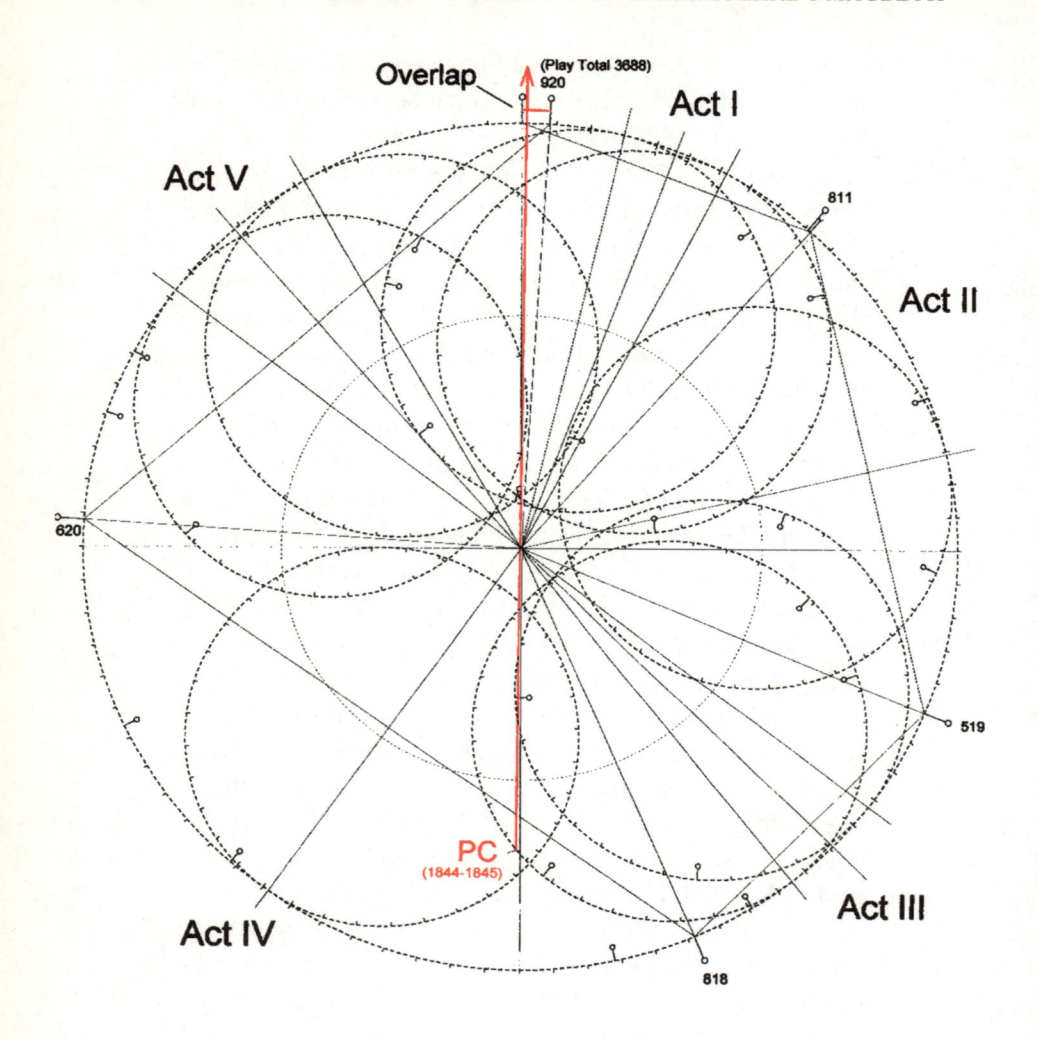

220   NUMBER AND GEOMETRY IN SHAKESPEARE'S *MACBETH*

Figure 38. The play centre and overlap of the Cymbeline 'figure.'

Thunder and Lightning. Enter three Witches.
    1   1. When shall we three meet againe?
    2   In Thunder, Lightning, or in Raine?
    3   2. When the Hurley-burley's done,
    4   When the Battaile's lost, and wonne.
    5   3. That will be ere the set of Sunne.
    6   1. Where the place?
    7   2. Vpon the Heath.

10. A WORK IN PROGRESS

<blockquote>

8   3. There to meet with *Macbeth*.
9   1. I come, *Gray-Malkin*.
10   *All. Padock* calls anon: faire is foule, and foule is faire,
11   Houer through the fogge and filthie ayre. *Exeunt*.

</blockquote>

As already noted by Sylvia in Chapter 2, these words can be seen as pointers to the end of the play; below, the trumpets sound and Malcolm's words resound with the power of acclaimed kingship. He is the man who destiny has now caught, and yet what of Macbeth? He is snatched by the ministering beings of another world, the world of the Spirit, who will lead him on to realms where his soul will be judged. Into the gates of the 'spirit land' enters one who was once a mediaeval king, the King of Scotland and, just as around Malcolm we hear the words 'Haile the King,' so we can imagine the call 'Haile the man!' around Macbeth. In a way the one event crowns the other at the place where the figure is crowned and displays its overlap — at its very summit. Although in the front space we hear of the crowning of a new king, behind this there is a potent gathering in the spirit world.[7]

In order to appreciate the vertical in a play's figure more fully we need to consider *Cymbeline,* the last play in the 1623 First Folio. Sylvia often worked on *Cymbeline*, yet hadn't created a figure until 1999, when we worked on it together as part of the preparation for a series of workshops.

Here too, in *Cymbeline*, the vertical line of the figure and the overlap reveal much that is interesting in connection with the play's essential inner meaning and direction. In *Cymbeline*, however, we notice an additional geometrical attribute in that the vertical line is *reinforced* by the positioning of the play centre. The play centre is actually placed very slightly to the left of the lower section of the vertical (see Figure 38).

Cymbeline is 3688 lines in length, a great deal longer than *Macbeth*. The lines at the centre of the play, lines 1844 and 1845, read as follows:

<blockquote>

A Conduct ouer Land, to Milford-Hauen.
Madam, all ioy befall your Grace, and you.   (3, 5)

</blockquote>

These two clearly-formed lines, are both spoken by the Roman General, Lucius, as he is about to take his leave from Cymbeline's court and bear to his master, the Emperor Augustus, news of the British refusal to pay the promised tribute; a deed forcing enmity and war between the two nations. The whole passage reads:

1828	*Cym.* Our Subiects (Sir)
1829	Will not endure his yoake; and for our selfe
1830	To shew lesse Soueraignty then they, must needs
1831	Appeare vn-Kinglike.
1832	*Luc.* So Sir: I desire of you
1833	A Conduct ouer Land, to Milford-Hauen.
1834	Madam, all ioy befall your Grace, and you.
1835	*Cym.* My Lords, you are appointed for that Office:
1836	The due of Honor, in no point omit:
1837	So farewell Noble *Lucius*.
1838	*Luc.* Your hand, my Lord.
1839	*Clot.* Receiue it friendly: but from this time forth
1840	I weare it as your Enemy.
1841	*Luc.* Sir, the Euent
1842	Is yet to name the winner. Fare you well.

When I first considered the words 'A Conduct ouer Land to Milford-Hauen ...' in relation to the figure, I felt immediately that I should investigate the direction from the play centre through the centre of the figure. It seemed fair to pick up the clue interpreting the first line of the play centre as 'Draw a line from here through the middle of the figure to the Mid-Heaven,' the highest point of the play-figure.

Once again, as in *Macbeth*, an overlap is reached but the particular line that is pointed to, line 2 of the play, commands our full attention:

    2   Our bloods no more obey the Heauens

I was intrigued to discover here that the word 'heavens' chimes out, echoing the word 'Haven' in the first line of the play centre, but what could be the significance of the words of this line, so subtly picked out?

The first scene of *Cymbeline* unfolds a dialogue between two gentlemen of Briton. It forms an extremely condensed synopsis of the context which will be unrolled and transformed during the course of the play. You could say it contains the 'raw material' of the play (the base substance of the Alchemist). The initial four lines are spoken by the First Gentleman, and their meaning is open to interpretation. In different editions of *Cymbeline* we find variations of punctuation as the editors have struggled to portray meaning in these somewhat ambiguous lines. However, the punctuation in the First Folio would seem correct and the resultant meaning significant.

> *Enter two Gentlemen.*
>   1. *Gent.*

1	You do not meet a man but Frownes.
2	Our bloods no more obey the Heauens
3	Then our Courtiers:
4	Still seeme, as do's the Kings.
5	2 *Gent.* But what's the matter?
6	1. His daughter, and the heire of's kingdome (whom
7	He purpos'd to his wiues sole Sonne, a Widdow
8	That late he married) hath referr'd her selfe
9	Vnto a poore, but worthy Gentleman. She's wedded,
10	Her Husband banish'd; she imprison'd, all
11	Is outward sorrow, though I thinke the King
12	Be touch'd at very heart.

The land is without vigour. A heaviness prevails and in the lives of people the pulse of the Heavens is not experienced. Even the King, Cymbeline, the one in whom the destiny and inspiration of his people resides, is out of touch. True spiritual sovereignty is blocked.

When we focus on line 2 alone — 'Our bloods no more obey the Heauens' — we are led to understand that at the heart of the play there will be a mystery concerning the faculty of man to sense the Divine through the blood; to bring alive once more the pulse of the Heavens into the pulse of man. It is a theme strongly developed throughout the course of the play yet one which we may only touch upon here as, in itself, it would form the basis of a further lengthy study.

In all the play figures that Sylvia discerned, there was always an overlap — the end always became a beginning and the beginning became an end. To our modern mind this circular configuration seems strange and yet, in the past, I am sure that this was a more familiar conception. This was explained beautifully by Walter Johannes Stein in connection with that great medieval work of German literature, *Parzival*, by Wolfram von Eschenbach:

As we read Wolfram's *Parzival*, we have the feeling that the opening chapters were written last, and this has been noticed by the commentators of Wolfram's *Parzival*. To obtain a complete survey of the poem, we must picture the sixteen adventures arranged diagrammatically in a circle, so that when the circle is complete the first adventure seems to be a continuation of the last. This kind of architecture will be found in all medieval writings; beginning and ending seems to be connected in a peculiar way, for example, Basilius Valentinus says, 'O beginning of the first beginning, remember the end, and end of the last end, remember the beginning, and allow the middle portion to be commended to you in all good faith. Thus will God the Father, Sun and Holy Spirit give unto you what you lack in Spirit, soul and body.[8]

Sylvia spoke of the geometrical play figures in a way that carried complete objectivity. In their construction she was always striving to render something which already existed and awaited discovery. She was at pains to state that these figures were not of her own invention; she had not *made* them, they were already there, intimately connected with the plays themselves. Once they were found a new chapter of investigation and discovery could begin and, at least in respect of *Macbeth*, this could open up new, radical directions of meaning. Sylvia was sure that the objective existence of the figures would one day be proven, not only as has been attempted here, through geometrical and literary analysis, but also through archaeological investigation. She was convinced that the figures were originally produced onto metal discs, at a time contemporary with Shakespeare himself. The means of their manufacture was certainly available due to the advances in the navigational sciences at that time, and the technical expertise, which had developed around the crafting, usually in brass, of accurate navigational instruments (see Plate 4). One such instrument, for instance, was the Mariner's Astrolabe, a device which, in some respects was not dissimilar in appearance to a play figure. It was Sylvia's firm conviction — though certainly unproven and highly controversial — that these discs would have been hidden, or buried, for safekeeping during what was to be a prolonged period of spiritual intolerance, distrust and fear (see Chapter 11).

The mention of the word 'Trifles' in the Dedicatory Epistle to the

Plate 1. The "Droeshout Portrait," from the First Folio of 1623.

To the great Variety of Readers.

From the most able, to him that can but spell. There you are number'd. We had rather you were weighd. Especially, when the fate of all Bookes depends vpon your capacities: and not of your heads alone, but of your purses. Well! It is now publique, & you wil stand for your priuiledges wee know: to read, and censure. Do so, but buy it first. That doth best commend a Booke, the Stationer saies. Then, how odde soeuer your braines be, or your wisedomes, make your licence the same, and spare not. Iudge your sixe-pen'orth, your shillings worth, your fiue shillings worth at a time, or higher, so you rise to the iust rates, and welcome. But, what euer you do, Buy. Censure will not driue a Trade, or make the Iacke go. And though you be a Magistrate of wit, and sit on the Stage at *Black-Friers*, or the *Cock-pit*, to arraigne Playes dailie, know, these Playes haue had their triall alreadie, and stood out all Appeales; and do now come forth quitted rather by a Decree of Court, then any purchas'd Letters of commendation.

It had bene a thing, we confesse, worthie to haue bene wished, that the Author himselfe had liu'd to haue set forth, and ouerseen his owne writings; But since it hath bin ordain'd otherwise, and he by death departed from that right, we pray you do not envie his Friends, the office of their care, and paine, to haue collected & publish'd them; and so to haue publish'd them, as where (before) you were abus'd with diuerse stolne, and surreptitious copies, maimed, and deformed by the frauds and stealthes of iniurious impostors, that expos'd them: euen those, are now offer'd to your view cur'd, and perfect of their limbes; and all the rest, absolute in their numbers, as he conceiued thē. Who, as he was a happie imitator of Nature, was a most gentle expresser of it. His mind and hand went together: And what he thought, he vttered with that easinesse, that wee haue scarse receiued from him a blot in his papers. But it is not our prouince, who onely gather his works, and giue them you, to praise him. It is yours that reade him. And there we hope, to your diuers capacities, you will finde enough, both to draw, and hold you: for his wit can no more lie hid, then it could be lost. Reade him, therefore; and againe, and againe: And if then you doe not like him, surely you are in some manifest danger, not to vnderstand him. And so we leaue you to other of his Friends, whom if you need, can bee your guides: if you neede them not, you can leade your selues, and others. And such Readers we wish him.

A 3

Iohn Heminge.
Henrie Condell.

Plate 2. Address "To the great Variety of Readers."

THE TRAGEDIE OF
MACBETH.

Actus Primus. Scœna Prima.

Thunder and Lightning. Enter three Witches.

1. Hen shall we three meet againe?
   In Thunder, Lightning, or in Raine?
2. When the Hurley-burley's done,
   When the Battaile's lost, and wonne.
3. That will be ere the set of Sunne.
1. Where the place?
2. Vpon the Heath.
3. There to meet with *Macbeth*.
1. I come, *Gray-Malkin*.
All. Padock calls anon: faire is foule, and foule is faire,
Houer through the fogge and filthie ayre. *Exeunt.*

Scena Secunda.

Alarum within. Enter King Malcome, Donalbaine, Lenox, with attendants, meeting a bleeding Captaine.

King. What bloody man is that? he can report,
As seemeth by his plight, of the Reuolt
The newest state.
  Mal. This is the Serieant,
Who like a good and hardie Souldier fought
'Gainst my Captiuitie: Haile braue friend;
Say to the King, the knowledge of the Broyle,
As thou didst leaue it.
  Cap. Doubtfull it stood,
As two spent Swimmers, that doe cling together,
And choake their Art: The mercilesse *Macdonwald*
(Worthie to be a Rebell, for to that
The multiplying Villanies of Nature
Doe swarme vpon him) from the Westerne Isles
Of Kernes and Gallowgrosses is supply'd,
And Fortune on his damned Quarry smiling,
Shew'd like a Rebells Whore: but all's too weake:
For braue *Macbeth* (well hee deserues that Name)
Disdayning Fortune, with his brandisht Steele,
Which smoak'd with bloody execution
(Like Valours Minion) caru'd out his passage,
Till hee fac'd the Slaue:
Which neu'r shooke hands, nor bad farwell to him,
Till he vnseam'd him from the Naue toth' Chops,
And fix'd his Head vpon our Battlements.

King. O valiant Cousin, worthy Gentleman.
  Cap. As whence the Sunne 'gins his reflection,
Shipwracking Stormes, and direfull Thunders:
So from that Spring, whence comfort seem'd to come,
Discomfort swells: Marke King of Scotland, marke,
No sooner Iustice had, with Valour arm'd,
Compell'd these skipping Kernes to trust their heeles,
But the Norweyan Lord, surueying vantage,
With furbusht Armes, and new supplyes of men,
Began a fresh assault.
  King. Dismay'd not this our Captaines, *Macbeth* and
Banquoh?
  Cap. Yes, as Sparrowes, Eagles;
Or the Hare, the Lyon:
If I say sooth, I must report they were
As Cannons ouer-charg'd with double Cracks,
So they doubly redoubled stroakes vpon the Foe:
Except they meant to bathe in reeking Wounds,
Or memorize another *Golgotha*,
I cannot tell: but I am faint,
My Gashes cry for helpe.
  King. So well thy words become thee, as thy wounds,
They smack of Honor both: Goe get him Surgeons.

Enter Rosse and Angus.

Who comes here?
  Mal. The worthy Thane of Rosse.
  Lenox. What a haste lookes through his eyes?
So should he looke, that seemes to speake things strange.
  Rosse. God saue the King.
  King. Whence cam'st thou, worthy *Thane*?
  Rosse. From Fiffe, great King,
Where the Norweyan Banners flowt the Skie,
And fanne our people cold.
Norway himselfe, with terrible numbers,
Assisted by that most disloyall Traytor,
The *Thane* of Cawdor, began a dismall Conflict,
Till that *Bellona's* Bridegroome, lapt in proofe,
Confronted him with selfe-comparisons,
Point against Point, rebellious Arme 'gainst Arme,
Curbing his lauish spirit: and to conclude,
The Victorie fell on vs.
  King. Great happinesse.
  Rosse. That now *Sweno*, the Norwayes King,
Craues composition:
Nor would we deigne him buriall of his men,
Till he disbursed, at Saint *Colmes* ynch,
Ten thousand Dollars, to our generall vse.
  King. No

721   1.2.62

Plate 3. Title page for "Macbeth," from First Folio of 1623.

LATITVDO
ÆQVATOR
Tropicus
Capri
cornii
ANDROMEDE
SINISTER PES ORIONIS
CANIS MAIOR
LVCIDA

Aquarius
Capricornus
Pisses
Februari
Ianneuari
December
Nouember
October
March
April
Iulie
Iunne
Augusti
September
Octobe
Nouember
Decembe
Ianneuarie
Februarie
Marche
Aprill
Maie

Plate 4 (opposite). Above: Gilded Brass astrolabe, made by Humphrey Cole, London, England, AD 1574, British Museum. Below: Astronomical Compendium made by James Kynvyn in c. 1593 for Robert Devereux, Earl of Essex, British Museum. © The Trustees of the British Museum.

Plate 5 (above). View of the South Front of Wilton House, Salisbury.

Plate 6 (above). "The most noble and incomparable payre of brethren." Portraits of (left) the 3rd and (right) 4th Earls of Pembroke and 1st Earl of Montgomery, by van Dyck hanging on either side of the elaborate marble chimney-piece in the Double Cube Room of Wilton House.

Plate 7 (opposite). The Double Cube Room, Wilton House, Salisbury

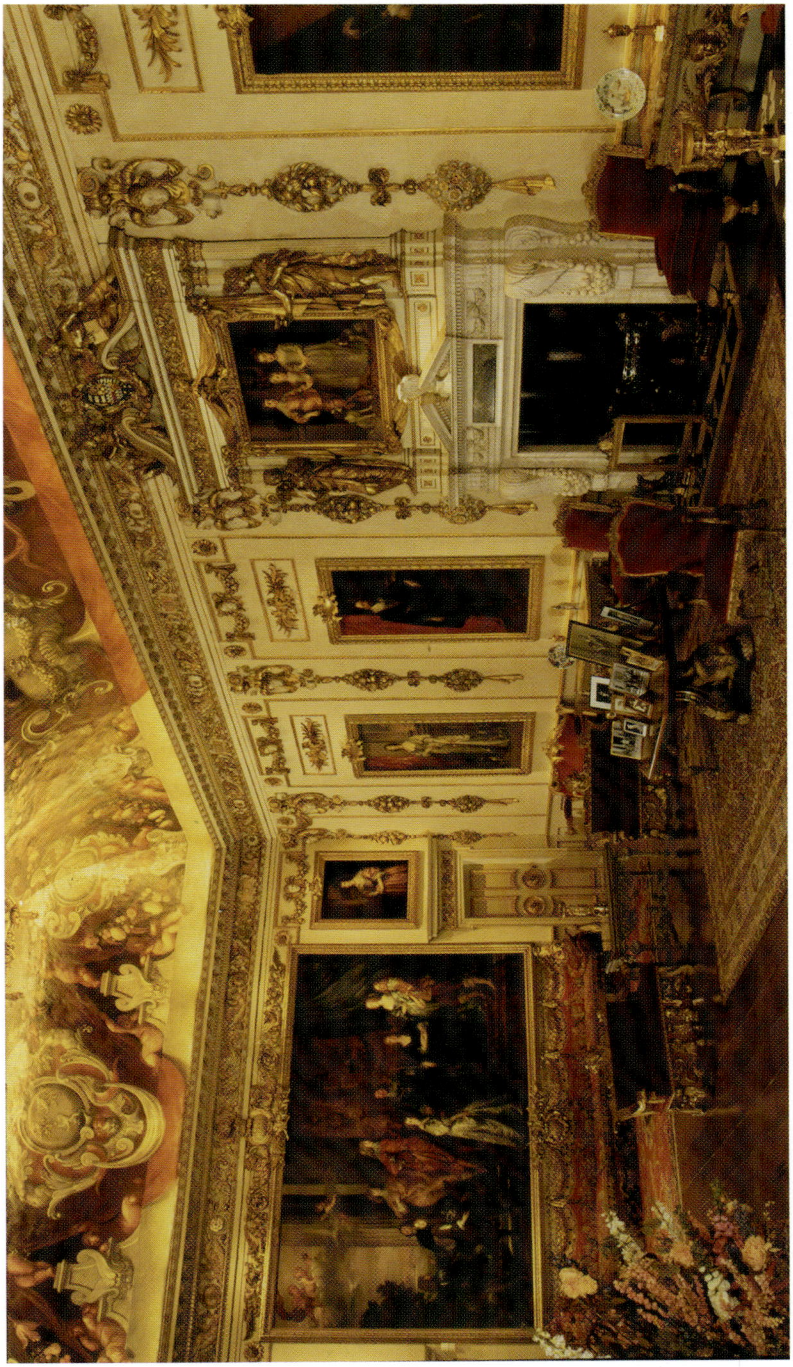

MACBETH

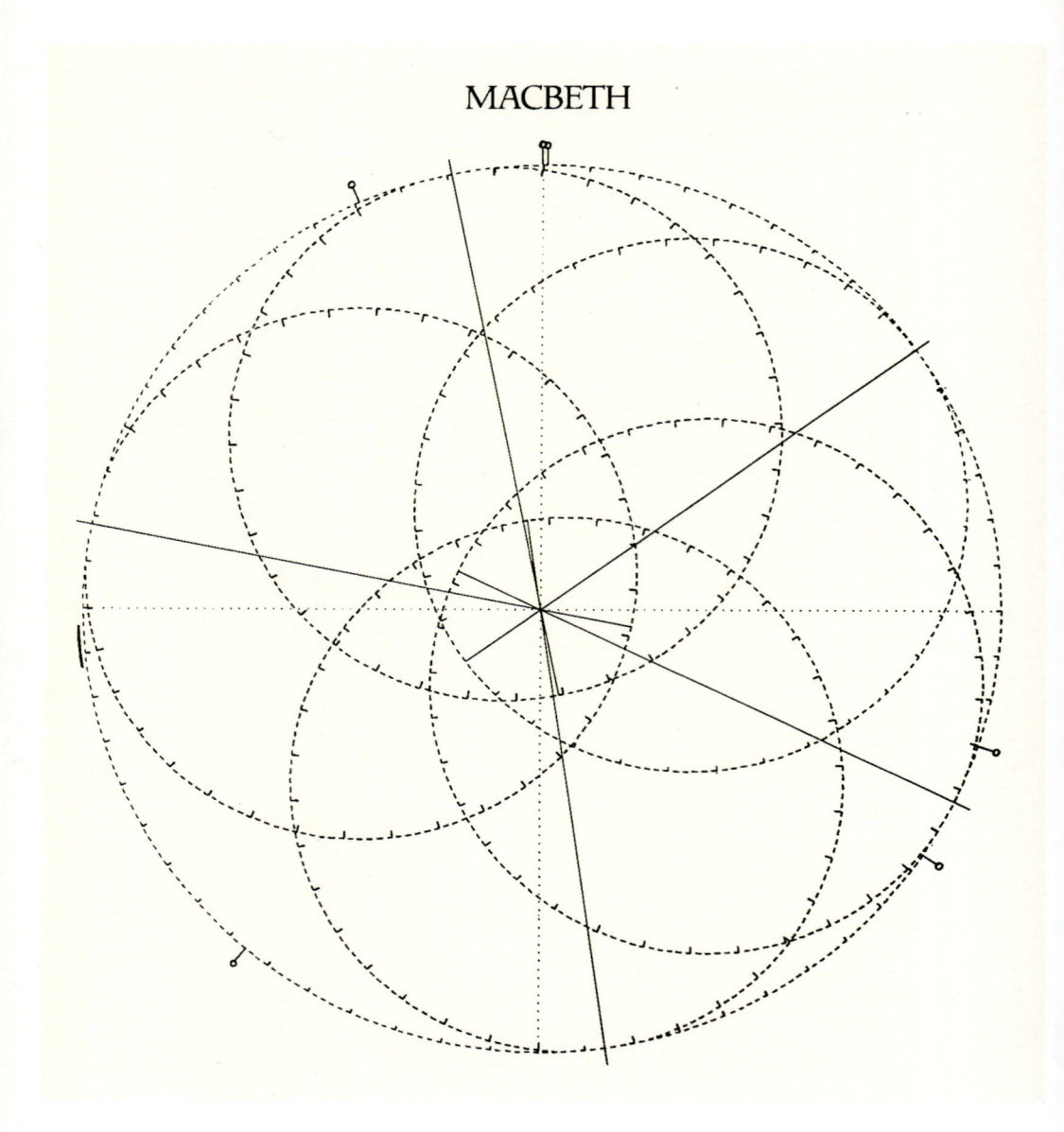

Plate 8. The Play Figure of William Shakespeare's Macbeth.

10. A WORK IN PROGRESS

1623 First Folio was for Sylvia a valuable clue to the existence of these discs:

> The language of the first part of the dedicatory epistle is the language of astrology and alchemy. 'Trifles' had many meanings: these did not as yet include 'confections of sponge, custard etc.' but they did include 'objects of pewter or of other alloys.' This might not be worth noticing if there were not already evidence that such trifles must have existed, and if a search for metal were not easier (and more hopeful) than a search for paper only.
>
> As for the strategy of such a burial, again the concept of a secret circle or order surrounding the playwright is strongly suggested. The preface to *Troilus and Cressida* refers to 'Grand Possessors' who seem to hold manuscripts and release them in their own time. These 'possessors' must have included in their number an occultist and mathematician as well as rich and powerful men, and they probably preserved both Rosicrucian and early Masonic traditions ... but much research is needed here.[9]

In the next chapter of this book Sylvia gives more background to these fascinating and far-reaching ideas, for it was certainly within Wilton House that Sylvia perceived that a great legacy of original work would be discovered.

11. Shakespeare and Wilton House

The subject of play-figures inscribed on discs was one that gained momentum for Sylvia during her later years, yet it was one that she was rather reluctant to put in the vanguard of her writing studies and public lectures. In July 1998, however, Sylvia was interviewed by Angela Turnbull of *The Salisbury Journal* (see article: 'Bard's clues may lie beneath Wilton' *Salisbury Journal,* July 30th, 1998), and there she spoke openly about the existence of the play-figures and how these would revolutionize the way we look at Shakespeare's plays. Regarding their preservation she said:

> They would have been inscribed on metal discs, and they would have been buried.

In the following chapter Sylvia describes the significance of Wilton house in relation to the works of Shakespeare and the preservation of his spiritual legacy. She leads us step by step towards an appreciation of the idea that a great Shakespearean treasury may lay buried beneath Wilton House. Yet we are now not only talking about play-figures inscribed on metal discs but also of the possibility of locating long-lost original manuscripts too.

Late in 1603, His Majesty's Players were summoned to present *As You Like It,* or some say *Twelfth Night,* to King James I, who was then visiting Salisbury and Wilton House (see Plate 5) during a time of plague in London. Legend has it that Lady Pembroke wrote a letter to her son at this time saying 'We have the man Shakespeare with us,' but no trace of this letter has been found and the story remains unverified. Nonetheless, Shakespeare's name and that of Wilton will always be linked, because the famous First Folio of the poet's collected works, published in 1623, was dedicated to the Third Earl of Pembroke and his younger brother.

The dedication is printed on the second page, following the Droushout portrait, and in it the two brothers, William and Philip, are addressed as 'The most noble and incomparable payre of brethren,' who, we gather, were patrons both of Shakespeare in his lifetime and of the book published seven years after his death.

Today the portraits of the brothers, the one of William thought to be posthumous, still hang on either side of the elaborate marble chimneypiece in the Double Cube Room of Wilton House, and form part of a series painted by Van Dyck in London in the 1630s, which was later brought to Wilton (see Plate 6).

In this chapter, I suggest that the link between Shakespeare and Wilton is even closer than has been suspected and that the dedication of the Folio to the Earls of Pembroke was a clue for posterity, rather than an end in itself. This is a high claim to make and a perilous one, in a world where new Shakespeare theories mushroom in the night and are apt to die as quickly, but let readers be the judges of the argument, or rather, of the story.

It has three elements: the First Shakespeare Folio; the Double Cube Room at Wilton House; and the brothers William and Philip, the third and fourth Earls of Pembroke, to whom the Folio was dedicated.

We may begin with the brothers, the sons of Mary Sidney, and the nephews of Sir Philip Sidney. William's reign as Earl of Pembroke lasted from 1604 until his sudden death in 1630, Philip's from 1630 to 1650, so that together they span the later part of Shakespeare's life, the publication of his collected works and the building of the Palladian house at Wilton.

William and Philip were brought up in the earlier Tudor house, built on the site of a nunnery by the first Earl of Pembroke. Later, both brothers became closely involved in the life of the Stuart Court; William as Lord Chamberlain and Philip as one of the early favourites of James I.

After William's death, Philip was appointed Lord Chamberlain by Charles I, and plans went ahead to replace the old Tudor house with a larger and grander one; in effect, a holiday palace for the king, who it si thought 'loved to visit Wilton.'

But when Philip lost his court appointment, and also had to return a £25,000 dowry to his son's widow, the house plans were much curtailed; the south elevation was actually halved, and the present end towers added. The result, however, can still be seen today, in this one part of the Palladian house undestroyed by James Wyatt.

Philip's reign as Earl coincided almost exactly with the building of that house.[1] William's name is connected more with that of Shakespeare. He is one of the candidates — though not a convincing one — for the title of 'Mr W. H.' to whom the sonnets were dedicated.

In Tresham Lever's book, *The Herberts of Wilton,* Chapter 5 is devoted to William and Philip.[2] The more we read about them, the more one salient fact emerges; they were extremely different from one another. William was gracious, learned and popular. Philip was violent tempered, 'ill-educated' and widely disliked. And though it has been said in Philip's favour that he was a great aesthete, as well as a sharp judge of men, the contrasting picture of the brothers is surely based on good evidence.

The book dedicated to both of them, the First Folio of Shakespeare's collected works, was published by two of the poet's fellow actors, John Hemynge and Henry Condell, who gathered together thirty-six plays and presumably supervised a slow editorial process. The book was finally printed in London by Isaac Jaggard (1623).

The first ten pages are taken up by prefatorial material: a short poem by Jonson opposite a mask-like engraving; the dedication and epistle to the Pembroke brothers; another epistle 'To the great variety of readers;' four poems; a list of actors; and a list of plays (with *Troilus and Cressida* missing from the list).

It is in the general epistle that the editors make their extraordinary claim:

> ... whereas (before) you were abus'd with deverse stol'ne and surreptitious copies ... even those are now offer'd to your view cur'd and perfect of their limbes and all the rest absolute in their numbers ...

Since the book is strewn with gross errors, beginning with the contents list and a zany confusion in the matter of act and scene divisions, readers and editors have been wondering ever since whether Hemynge and Condell were liars or fools. On the whole, we tend to be kind; they did their best, but their standards were simply not ours.

However, the debate continues, and though there is not room here for any proper argument, what follows will be clearer if I admit to a strong opinion. Essentially, Hemynge and Condell are speaking the truth, and if this is not yet recognised, in spite of all the work that has been done since Greg pioneered critical bibliography early in the twentieth century, it is only because the right trail has not been found. But perhaps I can leave the matter more as question than answer.

Why are we so condescending? Why do we look for wit in Shakespeare but none in his fellow actors, who lived and breathed his genius for most of their working lives? How, in fact, could anyone make a statement about the text so grossly at variance with the condition of that text, and not expect the discrepancy to be noticed? I submit that Hemynge and Condell not only expected it, but relied on it; they were indeed fools, but of the motley sort — fools, jokers, clowns and educators of humanity to boot.

The third element in the story is the Double Cube Room at Wilton House, a place that has been so fully described that here I will only attempt the briefest reminder.[3]

The Double Cube, sometimes called the banqueting room, lies roughly in the centre of the south part of the house, on the first floor, and is the largest of a sequence of state rooms. Its dimensions are given as 60 ft x 30 ft x 30 ft (18.3 m x 9.14 m x 9.14 m), and those of its sister room, the Single Cube (which lies further west), as 30 ft x 30 ft x 30 ft (9.14 m x 9.14 m x 9.14 m). But in fact both rooms have their upper edges cut off by the painted cove of the ceiling, making them casket-shaped.

If we enter the Double Cube by the Central Eastern door, the carved chimney-piece is on our right, the three high windows are on our left, and ahead is the vast canvas of Philip (the 4th Earl) and his family. Above us, the central shield of the ceiling, painted by Emmanuel de Critz, gives the illusion of a coffered dome with a big hole in the top, showing the sky (see Plate 7).

There are at least two aspects of this room that are surprising. One is that anything so lavish and spectacular should have come into existence at all in the days of a puritan revolution. The other is that such a room, in the setting of a Palladian house, should be markedly asymmetrical, for neither grand fireplace nor Venetian window is in the centre of its own long wall; both are out of step with the centre of the painted ceiling.

The date of the building makes us wonder whether perhaps the Pembroke family enjoyed some special privilege or protection; the lack of symmetry in the Double Cube room (and in adjoining rooms) can be looked at more closely. Christopher Hussey discussed it in some detail in the May 1963 edition of *Country Life* magazine. He drew attention to the fact that this asymmetry is 'not noticed' by Colen Campbell in his well-known plan of the house, published in 1717, which is curious because the room has not been essentially altered since about sixty years before that date.

It seems at first that, whether or not he had access to an early plan, Campbell simply disapproved of the actual shape of the Double Cube, and preferred to show an ideal one that fitted the title of his book, *Vitruvius Britannicus*. Christopher Hussey surmises that 'pre-existing structures or foundations' may have prevented the execution of this ideal plan; yet the theory is not too easy to accept.

The Double Cube was to be the great room in a great house; the showpiece of an ambitious earl with strong pretensions to aesthetic judgement. Surely Philip, though not quite as rich as he once hoped, could still command small armies of workmen to build, or 'unbuild,' at his wish? Later, large sums were spent on the interior decoration of all the south-facing staterooms. Since the concept of symmetry was still of fundamental importance in the late Renaissance, we should expect that getting it right would have taken precedence over almost all other considerations.

The shift is too great to be called a minor building error. It is as if a giant hand had deliberately pushed the end wall of the Double Cube two feet to the west (carrying other end walls with it) while the façade, with its ordered windows, stayed still.[4] But why? Philip, 4th Earl of Pembroke, must have known the answer, but his dark portrait cannot speak. Looking at it again, and remembering Tresham Lever's, *The Herberts of Wilton*, we are suddenly struck by the inappropriateness of that phrase in the Folio — 'incomparable pair.' It was, of course, an age of flattery and for William the epithet did well enough. But was it not absurd to apply it to Philip, with his very different reputation? Incomparable? To what, we may ask, might the two brothers not be compared? The answer can only be — to each other.

That the word 'incomparable' can have a second meaning is confirmed by the Oxford English Dictionary, which states: '1) matchless, peerless, and 2) not to be compared with or to. Both examples given under 2) fall in the first half of the seventeenth century.'[5]

When we look now at the two portraits and their position on either side of the fireplace, we begin to feel as if an old joke had been given a new varnish. William, to our left, looking upright, comfortable and rosy, commands the greater 'half' of the room; Philip, to our right, wearing an almost conspiratorial expression as he starts to climb a painted stair, is assigned the lesser half. William has plenty of space around him; Philip and the next portrait are somewhat squashed up into the north-east corner.[6]

Surely 'incomparable' is at once a comment on the brothers and on the room where their portraits were designed to hang? But if it is also a comment on the room then it is worth looking more closely at the proportions of that room.

The long north wall, with the off-centre fireplace is divided essentially into three parts: a longer part to the west; the hearth; and a shorter part to the east (see Plate 7).

TO THE MOST NOBLE
And
INCOMPARABLE PAIRE
OF BRETHREN.

William
Earle of Pembroke, &c. Lord Chamberlaine to the
Kings most Excellent Maiesty.

AND

Philip
Earle of Montgomery, &c. Gentleman of his Maiesties
Bed-Chamber. Both Knights of the most Noble Order
of the Garter, and our singular good
LORDS.

Right Honourable,

Hilst we studie to be thankful in our particular, for the many fauors we haue receiued from your L.L. we are falne vpon the ill fortune, to mingle two the most diuerse things that can bee, feare, and rashnesse; rashnesse in the enterprize, and feare of the successe. For, when we valew the places your H.H. sustaine, we cannot but know their dignity greater, then to descend to the reading of these trifles: and, vvhile we name them trifles, we haue depriu'd our selues of the defence of our Dedication. But since your L.L. haue beene pleas'd to thinke these trifles some-thing, heeretofore; and haue prosequuted both them, and their Authour liuing, vvith so much fauour: we hope, that (they out-liuing him, and he not hauing the fate, common with some, to be exequutor to his owne writings) you will vse the like indulgence toward them, you haue done

A 2 vnto

Figure 39. Page one 'To the Most Noble and Incomparable Pair'

The Epistle Dedicatorie.

vnto their parent. There is a great difference, vvhether any Booke choose his Patrones, or finde them: This hath done both. For, so much were your L. L. likings of the seuerall parts, vvhen they were acted, as before they vvere published, the Volume ask'd to be yours. We haue but collected them, and done an office to the dead, to procure his Orphanes, Guardians; vvithout ambition either of selfe-profit, or fame: onely to keepe the memory of so worthy a Friend, & Fellow aliue, as was our SHAKESPEARE, *by humble offer of his playes, to your most noble patronage. Wherein, as we haue iustly obserued, no man to come neere your L.L. but vvith a kind of religious addresse; it hath bin the height of our care, vvho are the Presenters, to make the present worthy of your H.H. by the perfection. But, there we must also craue our abilities to be considerd, my Lords. We cannot go beyond our owne powers. Country hands reach foorth milke, creame, fruites, or what they haue: and many Nations (we haue heard) that had not gummes & incense, obtained their requests with a leauened Cake. It vvas no fault to approch their Gods, by what meanes they could: And the most, though meanest, of things are made more precious, when they are dedicated to Temples. In that name therefore, we most humbly consecrate to your H. H. these remaines of your seruant Shakespeare; that what delight is in them, may be euer your L.L. the reputation his, & the faults ours, if any be committed, by a payre so carefull to shew their gratitude both to the liuing, and the dead, as is*

Your Lordshippes most bounden,

IOHN HEMINGE.
HENRY CONDELL.

Figure 40. Page two 'To the Most Noble and Incomparable Pair'

If we measure these parts and divide the long end plus hearthstone by the short end we come to 1.62. This is the shortened value usually given for the Golden Section.

Finding it here inscribed with such exactness suggests, though it does not prove, that the asymmetry of the room was not just a second-best; and the relevance of the word 'incomparable' (reminding us of 'incommensurable') makes us turn back to the Folio page where it is written (see Figure 39).[7]

> TO THE MOST NOBLE
> AND
> INCOMPARABLE PAIRE
> OF BRETHREN.
>
> WILLIAM
> Earle of Pembroke, &c. Lord Chamberlaine to the
> Kings most Excellent Maiesty.
>
> AND
>
> PHILIP
> Earle of Montgomery, &c. Gentleman of his Maiesties
> Bed-Chamber. Both Knights of the most Noble Order
> of the Garter, and our singular good
> LORDS.
>
> Right Honourable,
>
> Hilst we studie to be thankful in our particular, for the many favors we haue receiued from your L.L. we are falne vpon the ill fortune, to mingle two the most diuerse things that can bee, feare, and rashnesse; rashnesse in the enterprize, and feare of the successe. For, when we valew the places your H.H. sustaine, we cannot but know their dignity greater, then to descend to the reading of these trifles: and, while we name them trifles, we haue depriu'd our selues of the defence of our Dedication. But since your L.L. haue beene pleas'd to thinke these trifles some-thing, heeretofore; and haue prosequuted both them, and their Authour liuing with so much fauour: we hope, that (they out-liuing him, and he not hauing the fate, common with some, to be exequutor to his owne writings) you will vse the like indulgence toward them, you haue done
>
> A2 vnto

Figure 41

The first page of the Dedication is decorative, like a memorial stone, with an engraved headpiece above the names and titles of the two brothers. After a wide gap the letter proper begins well down the page with a large initial 'W' and continues overleaf. It is signed near the bottom of the second page by the editors, John Hemynge and Henry Condell. Compared to most other pages of the book, the first page of the Dedication looks very long and narrow. In fact, when we measure the print area, we find that the length is twice the breadth: it is a double square. Furthermore, the geometrical division between the two squares is clearly marked by a line of tiny print: 'of the Garter, and our singular good,' followed by 'Lords' below (see Figure 41).

But a double square is the ground plan of a double cube, and this dedication is addressed to men whose portraits hang in a Double Cube Room. Can this be a coincidence? The page too, is divided by the Golden Section at the point where the Epistle begins.

If we re-read that Epistle certain words now acquire a second meaning. A poet's 'remains,' for instance, may be his printed work; more naturally they are what is left behind when the printing is done. 'Patrones,' we discover, can also mean 'patterns;' so a book that finds its patterns seems to be a fellow who leads a successful paper-chase. The meaning of 'Temples,' where supplicants bring 'milk, cream, fruits ... and a leavened cake,' shifts from the general to the particular — the Double Cube Room has a double temple theme.

There are, of course, hundreds of fireplaces with marble architraves that are not unlike classical temples, but the great fireplace in the Double Cube at Wilton has fixed ornamental jugs ready to pour libations and, within the hearth, vestal flames, frozen in bronze. The smoke of the fire would lead the eye up the interior of another temple; for the particular episode in the legend of Perseus, painted on the central shield of the ceiling, is that in which the hero rescues his mother, Danae, who has fled to an altar for protection. There are also, it is true, other pages to be found where the print area is twice as long as it is wide; and even more where a rough, or exact, Golden Section appears. But if we make a more precise comparison here, by reducing the plan of the room to the scale of the page, the match of detail is also undeniable. It could be a coincidence, as some traditions in printing were similar to those in architecture — but is it? The words that are printed seem to argue against it.[8]

In that line of tiny print, for example, we may detect a second joke. It speaks of Knights of the Garter; but it is itself the garter of the page, holding up and crowding the lines above it, like wrinkles in a stocking, and leaving a smooth empty area below. It seems to be a hint that the Knights of the Garter are somehow involved. But in what? What exactly have we found?

West

TO THE MOST NOBLE
And
INCOMPARABLE PAIRE
OF BRETHREN.

WILLIAM
Earle of Pembroke, &c. Lord Chamberlaine to the
Kings most Excellent *Maiesty.*

AND

PHILIP
Earle of Montgomery, &c. Gentleman of his Maiesties
Bed-Chamber. Both Knights of the most Noble Order
of the Garter, and our singular good
LORDS.

Right Honourable,

Hilst we studie to be thankfull in our particular, for the many fauors we haue receiued from your L.L. we are falne vpon the ill fortune, to mingle two the most diuerse things that can bee, feare, and rashnesse; rashnesse in the enterprize, and feare of the successe. For, when we valew the places your H.H. sustaine, we cannot but know their dignity greater, then to descend to the reading of these trifles: and, while we name them trifles, we haue depriu'd our selues of the defence of our Dedication. But since your L.L. haue beene pleas'd to thinke these trifles some-thing, heeretofore; and haue prosequuted both them, and their *Authour* liuing, with so much fauour: we hope, that (they out-liuing him, and he not hauing the fate, common with some, to be exequutor to his owne writings) you will vse the like indulgence toward them, you haue done

A 2 vnto

South | *Venetian Window* | *Fireplace*

East

Figure 42. Ground plan of double cube room, Wilton House, superimposed onto page one of dedication

It is possibly a pattern and a signpost. Either the Double Cube Room was constructed to match the Folio Dedication, or page and room were conceived together, with one taking longer to make than the other. On page two of the epistle — the signpost — we read 'No man to come neere your L.L. But with a kind of religious addresse.' This falls just after the word 'SHAKESPEARE,' printed in small capitals, and seems to tell us both how and where. Perhaps a church, perhaps a cathedral, perhaps a great house built on the site of a nunnery; in any case, a place to be approached with awe.

Once we have arrived at the house, the print area of the dedication (page one) can reassure us; this is the right room, this is the most hopeful spot in England in which, or around which, to search for those unique literary remains whose total disappearance has always been a mystery. Hemynge and Condell had these remains in their hands, not only amended quartos but — since seventeen of the plays had never been published before — all kinds of manuscripts too; 'foul papers' probably, as well as fair copies and prompt copies. Did all this material vanish in one great fire? Was it so little valued that it was deliberately thrown away? Or was it so greatly valued that it was hidden?

I believe that the third answer is the most likely, but this belief springs from a study of the structure of the plays, contained, in part, within this book. Essentially, this structure is an architectural one, not entirely unlike that of many stanzaic poems of the same period.[9]

Architects, such as Alberti, Bramante and Palladio wrote publicly about the mathematical and geometrical aspect of their work.[10] Poets, immersed in the same Neo-Platonic tradition, commonly neither wrote, nor spoke of it, nor left any obvious clues behind. What makes this case a special one will appear either when the nature of the Shakespeare Folio is recognized, or when the 'copy' on which it was based turns up; which, of course, after the perilous passage of so many years it may well not do, even if it was once hidden carefully. Meanwhile, the theory should remain of interest, and even if the motive is not yet evident the question, 'How was it done?' may at least be approached.

A secret hiding place implies a secret plot; yet how could such a plot have been carried out? Does not the long gap of time between the publication of the Folio and the final completion of decorations in the Double Cube at Wilton House (around 1655) make the whole idea absurd? Not quite, if we think in terms of a temporary resting place for the papers (either in London or in the country), and, once again, of a circle of men, or a society, linked with the poet in his lifetime and still active for a number of years after his death. For the existence of such a circle we have in fact a small piece of evidence; a sentence near the end of the original Quarto preface to *Troilus and Cressida:*

> 'And believe this, that when he is gone and his comedies out of sale, you will scramble for them and set up a new English Inquisition. Take this for a warning, and at the peril of your pleasure's loss and judgement's, refuse not, nor like this the less for nor being sullied with the smoky breath of the multitude; but thank fortune for the 'scape it hath made amongst you, since by the grand possessors wills I believe you should have prayed for them rather than been prayed. And so I leave all such to be prayed for, for the state of their wits'healths that will not praise it. Vale.'

It is generally thought that 'grand possessors' meant the actor-sharers of the Kings Men, who may have tried to block publication of the play before it had had a run of public performance. But the early history of this play is wrapped in darkness and contradiction, and the true meaning of 'grand possessors' remains uncertain. Whoever they were, they seem to have had it in their power to hold or release plays at will.

The alteration to the great room at Wilton House was almost certainly conceived early on, at the drawing-board stage. No knocking down and rebuilding was involved. What was important was to leave firm evidence in *Vitruvius Brittanicus* for posterity, evidence that an alternative to Colen Campbell's plan had taken place, showing a symmetrical Double Cube (1717). If this was not the product of Campbell's fancy, it must have been based on an early plan, never executed.[11] We are led to wonder; which was surely the intention.

Just how the printer, Jaggard, was instructed, and how far he had to be 'in the know' is a question that takes us far into the field of bibliography. It concerns the printing of the plays, as well as the layout of the dedication and other prefatorial material. But an experienced editor would certainly have known the limitations within which a printer worked — how many spaces to a line and so forth — perhaps all that was required of Jaggard and his compositors was an exact obedience.

The theory gives rise to many speculations. How early in the century did William and Philip discuss the project of a new house at Wilton, to replace the Tudor one? Did a family tradition persist that whatever else was changed in that house the Double Cube was sacrosanct?[12] Above all, what exactly was destroyed in the great fire that swept through the newly-built south range in the winter of 1648? That part of the house, the diarist John Aubrey (1626–1697) tells us, had to be 're-edified,' and he speaks of a ceiling painting in the Double Cube that existed before the present one. But the Van Dyck portraits, planned for the room, were certainly not damaged; they arrived later, brought down from London in what must have been a slow, laborious procession. Other items could have come at the same time: perhaps a chest of wood or metal or a roll, wrapped in leather.

On Shakespeare's tomb in Holy Trinity Church, Stratford-on-Avon, is a curse warning off anyone who would disturb its contents.

> Good friend, for Jesus' sake forbear
> To dig the dust enclosed here.
> Blest be the man that spares these stones,
> And curst be he that moves my bones.

No one, so far, has gained permission to brave this curse, and we may read it now, with a certain hope, as a kind of 'anti-signpost:' not here, look elsewhere. At Wilton, in the Double Cube room, there is no curse; rather a setting of perfect aptness, theatrical, stunning, robed in classical allusions. There is even an open space of sky in the centre of the roof, only it is a painted one, and does not let in the rain as it did at the Globe Theatre.

In Shakespeare's day, the arts and sciences were still one. Though it will be said at first, by that great majority of scholars who regard the 1623 Folio as a botched printing job, that all this is 'such stuff as dreams are made on,' yet the final verdict of a circle of experts — or of a man with a chisel — may perhaps be different.

So far we have pointed to what is essentially a single clue: the curious match of a page and a room, but there are others, waiting to be looked at later. They include: the significance of the print area of the second page of the Folio dedication; a further interpretation of that four-line verse on the Stratford-on-Avon tomb; and the tracing of the recurring concept, or picture, in *Cymbeline*, the last play printed in the Folio. In that play, it can be argued, we find a last testament of the dramatist Shakespeare that is not less significant than the one many discover in *The Tempest* (the first play printed in the Folio) in which Prospero drowns his book. The recurring image in *Cymbeline,* together with the prophecy about the Lion's Whelp, answers our final question: 'Exactly where should we look in the Double Cube room?'[13] If anything is found, it will justify Philip, 4th Earl of Pembroke and 1st Earl of Montgomery, who is said to have backed the winning side in the Civil War 'for fear of losing Wilton House.'

12. Finding and Constructing the 'Figure' for a Shakespearean Play

The hidden plot of *Macbeth* arose from the discovery of symmetry, which we find wherever we look — in the whole play, in the single act, in the single scene. This symmetry — first perceptible as echoing sounds, images and meanings — was first demonstrated to the eye by means of scale maps, in which the proportion of the parts to the whole became visible (see Figures 1 and 2). In this demonstration the compass found a natural role.

However, a map does not entirely solve the mystery: we are still very far from having discovered the main-spring of the play's organisation. We are impelled to ask: is there indeed a further principle to be found within which the individual details of structure can be comprehended? The compass was first used to demonstrate known relationships: later to find new ones. In this way, the relationship appears as a curved line and the time-stream as a straight one. However, it may suddenly occur to us to ask, 'Why should it be this way round? Why should not the time-stream be curved and the relationships between its parts straight?'

The idea that time is curved is an old one. The heavenly bodies, which create and determine our human sense of time, move in ellipses. When we have journeyed right round the sun in a great curve we experience the same season; this spring we are reminded of last spring, this autumn of last autumn. Our memories of this time last year seem oddly closer than those of a few weeks back; we almost feel we could reach out a hand and touch them. Reason objects, of course, that we only have to look at the nature of memory to explain this phenomenon. Yet the signs and symbols of the year are themselves the children of time, and so is memory itself. Even if a mathematician could prove that *real* time has to be linear, we are dealing at present with *poetic* time, which might have its own inner laws.

Let us simply suppose then that the time-track of a play could be represented as a curve. We must ask next, what manner of curve?

To the ancient Greeks, and to those who inherited their thinking, the circle was the perfect curve. Could a Renaissance play be a great circle?

At the end of *Macbeth* we do indeed find strong echoes of the beginning. Yet the complex threefold symmetry, which is unquestionably there in the play, could hardly find complete expression in one great simple circle. We face, in fact, a curious kind of geometrical problem — how can the symmetry of a whole play, of the five acts within it, and each scene within those acts, find an elegant counterpart in a continuous curving line?

The problem found a solution, whose mode of arrival we have subsequently analyzed, in the introductory chapter of this book, but, as so often with 'scientific' discoveries, it did not entirely correspond to logical steps; it resembled more Kekule's dream of the carbon ring, or even the violent storm and shipwreck which lands us, astonished and rubbing our eyes, on the island of the *The Tempest*.[1]

In studying each play from a geometrical aspect I always asked the same question and kept to the same rules. The question was 'Do the numbers that the text reveals invite the construction of a figure similar in kind to, but different in proportions from, the one that arises from the text of *Macbeth?*' The rules were count one for each printed line of text, even if that line is no more than one syllable; for instance, the 'sure' of 'leysure' [leisure] in *Macbeth*, Act 1 Scene 3, which comes where Banquo says:

    Play-line 251   *Banq.* Worthy *Macbeth*, wee stay upon your ley-
            252   sure.

The act totals alone give enough information to find the basic proportions and outline of the figure. Most acts have the shape of the simple loop, which makes a simple circle and two *wings*, which are either exactly equal or differ by one line (with compensation later). But in some plays there are acts with the shape of a double loop as illustrated in Figure 43.

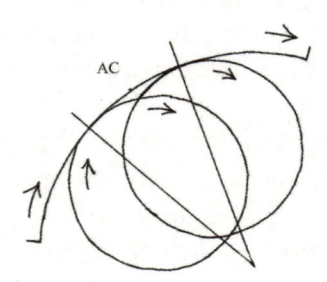

Figure 43

12. FINDING AND CONSTRUCTING "THE FIGURE"

This creates three sections along the great circle: a middle section, where the act centre lies, and two outer *wings*.

To find the size of the small circles in a particular play we must look first for the shortest act. The loop it makes must contain a circle with fewer lines than the act —and all the small circles in the other acts must be the same size.

Then we proceed by simple trial and error (though quite soon we guess correctly first time). Firstly, we try out the largest possible small circle out of the range of workable ones (the small circles must be easily related in number to 360 and so 240, 300, 400, 450, 540 would do, also 200, 600 and 520. See Figure 44).[2]

Figure 44

Possible number of lines in each small circle	Ratio between degrees and lines
240	360 : 240 = 3 : 2 Therefore there are 2 lines to every 3 degrees
300	360 : 300 = 6 : 5 Therefore there are 5 lines to every 6 degrees
360	360 : 360 = 1 : 1 Therefore there is 1 line to every 1 degree
400	360 : 400 = 9 : 10 Therefore there are 10 lines to every 9 degrees
450	360 : 450 = 4 : 5 Therefore there are 5 lines to every 4 degrees
540	360 : 540 = 2 : 3 Therefore there are 3 lines to every 2 degrees
200	360 : 200 = 9 : 5 Therefore there are 5 lines to every 9 degrees
600	360 : 600 = 3 : 5 Therefore there are 5 lines to every 3 degrees
520	360 : 520 = 9 : 13 Therefore there are 13 lines to every 9 degrees (this ratio is awkward)

We subtract a small circle of the chosen size from each act in turn, and add up the bits left over. If any act is so long that two circles can be subtracted from it, then we subtract two instead of one, because almost certainly we are looking at a double loop. To create the great circle, the loops or double loops 'take hands' and together should add up to a neat number, with a few lines over for the 'overlap' (see Figures 4 and 5). At the final addition of the 'bits over' (each representing two wings or a threefold area), we are holding our breath; either it will work or it won't. If it does, we have arrived at a great circle of such a size that it bears a simple ratio[3] to the small circles that will lie within it (I think great circles are unlikely ever to be less than 500 or greater than 1000, but there are many plays I have not studied). If it doesn't, we must choose small circles of a different size and recalculate the great circle by the same method. When it works — and it always does — it is as if dancers have been waiting in the wings of a theatre, ready to fall into place.

If all the acts are expressed in single loops then drawing the figure is relatively easy since the ratio of great diameter to small diameter is the same as the ratio of great circumference to small circumference. If one or more of the acts is expressed in a double loop, then the final form of the figure takes longer to establish, since we have to study the text with great care to find exactly where the axes of the twin circles lie. However, the main proportions of the figure are determined just as quickly as those of a one-loop-per-act figure. Very often the calibrations of the circles, great or small — at least down to 5 or 10 line sections — can be achieved by the pure geometrical construction of regular polygons; hexagons, pentagons, octagons and so on

When the figure has been constructed we may think that out of the mist of numbers this tangible shape has arrived. It is here, this is the end of the quest. But we are quite wrong, because it is only the beginning.[4] Not until one can directly relate the text to each position on the figure can one enter into the whole world of meaning, which the figures reveal. Certain laws begin to emerge; for instance, there always seems to be a relationship between the moment when one enters into a small circle, out of the great circle, and the moment when one leaves it. There is also a relationship between these crossing points and the nadir of the small circle (the point on the small circle which is nearest the centre point of the whole figure) which, when the small circles are single, is also the centre of the act.[5] Where there are two circles in an act, this relationship still holds good although the centre of the act will then come on the great

12. FINDING AND CONSTRUCTING "THE FIGURE"

circle. This characteristic of a double-circled act is also important when one is considering the problem of acts with an uneven total. A perfect act, containing a single inner circle, is theoretically only possibly where the act total is even. Then the *wings* of the act, which lie on the great circle, will be equal to one another, and the law of symmetry is obeyed. If, on the other hand, there are two circles in the act and the act centre falls on the great circle between them, then the act can happily be odd. The single central line points to a kind of general axis; this axis is not the diameter of a circle and does not require 180 degrees on each side of it and an even number of lines on each side. However, it is not exactly a rule to state that there are even numbers for single-circled acts, odd numbers for double-circled acts.

Anomalous situations can easily arise, for instance, where a single-circled act has an odd number of lines and an adjacent double-curved act has an even number of lines. But when they do it is quite clear that the number in the single-circled act is Janus-like: from the point of view that it obviously belongs where it is but, in fact, it also makes sense in connection with the odd numbered act, and can be borrowed by this act to make everything balance.

If the figure is more than an arbitrary construction we would expect the words, sounds and images the ten points of each concentric circle somehow to confirm those inter-act connections. Indeed, whatever is linked in the sphere of geometry, whether by invisible curves or straight lines or by actual intersections of the time-stream (as at the crossings of act-loops, or at the many crossings of act-circles with one another) we expect to find also linked in the sphere of verse.

In setting out to explore the geometrical relationships of a figure, in terms of the textual relationships of the play, it will be not unlike exploring the countryside with the help of a map. First, we pinpoint on the map the place where we want to go, then we go there in reality, and experience that place with all our senses. Finally, we compare it, using the instrument of memory, with other places we have been to lately, in some valley, or island or sea-girt kingdom.

Appendices

Appendix 1

The centre of *A Midsummer Night's Dream* is not immediately simple to locate; this is because the song, 'You Spotted Snakes with Doubled Tongue,' by which her attendants sing the Queen and the fairies asleep, can be measured in two ways. There are two verses each with a chorus beginning 'Philomel with melody.' After the first verse this chorus is given in full: Philomel with melody:

> Sing in our sweet lullaby.
> Lulla, lulla, lullaby, lulla, lulla, lullaby.
> Never harm, Nor spell, nor charm,
> Come our lovely Lady nigh.
> So good night, with lullaby.

But after the second verse they are simply indicated with the line 'Philomel with melody, etc.,' The first verse takes up 10 printed lines, the second only 5, with 5 more implied. The song ends with two more lines,
> Hence away, now all is well;
> One aloof, stand sentinel.

So, there are 17 printed lines altogether. However, the song as sung would have altogether 22 lines. The question is, how is this reality reflected in the numbering of the play? If we follow the rules it must be only 17 lines, because 'each printed line counts one,' but is there any way in which the writer indicated that this 17 was really 22? If we follow the rules, the total number of lines in the play is 2138 and the central lines fall at 1069 and 1070 which, as we have skipped out the extra chorus, fall at the words:

> For debt that bankrout slip doth sorrow owe,
> Which now in some slight measure it will pay,

Here the word 'measure' comes within the actual centre itself. If we add 5 for the second chorus of 'You Spotted Snakes,' then the total number of lines in the play becomes 2143, and the central single line of the play becomes line 1072. However, every line after 'You Spotted Snakes' is now increased by 5 and line 1072 falls before the original play centre; it falls at:

Here therefore for a while I will remain.

It would appear that this double way of counting is reflected in this central passage. So exactly what meaning can be attached to lines that are implied, but not printed, remains a question.

Appendix 2

Map of Macbeth, *Act I, Scene 3. Overview below, detail overleaf.*

Witches' Prologue
(38 lines)
{
1. Where hast thou been, Sister?

Wreck'd as homeward he did come.
Drum within — Beating Drum *(Line 30)*

Peace! The Charm's wound up.
Enter Lady Macbeth and Banquo
Macb. So foul and fair a day I have not seen
}

Prophecies
(43 lines)
{

Interlude of Wonder
(12 lines)
{
Speak, I charge you.   *Witches vanish*
Banq. The Earth hath bubbles, as the water ha's,

That takes the Reason Prisoner? — Scene Centre

Banq. To the self-same tune, and words: who's here?
Enter Ross and Angus
Ross. The king hath happily receiv'd, *Macbeth*
}

Fulfilment of Second Prophecy
(45 lines)
{

{ Soliloquy: Vision of Murder *(25 lines)*
(39 lines)
Macbeth takes command *(14 lines)*
}
{
Cousins, a word, I pray you.
Macb. Two Truths are told,

And make my seated Heart knock at my Ribs, — Beating Heart *(Line −30)*

Time, and the Hour, runs through the roughest Day.
Banq. Worthy *Macbeth*, we stay upoon your leysure.

Come friends.   *Exeunt*
}

Thunder. Enter the three Witches.

   1. Where hast thou been, Sister?
   2. Killing Swine.
   3. Sister, where thou?
   1. A Sailor's Wife had Chestnuts in her Lap,
And mouncht, & mouncht, and mouncht.
Give me, quoth I.
Aroint thee, Witch, the rump-fed Ronyon cries.
Her Husband's to Aleppo gone, Master o'th' Tiger:
But in a Sieve I'll thither sail,
And like a Rat without a tail,
I'll do, I'll do, and I'll do.
   2. I'll give thee a Wind.
   1. Th'art kind.
   3. And I another.
   1. I myself have all the other,
And the very Ports they blow,
All the Quarters that they know,
I'th' Ship-man's Card.
I'll drain him dry as Hay:
Sleep shall neither Night nor Day
Hang upon his Pent-house Lid:
He shall live a man forbid:
Weary sev'nights nine times nine,
Shall he dwindle, peak, and pine:
Though his Bark cannot be lost,
Yet it shall be Tempest-toss'd.
Look what I have.
   2. Show me, show me.
   1. Here I have a Pilot's Thumb,
Wreck'd, as homeward he did come.   *Drum within.*   × **Beating Drum**
   3. A Drum, a Drum: (line 30)
Macbeth doth come.
   All. The weyward Sisters, hand in hand,
Posters of the Sea and Land,
Thus do go, about, about,
Thrice to thine, and thrice to mine,
And thrice again, to make up nine,
Peace! The Charm's wound up.

Witches' Prologue (38 lines)

Enter Macbeth. and Banquo.

   Macb. So foul and fair a day I have not seen.
   Banq. How far is't call'd to Soris? What are these,
So wither'd, and so wild in their attire,
That look not like th'Inhabitants o' th'Earth,
And yet are on't? Live you, or are you aught
That man may question? you seem to understand me,
By each at once her choppy finger laying
Upon her skinny Lips: you should be Women,
And yet your Beards forbid me to interpret
That you are so.
   Macb. Speak, if you can: what are you?
   1. All hail *Macbeth*, hail to thee, *Thane* of Glamis.
   2. All hail *Macbeth*, hail to thee, *Thane* of Cawdor.
   3. All hail *Macbeth*, that shalt be King hereafter.
   Banq. Good Sir, why do you start, and seem to fear
Things that do sound so fair? I'th' name of truth
Are ye fantastical, or that indeed
Which outwardly ye show? My noble Partner
You greet with present Grace, and great prediction
Of Noble having, and of Royal hope,
That he seems rapt withal: To me you speak not.
If you can look into the Seeds of Time,
And say, which Grain will grow, and which will not,
Speak then to me, who neither beg, nor fear
Your favors, nor your hate.
   1. Hail.
   2. Hail.
   3. Hail.

Prophecies (43 lines)

APPENDICES 251

               1. Lesser than *Macbeth*, and greater.
               2. Not so happy, yet much happier.
               3. Thou shalt get Kings, though thou be none:
         So all hail *Macbeth*, and *Banquo*.
             1. *Banquo* and *Macbeth*, all hail.
           Macb. Stay, you imperfect Speakers, tell me more:
        By *Sinells* death, I know I am *Thane* of Glamis,
        But how, of Cawdor? the *Thane* of Cawdor lives
        A prosperous Gentleman: and to be King,
        Stands not within the prospect of belief,
        No more than to be Cawdor. Say from whence
        You owe this strange Intelligence, or why
        Upon this blasted Heath you stop our way
        With such Prophetic greeting?
        Speak, I charge you.   *Witches vanish.*
           Banq. The Earth hath bubbles, as the Water ha's,
Interlude   And these are of them: whither are they vanish'd?
of   *Macb.* Into the Air: and what seem'd corporal,
Wonder Melted, as breath into the Wind.
(12 lines) Would they had stay'd.
           Banq. Were such things here, as we do speak about?
        Or have we eaten on the insane Root,
        That takes the Reason Prisoner?   **× Scene Centre**
           Macb. Your Children shall be Kings.
           Banq. You shall be King.
           Macb. And *Thane* of Cawdor too: went it not so?
           Banq. To the self-same tune, and words: who's here?

               Enter Ross and Angus.

           Ross. The King hath happily receiv'd, *Macbeth*,
        The news of thy success: and when he reads
        Thy personal Venture in the Rebels fight,
        His Wonders and his Praises do contend
        Which should be thine, or his: silenc'd with that,
        In viewing o're the rest o'th' self-same day,
        He finds thee in the stout Norweyan Ranks,
        Nothing afeard of what thy self didst make
        Strange images of death, as thick as Tale
        Can post with post, and every one did bear
        Thy praises in his Kingdom's great defense,
        And pour'd them down before him.
           Ang. We are sent,
        To give thee from our Royal Master thanks;
        Only to herald thee into his sight,
        Not pay thee.
           Ross. And for an earnest of a greater Honor,
        He bade me, from him, call thee *Thane* of Cawdor:
        In which addition, hail most worthy *Thane*,
        For it is thine.
Fulfilment   *Banq.* What, can the Devil speak true?
of   *Macb.* The *Thane* of Cawdor lives:
Second Prophecy Why do you dress me in borrowed Robes?
(45 lines)   *Ang.* Who was the *Thane*, lives yet,
        But under heavy Judgement bears that Life,
        Which he deserves to lose.
        Whether he was combin'd with those of Norway,
        Or did line the Rebel with hidden help,
        And vantage; or that with both he labour'd
        In his Country's wreck, I know not:
        But Treasons Capital, confess'd and prov'd,
        Have overthrown him.
           Macb. Glamis, and *Thane* of Cawdor:
        The greatest is behind. Thanks for your pains.
        Do you not hope your Children shall be Kings,
        When those that gave the *Thane* of Cawdor to me,
        Promised no less to them.
           Banq. That trusted home,
        Might yet enkindle you unto the Crown,
        Besides the *Thane* of Cawdor. But 'tis strange:
        And oftentimes, to win us to our harm,
        The Instruments of Darkness tell us Truths,
        Win us with honest Trifles, to betray's
        In deepest consequence.
        Cousins, a word, I pray you.

252   NUMBER AND GEOMETRY IN SHAKESPEARE'S *MACBETH*

39 lines {

Soliloquy: the Vision of Murder (25 lines) {

Macb. Two Truths are told,
As happy Prologues to the swelling Act
Of the Imperial Theme. I thank you Gentlemen:
This supernatural soliciting
Cannot be ill, cannot be good.
If ill? why hath it given me earnest of success,
Commencing in a Truth? I am *Thane* of Cawdor.
If good? why do I yield to that suggestion,
Whose horrid Image doth unfix my Hair,   x Beating Heart
And make my seated Heart knock at my Ribs,   (line 30-)
Against the use of Nature? Present Fears
Are less than horrible Imaginings:
My Thought, whose Murther yet is but fantastical,
Shakes so my single state of Man,
That Function is smother'd in surmise,
And nothing is, but what is not.
  Banq. Look how our Partner's rapt.
  Macb. If Chance will have me King,
Why Chance may Crown me,
Without my stir.
  Banq. New Honors come upon him,
Like our strange Garments, cleave not to their mould,
But with the aid of use.
  Macb. Come what come may,
Time, and the Hour, runs through the roughest Day.
  Banq. Worthy *Macbeth*, we stay upon your ley-
sure.

Macbeth takes Command (14 lines) {

  Macb. Give me your favour:
My dull Brain was wrought with things forgotten.
Kind Gentlemen, your pains are registered,
Where every day I turn the Leaf,
To read them.
Let us toward the King: think upon
What hath chanc'd: and at more time,
The *Interim* having weigh'd it, let us speak
Our free Hearts each to other.
  Banq. Very gladly.
  Macb.. Till then, enough:
Come friends.   *Exeunt.*

Appendix 3

Below, we can see a comparison of the sections of the play to which we have been referring: Act 1 Scene 5, (the section which starts with prose — the letter — and which describes the summoning of spirits) arranged into lines as described, put against Act 5 Scene 1, (the prose section which shows the sleepwalking episode). Note, once again, that these sections are symmetrically opposite in the geometry of the whole play, and to compare them in terms of this symmetry we show the lines of Act 1 moving forwards alongside their partnering lines in Act 5 moving backwards.

```
                                                   324- Gent. Good night good Doctor. Exeunt.
                                                   325- I thinke, but dare not speake.
                                                   326- My minde she ha's mated, and amaz'd my sight.
                                                   327- And still keepe eyes vpon her: So goodnight,
                                                   328- Remoue from her the meanes of all annoyance,
                                                   329- God, God forgiue vs all. Looke after her,
                                                   330- More needs she the Diuine, then the Physitian:
                                                   331- To their deafe pillowes will discharge their Secrets:
                                                   332- Do breed vnnaturall troubles: infected mindes
                                                   333- Doct. Foule whisp'rings are abroad: vnnaturall deeds
                                                   334- Gent. Directly.
                                                   335- Doct. Will she go now to bed?
                                                                                          Exit Lady.
                                                   336- done, cannot be vndone. To bed, to bed, to bed.
                                                   337- Come, come, come, come, giue me your hand: What's
                                                   338- Lady. To bed, to bed: there's knocking at the gate:
                                                   339- Doct. Euen so?
                                                   340- he cannot come out on's graue.
                                                   341- looke not so pale: I tell you yet againe Banquo's buried;
                                                   342- Lad. Wash your hands, put on your Night-Gowne,
                                                   343- dyed holily in their beds.
                                                   344- knowne those which haue walkt in their sleep, who haue
                                                   345- Doct. This disease is beyond my practise: yet I haue
                                                   346- Gent. Pray God it be sir.
                                                   347- Doct. Well, well, well.
                                                   348- for the dignity of the whole body.
                                                   349- Gent. I would not haue such a heart in my bosome,
                                                   350- Doct. What a sigh is there? The hart is sorely charg'd.
```

```
                Scena Quinta.

       Enter Macbeths Wife alone with a Letter.

331 Lady. They met me in the day of successe: and I haue
332 learn'd by the perfect'st report, they haue more in them, then
333 mortall knowledge. When I burnt in desire to question them
334 further, they made themselues Ayre, into which they vanish'd.
335 Whiles I stood rapt in the wonder of it, came Missiues from
336 the King, who all-hail'd me Thane of Cawdor, by which Title
337 before, these weyward Sisters saluted me, and referr'd me to
338 the comming on of time, with haile King that shalt be. This
339 haue I thought good to deliuer thee (my dearest Partner of
340 Greatnesse) that thou might'st not loose the dues of reioycing
341 by being ignorant of what Greatnesse is promis'd thee. Lay
342 it to thy heart and farewell.
```

Below, are indications of a few of the interesting correspondences which can be gleaned by placing the two texts together.

Line 332 : Echo, 'per**fect** ... in**fect**.'
Line 335 : This coincides with the vanishing departure of Lady Macbeth.
Line 340 : 'grave ... greatness,' some echo there.
Line 342 : Both commands.
Line 344 : Echo of 'yet.'
Line 355 : Nice consonance of meaning, the relationship between speaking what she shouldn't and her thought about pouring spirits in her husbands ear, which will be speaking to him.
Line 357 : Sound echo, 'golden ... go to, go to'
Line 360 : 'What' sound echo.
Line 362 : This draws one's attention to the importance of her immediate reaction to the news about Duncan's arrival.
Line 371 : This also sounds like a comment on the position of the words, 'the raven himself is hoarse' which are a very important part in the text for they are a the centre of the scene, 'here's ... hoarse,' there is a certain consonance of sound.
Line 372 : 'croaks ... quarter,' sound echo.
Line 383 : 'you ...come,' repeated.
Line 387 : There is the sense that the words she won't repeat are just precisely those which are matched here which is her absolute spoken avowal that she means to murder Duncan.

APPENDICES

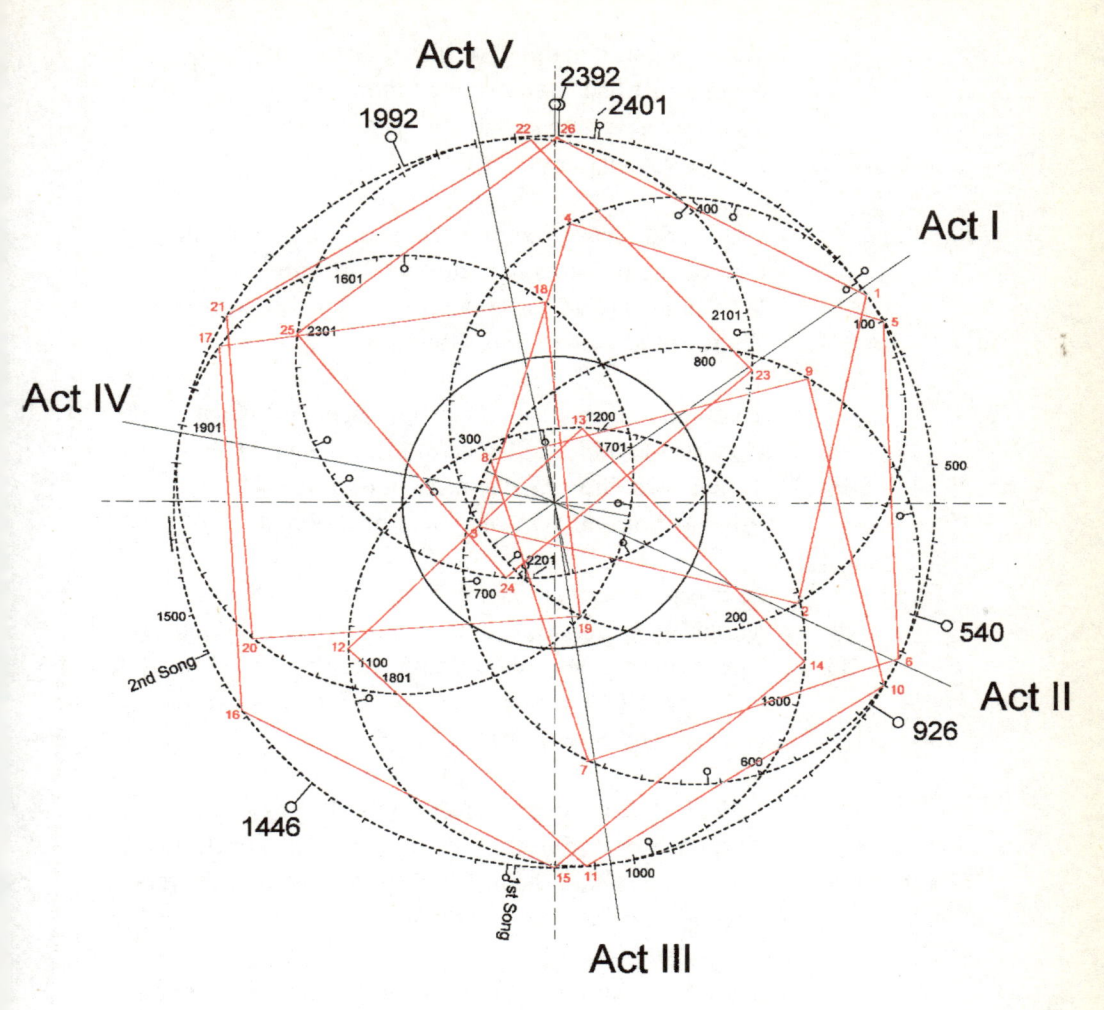

Appendix 4 The 92 rhythm

1 x 92

    1. A Saylors Wife had Chestnuts in her Lappe,
And mouncht, & mouncht, and mouncht:
Giue me, quoth I.
Aroynt thee, Witch, the rumpe-fed Ronyon cryes.

2 x 92 = 184

    Rosse. The King hath happily receiu'd, *Macbeth*,
The newes of thy successe: and when he reades
Thy personall Venture in the Rebels sight,
His Wonders and his Prayses doe contend,

3 × 92 = 276

> Which should be thine, or his: silenc'd with that,
> As one that had beene studied in his death,
> To throw away the dearest thing he ow'd,
> As 'twere a carelesse Trifle.

4 × 92 = 368

> *Mess.* So please you, it is true: our *Thane* is comming:
> One of my fellowes had the speed of him;
> Who almost dead for breath, had scarcely more
> Then would make vp his Message.

5 × 92 = 460

> To plague th' Inuenter. This euen-handed Iustice
> Commends th' Ingredience of our poyson'd Challice
> To our owne lips. Hee's heere in double trust;
> First, as I am his Kinsman, and his Subiect,

6 × 92 = 552

> And yet I would not sleepe:
> Mercifull Powers, restraine in me the cursed thoughts
> That Nature giues way to in repose.
>   *Enter Macbeth, and a Seruant with a Torch.*
> Giue me my Sword: who's there?

7 × 92 = 644

> *Macb.* There's one did laugh in's sleepe,
> And one cry'd Murther, that they did wake each other:
> I stood, and heard them: But they did say their Prayers,
> And addrest them againe to sleepe.

8 × 92 = 736

> and it takes him off; it perswades him, and dis-heartens
> him; makes him stand too, and not stand too: in conclu-
> sion, equiuocates him in a sleepe, and giuing him the Lye,
> leaues him.

9 × 92 = 828

> Th' expedition of my violent Loue
> Out-run the pawser, Reason. Here lay *Duncan*,
> His Siluer skinne, lac'd with His Golden Blood,
> And his gash'd Stabs, look'd like a Breach in Nature,

APPENDICES

                    Rosse. Will you to Scone?
10 x 92 = 920   *Macd.* No Cosin, Ile to Fife.
                    Rosse. Well, I will thither.
                    Macd. Well may you see things wel done there: Adieu

                    Macb. Well then,
                    Now haue you consider'd of my speeches:
11 x 92 = 1012 Know, that it was he, in the times past,
                    Which held you so vnder fortune,

                    Vsing those Thoughts, which should indeed haue dy'd
                    With them they thinke on: things without all remedie
12 x 92 = 1104 Should be without regard: what's done, is done.
                    Macb. We haue scorch'd the Snake, not kill'd it:

                    For my heart speakes, they are welcome.
                        Enter first Murtherer.
13 x 92 = 1196   *Macb.* See they encounter thee with their harts thanks
                    Both sides are euen: heere Ile sit i'th' mid'st,
                    Be large in mirth, anon wee'l drinke a Measure
                    The Table round. There's blood vpon thy face.

                    Macb. I do forget:
14 x 92 = 1288 Do not muse at me my most worthy Friends,
                    I haue a strange infirmity, which is nothing
                    To those that know me. Come, loue and health to all,

                    There hangs a vap'rous drop, profound,
15 x 92 = 1380 Ile catch it ere it come to ground;
                    And that distill'd by Magicke slights,
                    Shall raise such Artificiall Sprights,

                    Roote of Hemlocke, digg'd i'th' darke:
16 x 92 = 1472 Liuer of Blaspheming Iew,
                    Gall of Goate, and Slippes of Yew,
                    Sliuer'd in the Moones Ecclipse:

	Why sinkes that Caldron? & what noise is this? *Hoboyes*
17 x 92 = 1564	1 Shew.
	2 Shew.
	3 Shew.

Son. As Birds do Mother.
18 x 92 = 1656 *Wife.* What with Wormes, and Flyes?
Son. With what I get I meane, and so do they.
Wife. Poore Bird,

Why in that rawnesse left you Wife, and Childe?
19 x 92=1748   Those precious Motiues, those strong knots of Loue,
Without leaue-taking. I pray you,
Let not my Iealousies, be your Dishonors,

Was a most Sainted-King: the Queene that bore thee,
20 x 92 = 1840 Oftner vpon her knees, then on her feet,
Dy'de euery day she liu'd. Fare thee well,
These Euils thou repeat'st vpon thy selfe,

We are comming thither: Gracious England hath
21 x 92 = 1932 Lent vs good *Seyward*, and ten thousand men,
An older, and a better Souldier, none
That Christendome giues out.

Doct. Heark, she speaks, I will set downe what comes
22 x 92 = 2204 from her, to satisfie my remembrance the more strongly.
La. Out damned spot: out I say. One: Two: Why
then 'tis time to doo't: Hell is murky. Fye, my Lord, fie,

The minde I sway by, and the heart I beare,
23 x 92 = 2116 Shall neuer sagge with doubt, nor shake with feare.
Enter Seruant.
The diuell damne thee blacke, thou cream-fac'd Loone:
Where got'st thou that Goose-looke.

                    Till Famine and the Ague eate them vp:
24 x 92 = 2208 Were they not forc'd with those that should be ours,
                    We might haue met them darefull, beard to beard,
                    And beate them backward home. What is that noyse?

                    The Tyrants people, on both sides do fight,
25 x 92 = 2300 The Noble Thanes do brauely in the Warre,
                    The day almost it selfe professes yours,
                    And little is to do.

                    We will performe in measure, time, and place:
                    So thankes to all at once, and to each one,
26 x 92 = 2392 Whom we inuite, to see vs Crown'd at Scone.
                          Flourish.   *Exeunt Omnes.*

Appendix 5

Mirrored Text showing mirrored play-lines of Act 2 (play-lines 541 to 620) in the left-hand column (read downwards), and those of Act 4 (play-lines numbered from the end of the play, that is 541- to 620-; read upwards for continuity.

541	*Banq.* How goes the Night, Boy?	541-	Deale betweene thee and me; For euen now
542	*Fleance.* The Moone is downe: I haue not heard the	542-	From ouer-credulous hast: but God aboue
543	Clock.	543-	Into his power: and modest Wisedome pluckes me
544	*Banq.* And she goes downe at Twelue.	544-	By many of these traines, hath sought to win me
545	*Fleance.* I take't, 'tis later, Sir.	545-	To thy good Truth, and Honor. Diuellish *Macbeth*,
546	*Banq.* Hold, take my Sword:	546-	Wip'd the blacke Scruples, reconcil'd my thoughts
547	There's Husbandry in Heauen,	547-	Childe of integrity, hath from my soule
548	Their Candles are all out: take thee that too.	548-	*Mal. Macduff,* this Noble passion
549	A heauie Summons lyes like Lead vpon me,	549-	Thy hope ends heere.
550	And yet I would not sleepe:	550-	Hath banish'd me from Scotland. O my Brest,
551	Mercifull Powers, restraine in me the cursed thoughts	551-	These Euils thou repeat'st vpon thy selfe,
552	That Nature giues way to in repose.	552-	Dy'de euery day she liu'd. Fare thee well,
	Enter Macbeth, and a Seruant with a Torch.		
553	Giue me my Sword: who's there?	553-	Oftner vpon her knees, then on her feet,
554	*Macb.* A Friend.	554-	Was a most Sainted-King: the Queene that bore thee,
555	*Banq.* What Sir, not yet at rest? the King's a bed.	555-	And do's blaspheme his breed? Thy Royall Father
556	He hath beene in vnusuall Pleasure,	556-	By his owne Interdiction stands accust,
557	And sent forth great Largesse to your Offices.	557-	Since that the truest Issue of thy Throne
558	This Diamond he greetes your Wife withall,	558-	When shalt thou see thy wholsome dayes againe?
559	By the name of most kind Hostesse,	559-	With an vntitled Tyrant, bloody Sceptred,
560	And shut vp in measurelesse content.	560-	*Mac.* Fit to gouern? No not to liue. O Natiŏ miserable!
561	*Mac.* Being vnprepar'd,	561-	I am as I haue spoken.
562	Our will became the seruant to defect,	562-	*Mal.* If such a one be fit to gouerne, speake:
563	Which else should free haue wrought.	563-	*Macd.* O Scotland, Scotland.
564	*Banq.* All's well.	564-	All vnity on earth.
565	I dreamt last Night of the three weyward Sisters:	565-	Vprore the vniuersall peace, confound
566	To you they haue shew'd some truth.	566-	Poure the sweet Milke of Concord, into Hell,
567	*Macb.* I thinke not of them:	567-	Acting it many wayes. Nay, had I powre, I should
568	Yet when we can entreat an houre to serue,	568-	In the diuision of each seuerall Crime,
569	We would spend it in some words vpon that Businesse,	569-	I haue no rellish of them, but abound
570	If you would graunt the time.	570-	Deuotion, Patience, Courage, Fortitude,
571	*Banq.* At your kind'st leysure.	571-	Bounty, Perseuerance, Mercy, Lowlinesse,
572	*Macb.* If you shall cleaue to my consent,	572-	As Iustice, Verity, Temp'rance, Stablenesse,
573	When 'tis, it shall make Honor for you.	573-	*Mal.* But I haue none. The King-becoming Graces,
574	*Banq.* So I lose none,	574-	With other Graces weigh'd.
575	In seeking to augment it, but still keepe	575-	Of your meere Owne. All these are portable,
576	My Bosome franchis'd, and Allegeance cleare,	576-	Scotland hath Foysons, to fill vp your will
577	I shall be counsail'd.	577-	The Sword of our slaine Kings: yet do not feare,
578	*Macb.* Good repose the while.	578-	Then Summer-seeming Lust: and it hath bin
579	*Banq.* Thankes Sir: the like to you. *Exit Banquo.*	579-	stickes deeper: growes with more pernicious roote
580	*Macb.* Goe bid thy Mistresse, when my drinke is ready,	580-	*Macd.* This Auarice
581	She strike vpon the Bell. Get thee to bed. *Exit.*	581-	Destroying them for wealth.
582	Is this a Dagger, which I see before me,	582-	Quarrels vniust against the Good and Loyall,
583	The Handle toward my Hand? Come, let me clutch thee:	583-	To make me hunger more, that I should forge
584	I haue thee not, and yet I see thee still.	584-	And my more-hauing, would be as a Sawce

APPENDICES

85	Art thou not fatall Vision, sensible	585-	Desire his Iewels, and this others House,
86	To feeling, as to sight? or art thou but	586-	I should cut off the Nobles for their Lands,
87	A Dagger of the Minde, a false Creation,	587-	A stanchlesse Auarice, that were I King,
88	Proceeding from the heat-oppressed Braine?	588-	In my most ill-composd Affection, such
89	I see thee yet, in forme as palpable,	589-	*Mal.* With this, there growes
90	As this which now I draw.	590-	Finding it so inclinde.
91	Thou marshall'st me the way that I was going,	591-	As will to Greatnesse dedicate themselues,
92	And such an Instrument I was to vse.	592-	That Vulture in you, to deuoure so many
93	Mine Eyes are made the fooles o'th' other Sences,	593-	We haue willing Dames enough: there cannot be
94	Or else worth all the rest: I see thee still;	594-	And yet seeme cold. The time you may so hoodwinke:
95	And on thy Blade, and Dudgeon, Gouts of Blood,	595-	Conuey your pleasures in a spacious plenty,
96	Which was not so before. There's no such thing:	596-	To take vpon you what is yours: you may
97	It is the bloody Businesse, which informes	597-	And fall of many Kings. But feare not yet
98	Thus to mine Eyes. Now o're the one halfe World	598-	Th' vntimely emptying of the happy Throne
99	Nature seemes dead, and wicked Dreames abuse	599-	In Nature is a Tyranny: It hath beene
00	The Curtain'd sleepe: Witchcraft celebrates	600-	*Macd.* Boundlesse intemperance
01	Pale *Heccats* Offrings: and wither'd Murther,	601-	Then such an one to reigne.
02	Alarum'd by his Centinell, the Wolfe,	602-	That did oppose my will. Better *Macbeth*,
03	Whose howle's his Watch, thus with his stealthy pace,	603-	All continent Impediments would ore-beare
04	With *Tarquins* rauishing sides, towards his designe	604-	The Cesterne of my Lust, and my Desire
05	Moues like a Ghost. Thou sowre and firme-set Earth	605-	Your Matrons, and your Maides, could not fill vp
06	Heare not my steps, which they may walke, for feare	606-	In my Voluptuousnesse: Your Wiues, your Daughters,
07	Thy very stones prate of my where-about,	607-	That ha's a name. But there's no bottome, none
08	And take the present horror from the time,	608-	Sodaine, Malicious, smacking of euery sinne
09	Which now sutes with it. Whiles I threat, he liues:	609-	Luxurious, Auaricious, False, Deceitfull,
10	Words to the heat of deedes too cold breath giues.	610-	*Mal.* I grant him Bloody,
	A Bell rings.		
11	I goe, and it is done: the Bell inuites me.	611-	In euils, to top *Macbeth.*
12	Heare it not, Duncan, for it is a Knell,	612-	Of horrid Hell, can come a Diuell more damn'd
13	That summons thee to Heauen, or to Hell. *Exit.*	613-	*Macd.* Not in the Legions

Scena Secunda.

Enter Lady.

14	*La.* That which hath made thê drunk, hath made me bold:	614-	With my confinelesse harmes.
15	What hath quench'd them, hath giuen me fire.	615-	Esteeme him as a Lambe, being compar'd
16	Hearke, peace: it was the Owle that shriek'd,	616-	Will seeme as pure as Snow, and the poore State
17	The fatall Bell-man, which giues the stern'st good-night.	617-	That when they shall be open'd, blacke *Macbeth*
18	He is about it, the Doores are open:	618-	All the particulars of Vice so grafted,
19	And the surfeted Groomes doe mock their charge	619-	*Mal.* It is my selfe I meane: in whom I know
20	With Snores. I haue drugg'd their Possets,	620-	*Macd.* What should he be?

Appendix 6

The Venom of the Toad

At the beginning of Act 5, whose scene is a coven, the first witch directs the other two to circle the bubbling cauldron and cast into it the horrid ingredients that they have gathered. She herself makes the first throw. It is:

>   1452   Toad that under cold stone,
>   1453   Days and nights, has thirty one:
>   1454   Swelter'd venom sleeping got,

Since in this play numbers mentioned in the text seem invariably to point to numbers which underlie that text, (for example, the 'weary sev'nights' in Act 1 which can all be counted), we are impelled to look for a number here which represents thirty-one days and nights. We observe that the play line 'Fire burn and cauldron bubble,' which must mark the moment when the toad starts to cook, is play-line 1457, whose factors are 31 x 47. However, 47 does not seem an ideal number to represent a day and a night. It should be 48, which would be perfect, because it is twice 24, and two lines would then represent one hour. To arrive at 48 x 31 we have to add an extra 31 group, either after line 1457 or before the beginning of the play. Since the play is circular this is by no means impossible — in fact we have done it already in recognising that the last ten lines of the play function both as an epilogue and as a prologue. There is no reason why this principle should not be extended further backwards, so that the text at the end of the play represents two time-streams: the obvious immediate one which of course is later than the beginning of the play, and a second one which points to events that happened in that dark but very important time before the play begins.

If we add our extra 31 group after line 1457 in Act 4 we arrive at line 1488 — words that are spoken by Hecate:

>   Like elves and fairies in a ring,

She tells the witches to sing round the cauldron and enchant the ingredients they have cast into it. But this moment is clearly too late, since the first witch says the toad has already slept for thirty-one days and nights as she casts it into the cauldron near the beginning of the scene. Therefore, we are left with only one option; to add the 31-line group at the beginning of the play. By adding 31 backwards at the beginning of the play we arrive at line 32 back at the end of Act 5 Scene 7 (because of the overlap of one line at the end of the play). Line 32 back is spoken by Old Seyward:

    2361   Had I as many Sonnes, as I haue haires,

and it is preceded by the line:

    2360   Why then, Gods Soldier be he: (play—line)

The pause between these lines should mark the moment when the toad creeps under the stone and starts to brew its poison. The words here must point to some event in the life of Macbeth that leads to his downfall; an event perhaps that fills him with bitterness and hatred. Since, we think, 48 lines correspond to 24 hours, two lines must correspond to one hour, and 31 lines must correspond to 15½ hours — not, of course, that they are supposed to take that long to say, which would be absurd. But we are perhaps pointed to an event that took place 15½ hours before the opening of the play.

    Between the end and the beginning of the play there is a strong mirror, just as there is at the centre of the play. It is the outermost edges of that central mirror which have come together. Thus the report of young Seyward's death — the last part of it — mirrors the report of Macdonwald's death in Act 1 Scene 2. This ends with those very strange lines:

    34   Which neu'r shooke hands, nor bad farwell to him,
    35   Till he vnseam'd him from the Naue toth' Chops,
    36   And fix'd his Head vpon our Battlements.

I have long suspected that these lines hide a quite different meaning from the apparent one. I believe that he did shake hands and bid farewell to Macbeth because they were friends, and that the 'unseaming' points to the undoing of Macdonwald's armour after his death, when the head would be severed from the body to show as a trophy. Macbeth's plight, after all, was the same as Macdonwald's since both their wives had been seduced by the king, and we may think that, but for the toss of a coin, Macbeth might well have fought on the rebel side. Why he did not is another matter. Perhaps it was to please his wife whom he desperately loved. In any case, the killing of Macdonwald was the betrayal of a friendship, the first in a line of such betrayals. Macbeth will have felt deep guilt, making this day of battle a foul one as well as a fair one, and in suppressing that guilt he hardened himself for later deeds.

There is another aspect to these words 32 lines back from the end of the play. We do not know the number of old Seyward's sons, nor of his heirs, but clearly one comes nowhere near to matching the other. With King Duncan, however, the quantities were closer. The strong thought of Duncan's present here echoes the living Duncan, present in Act 1 Scene 2. His vice was lust and he had bastards all over the country.

There is in fact not merely a double reference, but a triple one in Old Seyward's words when he learns how his son died.

   2360   *Sey.* Why then, Gods Soldier be he:
   2361   Had I as many Sonnes, as I haue haires,
   2362   I would not wish them to a fairer death:
   2363   So his Knell is knoll'd.

There is a line-for-line mirroring between 'Why then, God's Soldier be he' which is 33 lines back, and 'Till hee fac'd the slaue' which is 33 lines forward, which seems to say that Macdonwald too will be God's soldier (this does not contradict the word 'slaue' which means somebody unfree — a man to be pitied, not necessarily an evil man). But those words of Seyward's — 'Why then God's Soldier be he' — we already sense refer to Macbeth as well, who also died bravely a moment since with his wounds 'on the front.'

At the beginning of the play he was a brave and innocent young soldier just like young Seyward. There is a strong sense of 'might-have-been' here, as well as a hint of an answer to that question did Shakespeare after all mean him to go to hell?

Appendix 7

The Soueraigne Flower

At the end of *Macbeth* Act 5 Scene 2 are the following lines:

2099	*Caithness*. Well, march we on,
2100	To giue Obedience, where 'tis truly ow'd:
2101	Meet we the Med'cine of the sickly Weale,
2102	And with him poure we in our Countries purge,
2103	Each drop of vs.
2104	*Lennox*. Or so much as it needes,
2105	To dew the Soueraigne Flower, and drowne the Weeds:
2106	Make we our March towards Birnan.*Exeunt marching*.

The 'Soueraigne Flower' and 'Med'cine of the sickly Weale' is of course Malcolm, who will soon inherit his rightful Kingdom. At the same time we suspect that these metaphors are not vague, but specific, and that Shakespeare had a particular flower in mind.

The word 'sovereign' indicates something of supreme power and in this context points clearly to the idea of a sovereign remedy. It also suggests something round and golden, like a coin (an early kind of sovereign did exist, dating from the time of Henry VIII), and this concept is confirmed by the passage that mirrors these lines across the centre of the play. We come to Act 1 Scene 4 and find King Duncan talking to Macbeth:

287	*King* ...onely I haue left to say,
288	More is thy due, then more than all can pay.

The word 'due' echoes the 'dew' that falls on flowers, confirms the link, and we realize that King Duncan is talking about money — gold coins. We are also searching for a flower that blooms around Whitsun, since other evidence points to the play ending around this season. So, we are looking for a golden flower with supreme healing qualities that flowers in the second half of May, or early June. It may also have a name indicating royalty. There are several candidates: St John's Wort; Penny Royal; Greater and Lesser Celandine; and King Cups.

St John's Wort, though a famous herb, reputed to chase off devils, is so much associated with midsummer and midsummer festivities that we cannot think it is the flower specially referred to at Whitsun. Penny Royal was a famous cure-all; good for coughs, gripe, the stone, jaundice, dropsy and hoarseness, as well as for driving away fleas. But its flowers are small and the name apparently refers to the royal silver penny, whereas we want a reference to something golden. In its favour is the possibility that Macbeth was growing fat and had dropsy. 'He cannot buckle his distempered cause within the belt of rule.'

The Lesser Celandine is interesting because one of its popular names is 'King's Evil,' a condition mentioned in *Macbeth,* and which it was reputed to cure. In Devon, the Lesser Celandine was called 'King Cup,' but elsewhere King Cup meant the beautiful Marsh Marigold, which seems to have been one of Shakespeare's favourite flowers, and which also had a reputation as a devil chaser, though not for other particular medicinal qualities.

Marsh Marigold reminds us of the true garden marigold, which certainly has great round yellow shining flowers like sovereigns. Its Latin name is *Calendula Officinalis,* and we are familiar today with Calendula as a remedy for cuts and wounds. This seems to be extremely appropriate in this context since the Scottish soldiers are going into battle, and some of them will be wounded. If their blood *dews* a marigold, that will be handy, because this flower will cure them if laid on their wounds. Thus, the garden marigold seems to be an excellent candidate, especially as there are so many references to marigolds in Shakespeare's plays. Some scholars think that by 'marigold' he always intended Marsh Marigold, others disagree. Perhaps he sometimes meant one and sometimes the other.

If the garden marigold is intended here then we must suppose that the Scottish army has lately passed by a village, town or castle where there would be gardens. It sounds as if they have all just met before setting out for the rendezvous, near Birnam Wood. It is likely that they are at the castle of one of the thanes. Since war was more or less endemic in Scotland the careful growing of marigolds, or calendula, in castle gardens also seems probable. The fresh or dried flowers would be ready when needed for treatment.

The Tragedie of Macbeth

by William Shakespeare

Numbered First Folio Text

The text of Macbeth here printed is that of the First Folio of 1623. It is presented in a quite particular way to show the line number of each spoken line of text in relation to where it is placed not only in the whole play, but also in each act and in each scene. Line numbers are shown to the left of the main column of text. In the columns to the right of the text we have the line numbers working backwards through the play, again for the whole play, each act and each scene. These reverse numbers, strange though they at first may seem, allow one to find and investigate matching symmetrical lines of text (sometimes referred to as 'mirrored' lines).

By presenting the text in this way the reader may use it not only as a companion to the previous chapters of this book, but also as a means for the researcher to explore further correspondences and layers of meaning within the numerical and geometrical architecture of the play.

Many thanks are given to Michael Best and 'Internet Shakespeare Editions' for the generous usage of the meticulously accurate First Folio Text of 'Macbeth' which was used as the basis for this presentation. The downloaded text was reformatted and, during the writing process, checked with a facsimile of the 1623 First Folio ('Facsimile Edition of First Folio' Kokeritz and Prouty, Geoffrey Cumberlege, Oxford University Press 1955). The letter forms employed by 'Internet Shakespeare Editions' (e.g. The modernisation of the long "s") have been retained as they provide the possibility of most readers being able to follow the text with flow and comfort.

It must be emphasised that it is important for the serious student/researcher to have a facsimile copy to hand (e.g. With regard to the exact setting out of the columns and pages in the original text) for, indeed, many questions still remain concerning the meaning and significance of the setting out of this wonderful book.

How to Use the Numbered Text

The numbers next to the text have been set out in such a way that they can be used not only to show the position of a line in relation to its scene, act, and the whole play, but also in order to find the matching, symmetrical lines of text. Each line may then be seen as part of a spacial/geometrical entity.

    1. Choose the line to be explored and note, in the columns on the left of the text, its playnumber, act-number and scene-number.

    2. Find the mirrored/symmetrical line by looking for the same number in the appropriate righthand column (this number will be marked by a dash to show that it has been counted in reverse).

    E.g. play-line 3 is, '2. When the Hurley-burley's done,' The play mirrored line is, 'We will performe in measure, time, and place:' play-line 3-.

Key to Numbered Text

S = scene centre
A = act centre
P = play centre
B = beginning of 'Weary Sev'nights'
E = end of 'Weary Sev'nights'
* = 'Weary Sev'nights'
Deg. = degrees of the Great Circle
° = degrees of act circles

THE TRAGEDIE OF MACBETH

Angle	Line Numbers Forwards				Line Numbers Backwards		
	Play	Act	Scene		Scene	Act	Play

Actus Primus. Scoena Prima.

Thunder and Lightning. Enter three Witches.

Angle	Play	Act	Scene		Scene	Act	Play
0 deg.							
	1	1	1	1. When shall we three meet againe?	11-	540-	2392-
	2	2	2	In Thunder, Lightning, or in Raine?	10-	539-	2391-
	3	3	3	2. When the Hurley-burley's done,	9-	538-	2390-
	4	4	4	When the Battaile's lost, and wonne.	8-	537-	2389-
3 deg.	5	5	5	3. That will be ere the set of Sunne.	7-	536-	2388-
	6	6	6 S	1. Where the place?	6-	535-	2387-
	7	7	7	2. Vpon the Heath.	5-	534-	2386-
	8	8	8	3. There to meet with *Macbeth*.	4-	533-	2385-
	9	9	9	1. I come, *Gray-Malkin*.	3-	532-	2384-
6 deg.	10	10	10	*All. Padock* calls anon: faire is foule, and foule is faire,	2-	531-	2383-
	11	11	11	Houer through the fogge and filthie ayre. *Exeunt*.	1-	530-	2382-

Scena Secunda.

*Alarum within. Enter King Malcome, Donal-
baine, Lenox, with attendants, meeting
a bleeding Captaine.*

	12	12	1	*King*. What bloody man is that? he can report,	76-	529-	2381-
	13	13	2	As seemeth by his plight, of the Reuolt	75-	528-	2380-
	14	14	3	The newest state.	74-	527-	2379-
9 deg.	15	15	4	*Mal*. This is the Serieant,	73-	526-	2378-
	16	16	5	Who like a good and hardie Souldier fought	72-	525-	2377-
	17	17	6	'Gainst my Captiuitie: Haile braue friend;	71-	524-	2376-
	18	18	7	Say to the King, the knowledge of the Broyle,	70-	523-	2375-
	19	19	8	As thou didst leaue it.	69-	522-	2374-
12 deg.	20	20	9	*Cap*. Doubtfull it stood	68-	521-	2373-

Angle	Play	Act	Scene		The Tragedie of Macbeth	Scene	Act	Play
	21	21	10		As two spent Swimmers, that doe cling together,	67-	520-	2372-
	22	22	11		And choake their Art: The mercilesse Macdonwald	66-	519-	2371-
	23	23	12		(Worthie to be a Rebell, for to that	65-	518-	2370-
	24	24	13		The multiplying Villanies of Nature	64-	517-	2369-
15 deg	25	25	14		Doe swarme vpon him) from the Westerne Isles	63-	516-	2368-
	26	26	15		Of Kernes and Gallowgrosses is supply'd,	62-	515-	2367-
	27	27	16		And Fortune on his damned Quarry smiling,	61-	514-	2366-
	28	28	17		Shew'd like a Rebells Whore: but all's too weake:	60-	513-	2365-
	29	29	18		For braue *Macbeth* (well hee deserues that Name)	59-	512-	2364-
18 deg	30	30	19		Disdayning Fortune, with his brandisht Steele,	58-	511-	2363-
	31	31	20		Which smoak'd with bloody execution	57-	510-	2362-
	32	32	21		(Like Valours Minion) caru'd out his passage,	56-	509-	2361-
	33	33	22		Till hee fac'd the Slaue:	55-	508-	2360-
	34	34	23		Which neu'r shooke hands, nor bad farwell to him,	54-	507-	2359-
21 deg	35	35	24		Till he vnseam'd him from the Naue toth' Chops,	53-	506-	2358-
	36	36	25		And fix'd his Head vpon our Battlements.	52-	505-	2357-
	37	37	26		*King.* O valiant Cousin, worthy Gentleman.	51-	504-	2356-
	38	38	27		*Cap.* As whence the Sunne 'gins his reflection,	50-	503-	2355-
	39	39	28		Shipwracking Stormes, and direfull Thunders:	49-	502-	2354-
24 deg	40	40	29		So from that Spring, whence comfort seem'd to come,	48-	501-	2353-
	41	41	30		Discomfort swells: Marke King of Scotland, marke,	47-	500-	2352-
	42	42	31		No sooner Iustice had, with Valour arm'd,	46-	499-	2351-
	43	43	32		Compell'd these skipping Kernes to trust their heeles,	45-	498-	2350-
	44	44	33		But the Norweyan Lord, surueying vantage,	44-	497-	2349-
27 deg	45	45	34		With furbusht Armes, and new supplyes of men,	43-	496-	2348-
	46	46	35		Began a fresh assault.	42-	495-	2347-
	47	47	36		*King.* Dismay'd not this our Captaines, *Macbeth* and	41-	494-	2346-
	48	48	37		*Banquoh*?	40-	493-	2345-
	49	49	38	S	*Cap.* Yes, as Sparrowes, Eagles;	39-	492-	2344-
30 deg	50	50	39	S	Or the Hare, the Lyon:	38-	491-	2343-
	51	51	40		If I say sooth, I must report they were	37-	490-	2342-
	52	52	41		As Cannons ouer-charg'd with double Cracks,	36-	489-	2341-
	53	53	42		So they doubly redoubled stroakes vpon the Foe:	35-	488-	2340-
	54	54	43		Except they meant to bathe in reeking Wounds,	34-	487-	2339-
33 deg	55	55	44		Or memorize another *Golgotha*,	33-	486-	2338-
	56	56	45		I cannot tell: but I am faint,	32-	485-	2337-
	57	57	46		My Gashes cry for helpe.	31-	484-	2336-
	58	58	47		*King.* So well thy words become thee, as thy wounds,	30-	483-	2335-

Angle	Play	Act	Scene	The Tragedie of Macbeth	Scene	Act	Play
	59	59	48	They smack of Honor both: Goe get him Surgeons.	29-	482-	2334-
				Enter Rosse and Angus			
36 deg	60	60	49	Who comes here?	28-	481-	2333-
	61	61	50	*Mal.* The worthy *Thane* of Rosse.	27-	480-	2332-
	62	62	51	*Lenox.* What a haste lookes through his eyes?	26-	479-	2331-
	63	63	52	So should he looke, that seemes to speake things strange.	25-	478-	2330-
	64	64	53	*Rosse.* God saue the King.	24-	477-	2329-
39 deg	65	65	54	*King.* Whence cam'st thou, worthy *Thane*?	23-	476-	2328-
	66	66	55	*Rosse.* From Fiffe, great King,	22-	475-	2327-
	67	67	56	Where the Norweyan Banners flowt the Skie,	21-	474-	2326-
	68	68	57	And fanne our people cold.	20-	473-	2325-
	69	69	58	Norway himselfe, with terrible numbers,	19-	472-	2324-
42 deg	70	70	59	Assisted by that most disloyall Traytor,	18-	471-	2323-
	71	71	60	The Thane of Cawdor, began a dismall Conflict,	17-	470-	2322-
	72	72	61	Till that *Bellona's* Bridegroome, lapt in proofe,	16-	469-	2321-
	73	73	62	Confronted him with selfe-comparisons,	15-	468-	2320-
	74	74	63	Point against Point, rebellious Arme 'gainst Arme,	14-	467-	2319-
45 deg	75	75	64	Curbing his lauish spirit: and to conclude,	13-	466-	2318-
	76	76	65	The Victorie fell on vs.	12-	465-	2317-
	77	77	66	*King.* Great happinesse.	11-	464-	2316-
	78	78	67	*Rosse.* That now *Sweno*, the Norwayes King,	10-	463-	2315-
	79	79	68	Craues composition:	9-	462-	2314-
48 deg	80	80	69	Nor would we deigne him buriall of his men,	8-	461-	2313-
	81	81	70	Till he disbursed, at Saint *Colmes* ynch,	7-	460-	2312-
	82	82	71	Ten thousand Dollars, to our generall vse.	6-	459-	2311-
	83	83	72	*King.* No more that *Thane* of Cawdor shall deceiue	5-	458-	2310-
	84	84	73	Our Bosome interest: Goe pronounce his present death,	4-	457-	2309-
51 deg	85	85	74	And with his former Title greet *Macbeth*.	3-	456-	2308-
	86	86	75	*Rosse.* Ile see it done.	2-	455-	2307-
	87	87	76	*King.* What he hath lost, Noble Macbeth hath wonne.	1-	454-	2306-
				Exeunt.			
				Scena Tertia.			
				Thunder. Enter the three Witches.			
	88	88	1	1. Where hast thou beene, Sister?	177-	453-	2305-

Angle	Play	Act	Scene	The Tragedie of Macbeth	Scene	Act	Play
	89	89	2	2. Killing Swine.	176-	452-	2304-
54 deg	90	90	3	3. Sister, where thou?	175-	451-	2303-
	91	91	4	1. A Saylors Wife had Chestnuts in her Lappe,	174-	450-	2302-
	92	92	5	And mounch, & mounch, and mounch:	173-	449-	2301-
	93	93	6	Giue me, quoth I.	172-	448-	2300-
	94	94	7	Aroynt thee, Witch, the rumpe-fed Ronyon cryes.	171-	447-	2299-
	95	95	8	Her Husband's to Aleppo gone, Master o'th' Tiger:	170-	446-	2298-
	96	96	9	But in a Syue Ile thither sayle,	169-	445-	2297-
	97	97	10	And like a Rat without a tayle,	168-	444-	2296-
	98	98	11	Ile doe, Ile doe, and Ile doe.	167-	443-	2295-
9 °	99	99	12	2. Ile giue thee a Winde.	166-	442-	2294-
	100	100	13	1. Th'art kinde.	165-	441-	2293-
	101	101	14	3. And I another.	164-	440-	2292-
	102	102	15	1. I my selfe haue all the other,	163-	439-	2291-
	103	103	16	And the very Ports they blow,	162-	438-	2290-
	104	104	17	All the Quarters that they know,	161-	437-	2289-
	105	105	18	I'th' Ship-mans Card.	160-	436-	2288-
	106	106	19	Ile dreyne him drie as Hay:	159-	435-	2287-
	107	107	20	Sleepe shall neyther Night nor Day	158-	434-	2286-
18 °	108	108	21	Hang vpon his Pent-house Lid:	157-	433-	2285-
	109	109	22	He shall liue a man forbid:	156-	432-	2284-
	110	110	23 B	Wearie Seu'nights, nine times nine,	155-	431-	2283-
	111	111	24	Shall he dwindle, peake, and pine:	154-	430-	2282-
	112	112	25	Though his Barke cannot be lost,	153-	429-	2281-
	113	113	26	Yet it shall be Tempest-tost.	152-	428-	2280-
	114	114	27	Looke what I haue.	151-	427-	2279-
	115	115	28	2. Shew me, shew me.	150-	426-	2278-
	116	116	29	1. Here I haue a Pilots Thumbe,	149-	425-	2277-
27 °	117	117	30	Wrackt, as homeward he did come. *Drum within.*	148-	424-	2276-
	118	118	31	3. A Drumme, a Drumme:	147-	423-	2275-
	119	119	32	*Macbeth* doth come.	146-	422-	2274-
	120	120	33	*All.* The weyward Sisters, hand in hand,	145-	421-	2273-
	121	121	34	Posters of the Sea and Land,	144-	420-	2272-
	122	122	35	Thus doe goe, about, about,	143-	419-	2271-
	123	123	36	Thrice to thine, and thrice to mine,	142-	418-	2270-
	124	124	37	And thrice againe, to make vp nine.	141-	417-	2269-
	125	125	38	Peace, the Charme's wound vp.	140-	416-	2268-
				Enter Macbeth and Banquo.			
36 °	126	126	39	*Macb.* So foule and faire a day I haue not seene.	139-	415-	2267-

Angle	Play	Act	Scene	The Tragedie of Macbeth	Scene	Act	Play
	127	127	40 *	*Banquo.* How farre is't call'd to Soris? What are these,	138-	414-	2266-
	128	128	41	So wither'd, and so wilde in their attyre,	137-	413-	2265-
	129	129	42	That looke not like th' Inhabitants o'th' Earth,	136-	412-	2264-
	130	130	43	And yet are on't? Liue you, or are you aught	135-	411-	2263-
	131	131	44	That man may question? you seeme to vnderstand me,	134-	410-	2262-
	132	132	45	By each at once her choppie finger laying	133-	409-	2261-
	133	133	46	Vpon her skinnie Lips: you should be Women,	132-	408-	2260-
	134	134	47	And yet your Beards forbid me to interprete	131-	407-	2259-
45°	135	135	48	That you are so.	130-	406-	2258-
	136	136	49	*Mac.* Speake if you can: what are you?	129-	405-	2257-
	137	137	50	1. All haile *Macbeth*, haile to thee *Thane* of Glamis.	128-	404-	2256-
	138	138	51	2. All haile *Macbeth*, haile to thee *Thane* of Cawdor.	127-	403-	2255-
	139	139	52	3. All haile *Macbeth*, that shalt be King hereafter.	126-	402-	2254-
	140	140	53	*Banq.* Good Sir, why doe you start, and seeme to feare	125-	401-	2253-
	141	141	54	Things that doe sound so faire? i'th' name of truth	124-	400-	2252-
	142	142	55	Are ye fantasticall, or that indeed	123-	399-	2251-
	143	143	56	Which outwardly ye shew? My Noble Partner	122-	398-	2250-
54°	144	144	57 *	You greet with present Grace, and great prediction	121-	397-	2249-
	145	145	58	Of Noble hauing, and of Royall hope,	120-	396-	2248-
	146	146	59	That he seemes wrapt withall: to me you speake not.	119-	395-	2247-
	147	147	60	If you can looke into the Seedes of Time,	118-	394-	2246-
	148	148	61	And say, which Graine will grow, and which will not,	117-	393-	2245-
	149	149	62	Speake then to me, who neyther begge, nor feare	116-	392-	2244-
	150	150	63	Your fauors, nor your hate.	115-	391-	2243-
	151	151	64	1. Hayle.	114-	390-	2242-
	152	152	65	2. Hayle.	113-	389-	2241-
63°	153	153	66	3. Hayle.	112-	388-	2240-
	154	154	67	1. Lesser than *Macbeth*, and greater.	111-	387-	2239-
	155	155	68	2. Not so happy, yet much happyer.	110-	386-	2238-
	156	156	69	3. Thou shalt get Kings, though thou be none:	109-	385-	2237-
	157	157	70	So all haile *Macbeth*, and *Banquo*.	108-	384-	2236-
	158	158	71	1. *Banquo*, and *Macbeth*, all haile.	107-	383-	2235-
	159	159	72	*Macb.* Stay you imperfect Speakers, tell me more:	106-	382-	2234-
	160	160	73	By Sinells death, I know I am *Thane* of Glamis,	105-	381-	2233-
	161	161	74 *	But how, of Cawdor? the *Thane* of Cawdor liues	104-	380-	2232-
72°	162	162	75	A prosperous Gentleman: And to be King,	103-	379-	2231-
	163	163	76	Stands not within the prospect of beleefe,	102-	378-	2230-
	164	164	77	No more then to be Cawdor. Say from whence	101-	377-	2229-
	165	165	78	You owe this strange Intelligence, or why	100-	376-	2228-

Angle	Play	Act	Scene	The Tragedie of Macbeth	Scene	Act	Play
	166	166	79	Vpon this blasted Heath you stop our way	99-	375-	2227-
	167	167	80	With such Prophetique greeting?	98-	374-	2226-
	168	168	81	Speake, I charge you. *Witches vanish.*	97-	373-	2225-
	169	169	82	*Banq.* The Earth hath bubbles, as the Water ha's,	96-	372-	2224-
	170	170	83	And these are of them: whither are they vanish'd?	95-	371-	2223-
81°	171	171	84	*Macb.* Into the Ayre: and what seem'd corporall,	94-	370-	2222-
	172	172	85	Melted, as breath into the Winde.	93-	369-	2221-
	173	173	86	Would they had stay'd.	92-	368-	2220-
	174	174	87	*Banq.* Were such things here, as we doe speake about?	91-	367-	2219-
	175	175	88	Or haue we eaten on the insane Root,	90-	366-	2218-
	176	176	89 S	That takes the Reason Prisoner?	89-	365-	2217-
	177	177	90	*Macb.* Your Children shall be Kings.	88-	364-	2216-
	178	178	91 *	*Banq.* You shall be King.	87-	363-	2215-
	179	179	92	*Macb.* And *Thane* of Cawdor too: went it not so?	86-	362-	2214-
90°	180	180	93	*Banq.* Toth' selfe-same tune and words: who's here?	85-	361-	2213-
				Enter Rosse and Angus.			
	181	181	94	*Rosse.* The King hath happily receiu'd, *Macbeth,*	84-	360-	2212-
	182	182	95	The newes of thy successe: and when he reades	83-	359-	2211-
	183	183	96	Thy personall Venture in the Rebels sight,	82-	358-	2210-
	184	184	97	His Wonders and his Prayses doe contend,	81-	357-	2209-
	185	185	98	Which should be thine, or his: silenc'd with that,	80-	356-	2208-
	186	186	99	In viewing o're the rest o'th' selfe-same day,	79-	355-	2207-
	187	187	100	He findes thee in the stout Norweyan Rankes,	78-	354-	2206-
	188	188	101	Nothing afeard of what thy selfe didst make	77-	353-	2205-
99°	189	189	102	Strange Images of death, as thick as Tale	76-	352-	2204-
	190	190	103	Can post with post, and euery one did beare	75-	351-	2203-
	191	191	104	Thy prayses in his Kingdomes great defence,	74-	350-	2202-
	192	192	105	And powr'd them downe before him.	73-	349-	2201-
	193	193	106	*Ang.* Wee are sent,	72-	348-	2200-
	194	194	107	To giue thee from our Royall Master thanks,	71-	347-	2199-
	195	195	108 *	Onely to harrold thee into his sight,	70-	346-	2198-
	196	196	109	Not pay thee.	69-	345-	2197-
	197	197	110	*Rosse.* And for an earnest of a greater Honor,	68-	344-	2196-
108°	198	198	111	He bad me, from him, call thee Thane of Cawdor:	67-	343-	2195-
	199	199	112	In which addition, haile most worthy Thane,	66-	342-	2194-
	200	200	113	For it is thine.	65-	341-	2193-
	201	201	114	*Banq.* What, can the Deuill speake true?	64-	340-	2192-
	202	202	115	*Macb.* The Thane of Cawdor liues:	63-	339-	2191-
	203	203	116	Why doe you dresse me in borrowed Robes?	62-	338-	2190-

NUMBERED FIRST FOLIO TEXT 275

Angle	Play	Act	Scene	The Tragedie of Macbeth	Scene	Act	Play
	204	204	117	*Ang.* Who was the *Thane*, liues yet,	61-	337-	2189-
	205	205	118	But vnder heauie Iudgement beares that Life,	60-	336-	2188-
	206	206	119	Which he deserues to loose.	59-	335-	2187-
117°	207	207	120	Whether he was combin'd with those of Norway,	58-	334-	2186-
	208	208	121	Or did lyne the Rebell with hidden helpe,	57-	333-	2185-
	209	209	122	And vantage; or that with both he labour'd	56-	332-	2184-
	210	210	123	In his Countreyes wracke, I know not:	55-	331-	2183-
	211	211	124	But Treasons Capitall, confess'd, and prou'd,	54-	330-	2182-
	212	212	125 *	Haue ouerthrowne him.	53-	329-	2181-
	213	213	126	*Macb.* Glamys, and *Thane* of Cawdor:	52-	328-	2180-
	214	214	127	The greatest is behinde. Thankes for your paines.	51-	327-	2179-
	215	215	128	Doe you not hope your Children shall be Kings,	50-	326-	2178-
126°	216	216	129	When those that gaue the *Thane* of Cawdor to me,	49-	325-	2177-
	217	217	130	Promis'd no lesse to them.	48-	324-	2176-
	218	218	131	*Banq.* That trusted home,	47-	323-	2175-
	219	219	132	Might yet enkindle you vnto the Crowne,	46-	322-	2174-
	220	220	133	Besides the Thane of Cawdor. But 'tis strange:	45-	321-	2173-
	221	221	134	And oftentimes, to winne vs to our harme,	44-	320-	2172-
	222	222	135	The Instruments of Darknesse tell vs Truths,	43-	319-	2171-
	223	223	136	Winne vs with honest Trifles, to betray's	42-	318-	2170-
	224	224	137	In deepest consequence.	41-	317-	2169-
135°	225	225	138	Cousins, a word, I pray you.	40-	316-	2168-
	226	226	139	*Macb.* Two Truths are told,	39-	315-	2167-
	227	227	140	As happy Prologues to the swelling Act	38-	314-	2166-
	228	228	141	Of the Imperiall Theame. I thanke you Gentlemen:	37-	313-	2165-
	229	229	142 *	This supernaturall solliciting	36-	312-	2164-
	230	230	143	Cannot be ill; cannot be good.	35-	311-	2163-
	231	231	144	If ill? why hath it giuen me earnest of successe,	34-	310-	2162-
	232	232	145	Commencing in a Truth? I am *Thane* of Cawdor.	33-	309-	2161-
	233	233	146	If good? why doe I yeeld to that suggestion,	32-	308-	2160-
144°	234	234	147	Whose horrid Image doth vnfixe my Heire,	31-	307-	2159-
	235	235	148	And make my seated Heart knock at my Ribbes,	30-	306-	2158-
	236	236	149	Against the vse of Nature? Present Feares	29-	305-	2157-
	237	237	150	Are lesse then horrible Imaginings:	28-	304-	2156-
	238	238	151	My Thought, whose Murther yet is but fantasticall,	27-	303-	2155-
	239	239	152	Shakes so my single state of Man,	26-	302-	2154-
	240	240	153	That Function is smother'd in surmise,	25-	301-	2153-
	241	241	154	And nothing is, but what is not.	24-	300-	2152-
	242	242	155	*Banq.* Looke how our Partner's rapt.	23-	299-	2151-

Angle	Play	Act	Scene	The Tragedie of Macbeth	Scene	Act	Play
153°	243	243	156	Macb. If Chance will haue me King,	22-	298-	2150-
	244	244	157	Why Chance may Crowne me,	21-	297-	2149-
	245	245	158	Without my stirre.	20-	296-	2148-
	246	246	159 *	Banq. New Honors come vpon him	19-	295-	2147-
	247	247	160	Like our strange Garments, cleaue not to their mould,	18-	294-	2146-
	248	248	161	But with the aid of vse.	17-	293-	2145-
	249	249	162	Macb. Come what come may,	16-	292-	2144-
	250	250	163	Time, and the Houre, runs through the roughest Day.	15-	291-	2143-
	251	251	164	Banq. Worthy Macbeth, wee stay vpon your ley-	14-	290-	2142-
162°	252	252	165	sure.	13-	289-	2141-
	253	253	166	Macb. Giue me your fauour:	12-	288-	2140-
	254	254	167	My dull Braine was wrought with things forgotten.	11-	287-	2139-
	255	255	168	Kinde Gentlemen, your paines are registred,	10-	286-	2138-
	256	256	169	Where euery day I turne the Leafe,	9-	285-	2137-
	257	257	170	To reade them.	8-	284-	2136-
	258	258	171	Let vs toward the King: thinke vpon	7-	283-	2135-
	259	259	172	What hath chanc'd: and at more time,	6-	282-	2134-
	260	260	173	The Interim hauing weigh'd it, let vs speake	5-	281-	2133-
171°	261	261	174	Our free Hearts each to other.	4-	280-	2132-
	262	262	175	Banq. Very gladly.	3-	279-	2131-
	263	263	176 *	Macb. Till then enough:	2-	278-	2130-
174°	264	264	177	Come friends. Exeunt.	1-	277-	2129-

Scena Quarta.

Flourish. Enter King, Lenox, Malcolme,
Donalbaine, and Attendants.

	265	265	1	King. Is execution done on Cawdor?	66-	276-	2128-
	266	266	2	Or not those in Commission yet return'd?	65-	275-	2127-
	267	267	3	Mal. My Liege, they are not yet come back.	64-	274-	2126-
	268	268	4	But I haue spoke with one that saw him die:	63-	273-	2125-
	269	269	5	Who did report, that very frankly hee	62-	272-	2124-
180°	270	270	6 A	Confess'd his Treasons, implor'd your Highnesse Pardon,	61-	271-	2123-
	271	271	7 A	And set forth a deepe Repentance:	60-	270-	2122-
	272	272	8	Nothing in his Life became him,	59-	269-	2121-
	273	273	9	Like the leauing it. Hee dy'de,	58-	268-	2120-

NUMBERED FIRST FOLIO TEXT 277

Angle	Play	Act	Scene		The Tragedie of Macbeth	Scene	Act	Play
	274	274	10		As one that had beene studied in his death,	57-	267-	2119-
	275	275	11		To throw away the dearest thing he ow'd,	56-	266-	2118-
	276	276	12		As 'twere a carelesse Trifle.	55-	265-	2117-
	277	277	13		*King.* There's no Art,	54-	264-	2116-
	278	278	14		To finde the Mindes construction in the Face.	53-	263-	2115-
189 °	279	279	15		He was a Gentleman, on whom I built	52-	262-	2114-
	280	280	16	*	An absolute Trust.	51-	261-	2113-
					Enter Macbeth, Banquo, Rosse, and Angus.			
	281	281	17		O worthyest Cousin,	50-	260-	2112-
	282	282	18		The sinne of my Ingratitude euen now	49-	259-	2111-
	283	283	19		Was heauie on me. Thou art so farre before,	48-	258-	2110-
	284	284	20		That swiftest Wing of Recompence is slow,	47-	257-	2109-
	285	285	21		To ouertake thee. Would thou hadst lesse deseru'd,	46-	256-	2108-
	286	286	22		That the proportion both of thanks, and payment,	45-	255-	2107-
	287	287	23		Might haue beene mine: onely I haue left to say,	44-	254-	2106-
198 °	288	288	24		More is thy due, then more then all can pay.	43-	253-	2105-
	289	289	25		*Macb.* The seruice, and the loyaltie I owe,	42-	252-	2104-
	290	290	26		In doing it, payes it selfe.	41-	251-	2103-
	291	291	27		Your Highnesse part, is to receiue our Duties:	40-	250-	2102-
	292	292	28		And our Duties are to your Throne, and State,	39-	249-	2101-
	293	293	29		Children, and Seruants; which doe but what they should,	38-	248-	2100-
	294	294	30		By doing euery thing safe toward your Loue	37-	247-	2099-
	295	295	31		And Honor.	36-	246-	2098-
	296	296	32		*King.* Welcome hither:	35-	245-	2097-
207 °	297	297	33	S*	I haue begun to plant thee, and will labour	34-	244-	2096-
	298	298	34	S	To make thee full of growing. Noble *Banquo*,	33-	243-	2095-
	299	299	35		That hast no lesse deseru'd, nor must be knowne	32-	242-	2094-
	300	300	36		No lesse to haue done so: Let me enfold thee,	31-	241-	2093-
	301	301	37		And hold thee to my Heart.	30-	240-	2092-
	302	302	38		*Banq.* There if I grow,	29-	239-	2091-
	303	303	39		The Haruest is your owne.	28-	238-	2090-
	304	304	40		*King.* My plenteous Ioyes,	27-	237-	2089-
	305	305	41		Wanton in fulnesse, seeke to hide themselues	26-	236-	2088-
216 °	306	306	42		In drops of sorrow. Sonnes, Kinsmen, *Thanes*,	25-	235-	2087-
	307	307	43		And you whose places are the nearest, know,	24-	234-	2086-
	308	308	44		We will establish our Estate vpon	23-	233-	2085-
	309	309	45		Our eldest, *Malcolme*, whom we name hereafter,	22-	232-	2084-
	310	310	46		The Prince of Cumberland: which Honor must	21-	231-	2083-
	311	311	47		Not vnaccompanied, inuest him onely,	20-	230-	2082-

Angle	Play	Act	Scene	The Tragedie of Macbeth	Scene	Act	Play
	312	312	48	But signes of Noblenesse, like Starres, shall shine	19-	229-	2081-
	313	313	49	On all deseruers. From hence to Envernes,	18-	228-	2080-
	314	314	50 *	And binde vs further to you.	17-	227-	2079-
225°	315	315	51	*Macb*. The Rest is Labor, which is not vs'd for you:	16-	226-	2078-
	316	316	52	Ile be my selfe the Herbenger, and make ioyfull	15-	225-	2077-
	317	317	53	The hearing of my Wife, with your approach:	14-	224-	2076-
	318	318	54	So humbly take my leaue.	13-	223-	2075-
	319	319	55	*King*. My worthy *Cawdor*.	12-	222-	2074-
	320	320	56	*Macb*. The Prince of Cumberland: that is a step,	11-	221-	2073-
	321	321	57	On which I must fall downe, or else o're-leape,	10-	220-	2072-
	322	322	58	For in my way it lyes. Starres hide your fires,	9-	219-	2071-
	323	323	59	Let not Light see my black and deepe desires:	8-	218-	2070-
234°	324	324	60	The Eye winke at the Hand: yet let that bee,	7-	217-	2069-
	325	325	61	Which the Eye feares, when it is done to see. *Exit*.	6-	216-	2068-
	326	326	62	*King*. True worthy Banquo: he is full so valiant,	5-	215-	2067-
	327	327	63	And in his commendations, I am fed:	4-	214-	2066-
	328	328	64	It is a Banquet to me. Let's after him,	3-	213-	2065-
	329	329	65	Whose care is gone before, to bid vs welcome:	2-	212-	2064-
240°	330	330	66	It is a peerelesse Kinsman. *Flourish*. *Exeunt*.	1-	211-	2063-

Scena Quinta.

Enter Macbeths Wife alone with a Letter.

	331	331	1 *	*Lady*. They met me in the day of successe: and I haue	81-	210-	2062-
	332	332	2	learn'd by the perfect'st report, they haue more in them, then	80-	209-	2061-
243°	333	333	3	mortall knowledge. When I burnt in desire to question them	79-	208-	2060-
	334	334	4	further, they made themselues Ayre, into which they vanish'd.	78-	207-	2059-
	335	335	5	Whiles I stood rapt in the wonder of it, came Missiues from	77-	206-	2058-
	336	336	6	the King, who all-hail'd me Thane of Cawdor, by which Title	76-	205-	2057-
	337	337	7	before, these weyward Sisters saluted me, and referr'd me to	75-	204-	2056-
	338	338	8	the comming on of time, with haile King that shalt be. This	74-	203-	2055-
	339	339	9	haue I thought good to deliuer thee (my dearest Partner of	73-	202-	2054-
	340	340	10	Greatnesse) that thou might'st not loose the dues of reioycing	72-	201-	2053-
	341	341	11	by being ignorant of what Greatnesse is promis'd thee. Lay	71-	200-	2052-
252°	342	342	12	it to thy heart and farewell.	70-	199-	2051-
	343	343	13	Glamys thou art, and Cawdor, and shalt be	69-	198-	2050-

Angle	Play	Act	Scene	The Tragedie of Macbeth	Scene	Act	Play
	344	344	14	What thou art promis'd: yet doe I feare thy Nature,	68-	197-	2049-
	345	345	15	It is too full o'th' Milke of humane kindnesse,	67-	196-	2048-
	346	346	16	To catch the neerest way. Thou would'st be great,	66-	195-	2047-
	347	347	17	Art not without Ambition, but without	65-	194-	2046-
	348	348	18 *	The illnesse should attend it. What thou would'st highly,	64-	193-	2045-
	349	349	19	That would'st thou holily: would'st not play false,	63-	192-	2044-
	350	350	20	And yet would'st wrongly winne.	62-	191-	2043-
261°	351	351	21	Thould'st haue, great Glamys, that which cryes,	61-	190-	2042-
	352	352	22	Thus thou must doe, if thou haue it;	60-	189-	2041-
	353	353	23	And that which rather thou do'st feare to doe,	59-	188-	2040-
	354	354	24	Then wishest should be vndone. High thee hither,	58-	187-	2039-
	355	355	25	That I may powre my Spirits in thine Eare,	57-	186-	2038-
	356	356	26	And chastise with the valour of my Tongue	56-	185-	2037-
	357	357	27	All that impeides thee from the Golden Round,	55-	184-	2036-
	358	358	28	Which Fate and Metaphysicall ayde doth seeme	54-	183-	2035-
	359	359	29	To haue thee crown'd withall. *Enter Messenger.*	53-	182-	2034-
270°	360	360	30	What is your tidings?	52-	181-	2033-
	361	361	31	*Mess.* The King comes here to Night.	51-	180-	2032-
	362	362	32	*Lady.* Thou'rt mad to say it.	50-	179-	2031-
	363	363	33	Is not thy Master with him? who, wer't so,	49-	178-	2030-
	364	364	34	Would haue inform'd for preparation.	48-	177-	2029-
	365	365	35 *	*Mess.* So please you, it is true: our *Thane* is comming:	47-	176-	2028-
	366	366	36	One of my fellowes had the speed of him;	46-	175-	2027-
	367	367	37	Who almost dead for breath, had scarcely more	45-	174-	2026-
	368	368	38	Then would make vp his Message.	44-	173-	2025-
279°	369	369	39	*Lady.* Giue him tending,	43-	172-	2024-
	370	370	40	He brings great newes, *Exit Messenger.*	42-	171-	2023-
	371	371	41 S	The Rauen himselfe is hoarse,	41-	170-	2022-
	372	372	42	That croakes the fatall entrance of *Duncan*	40-	169-	2021-
	373	373	43	Vnder my Battlements. Come you Spirits,	39-	168-	2020-
	374	374	44	That tend on mortall thoughts, vnsex me here,	38-	167-	2019-
	375	375	45	And fill me from the Crowne to the Toe, top-full	37-	166-	2018-
	376	376	46	Of direst Crueltie: make thick my blood,	36-	165-	2017-
	377	377	47	Stop vp th' accesse, and passage to Remorse,	35-	164-	2016-
288°	378	378	48	That no compunctious visitings of Nature	34-	163-	2015-
	379	379	49	Shake my fell purpose, nor keepe peace betweene	33-	162-	2014-
	380	380	50	Th' effect, and hit. Come to my Womans Brests,	32-	161-	2013-
	381	381	51	And take my Milke for Gall, you murth'ring Ministers,	31-	160-	2012-
	382	382	52 *	Where-euer, in your sightlesse substances,	30-	159-	2011-

Angle	Play	Act	Scene	The Tragedie of Macbeth	Scene	Act	Play
	383	383	53	You wait on Natures Mischiefe. Come thick Night,	29-	158-	2010-
	384	384	54	And pall thee in the dunnest smoake of Hell,	28-	157-	2009-
	385	385	55	That my keene Knife see not the Wound it makes,	27-	156-	2008-
	386	386	56	Nor Heauen peepe through the Blanket of the darke,	26-	155-	2007-
297°	387	387	57	To cry, hold, hold. *Enter Macbeth*.	25-	154-	2006-
	388	388	58	Great Glamys, worthy Cawdor,	24-	153-	2005-
	389	389	59	Greater then both, by the all-haile hereafter,	23-	152-	2004-
	390	390	60	Thy Letters haue transported me beyond	22-	151-	2003-
	391	391	61	This ignorant present, and I feele now	21-	150-	2002-
	392	392	62	The future in the instant.	20-	149-	2001-
	393	393	63	*Macb*. My dearest Loue,	19-	148-	2000-
	394	394	64	Duncan comes here to Night.	18-	147-	1999-
	395	395	65	*Lady*. And when goes hence?	17-	146-	1998-
306°	396	396	66	*Macb*. To morrow, as he purposes.	16-	145-	1997-
	397	397	67	*Lady*. O neuer,	15-	144-	1996-
	398	398	68	Shall Sunne that Morrow see.	14-	143-	1995-
	399	399	69 *	Your Face, my *Thane*, is as a Booke, where men	13-	142-	1994-
	400	400	70	May reade strange matters, to beguile the time.	12-	141-	1993-
	401	401	71	Looke like the time, beare welcome in your Eye,	11-	140-	1992-
	402	402	72	Your Hand, your Tongue: looke like th' innocent flower,	10-	139-	1991-
	403	403	73	But be the Serpent vnder't. He that's comming,	9-	138-	1990-
	404	404	74	Must be prouided for: and you shall put	8-	137-	1989-
315°	405	405	75	This Nights great Businesse into my dispatch,	7-	136-	1988-
	406	406	76	Which shall to all our Nights, and Dayes to come,	6-	135-	1987-
	407	407	77	Giue solely soueraigne sway, and Masterdome.	5-	134-	1986-
	408	408	78	*Macb*. We will speake further,	4-	133-	1985-
	409	409	79	*Lady*. Onely looke vp cleare:	3-	132-	1984-
	410	410	80	To alter fauor, euer is to feare:	2-	131-	1983-
321°	411	411	81	Leaue all the rest to me. *Exeunt*.	1-	130-	1982-

Scena Sexta.

Hoboyes, and Torches. Enter King, Malcolme,
Donalbaine, Banquo, Lenox, Macduff,
Rosse, Angus, and Attendants.

| | 412 | 412 | 1 | *King*. This Castle hath a pleasant seat, | 37- | 129- | 1981- |

NUMBERED FIRST FOLIO TEXT 281

Angle	Play	Act	Scene	The Tragedie of Macbeth	Scene	Act	Play
	413	413	2	The ayre nimbly and sweetly recommends it selfe	36-	128-	1980-
324 °	414	414	3	Vnto our gentle sences.	35-	127-	1979-
	415	415	4	*Banq.* This Guest of Summer,	34-	126-	1978-
	416	416	5	* The Temple-haunting Barlet does approue,	33-	125-	1977-
	417	417	6	By his loued Mansonry, that the Heauens breath	32-	124-	1976-
	418	418	7	Smells wooingly here: no Iutty frieze,	31-	123-	1975-
	419	419	8	Buttrice, nor Coigne of Vantage, but this Bird	30-	122-	1974-
	420	420	9	Hath made his pendant Bed, and procreant Cradle,	29-	121-	1973-
	421	421	10	Where they must breed, and haunt: I haue obseru'd	28-	120-	1972-
	422	422	11	The ayre is delicate. *Enter Lady.*	27-	119-	1971-
333 °	423	423	12	*King.* See, see, our honor'd Hostesse:	26-	118-	1970-
	424	424	13	The Loue that followes vs, sometime is our trouble,	25-	117-	1969-
	425	425	14	Which still we thanke as Loue. Herein I teach you,	24-	116-	1968-
	426	426	15	How you shall bid God-eyld vs for your paines,	23-	115-	1967-
	427	427	16	And thanke vs for your trouble.	22-	114-	1966-
	428	428	17	*Lady.* All our seruice,	21-	113-	1965-
	439	439	18	In euery point twice done, and then done double,	20-	112-	1964-
	430	430	19	S Were poore, and single Businesse, to contend	19-	111-	1963-
	431	431	20	Against those Honors deepe, and broad,	18-	110-	1962-
342 °	432	432	21	Wherewith your Maiestie loades our House:	17-	109-	1961-
	433	433	22	* For those of old, and the late Dignities,	16-	108-	1960-
	434	434	23	Heap'd vp to them, we rest your Ermites.	15-	107-	1959-
	435	435	24	*King.* Where's the Thane of Cawdor?	14-	106-	1958-
	436	436	25	We courst him at the heeles, and had a purpose	13-	105-	1957-
	437	437	26	To be his Purueyor: But he rides well,	12-	104-	1956-
	438	438	27	And his great Loue (sharpe as his Spurre) hath holp him	11-	103-	1955-
	449	449	28	To his home before vs: Faire and Noble Hostesse	10-	102-	1954-
	440	440	29	We are your guest to night.	9-	101-	1953-
351 °	441	441	30	*La.* Your Seruants euer,	8-	100-	1952-
	442	442	31	Haue theirs, themselues, and what is theirs in compt,	7-	99-	1951-
	443	443	32	To make their Audit at your Highnesse pleasure,	6-	98-	1950-
	444	444	33	Still to returne your owne.	5-	97-	1949-
	445	445	34	*King.* Giue me your hand:	4-	96-	1948-
	446	446	35	Conduct me to mine Host we loue him highly,	3-	95-	1947-
	447	447	36	And shall continue, our Graces towards him.	2-	94-	1946-
358 °	448	448	37	By your leaue Hostesse. *Exeunt*	1-	93-	1945-

282   NUMBER AND GEOMETRY IN SHAKESPEARE'S *MACBETH*

Angle	Play	Act	Scene	The Tragedie of Macbeth	Scene	Act	Play
				Scena Septima.			
				Ho-boyes. Torches.			
				Enter a Sewer, and diuers Seruants with Dishes and Seruice ouer the Stage. Then enter Macbeth.			
	449	449	1	*Macb*. If it were done, when 'tis done, then 'twer well,	92-	92-	1944-
360 °	450	450	2	* It were done quickly: If th' Assassination	91-	91-	1943-
	451	451	3	Could trammell vp the Consequence, and catch	90-	90-	1942-
	452	452	4	With his surcease, Successe: that but this blow	89-	89-	1941-
	453	453	5	Might be the be all, and the end all. Heere,	88-	88-	1940-
	454	454	6	But heere, vpon this Banke and Schoole of time,	87-	87-	1939-
57 deg	455	455	7	Wee'ld iumpe the life to come. But in these Cases,	86-	86-	1938-
	456	456	8	We still haue iudgement heere, that we but teach	85-	85-	1937-
	457	457	9	Bloody Instructions, which being taught, returne	84-	84-	1936-
	458	458	10	To plague th' Inuenter. This euen-handed Iustice	83-	83-	1935-
	459	459	11	Commends th' Ingredience of our poyson'd Challice	82-	82-	1934-
60 deg	460	460	12	To our owne lips. Hee's heere in double trust;	81-	81-	1933-
	461	461	13	First, as I am his Kinsman, and his Subiect,	80-	80-	1932-
	462	462	14	Strong both against the Deed: Then, as his Host,	79-	79-	1931-
	463	463	15	Who should against his Murtherer shut the doore,	78-	78-	1930-
	464	464	16	Not beare the knife my selfe. Besides, this *Duncane*	77-	77-	1929-
63 deg	465	465	17	Hath borne his Faculties so meeke; hath bin	76-	76-	1928-
	466	466	18	So cleere in his great Office, that his Vertues	75-	75-	1927-
	467	467	19	* Will pleade like Angels, Trumpet-tongu'd against	74-	74-	1926-
	468	468	20	The deepe damnation of his taking off:	73-	73-	1925-
	469	469	21	And Pitty, like a naked New-borne-Babe,	72-	72-	1924-
66 deg	470	470	22	Striding the blast, or Heauens Cherubin, hors'd	71-	71-	1923-
	471	471	23	Vpon the sightlesse Curriors of the Ayre,	70-	70-	1922-
	472	472	24	Shall blow the horrid deed in euery eye,	69-	69-	1921-
	473	473	25	That teares shall drowne the winde. I haue no Spurre	68-	68-	1920-
	474	474	26	To pricke the sides of my intent, but onely	67-	67-	1919-
69 deg	475	475	27	Vaulting Ambition, which ore-leapes it selfe,	66-	66-	1918-
	476	476	28	And falles on th' other. *Enter Lady.*	65-	65-	1917-
	477	477	29	How now? What Newes?	64-	64-	1916-
	478	478	30	*La*. He has almost supt: why haue you left the chamber?	63-	63-	1915-

Angle	Play	Act	Scene		The Tragedie of Macbeth	Scene	Act	Play
	479	479	31		*Mac.* Hath he ask'd for me?	62-	62-	1914-
72 deg	480	480	32		*La.* Know you not, he ha's?	61-	61-	1913-
	481	481	33		*Mac.* We will proceed no further in this Businesse:	60-	60-	1912-
	482	482	34		He hath Honour'd me of late, and I haue bought	59-	59-	1911-
	483	483	35		Golden Opinions from all sorts of people,	58-	58-	1910-
	484	484	36	*	Which would be worne now in their newest glosse,	57-	57-	1909-
75 deg	485	485	37		Not cast aside so soone.	56-	56-	1908-
	486	486	38		*La.* Was the hope drunke,	55-	55-	1907-
	487	487	39		Wherein you drest your selfe? Hath it slept since?	54-	54-	1906-
	488	488	40		And wakes it now to looke so greene, and pale,	53-	53-	1905-
	489	489	41		At what it did so freely? From this time,	52-	52-	1904-
78 deg	490	490	42		Such I account thy loue. Art thou affeard	51-	51-	1903-
	491	491	43		To be the same in thine owne Act, and Valour,	50-	50-	1902-
	492	492	44		As thou art in desire? Would'st thou haue that	49-	49-	1901-
	493	493	45		Which thou esteem'st the Ornament of Life,	48-	48-	1900-
	494	494	46	S	And liue a Coward in thine owne Esteeme?	47-	47-	1899-
81 deg	495	495	47	S	Letting I dare not, wait vpon I would,	46-	46-	1898-
	496	496	48		Like the poore Cat i'th' Addage.	45-	45-	1897-
	497	497	49		*Macb.* Prythee peace:	44-	44-	1896-
	498	498	50		I dare do all that may become a man,	43-	43-	1895-
	499	499	51		Who dares do more, is none.	42-	42-	1894-
84 deg	500	500	52		*La.* What Beast was't then	41-	41-	1893-
	501	501	53	*	That made you breake this enterprize to me?	40-	40-	1892-
	502	502	54		When you durst do it, then you were a man:	39-	39-	1891-
	503	503	55		And to be more then what you were, you would	38-	38-	1890-
	504	504	56		Be so much more the man. Nor time, nor place	37-	37-	1889-
87 deg	505	505	57		Did then adhere, and yet you would make both:	36-	36-	1888-
	506	506	58		They haue made themselues, and that their fitnesse now	35-	35-	1887-
	507	507	59		Do's vnmake you. I haue giuen Sucke, and know	34-	34-	1886-
	508	508	60		How tender 'tis to loue the Babe that milkes me,	33-	33-	1885-
	509	509	61		I would, while it was smyling in my Face,	32-	32-	1884-
90 deg	510	510	62		Haue pluckt my Nipple from his Bonelesse Gummes,	31-	31-	1883-
	511	511	63		And dasht the Braines out, had I so sworne	30-	30-	1882-
	512	512	64		As you haue done to this.	29-	29-	1881-
	513	513	65		*Macb.* If we should faile?	28-	28-	1880-
	514	514	66		*Lady.* We faile?	27-	27-	1879-
93 deg	515	515	67		But screw your courage to the sticking place,	26-	26-	1878-
	516	516	68		And wee'le not fayle: when Duncan is asleepe,	25-	25-	1877-
	517	517	69		(Whereto the rather shall his dayes hard Iourney	24-	24-	1876-

Angle	Play	Act	Scene	The Tragedie of Macbeth	Scene	Act	Play
	518	518	70 *	Soundly inuite him) his two Chamberlaines	23-	23-	1875-
	519	519	71	Will I with Wine, and Wassell, so conuince,	22-	22-	1874-
96 deg	520	520	72	That Memorie, the Warder of the Braine,	21-	21-	1873-
	521	521	73	Shall be a Fume, and the Receit of Reason	20-	20-	1872-
	522	522	74	A Lymbeck onely: when in Swinish sleepe,	19-	19-	1871-
	523	523	75	Their drenched Natures lyes as in a Death,	18-	18-	1870-
	524	524	76	What cannot you and I performe vpon	17-	17-	1869-
99 deg	525	525	77	Th' vnguarded *Duncan*? What not put vpon	16-	16-	1868-
	526	526	78	His spungie Officers? who shall beare the guilt	15-	15-	1867-
	527	527	79	Of our great quell.	14-	14-	1866-
	528	528	80	*Macb*. Bring forth Men-Children onely:	13-	13-	1865-
	529	529	81	For thy vndaunted Mettle should compose	12-	12-	1864-
102 deg	530	530	82	Nothing but Males. Will it not be receiu'd,	11-	11-	1863-
	531	531	83	When we haue mark'd with blood those sleepie two	10-	10-	1862-
	532	532	84	Of his owne Chamber, and vs'd their very Daggers,	9-	9-	1861-
	533	533	85	That they haue don't?	8-	8-	1860-
	534	534	86	*Lady*. Who dares receiue it other,	7-	7-	1859-
105 deg	535	535	87 *	As we shall make our Griefes and Clamor rore,	6-	6-	1858-
	536	536	88	Vpon his Death?	5-	5-	1857-
	537	537	89	*Macb*. I am settled, and bend vp	4-	4-	1856-
	538	538	90	Each corporall Agent to this terrible Feat.	3-	3-	1855-
	539	539	91	Away, and mock the time with fairest show,	2-	2-	1854-
108 deg	540	540	92	False Face must hide what the false Heart doth know.	1-	1-	1853-

Exeunt.

Actus Secundus. Scena Prima.

Enter Banquo, and Fleance, with a Torch before him.

	541	1	1	*Banq*. How goes the Night, Boy?	73-	386-	1852-
	542	2	2	*Fleance*. The Moone is downe: I haue not heard the	72-	385-	1851-
	543	3	3	Clock.	71-	384-	1850-
	544	4	4	*Banq*. And she goes downe at Twelue.	70-	383-	1849-
111 deg	545	5	5	*Fleance*. I take't, 'tis later, Sir.	69-	382-	1848-
	546	6	6	*Banq*. Hold, take my Sword:	68-	381-	1847-
	547	7	7	There's Husbandry in Heauen,	67-	380-	1846-

NUMBERED FIRST FOLIO TEXT   285

Angle	Play	Act	Scene		The Tragedie of Macbeth	Scene	Act	Play
	548	8	8		Their Candles are all out: take thee that too.	66-	379-	1845-
	549	9	9		A heauie Summons lyes like Lead vpon me,	65-	378-	1844-
114 deg	550	10	10		And yet I would not sleepe:	64-	377-	1843-
	551	11	11		Mercifull Powers, restraine in me the cursed thoughts	63-	376-	1842-
	552	12	12	*	That Nature giues way to in repose.	62-	375-	1841-
					Enter Macbeth, and a Seruant with a Torch.			
0°	553	13	13		Giue me my Sword: who's there?	61-	374-	1840-
	554	14	14		*Macb.* A Friend.	60-	373-	1839-
	555	15	15		*Banq.* What Sir, not yet at rest? the King's a bed.	59-	372-	1838-
	556	16	16		He hath beene in vnusuall Pleasure,	58-	371-	1837-
	557	17	17		And sent forth great Largesse to your Offices.	57-	370-	1836-
	558	18	18		This Diamond he greetes your Wife withall,	56-	369-	1835-
	559	19	19		By the name of most kind Hostesse,	55-	368-	1834-
	560	20	20		And shut vp in measurelesse content.	54-	367-	1833-
	561	21	21		*Mac.* Being vnprepar'd,	53-	366-	1832-
9 °	562	22	22		Our will became the seruant to defect,	52-	365-	1831-
	563	23	23		Which else should free haue wrought.	51-	364-	1830-
	564	24	24		*Banq.* All's well.	50-	363-	1829-
	565	25	25		I dreamt last Night of the three weyward Sisters:	49-	362-	1828-
	566	26	26		To you they haue shew'd some truth.	48-	361-	1827-
	567	27	27		*Macb.* I thinke not of them:	47-	360-	1826-
	568	28	28		Yet when we can entreat an houre to serue,	46-	359-	1825-
	569	29	29	*	We would spend it in some words vpon that Businesse,	45-	358-	1824-
	570	30	30		If you would graunt the time.	44-	357-	1823-
18 °	571	31	31		*Banq.* At your kind'st leysure.	43-	356-	1822-
	572	32	32		*Macb.* If you shall cleaue to my consent,	42-	355-	1821-
	573	33	33		When 'tis, it shall make Honor for you.	41-	354-	1820-
	574	34	34		*Banq.* So I lose none,	40-	353-	1819-
	575	35	35		In seeking to augment it, but still keepe	39-	352-	1818-
	576	36	36		My Bosome franchis'd, and Allegeance cleare,	38-	351-	1817-
	577	37	37	S	I shall be counsail'd.	37-	350-	1816-
	578	38	38		*Macb.* Good repose the while.	36-	349-	1815-
	579	39	39		*Banq.* Thankes Sir: the like to you. *Exit Banquo.*	35-	348-	1814-
27 °	580	40	40		*Macb.* Goe bid thy Mistresse, when my drinke is ready,	34-	347-	1813-
	581	41	41		She strike vpon the Bell. Get thee to bed. *Exit.*	33-	346-	1812-
	582	42	42		Is this a Dagger, which I see before me,	32-	345-	1811-
	583	43	43		The Handle toward my Hand? Come, let me clutch thee:	31-	344-	1810-
	584	44	44		I haue thee not, and yet I see thee still.	30-	343-	1809-
	585	45	45		Art thou not fatall Vision, sensible	29-	342-	1808-

Angle	Play	Act	Scene		The Tragedie of Macbeth	Scene	Act	Play
	586	46	46	*	To feeling, as to sight? or art thou but	28-	341-	1807-
	587	47	47		A Dagger of the Minde, a false Creation,	27-	340-	1806-
	588	48	48		Proceeding from the heat-oppressed Braine?	26-	339-	1805-
36°	589	49	49		I see thee yet, in forme as palpable,	25-	338-	1804-
	590	50	50		As this which now I draw.	24-	337-	1803-
	591	51	51		Thou marshall'st me the way that I was going,	23-	336-	1802-
	592	52	52		And such an Instrument I was to vse.	22-	335-	1801-
	593	53	53		Mine Eyes are made the fooles o'th' other Sences,	21-	334-	1800-
	594	54	54		Or else worth all the rest: I see thee still;	20-	333-	1799-
	595	55	55		And on thy Blade, and Dudgeon, Gouts of Blood,	19-	332-	1798-
	596	56	56		Which was not so before. There's no such thing:	18-	331-	1797-
	597	57	57		It is the bloody Businesse, which informes	17-	330-	1796-
45°	598	58	58		Thus to mine Eyes. Now o're the one halfe World	16-	329-	1795-
	599	59	59		Nature seemes dead, and wicked Dreames abuse	15-	328-	1794-
	600	60	60		The Curtain'd sleepe: Witchcraft celebrates	14-	327-	1793-
	601	61	61		Pale *Heccats* Offrings: and wither'd Murther,	13-	326-	1792-
	602	62	62		Alarum'd by his Centinell, the Wolfe,	12-	325-	1791-
	603	63	63	*	Whose howle's his Watch, thus with his stealthy pace,	11-	324-	1790-
	604	64	64		With *Tarquins* rauishing sides, towards his designe	10-	323-	1789-
	605	65	65		Moues like a Ghost. Thou sowre and firme-set Earth	9-	322-	1788-
	606	66	66		Heare not my steps, which they may walke, for feare	8-	321-	1787-
54°	607	67	67		Thy very stones prate of my where-about,	7-	320-	1786-
	608	68	68		And take the present horror from the time,	6-	319-	1785-
	609	69	69		Which now sutes with it. Whiles I threat, he liues:	5-	318-	1784-
	610	70	70		Words to the heat of deedes too cold breath giues.	4-	317-	1783-
					A Bell rings.			
	611	71	71		I goe, and it is done: the Bell inuites me.	3-	316-	1782-
	612	72	72		Heare it not, Duncan, for it is a Knell,	2-	315-	1781-
	613	73	73		That summons thee to Heauen, or to Hell. *Exit*.	1-	314-	1780-

---

Scena Secunda.

Enter Lady.

	614	74	1		*La.* That which hath made thê drunk, hath made me bold:	90-	313-	1779-
	615	75	2		What hath quench'd them, hath giuen me fire.	89-	312-	1778-
63°	616	76	3		Hearke, peace: it was the Owle that shriek'd,	88-	311-	1777-

Angle	Play	Act	Scene	The Tragedie of Macbeth	Scene	Act	Play
	617	77	4	The fatall Bell-man, which giues the stern'st good-night.	87-	310-	1776-
	618	78	5	He is about it, the Doores are open:	86-	309-	1775-
	619	79	6	And the surfeted Groomes doe mock their charge	85-	308-	1774-
	620	80	7 *	With Snores. I haue drugg'd their Possets,	84-	307-	1773-
	621	81	8	That Death and Nature doe contend about them,	83-	306-	1772-
	622	82	9	Whether they liue, or dye.	82-	305-	1771-
				Enter Macbeth.			
	623	83	10	*Macb.* Who's there? what hoa?	81-	304-	1770-
	624	84	11	*Lady.* Alack, I am afraid they haue awak'd,	80-	303-	1769-
72°	625	85	12	And 'tis not done: th' attempt, and not the deed,	79-	302-	1768-
	626	86	13	Confounds vs: hearke: I lay'd their Daggers ready,	78-	301-	1767-
	627	87	14	He could not misse 'em. Had he not resembled	77-	300-	1766-
	628	88	15	My Father as he slept, I had don't.	76-	299-	1765-
	629	89	16	My Husband?	75-	298-	1764-
	630	90	17	*Macb.* I haue done the deed:	74-	297-	1763-
	631	91	18	Didst thou not heare a noyse?	73-	296-	1762-
	632	92	19	*Lady.* I heard the Owle schreame, and the Crickets cry.	72-	295-	1761-
	633	93	20	Did not you speake?	71-	294-	1760-
81°	634	94	21	*Macb.* When?	70-	293-	1759-
	635	95	22	*Lady.* Now.	69-	292-	1758-
	636	96	23	*Macb.* As I descended?	68-	291-	1757-
	637	97	24 *	*Lady.* I.	67-	290-	1756-
	638	98	25	*Macb.* Hearke, who lyes i'th' second Chamber?	66-	289-	1755-
	639	99	26	*Lady.* Donalbaine.	65-	288-	1754-
	640	100	27	*Mac.* This is a sorry sight.	64-	287-	1753-
	641	101	28	*Lady.* A foolish thought, to say a sorry sight.	63-	286-	1752-
	642	102	29	*Macb.* There's one did laugh in's sleepe,	62-	285-	1751-
90°	643	103	30	And one cry'd Murther, that they did wake each other:	61-	284-	1750-
	644	104	31	I stood, and heard them: But they did say their Prayers,	60-	283-	1749-
	645	105	32	And addrest them againe to sleepe.	59-	282-	1748-
	646	106	33	*Lady.* There are two lodg'd together.	58-	281-	1747-
	647	107	34	*Macb.* One cry'd God blesse vs, and Amen the other,	57-	280-	1746-
	648	108	35	As they had seene me with these Hangmans hands:	56-	279-	1745-
	649	109	36	Listning their feare, I could not say Amen,	55-	278-	1744-
	650	110	37	When they did say God blesse vs.	54-	277-	1743-
	651	111	38	*Lady.* Consider it not so deepely.	53-	276-	1742-
99°	652	112	39	*Mac.* But wherefore could not I pronounce Amen?	52-	275-	1741-
	653	113	40	I had most need of Blessing, and Amen stuck in my throat.	51-	274-	1740-
	654	114	41 *	*Lady.* These deeds must not be thought	50-	273-	1739-

Angle	Play	Act	Scene		The Tragedie of Macbeth	Scene	Act	Play
	655	115	42		After these wayes: so, it will make vs mad.	49-	272-	1738-
	656	116	43		*Macb.* Me thought I heard a voyce cry, Sleep no more:	48-	271-	1737-
	657	117	44		Macbeth does murther Sleepe, the innocent Sleepe,	47-	270-	1736-
	658	118	45	S	Sleepe that knits vp the rauel'd Sleeue of Care,	46-	269-	1735-
	659	119	46	S	The death of each dayes Life, sore Labors Bath,	45-	268-	1734-
	660	120	47		Balme of hurt Mindes, great Natures second Course,	44-	267-	1733-
108°	661	121	48		Chiefe nourisher in Life's Feast.	43-	266-	1732-
	662	122	49		*Lady.* What doe you meane?	42-	265-	1731-
	663	123	50		*Macb.* Still it cry'd, Sleepe no more to all the House:	41-	264-	1730-
	664	124	51		Glamis hath murther'd Sleepe, and therefore *Cawdor*	40-	263-	1729-
	665	125	52		Shall sleepe no more: *Macbeth* shall sleepe no more.	39-	262-	1728-
	666	126	53		Lady. Who was it, that thus cry'd? why worthy *Thane*,	38-	261-	1727-
	667	127	54		You doe vnbend your Noble strength, to thinke	37-	260-	1726-
	668	128	55		So braine-sickly of things: Goe get some Water,	36-	259-	1725-
	669	129	56		And wash this filthie Witnesse from your Hand.	35-	258-	1724-
117°	670	130	57		Why did you bring these Daggers from the place?	34-	257-	1723-
	671	131	58	*	They must lye there: goe carry them, and smeare	33-	256-	1722-
	672	132	59		The sleepie Groomes with blood.	32-	255-	1721-
	673	133	60		*Macb.* Ile goe no more:	31-	254-	1720-
	674	134	61		I am afraid, to thinke what I haue done:	30-	253-	1719-
	675	135	62		Looke on't againe, I dare not.	29-	252-	1718-
	676	136	63		*Lady.* Infirme of purpose:	28-	251-	1717-
	677	137	64		Giue me the Daggers: the sleeping, and the dead,	27-	250-	1716-
	678	138	65		Are but as Pictures: 'tis the Eye of Child-hood,	26-	249-	1715-
126°	679	139	66		That feares a painted Deuill. If he doe bleed,	25-	248-	1714-
	680	140	67		Ile guild the Faces of the Groomes withall,	24-	247-	1713-
	681	141	68		For it must seeme their Guilt. *Exit.*	23-	246-	1712-
					Knocke within.			
	682	142	69		*Macb.* Whence is that knocking?	22-	245-	1711-
	683	143	70		How is't with me, when euery noyse appalls me?	21-	244-	1710-
	684	144	71		What Hands are here? hah: they pluck out mine Eyes.	20-	243-	1709-
	685	145	72		Will all great Neptunes Ocean wash this blood	19-	242-	1708-
	686	146	73		Cleane from my Hand? no: this my Hand will rather	18-	241-	1707-
	687	147	74		The multitudinous Seas incarnardine,	17-	240-	1706-
135°	688	148	75	*	Making the Greene one, Red.	16-	239-	1705-
					Enter Lady.			
	689	149	76		*Lady.* My Hands are of your colour: but I shame	15-	238-	1704-
	690	150	77		To weare a Heart so white. *Knocke.*	14-	237-	1703-
	691	151	78		I heare a knocking at the South entry:	13-	236-	1702-

NUMBERED FIRST FOLIO TEXT   289

Angle	Play	Act	Scene	The Tragedie of Macbeth	Scene	Act	Play
	692	152	79	Retyre we to our Chamber:	12-	235-	1701-
	693	153	80	A little Water cleares vs of this deed.	11-	234-	1700-
	694	154	81	How easie is it then? your Constancie	10-	233-	1699-
	695	155	82	Hath left you vnattended. *Knocke.*	9-	232-	1698-
	696	156	83	Hearke, more knocking.	8-	231-	1697-
144°	697	157	84	Get on your Night-Gowne, least occasion call vs,	7-	230-	1696-
	698	158	85	And shew vs to be Watchers: be not lost	6-	229-	1695-
	699	159	86	So poorely in your thoughts.	5-	228-	1694-
	700	160	87	*Macb.* To know my deed, *Knocke.*	4-	227-	1693-
	701	161	88	'Twere best not know my selfe.	3-	226-	1692-
	702	162	89	Wake *Duncan* with thy knocking:	2-	225-	1691-
150°	703	163	90	I would thou could'st. *Exeunt.*	1-	224-	1690-

Scena Tertia.

Enter a Porter.
                                        Knocking within.

	704	164	1		*Porter.* Here's a knocking indeede: if a man were	170-	223-	1689-
	705	165	2	*	Porter of Hell Gate, hee should haue old turning the	169-	222-	1688-
153°	706	166	3		Key. *Knock.* Knock, Knock, Knock. Who's there	168-	221-	1687-
	707	167	4		i'th' name of *Belzebub*? Here's a Farmer, that hang'd	167-	220-	1686-
	708	168	5		himselfe on th' expectation of Plentie: Come in time, haue	166-	219-	1685-
	709	169	6		Napkins enow about you, here you'le sweat for't. *Knock.*	165-	218-	1684-
	710	170	7		Knock, knock. Who's there in th' other Deuils Name?	164-	217-	1683-
	711	171	8		Faith here's an Equiuocator, that could sweare in both	163-	216-	1682-
	712	172	9		the Scales against eyther Scale, who committed Treason	162-	215-	1681-
	713	173	10		enough for Gods sake, yet could not equiuocate to Hea-	161-	214-	1680-
	714	174	11		uen: oh come in, Equiuocator. *Knock.* Knock,	160-	213-	1679-
162°	715	175	12		Knock, Knock. Who's there? 'Faith here's an English	159-	212-	1678-
	716	176	13		Taylor come hither, for stealing out of a French Hose:	158-	211-	1677-
	717	177	14		Come in Taylor, here you may rost your Goose. *Knock.*	157-	210-	1676-
	718	178	15		Knock, Knock. Neuer at quiet: What are you? but this	156-	209-	1675-
	719	179	16		place is too cold for Hell. Ile Deuill-Porter it no further:	155-	208-	1674-
	720	180	17		I had thought to haue let in some of all Professions, that	154-	207-	1673-
	721	181	18		goe the Primrose way to th' euerlasting Bonfire. *Knock.*	153-	206-	1672-
	722	182	19	*	Anon, anon, I pray you remember the Porter.	152-	205-	1671-

Enter Macduff, and Lenox

Angle	Play	Act	Scene	The Tragedie of Macbeth	Scene	Act	Play
	723	183	20	*Macd.* Was it so late, friend, ere you went to Bed,	151-	204-	1670-
171°	724	184	21	That you doe lye so late?	150-	203-	1669-
	725	185	22	*Port.* Faith Sir, we were carowsing till the second Cock:	149-	202-	1668-
	726	186	23	And Drinke, Sir, is a great prouoker of three things.	148-	201-	1667-
	727	187	24	*Macd.* What three things does Drinke especially	147-	200-	1666-
	728	188	25	prouoke?	146-	199-	1665-
	729	189	26	*Port.* Marry, Sir, Nose-painting, Sleepe, and Vrine.	145-	198-	1664-
	730	190	27	Lecherie, Sir, it prouokes, and vnprouokes: it prouokes	144-	197-	1663-
	731	191	28	the desire, but it takes away the performance. Therefore	143-	196-	1662-
	732	192	29	much Drinke may be said to be an Equiuocator with Le-	142-	195-	1661-
180°	733	193	30 A	cherie: it makes him, and it marres him; it sets him on,	141-	194-	1660-
	734	194	31 A	and it takes him off; it perswades him, and dis-heartens	140-	193-	1659-
	735	195	32	him; makes him stand too, and not stand too: in conclu-	139-	192-	1658-
	736	196	33	sion, equiuocates him in a sleepe, and giuing him the Lye,	138-	191-	1657-
	737	197	34	leaues him.	137-	190-	1656-
	738	198	35	*Macd.* I beleeue, Drinke gaue thee the Lye last Night.	136-	189-	1655-
	739	199	36 *	*Port.* That it did, Sir, i'the very Throat on me: but I	135-	188-	1654-
	740	200	37	requited him for his Lye, and (I thinke) being too strong	134-	187-	1653-
	741	201	38	for him, though he tooke vp my Legges sometime, yet I	133-	186-	1652-
189°	742	202	39	made a Shift to cast him.	132-	185-	1651-
				Enter Macbeth.			
	743	203	40	*Macd.* Is thy Master stirring?	131-	184-	1650-
	744	204	41	Our knocking ha's awak'd him: here he comes.	130-	183-	1649-
	745	205	42	*Lenox.* Good morrow, Noble Sir.	129-	182-	1648-
	746	206	43	*Macb.* Good morrow both.	128-	181-	1647-
	747	207	44	*Macd.* Is the King stirring, worthy *Thane*?	127-	180-	1646-
	748	208	45	*Macb.* Not yet.	126-	179-	1645-
	749	209	46	*Macd.* He did command me to call timely on him,	125-	178-	1644-
	750	210	47	I haue almost slipt the houre.	124-	177-	1643-
198°	751	211	48	*Macb.* Ile bring you to him.	123-	176-	1642-
	752	212	49	*Macd.* I know this is a ioyfull trouble to you:	122-	175-	1641-
	753	213	50	But yet 'tis one.	121-	174-	1640-
	754	214	51	*Macb.* The labour we delight in, Physicks paine:	120-	173-	1639-
	755	215	52	This is the Doore.	119-	172-	1638-
	756	216	53 *	*Macd.* Ile make so bold to call, for 'tis my limitted	118-	171-	1637-
	757	217	54	seruice. *Exit Macduffe.*	117-	170-	1636-
	758	218	55	*Lenox.* Goes the King hence to day?	116-	169-	1635-
	759	219	56	*Macb.* He does: he did appoint so.	115-	168-	1634-
207°	760	220	57	*Lenox.* The Night ha's been vnruly:	114-	167-	1633-

Angle	Play	Act	Scene		The Tragedie of Macbeth	Scene	Act	Play
	761	221	58		Where we lay, our Chimneys were blowne downe,	113-	166-	1632-
	762	222	59		And (as they say) lamentings heard i'th' Ayre;	112-	165-	1631-
	763	223	60		Strange Schreemes of Death,	111-	164-	1630-
	764	224	61		And Prophecying, with Accents terrible,	110-	163-	1629-
	765	225	62		Of dyre Combustion, and confus'd Euents,	109-	162-	1628-
	766	226	63		New hatch'd toth' wofull time.	108-	161-	1627-
	767	227	64		The obscure Bird clamor'd the liue-long Night.	107-	160-	1626-
	768	228	65		Some say, the Earth was Feuorous,	106-	159-	1625-
216°	769	229	66		And did shake.	105-	158-	1624-
	770	230	67		*Macb.* 'Twas a rough Night.	104-	157-	1623-
	771	231	68		*Lenox.* My young remembrance cannot paralell	103-	156-	1622-
	772	232	69		A fellow to it.	102-	155-	1621-
					Enter Macduff.			
	773	233	70	*	*Macd.* O horror, horror, horror.	101-	154-	1620-
	774	234	71		Tongue nor Heart cannot conceiue, nor name thee.	100-	153-	1619-
	775	235	72		*Macb. and Lenox.* What's the matter?	99-	152-	1618-
	776	236	73		*Macd.* Confusion now hath made his Master-peece:	98-	151-	1617-
	777	237	74		Most sacrilegious Murther hath broke ope	97-	150-	1616-
225°	778	238	75		The Lords anoynted Temple, and stole thence	96-	149-	1615-
	779	239	76		The Life o'th' Building.	95-	148-	1614-
	780	240	77		*Macb.* What is't you say, the Life?	94-	147-	1613-
	781	241	78		*Lenox.* Meane you his Maiestie?	93-	146-	1612-
	782	242	79		*Macd.* Approch the Chamber, and destroy your sight	92-	145-	1611-
	783	243	80		With a new *Gorgon*. Doe not bid me speake:	91-	144-	1610-
	784	244	81		See, and then speake your selues: awake, awake,	90-	143-	1609-
					Exeunt Macbeth and Lenox.			
	785	245	82		Ring the Alarum Bell: Murther, and Treason,	89-	142-	1608-
	786	246	83		*Banquo,* and *Donalbaine: Malcolme* awake,	88-	141-	1607-
234°	787	247	84		Shake off this Downey sleepe, Deaths counterfeit,	87-	140-	1606-
	788	248	85	S	And looke on Death it selfe: vp, vp, and see	86-	139-	1605-
	789	249	86	S	The great Doomes Image: *Malcolme, Banquo,*	85-	138-	1604-
	790	250	87	*	As from your Graues rise vp, and walke like Sprights,	84-	137-	1603-
	791	251	88		To countenance this horror. Ring the Bell.	83-	136-	1602-
					Bell rings. Enter Lady.			
	792	252	89		*Lady.* What's the Businesse?	82-	135-	1601-
	793	253	90		That such a hideous Trumpet calls to parley	81-	134-	1600-
	794	254	91		The sleepers of the House? speake, speake.	80-	133-	1599-
	795	255	92		*Macd.* O gentle Lady,	79-	132-	1598-
243°	796	256	93		'Tis not for you to heare what I can speake:	78-	131-	1597-

Angle	Play	Act	Scene	The Tragedie of Macbeth	Scene	Act	Play
	797	257	94	The repetition in a Womans eare,	77-	130-	1596-
	798	258	95	Would murther as it fell.	76-	129-	1595-
				Enter Banquo.			
	799	259	96	O *Banquo, Banquo,* Our Royall Master's murther'd.	75-	128-	1594-
	800	260	97	*Lady.* Woe, alas:	74-	127-	1593-
	801	261	98	What, in our House?	73-	126-	1592-
	802	262	99	*Ban.* Too cruell, any where.	72-	125-	1591-
	803	263	100	Deare *Duff,* I prythee contradict thy selfe,	71-	124-	1590-
	804	264	101	And say, it is not so.	70-	123-	1589-
				Enter Macbeth, Lenox, and Rosse.			
252 °	805	265	102	*Macb.* Had I but dy'd an houre before this chance,	69-	122-	1588-
	806	266	103	I had liu'd a blessed time: for from this instant,	68-	121-	1587-
	807	267	104 *	There's nothing serious in Mortalitie:	67-	120-	1586-
	808	268	105	All is but Toyes: Renowne and Grace is dead	66-	119-	1585-
	809	269	106	The Wine of Life is drawne, and the meere Lees	65-	118-	1584-
	810	270	107	Is left this Vault, to brag of.	64-	117-	1583-
				Enter Malcolme and Donalbaine.			
	811	271	108	*Donal.* What is amisse?	63-	116-	1582-
	812	272	109	*Macb.* You are, and doe not know't:	62-	115-	1581-
	813	273	110	The Spring, the Head, the Fountaine of your Blood	61-	114-	1580-
261 °	814	274	111	Is stopt, the very Source of it is stopt.	60-	113-	1579-
	815	275	112	*Macd.* Your Royall Father's murther'd.	59-	112-	1578-
	816	276	113	*Mal.* Oh, by whom?	58-	111-	1577-
	817	277	114	*Lenox.* Those of his Chamber, as it seem'd, had don't:	57-	110-	1576-
	818	278	115	Their Hands and Faces were all badg'd with blood,	56-	109-	1575-
	819	279	116	So were their Daggers, which vnwip'd, we found	55-	108-	1574-
	820	280	117	Vpon their Pillowes: they star'd, and were distracted,	54-	107-	1573-
	821	281	118	No mans Life was to be trusted with them.	53-	106-	1572-
	822	282	119	*Macb.* O, yet I doe repent me of my furie,	52-	105-	1571-
270 °	823	283	120	That I did kill them.	51-	104-	1570-
	824	284	121 *	*Macd.* Wherefore did you so?	50-	103-	1569-
	825	285	122	*Macb.* Who can be wise, amaz'd, temp'rate, & furious,	49-	102-	1568-
	826	286	123	Loyall, and Neutrall, in a moment? No man:	48-	101-	1567-
	827	287	124	Th' expedition of my violent Loue	47-	100-	1566-
	828	288	125	Out-run the pawser, Reason. Here lay *Duncan,*	46-	99-	1565-
	829	289	126	His Siluer skinne, lac'd with His Golden Blood,	45-	98-	1564-
	830	290	127	And his gash'd Stabs, look'd like a Breach in Nature,	44-	97-	1563-
	831	291	128	For Ruines wastfull entrance: there the Murtherers,	43-	96-	1562-
279 °	832	292	129	Steep'd in the Colours of their Trade; their Daggers	42-	95-	1561-

NUMBERED FIRST FOLIO TEXT 293

The Tragedie of Macbeth

Angle	Play	Act	Scene		Scene	Act	Play
	833	293	130	Vnmannerly breech'd with gore: who could refraine,	41-	94-	1560-
	834	294	131	That had a heart to loue; and in that heart,	40-	93-	1559-
	835	295	132	Courage, to make's loue knowne?	39-	92-	1558-
	836	296	133	*Lady.* Helpe me hence, hoa.	38-	91-	1557-
	837	297	134	*Macd.* Looke to the Lady.	37-	90-	1556-
	838	298	135	*Mal.* Why doe we hold our tongues,	36-	89-	1555-
	839	299	136	That most may clayme this argument for ours?	35-	88-	1554-
	840	300	137	*Donal.* What should be spoken here,	34-	87-	1553-
288°	841	301	138 *	Where our Fate hid in an augure hole,	33-	86-	1552-
	842	302	139	May rush, and seize vs? Let's away,	32-	85-	1551-
	843	303	140	Our Teares are not yet brew'd.	31-	84-	1550-
	844	304	141	*Mal.* Nor our strong Sorrow	30-	83-	1549-
	845	305	142	Vpon the foot of Motion.	29-	82-	1548-
	846	306	143	*Banq.* Looke to the Lady:	28-	81-	1547-
	847	307	144	And when we haue our naked Frailties hid,	27-	80-	1546-
	848	308	145	That suffer in exposure; let vs meet,	26-	79-	1545-
	849	309	146	And question this most bloody piece of worke,	25-	78-	1544-
297°	850	310	147	To know it further. Feares and scruples shake vs:	24-	77-	1543-
	851	311	148	In the great Hand of God I stand, and thence,	23-	76-	1542-
	852	312	149	Against the vndivulg'd pretence, I fight	22-	75-	1541-
	853	313	150	Of Treasonous Mallice.	21-	74-	1540-
	854	314	151	*Macd.* And so doe I.	20-	73-	1539-
	855	315	152	*All.* So all.	19-	72-	1538-
	856	316	153	*Macb.* Let's briefely put on manly readinesse,	18-	71-	1537-
	857	317	154	And meet i'th' Hall together.	17-	70-	1536-
	858	318	155 *	*All.* Well contented. *Exeunt.*	16-	69-	1535-
306°	859	319	156	*Malc.* What will you doe?	15-	68-	1534-
	860	320	157	Let's not consort with them:	14-	67-	1533-
	861	321	158	To shew an vnfelt Sorrow, is an Office	13-	66-	1532-
	862	322	159	Which the false man do's easie.	12-	65-	1531-
	863	323	160	Ile to England.	11-	64-	1530-
	864	324	161	*Don.* To Ireland, I:	10-	63-	1529-
	865	325	162	Our seperated fortune shall keepe vs both the safer:	9-	62-	1528-
	866	326	163	Where we are, there's Daggers in mens smiles;	8-	61-	1527-
	867	327	164	The neere in blood, the neerer bloody.	7-	60-	1526-
315°	868	328	165	*Malc.* This murtherous Shaft that's shot,	6-	59-	1525-
	869	329	166	Hath not yet lighted: and our safest way,	5-	58-	1524-
	870	330	167	Is to auoid the ayme. Therefore to Horse,	4-	57-	1523-
	871	331	168	And let vs not be daintie of leaue-taking,	3-	56-	1522-

Angle	Play	Act	Scene	The Tragedie of Macbeth	Scene	Act	Play
	872	332	169	But shift away: there's warrant in that Theft,	2-	55-	1521-
320°	873	333	170	Which steales it selfe, when there's no mercie left.	1-	54-	1520-
				Exeunt.			
				Scena Quarta.			
				Enter Rosse, with an Old man.			
	874	334	1	*Old man.* Threescore and ten I can remember well,	53-	53-	1519-
	875	335	2 *	Within the Volume of which Time, I haue seene	52-	52-	1518-
	876	336	3	Houres dreadfull, and things strange: but this sore Night	51-	51-	1517-
324°	877	337	4	Hath trifled former knowings.	50-	50-	1516-
	878	338	5	*Rosse.* Ha, good Father,	49-	49-	1515-
	879	339	6	Thou seest the Heauens, as troubled with mans Act,	48-	48-	1514-
	880	340	7	Threatens his bloody Stage: byth' Clock 'tis Day,	47-	47-	1513-
	881	341	8	And yet darke Night strangles the trauailing Lampe:	46-	46-	1512-
	882	342	9	Is't Nights predominance, or the Dayes shame,	45-	45-	1511-
	883	343	10	That Darknesse does the face of Earth intombe,	44-	44-	1510-
	884	344	11	When liuing Light should kisse it?	43-	43-	1509-
	885	345	12	*Old man.* 'Tis vnnaturall,	42-	42-	1508-
333°	886	346	13	Euen like the deed that's done: On Tuesday last,	41-	41-	1507-
	887	347	14	A Faulcon towring in her pride of place,	40-	40-	1506-
	888	348	15	Was by a Mowsing Owle hawkt at, and kill'd.	39-	39-	1505-
	889	349	16	*Rosse.* And *Duncans* Horses,	38-	38-	1504-
	890	350	17	(A thing most strange, and certaine)	37-	37-	1503-
	891	351	18	Beauteous, and swift, the Minions of their Race,	36-	36-	1502-
	892	352	19 *	Turn'd wilde in nature, broke their stalls, flong out,	35-	35-	1501-
	893	353	20	Contending 'gainst Obedience, as they would	34-	34-	1500-
	894	354	21	Make Warre with Mankinde.	33-	33-	1499-
342°	895	355	22	*Old man.* 'Tis said, they eate each other.	32-	32-	1498-
	896	356	23	*Rosse.* They did so:	31-	31-	1497-
	897	357	24	To th' amazement of mine eyes that look'd vpon't.	30-	30-	1496-
				Enter Macduffe.			
	898	358	25	Heere comes the good *Macduffe.*	29-	29-	1495-
	899	359	26	How goes the world Sir, now?	28-	28-	1494-
	900	360	27 S	*Macd.* Why see you not?	27-	27-	1493-
	901	361	28	*Ross.* Is't known who did this more then bloody deed?	26-	26-	1492-

NUMBERED FIRST FOLIO TEXT 295

Angle	Play	Act	Scene	The Tragedie of Macbeth	Scene	Act	Play
	902	362	29	Macd. Those that *Macbeth* hath slaine.	25-	25-	1491-
	903	363	30	*Ross.* Alas the day,	24-	24-	1490-
351°	904	364	31	What good could they pretend?	23-	23-	1489-
	905	365	32	*Macd.* They were subborned,	22-	22-	1488-
	906	366	33	*Malcolme,* and *Donalbaine* the Kings two Sonnes	21-	21-	1487-
	907	367	34	Are stolne away and fled, which puts vpon them	20-	20-	1486-
	908	368	35	Suspition of the deed.	19-	19-	1485-
	909	369	36 *	*Rosse.* 'Gainst Nature still,	18-	18-	1484-
	910	370	37	Thriftlesse Ambition, that will rauen vp	17-	17-	1483-
	911	371	38	Thine owne liues meanes: Then 'tis most like,	16-	16-	1482-
	912	372	39	The Soueraignty will fall vpon *Macbeth.*	15-	15-	1481-
360°	913	373	40	*Macd.* He is already nam'd, and gone to Scone	14-	14-	1480-
	914	374	41	To be inuested.	13-	13-	1479-
117 deg	915	375	42	*Rosse.* Where is *Duncans* body?	12-	12-	1478-
	916	376	43	*Macd.* Carried to Colmekill,	11-	11-	1477-
	917	377	44	The Sacred Store-house of his Predecessors,	10-	10-	1476-
	918	378	45	And Guardian of their Bones.	9-	9-	1475-
	919	379	46	*Rosse.* Will you to Scone?	8-	8-	1474-
120 deg	920	380	47	*Macd.* No Cosin, Ile to Fife.	7-	7-	1473-
	921	381	48	*Rosse.* Well, I will thither.	6-	6-	1472-
	922	382	49	*Macd.* Well may you see things wel done there: Adieu	5-	5-	1471-
	923	383	50	Least our old Robes sit easier then our new.	4-	4-	1470-
	924	384	51	*Rosse.* Farewell, Father.	3-	3-	1469-
123 deg	925	385	52	Old *M.* Gods benyson go with you, and with those	2-	2-	1468-
	926	386	53 *	That would make good of bad, and Friends of Foes.	1-	1-	1467-
				Exeunt omnes			

Actus Tertius. Scena Prima.

Enter Banquo.

	927	1	1	*Banq.* Thou hast it now, King, Cawdor, Glamis, all,	164-	520-	1466-
	928	2	2	As the weyard Women promis'd, and I feare	163-	519-	1465-
	929	3	3	Thou playd'st most fowly for't: yet it was saide	162-	518-	1464-
126 deg	930	4	4	It should not stand in thy Posterity,	161-	517-	1463-
	931	5	5	But that my selfe should be the Roote, and Father	160-	516-	1462-
	932	6	6	Of many Kings. If there come truth from them,	159-	515-	1461-

296 NUMBER AND GEOMETRY IN SHAKESPEARE'S *MACBETH*

Angle	Play	Act	Scene	The Tragedie of Macbeth	Scene	Act	Play
	933	7	7	As vpon thee Macbeth, their Speeches shine,	158-	514-	1460-
	934	8	8	Why by the verities on thee made good,	157-	513-	1459-
129 deg	935	9	9	May they not be my Oracles as well,	156-	512-	1458-
	936	10	10	And set me vp in hope. But hush, no more.	155-	511-	1457-
				Senit sounded. Enter Macbeth as King, Lady Lenox, Rosse, Lords, and Attendants.			
	937	11	11	Macb. Heere's our chiefe Guest.	154-	510-	1456-
	938	12	12	La. If he had beene forgotten,	153-	509-	1455-
	939	13	13	It had bene as a gap in our great Feast,	152-	508-	1454-
132 deg	940	14	14	And all-thing vnbecomming.	151-	507-	1453-
	941	15	15	*Macb.* To night we hold a solemne Supper sir,	150-	506-	1452-
	942	16	16	And Ile request your presence.	149-	505-	1451-
	943	17	17 *	*Banq.* Let your Highnesse	148-	504-	1450-
	944	18	18	Command vpon me, to the which my duties	147-	503-	1449-
135 deg	945	19	19	Are with a most indissoluble tye	146-	502-	1448-
	946	20	20	For euer knit.	145-	501-	1447-
	947	21	21	*Macb.* Ride you this afternoone?	144-	500-	1446-
	948	22	22	*Ban.* I, my good Lord.	143-	499-	1445-
	949	23	23	*Macb.* We should haue else desir'd your good aduice	142-	498-	1444-
138 deg	950	24	24	(Which still hath been both graue, and prosperous)	141-	497-	1443-
	951	25	25	In this dayes Councell: but wee'le take to morrow.	140-	496-	1442-
	952	26	26	Is't farre you ride?	139-	495-	1441-
	953	27	27	*Ban.* As farre, my Lord, as will fill vp the time	138-	494-	1440-
	954	28	28	'Twixt this, and Supper. Goe not my Horse the better,	137-	493-	1439-
141 deg	955	29	29	I must become a borrower of the Night,	136-	492-	1438-
	956	30	30	For a darke houre, or twaine.	135-	491-	1437-
	957	31	31	*Macb.* Faile not our Feast.	134-	490-	1436-
	958	32	32	*Ban.* My Lord, I will not.	133-	489-	1435-
	959	33	33	*Macb.* We heare our bloody Cozens are bestow'd	132-	488-	1434-
144 deg	960	34	34 *	In England, and in Ireland, not confessing	131-	487-	1433-
	961	35	35	Their cruell Parricide, filling their hearers	130-	486-	1432-
	962	36	36	With strange inuention. But of that to morrow,	129-	485-	1431-
	963	37	37	When therewithall, we shall haue cause of State,	128-	484-	1430-
	964	38	38	Crauing vs ioyntly. Hye you to Horse:	127-	483-	1429-
147 deg	965	39	39	Adieu, till you returne at Night.	126-	482-	1428-
	966	40	40	Goes *Fleance* with you?	125-	481-	1427-
	967	41	41	*Ban.* I, my good Lord: our time does call vpon's.	124-	480-	1426-

NUMBERED FIRST FOLIO TEXT 297

The Tragedie of Macbeth

Angle	Play	Act	Scene		Scene	Act	Play
	968	42	42	*Macb.* I wish your Horses swift, and sure of foot:	123-	479-	1425-
	969	43	43	And so I doe commend you to their backs.	122-	478-	1424-
150 deg	970	44	44	Farewell. *Exit Banquo.*	121-	477-	1423-
	971	45	45	Let euery man be master of his time,	120-	476-	1422-
	972	46	46	Till seuen at Night, to make societie	119-	475-	1421-
	973	47	47	The sweeter welcome:	118-	474-	1420-
	974	48	48	We will keepe our selfe till Supper time alone:	117-	473-	1419-
153 deg	975	49	49	While then, God be with you. *Exeunt Lords.*	116-	472-	1418-
	976	50	50	Sirrha, a word with you: Attend those men	115-	471-	1417-
	977	51	51 *	Our pleasure?	114-	470-	1416-
	978	52	52	*Seruant.* They are, my Lord, without the Pallace	113-	469-	1415-
	979	53	53	Gate.	112-	468-	1414-
156 deg	980	54	54	*Macb.* Bring them before vs. *Exit Seruant.*	111-	467-	1413-
	981	55	55	To be thus, is nothing, but to be safely thus	110-	466-	1412-
	982	56	56	Our feares in *Banquo* sticke deepe,	109-	465-	1411-
	983	57	57	And in his Royaltie of Nature reignes that	108-	464-	1410-
	984	58	58	Which would be fear'd. 'Tis much he dares,	107-	463-	1409-
159 deg	985	59	59	And to that dauntlesse temper of his Minde,	106-	462-	1408-
	986	60	60	He hath a Wisdome, that doth guide his Valour,	105-	461-	1407-
	987	61	61	To act in safetie. There is none but he,	104-	460-	1406-
	988	62	62	Whose being I doe feare: and vnder him,	103-	459-	1405-
	989	63	63	My Genius is rebuk'd, as it is said	102-	458-	1404-
162 deg	990	64	64	*Mark Anthonies* was by *Caesar*. He chid the Sisters,	101-	457-	1403-
	991	65	65	When first they put the Name of King vpon me,	100-	456-	1402-
	992	66	66	And bad them speake to him. Then Prophet-like,	99-	455-	1401-
	993	67	67	They hayl'd him Father to a Line of Kings.	98-	454-	1400-
	994	68	68 *	Vpon my Head they plac'd a fruitlesse Crowne,	97-	453-	1399-
165 deg	995	69	69	And put a barren Scepter in my Gripe,	96-	452-	1398-
	996	70	70	Thence to be wrencht with an vnlineall Hand,	95-	451-	1397-
	997	71	71	No Sonne of mine succeeding: if't be so,	94-	450-	1396-
	998	72	72	For *Banquo's* Issue haue I fil'd my Minde,	93-	449-	1395-
	999	73	73	For them, the gracious Duncan haue I murther'd,	92-	448-	1394-
168 deg	1000	74	74	Put Rancours in the Vessell of my Peace	91-	447-	1393-
	1001	75	75	Onely for them, and mine eternall Iewell	90-	446-	1392-
	1002	76	76	Giuen to the common Enemie of Man,	89-	445-	1391-
	1003	77	77	To make them Kings, the Seedes of *Banquo* Kings.	88-	444-	1390-
	1004	78	78	Rather then so, come Fate into the Lyst,	87-	443-	1389-
171 deg	1005	79	79	And champion me to th' vtterance.	86-	442-	1388-
0°	1006	80	80	Who's there?	85-	441-	1387-

Angle	Play	Act	Scene		The Tragedie of Macbeth	Scene	Act	Play
					Enter Seruant, and two Murtherers.			
	1007	81	81		Now goe to the Doore, and stay there till we call.	84-	440-	1386-
					Exit Seruant.			
	1008	82	82	S	Was it not yesterday we spoke together?	83-	439-	1385-
	1009	83	83	S	*Murth.* It was, so please your Highnesse.	82-	438-	1384-
	1010	84	84		*Macb.* Well then,	81-	437-	1383-
	1011	85	85	*	Now haue you consider'd of my speeches:	80-	436-	1382-
	1012	86	86		Know, that it was he, in the times past,	79-	435-	1381-
	1013	87	87		Which held you so vnder fortune,	78-	434-	1380-
	1014	88	88		Which you thought had been our innocent selfe.	77-	433-	1379-
9°	1015	89	89		This I made good to you, in our last conference,	76-	432-	1378-
	1016	90	90		Past in probation with you:	75-	431-	1377-
	1017	91	91		How you were borne in hand, how crost:	74-	430-	1376-
	1018	92	92		The Instruments: who wrought with them:	73-	429-	1375-
	1019	93	93		And all things else, that might	72-	428-	1374-
	1020	94	94		To halfe a Soule, and to a Notion craz'd,	71-	427-	1373-
	1021	95	95		Say, Thus did *Banquo.*	70-	426-	1372-
	1022	96	96		*1. Murth.* You made it knowne to vs.	69-	425-	1371-
	1023	97	97		*Macb.* I did so:	68-	424-	1370-
18°	1024	98	98		And went further, which is now	67-	423-	1369-
	1025	99	99		Our point of second meeting.	66-	422-	1368-
	1026	100	100		Doe you finde your patience so predominant,	65-	421-	1367-
	1027	101	101		In your nature, that you can let this goe?	64-	420-	1366-
	1028	102	102	*	Are you so Gospell'd, to pray for this good man,	63-	419-	1365-
	1029	103	103		And for his Issue, whose heauie hand	62-	418-	1364-
	1030	104	104		Hath bow'd you to the Graue, and begger'd	61-	417-	1363-
	1031	105	105		Yours for euer?	60-	416-	1362-
	1032	106	106		*1. Murth.* We are men, my Liege.	59-	415-	1361-
27°	1033	107	107		*Macb.* I, in the Catalogue ye goe for men,	58-	414-	1360-
	1034	108	108		As Hounds, and Greyhounds, Mungrels, Spaniels, Curres,	57-	413-	1359-
	1035	109	109		Showghes, Water-Rugs, and Demy-Wolues are clipt	56-	412-	1358-
	1036	110	110		All by the Name of Dogges: the valued file	55-	411-	1357-
	1037	111	111		Distinguishes the swift, the slow, the subtle,	54-	410-	1356-
	1038	112	112		The House-keeper, the Hunter, euery one	53-	409-	1355-
	1039	113	113		According to the gift, which bounteous Nature	52-	408-	1354-
	1040	114	114		Hath in him clos'd: whereby he does receiue	51-	407-	1353-
	1041	115	115		Particular addition, from the Bill,	50-	406-	1352-
36°	1042	116	116		That writes them all alike: and so of men.	49-	405-	1351-
	1043	117	117		Now, if you haue a station in the file,	48-	404-	1350-

NUMBERED FIRST FOLIO TEXT 299

Angle	Play	Act	Scene		The Tragedie of Macbeth	Scene	Act	Play
	1044	118	118		Not i'th' worst ranke of Manhood, say't,	47-	403-	1349-
	1045	119	119	*	And I will put that Businesse in your Bosomes,	46-	402-	1348-
	1046	120	120		Whose execution takes your Enemie off,	45-	401-	1347-
	1047	121	121		Grapples you to the heart; and loue of vs,	44-	400-	1346-
	1048	122	122		Who weare our Health but sickly in his Life,	43-	399-	1345-
	1049	123	123		Which in his Death were perfect.	42-	398-	1344-
	1050	124	124		2. *Murth*. I am one, my Liege,	41-	397-	1343-
45°	1051	125	125		Whom the vile Blowes and Buffets of the World	40-	396-	1342-
	1052	126	126		Hath so incens'd, that I am recklesse what I doe,	39-	395-	1341-
	1053	127	127		To spight the World.	38-	394-	1340-
	1054	128	128		1. *Murth*. And I another,	37-	393-	1339-
	1055	129	129		So wearie with Disasters, tugg'd with Fortune,	36-	392-	1338-
	1056	130	130		That I would set my Life on any Chance,	35-	391-	1337-
	1057	131	131		To mend it, or be rid on't.	34-	390-	1336-
	1058	132	132		*Macb*. Both of you know *Banquo* was your Enemie.	33-	389-	1335-
	1059	133	133		*Murth*. True, my Lord.	32-	388-	1334-
54°	1060	134	134		*Macb*. So is he mine: and in such bloody distance,	31-	387-	1333-
	1061	135	135		That euery minute of his being, thrusts	30-	386-	1332-
	1062	136	136	*	Against my neer'st of Life: and though I could	29-	385-	1331-
	1063	137	137		With bare-fac'd power sweepe him from my sight,	28-	384-	1330-
	1064	138	138		And bid my will auouch it; yet I must not,	27-	383-	1329-
	1065	139	139		For certaine friends that are both his, and mine,	26-	382-	1328-
	1066	140	140		Whose loues I may not drop, but wayle his fall,	25-	381-	1327-
	1067	141	141		Who I my selfe struck downe: and thence it is,	24-	380-	1326-
	1068	142	142		That I to your assistance doe make loue,	23-	379-	1325-
63°	1069	143	143		Masking the Businesse from the common Eye,	22-	378-	1324-
	1070	144	144		For sundry weightie Reasons.	21-	377-	1323-
	1071	145	145		2. *Murth*. We shall, my Lord,	20-	376-	1322-
	1072	146	146		Performe what you command vs.	19-	375-	1321-
	1073	147	147		1. *Murth*. Though our Liues--	18-	374-	1320-
	1074	148	148		*Macb*. Your Spirits shine through you.	17-	373-	1319-
	1075	149	149		Within this houre, at most,	16-	372-	1318-
	1076	150	150		I will aduise you where to plant your selues,	15-	371-	1317-
	1077	151	151		Acquaint you with the perfect Spy o'th' time,	14-	370-	1316-
72°	1078	152	152		The moment on't, for't must be done to Night,	13-	369-	1315-
	1079	153	153	*	And something from the Pallace: alwayes thought,	12-	368-	1314-
	1080	154	154		That I require a clearenesse; and with him,	11-	367-	1313-
	1081	155	155		To leaue no Rubs nor Botches in the Worke:	10-	366-	1312-
	1082	156	156		*Fleans*, his Sonne, that keepes him companie,	9-	365-	1311-

Angle	Play	Act	Scene	The Tragedie of Macbeth	Scene	Act	Play
	1083	157	157	Whose absence is no lesse materiall to me,	8-	364-	1310-
	1084	158	158	Then is his Fathers, must embrace the fate	7-	363-	1309-
	1085	159	159	Of that darke houre: resolue your selues apart,	6-	362-	1308-
	1086	160	160	Ile come to you anon.	5-	361-	1307-
81 °	1087	161	161	*Murth*. We are resolu'd, my Lord.	4-	360-	1306-
	1088	162	162	*Macb*. Ile call vpon you straight: abide within,	3-	359-	1305-
	1089	163	163	It is concluded: *Banquo*, thy Soules flight,	2-	358-	1304-
84 °	1090	164	164	If it finde Heauen, must finde it out to Night. *Exeunt*.	1-	357-	1303-

Scena Secunda.

Enter Macbeths Lady, and a Seruant.

Angle	Play	Act	Scene		Scene	Act	Play
	1091	165	1	*Lady*. Is Banquo gone from Court?	63-	356-	1302-
	1092	166	2	*Seruant*. I, Madame, but returnes againe to Night.	62-	355-	1301-
	1093	167	3	*Lady*. Say to the King, I would attend his leysure,	61-	354-	1300-
	1094	168	4	For a few words.	60-	353-	1299-
	1095	169	5	*Seruant*. Madame, I will. *Exit*.	59-	352-	1298-
90 °	1096	170	6 *	*Lady*. Nought's had, all's spent.	58-	351-	1297-
	1097	171	7	Where our desire is got without content:	57-	350-	1296-
	1098	172	8	'Tis safer, to be that which we destroy,	56-	349-	1295-
	1099	173	9	Then by destruction dwell in doubtfull ioy.	55-	348-	1294-

Enter Macbeth.

Angle	Play	Act	Scene		Scene	Act	Play
	1100	174	10	How now, my Lord, why doe you keepe alone?	54-	347-	1293-
	1101	175	11	Of sorryest Fancies your Companions making,	53-	346-	1292-
	1102	176	12	Vsing those Thoughts, which should indeed haue dy'd	52-	345-	1291-
	1103	177	13	With them they thinke on: things without all remedie	51-	344-	1290-
	1104	178	14	Should be without regard: what's done, is done.	50-	343-	1289-
99 °	1105	179	15	*Macb*. We haue scorch'd the Snake, not kill'd it:	49-	342-	1288-
	1106	180	16	Shee'le close, and be her selfe, whilest our poore Mallice	48-	341-	1287-
	1107	181	17	Remaines in danger of her former Tooth.	47-	340-	1286-
	1108	182	18	But let the frame of things dis-ioynt,	46-	339-	1285-
	1109	183	19	Both the Worlds suffer,	45-	338-	1284-
	1110	184	20	Ere we will eate our Meale in feare, and sleepe	44-	337-	1283-
	1111	185	21	In the affliction of these terrible Dreames,	43-	336-	1282-
	1112	186	22	That shake vs Nightly: Better be with the dead,	42-	335-	1281-

NUMBERED FIRST FOLIO TEXT   301

Angle	Play	Act	Scene		The Tragedie of Macbeth	Scene	Act	Play
	1113	187	23	*	Whom we, to gayne our peace, haue sent to peace,	41-	334-	1280-
108°	1114	188	24		Then on the torture of the Minde to lye	40-	333-	1279-
	1115	189	25		In restlesse extasie.	39-	332-	1278-
	1116	190	26		*Duncane* is in his Graue:	38-	331-	1277-
	1117	191	27		After Lifes fitfull Feuer, he sleepes well,	37-	330-	1276-
	1118	192	28		Treason ha's done his worst: nor Steele, nor Poyson,	36-	329-	1275-
	1119	193	29		Mallice domestique, forraine Leuie, nothing,	35-	328-	1274-
	1120	194	30		Can touch him further.	34-	327-	1273-
	1121	195	31		*Lady.* Come on:	33-	326-	1272-
	1122	196	32	S	Gentle my Lord, sleeke o're your rugged Lookes,	32-	325-	1271-
117°	1123	197	33		Be bright and Iouiall among your Guests to Night.	31-	324-	1270-
	1124	198	34		*Macb.* So shall I Loue, and so I pray be you:	30-	323-	1269-
	1125	199	35		Let your remembrance apply to *Banquo*,	29-	322-	1268-
	1126	200	36		Present him Eminence, both with Eye and Tongue:	28-	321-	1267-
	1127	201	37		Vnsafe the while, that wee must laue	27-	320-	1266-
	1128	202	38		Our Honors in these flattering streames,	26-	319-	1265-
	1129	203	39		And make our Faces Vizards to our Hearts,	25-	318-	1264-
	1130	204	40	*	Disguising what they are.	24-	317-	1263-
	1131	205	41		*Lady.* You must leaue this.	23-	316-	1262-
126°	1132	206	42		*Macb.* O, full of Scorpions is my Minde, deare Wife:	22-	315-	1261-
	1133	207	43		Thou know'st, that *Banquo* and his *Fleans* liues.	21-	314-	1260-
	1134	208	44		*Lady.* But in them, Natures Coppie's not eterne.	20-	313-	1259-
	1135	209	45		*Macb.* There's comfort yet, they are assaileable,	19-	312-	1258-
	1136	210	46		Then be thou iocund: ere the Bat hath flowne	18-	311-	1257-
	1137	211	47		His Cloyster'd flight, ere to black *Heccats* summons	17-	310-	1256-
	1138	212	48		The shard-borne Beetle, with his drowsie hums,	16-	309-	1255-
	1139	213	49		Hath rung Nights yawning Peale,	15-	308-	1254-
	1140	214	50		There shall be done a deed of dreadfull note.	14-	307-	1253-
135°	1141	215	51		*Lady.* What's to be done?	13-	306-	1252-
	1142	216	52		*Macb.* Be innocent of the knowledge, dearest Chuck,	12-	305-	1251-
	1143	217	53		Till thou applaud the deed: Come, seeling Night,	11-	304-	1250-
	1144	218	54		Skarfe vp the tender Eye of pittifull Day,	10-	303-	1249-
	1145	219	55		And with thy bloodie and inuisible Hand	9-	302-	1248-
	1146	220	56		Cancell and teare to pieces that great Bond,	8-	301-	1247-
	1147	221	57	*	Which keepes me pale. Light thickens,	7-	300-	1246-
	1148	222	58		And the Crow makes Wing toth' Rookie Wood:	6-	299-	1245-
	1149	223	59		Good things of Day begin to droope, and drowse,	5-	298-	1244-
144°	1150	224	60		Whiles Nights black Agents to their Prey's doe rowse.	4-	297-	1243-
	1151	225	61		Thou maruell'st at my words: but hold thee still,	3-	296-	1242-

Angle	Play	Act	Scene	The Tragedie of Macbeth	Scene	Act	Play
	1152	226	62	Things bad begun, make strong themselues by ill:	2-	295-	1241-
147°	1153	227	63	So prythee goe with me. *Exeunt.*	1-	294-	1240-

Scena Tertia.

Enter three Murtherers.

Angle	Play	Act	Scene	Text	Scene	Act	Play
	1154	228	1	1. But who did bid thee ioyne with vs?	33-	293-	1239-
	1155	229	2	3. *Macbeth.*	32-	292-	1238-
	1156	230	3	2. He needes not our mistrust, since he deliuers	31-	291-	1237-
	1157	231	4	Our Offices, and what we haue to doe,	30-	290-	1236-
	1158	232	5	To the direction iust.	29-	289-	1235-
153°	1159	233	6	1. Then stand with vs:	28-	288-	1234-
	1160	234	7	The West yet glimmers with some streakes of Day.	27-	287-	1233-
	1161	235	8	Now spurres the lated Traueller apace,	26-	286-	1232-
	1162	236	9	To gayne the timely Inne, and neere approches	25-	285-	1231-
	1163	237	10	The subiect of our Watch.	24-	284-	1230-
	1164	238	11 *	3. Hearke, I heare Horses.	23-	283-	1229-
	1165	239	12	Banquo within. Giue vs a Light there, hoa.	22-	282-	1228-
	1166	240	13	2. Then 'tis hee:	21-	281-	1227-
	1167	241	14	The rest, that are within the note of expectation,	20-	280-	1226-
162°	1168	242	15	Alreadie are i'th' Court.	19-	279-	1225-
	1169	243	16	1. His Horses goe about.	18-	278-	1224-
	1170	244	17 SC	3. Almost a mile: but he does vsually,	17-	277-	1223-
	1171	245	18	So all men doe, from hence toth' Pallace Gate	16-	276-	1222-
	1172	246	19	Make it their Walke.	15-	275-	1221-

Enter Banquo and Fleans, with a Torch.

Angle	Play	Act	Scene	Text	Scene	Act	Play
	1173	247	20	2. A Light, a Light.	14-	274-	1220-
	1174	248	21	3. 'Tis hee.	13-	273-	1219-
	1175	249	22	1. Stand too't.	12-	272-	1218-
	1176	250	23	Ban. It will be Rayne to Night.	11-	271-	1217-
171°	1177	251	24	1. Let it come downe.	10-	270-	1216-
	1178	252	25	Ban. O, Trecherie!	9-	269-	1215-
	1179	253	26	Flye good *Fleans*, flye, flye, flye,	8-	268-	1214-
	1180	254	27	Thou may'st reuenge. O Slaue!	7-	267-	1213-
	1181	255	28 *	3. Who did strike out the Light?	6-	266-	1212-

NUMBERED FIRST FOLIO TEXT   303

Angle	Play	Act	Scene	The Tragedie of Macbeth	Scene	Act	Play
	1182	256	29	1. Was't not the way?	5-	265-	1211-
	1183	257	30	3. There's but one downe: the Sonne is fled.	4-	264-	1210-
	1184	258	31	2. We haue lost	3-	263-	1209-
	1185	259	32	Best halfe of our Affaire.	2-	262-	1208-
180°	1186	260	33 A	1. Well, let's away, and say how much is done.	1-	261-	1207-
				Exeunt.			

Scena Quarta.

Banquet prepar'd. Enter Macbeth, Lady, Rosse, Lenox, Lords, and Attendants.

	1187	261	1 A	*Macb.* You know your owne degrees, sit downe:	169-	260-	1206-
	1188	262	2	At first and last, the hearty welcome.	168-	259-	1205-
	1189	263	3	*Lords.* Thankes to your Maiesty.	167-	258-	1204-
	1190	264	4	*Macb.* Our selfe will mingle with Society,	166-	257-	1203-
	1191	265	5	And play the humble Host:	165-	256-	1202-
	1192	266	6	Our Hostesse keepes her State, but in best time	164-	255-	1201-
	1193	267	7	We will require her welcome.	163-	254-	1200-
	1194	268	8	*La.* Pronounce it for me Sir, to all our Friends,	162-	253-	1199-
189°	1195	269	9	For my heart speakes, they are welcome.	161-	252-	1198-
				Enter first Murtherer.			
	1196	270	10 P	*Macb.* See they encounter thee with their harts thanks	160-	251-	1197-
	1197	271	11 P	Both sides are euen: heere Ile sit i'th' mid'st,	159-	250-	1196-
	1198	272	12 *	Be large in mirth, anon wee'l drinke a Measure	158-	249-	1195-
	1199	273	13	The Table round. There's blood vpon thy face.	157-	248-	1194-
	1200	274	14	*Mur.* 'Tis *Banquo's* then.	156-	247-	1193-
	1201	275	15	*Macb.* 'Tis better thee without, then he within.	155-	246-	1192-
	1202	276	16	Is he dispatch'd?	154-	245-	1191-
	1203	277	17	*Mur.* My Lord his throat is cut, that I did for him.	153-	244-	1190-
198°	1204	278	18	*Mac.* Thou art the best o'th' Cut-throats,	152-	243-	1189-
	1205	279	19	Yet hee's good that did the like for *Fleans*:	151-	242-	1188-
	1206	280	20	If thou did'st it, thou art the Non-pareill.	150-	241-	1187-
	1207	281	21	*Mur.* Most Royall Sir	149-	240-	1186-
	1208	282	22	*Fleans* is scap'd.	148-	239-	1185-
	1209	283	23	*Macb.* Then comes my Fit againe:	147-	238-	1184-
	1210	284	24	I had else beene perfect;	146-	237-	1183-

304 NUMBER AND GEOMETRY IN SHAKESPEARE'S *MACBETH*

Angle	Play	Act	Scene		The Tragedie of Macbeth	Scene	Act	Play
	1211	285	25		Whole as the Marble, founded as the Rocke,	145-	236-	1182-
	1212	286	26		As broad, and generall, as the casing Ayre:	144-	235-	1181-
207 °	1213	287	27		But now I am cabin'd, crib'd, confin'd, bound in	143-	234-	1180-
	1214	288	28		To sawcy doubts, and feares. But *Banquo's* safe?	142-	233-	1179-
	1215	289	29	*	*Mur*. I, my good Lord: safe in a ditch he bides,	141-	232-	1178-
	1216	290	30		With twenty trenched gashes on his head;	140-	231-	1177-
	1217	291	31		The least a Death to Nature.	139-	230-	1176-
	1218	292	32		*Macb*. Thankes for that:	138-	229-	1175-
	1219	293	33		There the growne Serpent lyes, the worme that's fled	137-	228-	1174-
	1220	294	34		Hath Nature that in time will Venom breed,	136-	227-	1173-
	1221	295	35		No teeth for th' present. Get thee gone, to morrow	135-	226-	1172-
216 °	1222	296	36		Wee'l heare our selues againe. *Exit Murderer*.	134-	225-	1171-
	1223	297	37		*Lady*. My Royall Lord,	133-	224-	1170-
	1224	298	38		You do not giue the Cheere, the Feast is sold	132-	223-	1169-
	1225	299	39		That is not often vouch'd, while 'tis a making:	131-	222-	1168-
	1226	300	40		'Tis giuen, with welcome: to feede were best at home:	130-	221-	1167-
	1227	301	41		From thence, the sawce to meate is Ceremony,	129-	220-	1166-
	1228	302	42		Meeting were bare without it.	128-	219-	1165-
					Enter the Ghost of Banquo, and sits in Macbeths place.			
	1229	303	43		*Macb*. Sweet Remembrancer:	127-	218-	1164-
	1230	304	44		Now good digestion waite on Appetite,	126-	217-	1163-
225 °	1231	305	45		And health on both.	125-	216-	1162-
	1232	306	46	*	*Lenox*. May't please your Highnesse sit.	124-	215-	1161-
	1233	307	47		*Macb*. Here had we now our Countries Honor, roof'd,	123-	214-	1160-
	1234	308	48		Were the grac'd person of our *Banquo* present:	122-	213-	1159-
	1235	309	49		Who, may I rather challenge for vnkindnesse,	121-	212-	1158-
	1236	310	50		Then pitty for Mischance.	120-	211-	1157-
	1237	311	51		*Rosse*. His absence (Sir)	119-	210-	1156-
	1238	312	52		Layes blame vpon his promise. Pleas't your Highnesse	118-	209-	1155-
	1239	313	53		To grace vs with your Royall Company?	117-	208-	1154-
234 °	1240	314	54		*Macb*. The Table's full.	116-	207-	1153-
	1241	315	55		*Lenox*. Heere is a place reseru'd Sir.	115-	206-	1152-
	1242	316	56		*Macb*. Where?	114-	205-	1151-
	1243	317	57		*Lenox*. Heere my good Lord.	113-	204-	1150-
	1244	318	58		What is't that moues your Highnesse?	112-	203-	1149-
	1245	319	59		*Macb*. Which of you haue done this?	111-	202-	1148-
	1246	320	60		*Lords*. What, my good Lord?	110-	201-	1147-

NUMBERED FIRST FOLIO TEXT   305

Angle	Play	Act	Scene		The Tragedie of Macbeth	Scene	Act	Play
	1247	321	61		*Macb.* Thou canst not say I did it: neuer shake	109-	200-	1146-
	1248	322	62		Thy goary lockes at me.	108-	199-	1145-
243°	1249	323	63	*	*Rosse.* Gentlemen rise, his Highnesse is not well.	107-	198-	1144-
	1250	324	64		*Lady.* Sit worthy Friends: my Lord is often thus,	106-	197-	1143-
	1251	325	65		And hath beene from his youth. Pray you keepe Seat,	105-	196-	1142-
	1252	326	66		The fit is momentary, vpon a thought	104-	195-	1141-
	1253	327	67		He will againe be well. If much you note him	103-	194-	1140-
	1254	328	68		You shall offend him, and extend his Passion,	102-	193-	1139-
	1255	329	69		Feed, and regard him not. Are you a man?	101-	192-	1138-
	1256	330	70		*Macb.* I, and a bold one, that dare looke on that	100-	191-	1137-
	1257	331	71		Which might appall the Diuell.	99-	190-	1136-
252°	1258	332	72		*La.* O proper stuffe:	98-	189-	1135-
	1259	333	73		This is the very painting of your feare:	97-	188-	1134-
	1260	334	74		This is the Ayre-drawne-Dagger which you said	96-	187-	1133-
	1261	335	75		Led you to *Duncan.* O, these flawes and starts	95-	186-	1132-
	1262	336	76		(Impostors to true feare) would well become	94-	185-	1131-
	1263	337	77		A womans story, at a Winters fire	93-	184-	1130-
	1264	338	78		Authoriz'd by her Grandam: shame it selfe,	92-	183-	1129-
	1265	339	79		Why do you make such faces? When all's done	91-	182-	1128-
	1266	340	80	*	You looke but on a stoole.	90-	181-	1127-
261°	1267	341	81		*Macb.* Prythee see there:	89-	180-	1126-
	1268	342	82		Behold, looke, loe, how say you:	88-	179-	1125-
	1269	343	83		Why what care I, if thou canst nod, speake too.	87-	178-	1124-
	1270	344	84		If Charnell houses, and our Graues must send	86-	177-	1123-
	1271	345	85	S	Those that we bury, backe; our Monuments	85-	176-	1122-
	1272	346	86		Shall be the Mawes of Kytes.	84-	175-	1121-
	1273	347	87		*La.* What? quite vnmann'd in folly.	83-	174-	1120-
	1274	348	88		*Macb.* If I stand heere, I saw him.	82-	173-	1119-
	1275	349	89		*La.* Fie for shame.	81-	172-	1118-
270°	1276	350	90		*Macb.* Blood hath bene shed ere now, i'th' olden time	80-	171-	1117-
	1277	351	91		Ere humane Statute purg'd the gentle Weale:	79-	170-	1116-
	1278	352	92		I, and since too, Murthers haue bene perform'd	78-	169-	1115-
	1279	353	93		Too terrible for the eare. The times has bene,	77-	168-	1114-
	1280	354	94		That when the Braines were out, the man would dye,	76-	167-	1113-
	1281	355	95		And there an end: But now they rise againe	75-	166-	1112-
	1282	356	96		With twenty mortall murthers on their crownes,	74-	165-	1111-
	1283	357	97	*	And push vs from our stooles. This is more strange	73-	164-	1110-
	1284	358	98		Then such a murther is.	72-	163-	1109-
279°	1285	359	99		*La.* My worthy Lord	71-	162-	1108-

Angle	Play	Act	Scene	The Tragedie of Macbeth	Scene	Act	Play
	1286	360	100	Your Noble Friends do lacke you.	70-	161-	1107-
	1287	361	101	*Macb*. I do forget:	69-	160-	1106-
	1288	362	102	Do not muse at me my most worthy Friends,	68-	159-	1105-
	1289	363	103	I haue a strange infirmity, which is nothing	67-	158-	1104-
	1290	364	104	To those that know me. Come, loue and health to all,	66-	157-	1103-
	1291	365	105	Then Ile sit downe: Giue me some Wine, fill full:	65-	156-	1102-
				Enter Ghost.			
	1292	366	106	I drinke to th' generall ioy o'th' whole Table,	64-	155-	1101-
	1293	367	107	And to our deere Friend *Banquo*, whom we misse:	63-	154-	1100-
288 °	1294	368	108	Would he were heere: to all, and him we thirst,	62-	153-	1099-
	1295	369	109	And all to all.	61-	152-	1098-
	1296	370	110	*Lords*. Our duties, and the pledge.	60-	151-	1097-
	1297	371	111	*Mac*. Auant, & quit my sight, let the earth hide thee:	59-	150-	1096-
	1298	372	112	Thy bones are marrowlesse, thy blood is cold:	58-	149-	1095-
	1299	373	113	Thou hast no speculation in those eyes	57-	148-	1094-
	1300	374	114 *	Which thou dost glare with.	56-	147-	1093-
	1301	375	115	*La*. Thinke of this good Peeres	55-	146-	1092-
	1302	376	116	But as a thing of Custome: 'Tis no other,	54-	145-	1091-
297 °	1303	377	117	Onely it spoyles the pleasure of the time.	53-	144-	1090-
	1304	378	118	*Macb*. What man dare, I dare:	52-	143-	1089-
	1305	379	119	Approach thou like the rugged Russian Beare,	51-	142-	1088-
	1306	380	120	The arm'd Rhinoceros, or th' Hircan Tiger,	50-	141-	1087-
	1307	381	121	Take any shape but that, and my firme Nerues	49-	140-	1086-
	1308	382	122	Shall neuer tremble. Or be aliue againe,	48-	139-	1085-
	1309	383	123	And dare me to the Desart with thy Sword:	47-	138-	1084-
	1310	384	124	If trembling I inhabit then, protest mee	46-	137-	1083-
	1311	385	125	The Baby of a Girle. Hence horrible shadow,	45-	136-	1082-
306 °	1312	386	126	Vnreall mock'ry hence. Why so, being gone	44-	135-	1081-
	1313	387	127	I am a man againe: pray you sit still.	43-	134-	1080-
	1314	388	128	*La*. You haue displac'd the mirth,	42-	133-	1079-
	1315	389	129	Broke the good meeting, with most admir'd disorder.	41-	132-	1078-
	1316	390	130	*Macb*. Can such things be,	40-	131-	1077-
	1317	391	131 *	And ouercome vs like a Summers Clowd,	39-	130-	1076-
	1318	392	132	Without our speciall wonder? You make me strange	38-	129-	1075-
	1319	393	133	Euen to the disposition that I owe,	37-	128-	1074-
	1320	394	134	When now I thinke you can behold such sights,	36-	127-	1073-
315 °	1321	395	135	And keepe the naturall Rubie of your Cheekes,	35-	126-	1072-
	1322	396	136	When mine is blanch'd with feare.	34-	125-	1071-
	1323	397	137	*Rosse*. What sights, my Lord?	33-	124-	1070-

NUMBERED FIRST FOLIO TEXT   307

Angle	Play	Act	Scene	The Tragedie of Macbeth	Scene	Act	Play
	1324	398	138	La. I pray you speake not: he growes worse & worse	32-	123-	1069-
	1325	399	139	Question enrages him: at once, goodnight.	31-	122-	1068-
	1326	400	140	Stand not vpon the order of your going,	30-	121-	1067-
	1327	401	141	But go at once.	29-	120-	1066-
	1328	402	142	Len. Good night, and better health	28-	119-	1065-
	1329	403	143	Attend his Maiesty.	27-	118-	1064-
324 °	1330	404	144	La. A kinde goodnight to all. Exit Lords.	26-	117-	1063-
	1331	405	145	Macb. It will haue blood they say:	25-	116-	1062-
	1332	406	146	Blood will haue Blood:	24-	115-	1061-
	1333	407	147	Stones haue beene knowne to moue, & Trees to speake:	23-	114-	1060-
	1334	408	148 *	Augures, and vnderstood Relations, haue	22-	113-	1059-
	1335	409	149	By Maggot Pyes, & Choughes, & Rookes brought forth	21-	112-	1058-
	1336	410	150	The secret'st man of Blood. What is the night?	20-	111-	1057-
	1337	411	151	La. Almost at oddes with morning, which is which.	19-	110-	1056-
	1338	412	152	Macb. How say'st thou that *Macduff* denies his person	18-	109-	1055-
333 °	1339	413	153	At our great bidding.	17-	108-	1054-
	1340	414	154	La. Did you send to him Sir?	16-	107-	1053-
	1341	415	155	Macb. I heare it by the way: But I will send:	15-	106-	1052-
	1342	416	156	There's not a one of them but in his house	14-	105-	1051-
	1343	417	157	I keepe a Seruant Feed. I will to morrow	13-	104-	1050-
	1344	418	158	(And betimes I will) to the weyard Sisters.	12-	103-	1049-
	1345	419	159	More shall they speake: for now I am bent to know	11-	102-	1048-
	1346	420	160	By the worst meanes, the worst, for mine owne good,	10-	101-	1047-
	1347	421	161	All causes shall giue way. I am in blood	9-	100-	1046-
342 °	1348	422	162	Stept in so farre, that should I wade no more,	8-	99-	1045-
	1349	423	163	Returning were as tedious as go ore:	7-	98-	1044-
	1350	424	164	Strange things I haue in head, that will to hand,	6-	97-	1043-
	1351	425	165 *	Which must be acted, ere they may be scand.	5-	96-	1042-
	1352	426	166	La. You lacke the season of all Natures, sleepe.	4-	95-	1041-
	1353	427	167	Macb. Come, wee'l to sleepe: My strange & self-abuse	3-	94-	1040-
	1354	428	168	Is the initiate feare, that wants hard vse:	2-	93-	1039-
349 °	1355	439	169	We are yet but yong indeed. Exeunt.	1-	92-	1038-

Scena Quinta.

Thunder. Enter the three Witches, meeting Hecat.

Angle	Play	Act	Scene		The Tragedie of Macbeth	Scene	Act	Play
	1356	430	1		1. Why how now *Hecat*, you looke angerly?	37-	91-	1037-
351°	1357	431	2		*Hec.* Haue I not reason (Beldams) as you are?	36-	90-	1036-
	1358	432	3		Sawcy, and ouer-bold, how did you dare	35-	89-	1035-
	1359	433	4		To Trade, and Trafficke with *Macbeth*,	34-	88-	1034-
	1360	434	5		In Riddles, and Affaires of death;	33-	87-	1033-
	1361	435	6		And I the Mistris of your Charmes,	32-	86-	1032-
	1362	436	7		The close contriuer of all harmes,	31-	85-	1031-
	1363	437	8		Was neuer call'd to beare my part,	30-	84-	1030-
	1364	438	9		Or shew the glory of our Art?	29-	83-	1029-
	1365	449	10		And which is worse, all you haue done	28-	82-	1028-
360°	1366	440	11		Hath bene but for a wayward Sonne,	27-	81-	1027-
	1367	441	12		Spightfull, and wrathfull, who (as others do)	26-	80-	1026-
	1368	442	13	*	Loues for his owne ends, not for you.	25-	79-	1025-
	1369	443	14		But make amends now: Get you gon,	24-	78-	1024-
174 deg	1370	444	15		And at the pit of Acheron	23-	77-	1023-
	1371	445	16		Meete me i'th' Morning: thither he	22-	76-	1022-
	1372	446	17		Will come, to know his Destinie.	21-	75-	1021-
	1373	447	18		Your Vessels, and your Spels prouide,	20-	74-	1020-
	1374	448	19	S	Your Charmes, and euery thing beside;	19-	73-	1019-
177 deg	1375	449	20		I am for th' Ayre: This night Ile spend	18-	72-	1018-
	1376	450	21		Vnto a dismall, and a Fatall end.	17-	71-	1017-
	1377	451	22		Great businesse must be wrought ere Noone.	16-	70-	1016-
	1378	452	23		Vpon the Corner of the Moone	15-	69-	1015-
	1379	453	24		There hangs a vap'rous drop, profound,	14-	68-	1014-
180 deg	1380	454	25		Ile catch it ere it come to ground;	13-	67-	1013-
	1381	455	26		And that distill'd by Magicke slights,	12-	66-	1012-
	1382	456	27		Shall raise such Artificiall Sprights,	11-	65-	1011-
	1383	457	28		As by the strength of their illusion,	10-	64-	1010-
	1384	458	29		Shall draw him on to his Confusion.	9-	63-	1009-
183 deg	1385	459	30	*	He shall spurne Fate, scorne Death, and beare	8-	62-	1008-
	1386	460	31		His hopes 'boue Wisedome, Grace, and Feare:	7-	61-	1007-
	1387	461	32		And you all know, Security	6-	60-	1006-
	1388	462	33		Is Mortals cheefest Enemie.	5-	59-	1005-
					Musicke, and a Song.			
	1389	463	34		Hearke, I am call'd: my little Spirit see	4-	58-	1004-
186 deg	1390	464	35		Sits in Foggy cloud, and stayes for me.	3-	57-	1003-
					Sing within. Come away, come away, &c.			
	1391	465	36		1 Come, let's make hast, shee'l soone be	2-	56-	1002-

Angle	Play	Act	Scene	The Tragedie of Macbeth	Scene	Act	Play
	1392	466	37	Backe againe. *Exeunt.*	1-	55-	1001-

Scena Sexta.

Enter Lenox, and another Lord.

Angle	Play	Act	Scene		Scene	Act	Play
	1393	467	1	*Lenox.* My former Speeches,	54-	54-	1000-
	1394	468	2	Haue but hit your Thoughts	53-	53-	999-
189 deg	1395	469	3	Which can interpret farther: Onely I say	52-	52-	998-
	1396	470	4	Things haue bin strangely borne. The gracious *Duncan*	51-	51-	997-
	1397	471	5	Was pittied of *Macbeth*: marry he was dead:	50-	50-	996-
	1398	472	6	And the right valiant *Banquo* walk'd too late,	49-	49-	995-
	1399	473	7	Whom you may say (if't please you) *Fleans* kill'd,	48-	48-	994-
192 deg	1400	474	8	For *Fleans* fled: Men must not walke too late.	47-	47-	993-
	1401	475	9	Who cannot want the thought, how monstrous	46-	46-	992-
	1402	476	10 *	It was for *Malcolme*, and for *Donalbane*	45-	45-	991-
	1403	477	11	To kill their gracious Father? Damned Fact,	44-	44-	990-
	1404	478	12	How it did greeue *Macbeth*? Did he not straight	43-	43-	989-
195 deg	1405	479	13	In pious rage, the two delinquents teare,	42-	42-	988-
	1406	480	14	That were the Slaues of drinke, and thralles of sleepe?	41-	41-	987-
	1407	481	15	Was not that Nobly done? I, and wisely too:	40-	40-	986-
	1408	482	16	For 'twould haue anger'd any heart aliue	39-	39-	985-
	1409	483	17	To heare the men deny't. So that I say,	38-	38-	984-
198 deg	1410	484	18	He ha's borne all things well, and I do thinke,	37-	37-	983-
	1411	485	19	That had he *Duncans* Sonnes vnder his Key,	36-	36-	982-
	1412	486	20	(As, and't please Heauen he shall not) they should finde	35-	35-	981-
	1413	487	21	What 'twere to kill a Father: So should *Fleans*.	34-	34-	980-
	1414	488	22	But peace; for from broad words, and cause he fayl'd	33-	33-	979-
201 deg	1415	489	23	His presence at the Tyrants Feast, I heare	32-	32-	978-
	1416	490	24	*Macduffe* liues in disgrace. Sir, can you tell	31-	31-	977-
	1417	491	25	Where he bestowes himselfe?	30-	30-	976-
	1418	492	26	*Lord.* The Sonnes of *Duncane*	29-	29-	975-
	1419	493	27 S*	(From whom this Tyrant holds the due of Birth)	28-	28-	974-
204 deg	1420	494	28 S	Liues in the English Court, and is receyu'd	27-	27-	973-
	1421	495	29	Of the most Pious *Edward*, with such grace,	26-	26-	972-
	1422	496	30	That the maleuolence of Fortune, nothing	25-	25-	971-

Angle	Play	Act	Scene	The Tragedie of Macbeth	Scene	Act	Play
	1423	497	31	Takes from his high respect. Thither *Macduffe*	24-	24-	970-
	1424	498	32	Is gone, to pray the Holy King, vpon his ayd	23-	23-	969-
207 deg	1425	499	33	To wake Northumberland, and warlike *Seyward*,	22-	22-	968-
	1426	500	34	That by the helpe of these (with him aboue)	21-	21-	967-
	1427	501	35	To ratifie the Worke) we may againe	20-	20-	966-
	1428	502	36	Giue to our Tables meate, sleepe to our Nights:	19-	19-	965-
	1439	503	37	Free from our Feasts, and Banquets bloody kniues;	18-	18-	964-
210 deg	1430	504	38	Do faithfull Homage, and receiue free Honors,	17-	17-	963-
	1431	505	39	All which we pine for now. And this report	16-	16-	962-
	1432	506	40	Hath so exasperate their King, that hee	15-	15-	961-
	1433	507	41	Prepares for some attempt of Warre.	14-	14-	960-
	1434	508	42	Len. Sent he to *Macduffe*?	13-	13-	959-
213 deg	1435	509	43	Lord. He did: and with an absolute Sir, not I	12-	12-	958-
	1436	510	44	* The clowdy Messenger turnes me his backe,	11-	11-	957-
	1437	511	45	And hums; as who should say, you'l rue the time	10-	10-	956-
	1438	512	46	That clogges me with this Answer.	9-	9-	955-
	1439	513	47	Lenox. And that well might	8-	8-	954-
216 deg	1440	514	48	Aduise him to a Caution, t' hold what distance	7-	7-	953-
	1441	515	49	His wisedome can prouide. Some holy Angell	6-	6-	952-
	1442	516	50	Flye to the Court of England, and vnfold	5-	5-	951-
	1443	517	51	His Message ere he come, that a swift blessing	4-	4-	950-
	1444	518	52	May soone returne to this our suffering Country,	3-	3-	949-
219 deg	1445	519	53	Vnder a hand accurs'd.	2-	2-	948-
	1446	520	54	Lord. Ile send my Prayers with him. *Exeunt*	1-	1-	947-

Actus Quartus. Scena Prima.

Thunder. Enter the three Witches.

	1447	1	1	1 Thrice the brinded Cat hath mew'd.	172-	546-	946-
	1448	2	2	2 Thrice, and once the Hedge-Pigge whin'd.	171-	545-	945-
	1449	3	3	3 Harpier cries, 'tis time, 'tis time.	170-	544-	944-
222 deg	1450	4	4	1 Round about the Caldron go:	169-	543-	943-
	1451	5	5	In the poysond Entrailes throw	168-	542-	942-
	1452	6	6	Toad, that vnder cold stone,	167-	541-	941-
	1453	7	7	* Dayes and Nights, ha's thirty one:	166-	540-	940-
	1454	8	8	Sweltred Venom sleeping got,	165-	539-	939-

NUMBERED FIRST FOLIO TEXT   311

Angle	Play	Act	Scene		The Tragedie of Macbeth	Scene	Act	Play
225 deg	1455	9	9		Boyle thou first i'th' charmed pot.	164-	538-	938-
	1456	10	10		*All.* Double, double, toile and trouble;	163-	537-	937-
	1457	11	11		Fire burne, and Cauldron bubble.	162-	536-	936-
	1458	12	12		2 Fillet of a Fenny Snake,	161-	535-	935-
	1459	13	13		In the Cauldron boyle and bake:	160-	534-	934-
228 deg	1460	14	14		Eye of Newt, and Toe of Frogge,	159-	533-	933-
	1461	15	15		Wooll of Bat, and Tongue of Dogge:	158-	532-	932-
	1462	16	16		Adders Forke, and Blinde-wormes Sting,	157-	531-	931-
	1463	17	17		Lizards legge, and Howlets wing:	156-	530-	930-
	1464	18	18		For a Charme of powrefull trouble,	155-	529-	929-
231 deg	1465	19	19		Like a Hell-broth, boyle and bubble.	154-	528-	928-
	1466	20	20		All. Double, double, toyle and trouble,	153-	527-	927-
	1467	21	21		Fire burne, and Cauldron bubble.	152-	526-	926-
	1468	22	22		3 Scale of Dragon, Tooth of Wolfe,	151-	525-	925-
	1469	23	23		Witches Mummey, Maw, and Gulfe	150-	524-	924-
234 deg	1470	24	24	*	Of the rauin'd salt Sea sharke:	149-	523-	923-
	1471	25	25		Roote of Hemlocke, digg'd i'th' darke:	148-	522-	922-
	1472	26	26		Liuer of Blaspheming Iew,	147-	521-	921-
	1473	27	27		Gall of Goate, and Slippes of Yew,	146-	520-	920-
	1474	28	28		Sliuer'd in the Moones Ecclipse:	145-	519-	919-
237 deg	1475	29	29		Nose of Turke, and Tartars lips:	144-	518-	918-
	1476	30	30		Finger of Birth-strangled Babe,	143-	517-	917-
	1477	31	31		Ditch-deliuer'd by a Drab,	142-	516-	916-
	1478	32	32		Make the Grewell thicke, and slab.	141-	515-	915-
	1479	33	33		Adde thereto a Tigers Chawdron,	140-	514-	914-
240 deg	1480	34	34		For th' Ingredience of our Cawdron.	139-	513-	913-
	1481	35	35		All. Double, double, toyle and trouble,	138-	512-	912-
	1482	36	36		Fire burne, and Cauldron bubble.	137-	511-	911-
	1483	37	37		2 Coole it with a Baboones blood,	136-	510-	910-
	1484	38	38		Then the Charme is firme and good.	135-	509-	909-
					Enter Hecat, and the other three Witches.			
243 deg	1485	39	39		*Hec.* O well done: I commend your paines,	134-	508-	908-
	1486	40	40	E	And euery one shall share i'th' gaines:	133-	507-	907-
	1487	41	41		And now about the Cauldron sing	132-	506-	906-
	1488	42	42		Like Elues and Fairies in a Ring,	131-	505-	905-
	1489	43	43		Inchanting all that you put in.	130-	504-	904-
					Musicke and a Song. Blacke Spirits, &c.			
246 deg	1490	44	44		2 By the pricking of my Thumbes,	129-	503-	903-
	1491	45	45		Something wicked this way comes:	128-	502-	902-

Angle	Play	Act	Scene	The Tragedie of Macbeth	Scene	Act	Play
	1492	46	46	Open Lockes, who euer knockes.	127-	501-	901-
				Enter Macbeth.			
	1493	47	47	*Macb.* How now you secret, black, & midnight Hags?	126-	500-	900-
	1494	48	48	What is't you do?	125-	499-	899-
249 deg	1495	49	49	*All.* A deed without a name.	124-	498-	898-
	1496	50	50	*Macb.* I coniure you, by that which you Professe,	123-	497-	897-
	1497	51	51	(How ere you come to know it) answer me:	122-	496-	896-
	1498	52	52	Though you vntye the Windes, and let them fight	121-	495-	895-
	1499	53	53	Against the Churches: Though the yesty Waues	120-	494-	894-
252 deg	1500	54	54	Confound and swallow Nauigation vp:	119-	493-	893-
	1501	55	55	Though bladed Corne be lodg'd, & Trees blown downe,	118-	492-	892-
	1502	56	56	Though Castles topple on their Warders heads:	117-	491-	891-
	1503	57	57	Though Pallaces, and Pyramids do slope	116-	490-	890-
	1504	58	58	Their heads to their Foundations: Though the treasure	115-	489-	889-
255 deg	1505	59	59	Of Natures Germaine, tumble altogether,	114-	488-	888-
	1506	60	60	Euen till destruction sicken: Answer me	113-	487-	887-
	1507	61	61	To what I aske you.	112-	486-	886-
	1508	62	62	1 Speake.	111-	485-	885-
	1509	63	63	2 Demand.	110-	484-	884-
258 deg	1510	64	64	3 Wee'l answer.	109-	483-	883-
	1511	65	65	1 Say, if th'hadst rather heare it from our mouthes,	108-	482-	882-
	1512	66	66	Or from our Masters.	107-	481-	881-
	1513	67	67	*Macb.* Call 'em: let me see 'em.	106-	480-	880-
	1514	68	68	1 Powre in Sowes blood, that hath eaten	105-	479-	879-
261deg	1515	69	69	Her nine Farrow: Greaze that's sweaten	104-	478-	878-
	1516	70	70	From the Murderers Gibbet, throw	103-	477-	877-
	1517	71	71	Into the Flame.	102-	476-	876-
	1518	72	72	*All.* Come high or low:	101-	475-	875-
	1519	73	73	Thy Selfe and Office deaftly show. *Thunder.*	100-	474-	874-
				1. Apparation, an Armed Head.			
	1520	74	74	*Macb.* Tell me, thou vnknowne power.	99-	473-	873-
270 deg	1521	75	75	1 He knowes thy thought:	98-	472-	872-
	1522	76	76	Heare his speech, but say thou nought.	97-	471-	871-
	1523	77	77	1 *Appar.* Macbeth, Macbeth, Macbeth:	96-	470-	870-
	1524	78	78	Beware *Macduffe,*	95-	469-	869-
	1525	79	79	Beware the Thane of Fife: dismisse me. Enough.	94-	468-	868-
				He Descends.			
273 deg	1526	80	80	*Macb.* What ere thou art, for thy good caution, thanks	93-	467-	867-
	1527	81	81	Thou hast harp'd my feare aright. But one word more.	92-	466-	866-

NUMBERED FIRST FOLIO TEXT 313

Angle	Play	Act	Scene		The Tragedie of Macbeth		Scene	Act	Play
	1528	82	82		1 He will not be commanded: heere's another		91-	465-	865-
	1529	83	83		More potent then the first.	*Thunder.*	90-	464-	864-
					2 *Apparition, a Bloody Childe.*				
	1530	84	84		2 *Appar.* Macbeth, Macbeth, Macbeth.		89-	463-	863-
276 deg	1531	85	85		*Macb.* Had I three eares, Il'd heare thee.		88-	462-	862-
	1532	86	86	S	*Appar.* Be bloody, bold, & resolute:		87-	461-	861-
	1533	87	87	S	Laugh to scorne		86-	460-	860-
	1534	88	88		The powre of man: For none of woman borne		85-	459-	859-
	1535	89	89		Shall harme *Macbeth.*	*Descends.*	84-	458-	858-
279 deg	1536	90	90		*Mac.* Then liue *Macduffe*: what need I feare of thee?		83-	457-	857-
	1537	91	91		But yet Ile make assurance: double sure,		82-	456-	856-
	1538	92	92		And take a Bond of Fate: thou shalt not liue,		81-	455-	855-
0°	1539	93	93		That I may tell pale-hearted Feare, it lies;		80-	454-	854-
	1540	94	94		And sleepe in spight of Thunder.	*Thunder*	79-	453-	853-
					3 *Apparation, a Childe Crowned, with a Tree in his hand.*				
	1541	95	95		What is this, that rises like the issue of a King,		78-	452-	852-
	1542	96	96		And weares vpon his Baby-brow, the round		77-	451-	851-
	1543	97	97		And top of Soueraignty?		76-	450-	850-
	1544	98	98		*All.* Listen, but speake not too't.		75-	449-	849-
	1545	99	99		3 *Appar.* Be Lyon metled, proud, and take no care:		74-	448-	848-
	1546	100	100		Who chafes, who frets, or where Conspirers are:		73-	447-	847-
	1547	101	101		*Macbeth* shall neuer vanquish'd be, vntill		72-	446-	846-
9°	1548	102	102		Great Byrnam Wood, to high Dunsmane Hill		71-	445-	845-
	1549	103	103		Shall come against him.	*Descend.*	70-	444-	844-
	1550	104	104		*Macb.* That will neuer bee:		69-	443-	843-
	1551	105	105		Who can impresse the Forrest, bid the Tree		68-	442-	842-
	1552	106	106		Vnfixe his earth-bound Root? Sweet boadments, good:		67-	441-	841-
	1553	107	107		Rebellious dead, rise neuer till the Wood		66-	440-	840-
	1554	108	108		Of Byrnan rise, and our high plac'd *Macbeth*		65-	439-	839-
	1555	109	109		Shall liue the Lease of Nature, pay his breath		64-	438-	838-
	1556	110	110		To time, and mortall Custome. Yet my Hart		63-	437-	837-
18°	1557	111	111		Throbs to know one thing: Tell me, if your Art		62-	436-	836-
	1558	112	112		Can tell so much: Shall *Banquo's* issue euer		61-	435-	835-
	1559	113	113		Reigne in this Kingdome?		60-	434-	834-
	1560	114	114		*All.* Seeke to know no more.		59-	433-	833-
	1561	115	115		*Macb.* I will be satisfied. Deny me this,		58-	432-	832-
	1562	116	116		And an eternall Curse fall on you: Let me know.		57-	431-	831-
	1563	117	117		Why sinkes that Caldron? & what noise is this?	*Hoboyes*	56-	430-	830-
	1564	118	118		1 Shew.		55-	429-	829-

Angle	Play	Act	Scene	The Tragedie of Macbeth	Scene	Act	Play
	1565	119	119	2 Shew.	54-	428-	828-
27°	1566	120	120	3 Shew.	53-	427-	827-
	1567	121	121	*All.* Shew his Eyes, and greeue his Hart,	52-	426-	826-
	1568	122	122	Come like shadowes, so depart.	51-	425-	825-
				A shew of eight Kings, and Banquo last, with a glasse in his hand.			
	1569	123	123	*Macb.* Thou art too like the Spirit of *Banquo*: Down:	50-	424-	824-
	1570	124	124	Thy Crowne do's seare mine Eye-bals. And thy haire	49-	423-	823-
	1571	125	125	Thou other Gold-bound-brow, is like the first:	48-	422-	822-
	1572	126	126	A third, is like the former. Filthy Hagges,	47-	421-	821-
	1573	127	127	Why do you shew me this? ___ A fourth? Start eyes!	46-	420-	820-
	1574	128	128	What will the Line stretch out to'th' cracke of Doome?	45-	419-	819-
36°	1575	129	129	Another yet? A seauenth? Ile see no more:	44-	418-	818-
	1576	130	130	And yet the eighth appeares, who beares a glasse,	43-	417-	817-
	1577	131	131	Which shewes me many more: and some I see,	42-	416-	816-
	1578	132	132	That two-fold Balles, and trebble Scepters carry.	41-	415-	815-
	1579	133	133	Horrible sight: Now I see 'tis true,	40-	414-	814-
	1580	134	134	For the Blood-bolter'd *Banquo* smiles vpon me,	39-	413-	813-
	1581	135	135	And points at them for his. What? is this so?	38-	412-	812-
	1582	136	136	1 I Sir, all this is so. But why	37-	411-	811-
	1583	137	137	Stands *Macbeth* thus amazedly?	36-	410-	810-
45°	1584	138	138	Come Sisters, cheere we vp his sprights,	35-	409-	809-
	1585	139	139	And shew the best of our delights.	34-	408-	808-
	1586	140	140	Ile Charme the Ayre to giue a sound,	33-	407-	807-
	1587	141	141	While you performe your Antique round:	32-	406-	806-
	1588	142	142	That this great King may kindly say,	31-	405-	805-
	1589	143	143	Our duties, did his welcome pay. *Musicke.*	30-	404-	804-
				The Witches Dance, and vanish.			
	1590	144	144	*Macb.* Where are they? Gone?	29-	403-	803-
	1591	145	145	Let this pernitious houre,	28-	402-	802-
	1592	146	146	Stand aye accursed in the Kalender.	27-	401-	801-
54°	1593	147	147	Come in, without there. *Enter Lenox.*	26-	400-	800-
	1594	148	148	*Lenox.* What's your Graces will.	25-	399-	799-
	1595	149	149	*Macb.* Saw you the Weyard Sisters?	24-	398-	798-
	1596	150	150	*Lenox.* No my Lord.	23-	397-	797-
	1597	151	151	*Macb.* Came they not by you?	22-	396-	796-
	1598	152	152	*Lenox.* No indeed my Lord.	21-	395-	795-
	1599	153	153	*Macb.* Infected be the Ayre whereon they ride,	20-	394-	794-
	1600	154	154	And damn'd all those that trust them. I did heare	19-	393-	793-

Angle	Play	Act	Scene	The Tragedie of Macbeth	Scene	Act	Play
	1601	155	155	The gallopping of Horse. Who was't came by?	18-	392-	792-
63°	1602	156	156	*Len.* 'Tis two or three my Lord, that bring you word:	17-	391-	791-
	1603	157	157	*Macduff* is fled to England.	16-	390-	790-
	1604	158	158	*Macb.* Fled to England?	15-	389-	789-
	1605	159	159	*Len.* I, my good Lord.	14-	388-	788-
	1606	160	160	*Macb.* Time, thou anticipat'st my dread exploits:	13-	387-	787-
	1607	161	161	The flighty purpose neuer is o're-tooke	12-	386-	786-
	1608	162	162	Vnlesse the deed go with it. From this moment,	11-	385-	785-
	1609	163	163	The very firstlings of my heart shall be	10-	384-	784-
	1610	164	164	The firstlings of my hand. And euen now	9-	383-	783-
72°	1611	165	165	To Crown my thoughts with Acts: be it thoght & done:	8-	382-	782-
	1612	166	166	The Castle of *Macduff*, I will surprize.	7-	381-	781-
	1613	167	167	Seize vpon Fife; giue to th' edge o'th' Sword	6-	380-	780-
	1614	168	168	His Wife, his Babes, and all vnfortunate Soules	5-	379-	779-
	1615	169	169	That trace him in his Line. No boasting like a Foole,	4-	378-	778-
	1616	170	170	This deed Ile do, before this purpose coole,	3-	377-	777-
	1617	171	171	But no more sights. Where are these Gentlemen?	2-	376-	776-
79°	1618	172	172	Come bring me where they are. *Exeunt*	1-	375-	775-

Scena Secunda.

Enter Macduffes Wife, her Son, and Rosse.

	1619	173	1	*Wife.* What had he done, to make him fly the Land?	98-	374-	774-
81°	1620	174	2	*Rosse.* You must haue patience Madam.	97-	373-	773-
	1621	175	3	*Wife.* He had none:	96-	372-	772-
	1622	176	4	His flight was madnesse: when our Actions do not,	95-	371-	771-
	1623	177	5	Our feares do make vs Traitors.	94-	370-	770-
	1624	178	6	*Rosse.* You know not	93-	369-	769-
	1625	179	7	Whether it was his wisedome, or his feare.	92-	368-	768-
	1626	180	8	*Wife.* Wisedom? to leaue his wife, to leaue his Babes,	91-	367-	767-
	1627	181	9	His Mansion, and his Titles, in a place	90-	366-	766-
	1628	182	10	From whence himselfe do's flye? He loues vs not,	89-	365-	765-
90°	1629	183	11	He wants the naturall touch. For the poore Wren	88-	364-	764-
	1630	184	12	(The most diminitiue of Birds) will fight,	87-	363-	763-
	1631	185	13	Her yong ones in her Nest, against the Owle:	86-	362-	762-
	1632	186	14	All is the Feare, and nothing is the Loue;	85-	361-	761-

Angle	Play	Act	Scene	The Tragedie of Macbeth	Scene	Act	Play
	1633	187	15	As little is the Wisedome, where the flight	84-	360-	760-
	1634	188	16	So runnes against all reason.	83-	359-	759-
	1635	189	17	*Rosse.* My deerest Cooz,	82-	358-	758-
	1636	190	18	I pray you schoole your selfe. But for your Husband,	81-	357-	757-
	1637	191	19	He is Noble, Wise, Iudicious, and best knowes	80-	356-	756-
99°	1638	192	20	The fits o'th' Season. I dare not speake much further,	79-	355-	755-
	1639	193	21	But cruell are the times, when we are Traitors	78-	354-	754-
	1640	194	22	And do not know our selues: when we hold Rumor	77-	353-	753-
	1641	195	23	From what we feare, yet know not what we feare,	76-	352-	752-
	1642	196	24	But floate vpon a wilde and violent Sea	75-	351-	751-
	1643	197	25	Each way, and moue. I take my leaue of you:	74-	350-	750-
	1644	198	26	Shall not be long but Ile be heere againe:	73-	349-	749-
	1645	199	27	Things at the worst will cease, or else climbe vpward,	72-	348-	748-
	1646	200	28	To what they were before. My pretty Cosine,	71-	347-	747-
108°	1647	201	29	Blessing vpon you.	70-	346-	746-
	1648	202	30	*Wife.* Father'd he is,	69-	345-	745-
	1649	203	31	And yet hee's Father-lesse.	68-	344-	744-
	1650	204	32	*Rosse.* I am so much a Foole, should I stay longer	67-	343-	743-
	1651	205	33	It would be my disgrace, and your discomfort.	66-	342-	742-
	1652	206	34	I take my leaue at once. *Exit Rosse.*	65-	341-	741-
	1653	207	35	*Wife.* Sirra, your Fathers dead,	64-	340-	740-
	1654	208	36	And what will you do now? How will you liue?	63-	339-	739-
	1655	209	37	*Son.* As Birds do Mother.	62-	338-	738-
117°	1656	210	38	*Wife.* What with Wormes, and Flyes?	61-	337-	737-
	1657	211	39	*Son.* With what I get I meane, and so do they.	60-	336-	736-
	1658	212	40	*Wife.* Poore Bird,	59-	335-	735-
	1659	213	41	Thou'dst neuer Feare the Net, nor Lime,	58-	334-	734-
	1660	214	42	The Pitfall, nor the Gin.	57-	333-	733-
	1661	215	43	*Son.* Why should I Mother?	56-	332-	732-
	1662	216	44	Poore Birds they are not set for:	55-	331-	731-
	1663	217	45	My Father is not dead for all your saying.	54-	330-	730-
	1664	218	46	*Wife.* Yes, he is dead:	53-	329-	729-
126°	1665	219	47	How wilt thou do for a Father?	52-	328-	728-
	1666	220	48	*Son.* Nay how will you do for a Husband?	51-	327-	727-
	1667	221	49 S	*Wife.* Why I can buy me twenty at any Market.	50-	326-	726-
	1668	222	50 S	*Son.* Then you'l by 'em to sell againe.	49-	325-	725-
	1669	223	51	*Wife.* Thou speak'st withall thy wit,	48-	324-	724-
	1670	224	52	And yet I'faith with wit enough for thee.	47-	323-	723-
	1671	225	53	*Son.* Was my Father a Traitor, Mother?	46-	322-	722-

NUMBERED FIRST FOLIO TEXT   317

Angle	Play	Act	Scene	The Tragedie of Macbeth	Scene	Act	Play
	1672	226	54	*Wife.* I, that he was.	45-	321-	721-
	1673	227	55	*Son.* What is a Traitor?	44-	320-	720-
135°	1674	228	56	*Wife.* Why one that sweares, and lyes.	43-	319-	719-
	1675	229	57	*Son.* And be all Traitors, that do so.	42-	318-	718-
	1676	230	58	*Wife.* Euery one that do's so, is a Traitor,	41-	317-	717-
	1677	231	59	And must be hang'd.	40-	316-	716-
	1678	232	60	*Son.* And must they all be hang'd, that swear and lye?	39-	315-	715-
	1679	233	61	*Wife.* Euery one.	38-	314-	714-
	1680	234	62	*Son.* Who must hang them?	37-	313-	713-
	1681	235	63	*Wife.* Why, the honest men.	36-	312-	712-
	1682	236	64	*Son.* Then the Liars and Swearers are Fools: for there	35-	311-	711-
144°	1683	237	65	are Lyars and Swearers enow, to beate the honest men,	34-	310-	710-
	1684	238	66	and hang vp them.	33-	309-	709-
	1685	239	67	*Wife.* Now God helpe thee, poore Monkie:	32-	308-	708-
	1686	240	68	But how wilt thou do for a Father?	31-	307-	707-
	1687	241	69	*Son.* If he were dead, you'ld weepe for him: if you	30-	306-	706-
	1688	242	70	would not, it were a good signe, that I should quickely	29-	305-	705-
	1689	243	71	haue a new Father.	28-	304-	704-
	1690	244	72	*Wife.* Poore pratler, how thou talk'st?	27-	303-	703-
				Enter a Messenger.			
	1691	245	73	*Mes.* Blesse you faire Dame: I am not to you known,	26-	302-	702-
153°	1692	246	74	Though in your state of Honor I am perfect;	25-	301-	701-
	1693	247	75	I doubt some danger do's approach you neerely.	24-	300-	700-
	1694	248	76	If you will take a homely mans aduice,	23-	299-	699-
	1695	249	77	Be not found heere: Hence with your little ones	22-	298-	698-
	1696	250	78	To fright you thus. Me thinkes I am too sauage:	21-	297-	697-
	1697	251	79	To do worse to you, were fell Cruelty,	20-	296-	696-
	1698	252	80	Which is too nie your person. Heauen preserue you,	19-	295-	695-
	1699	253	81	I dare abide no longer. *Exit Messenger.*	18-	294-	694-
	1700	254	82	*Wife.* Whether should I flye?	17-	293-	693-
162°	1701	255	83	I haue done no harme. But I remember now	16-	292-	692-
	1702	256	84	I am in this earthly world: where to do harme	15-	291-	691-
	1703	257	85	Is often laudable, to do good sometime	14-	290-	690-
	1704	258	86	Accounted dangerous folly. Why then (alas)	13-	289-	689-
	1705	259	87	Do I put vp that womanly defence,	12-	288-	688-
	1706	260	88	To say I haue done no harme?	11-	287-	687-
	1707	261	89	What are these faces?	10-	286-	686-
				Enter Murtherers.			
	1708	262	90	*Mur.* Where is your Husband?	9-	285-	685-

Angle	Play	Act	Scene		The Tragedie of Macbeth	Scene	Act	Play
	1709	263	91		*Wife*. I hope in no place so vnsanctified,	8-	284-	684-
171°	1710	264	92		Where such as thou may'st finde him.	7-	283-	683-
	1711	265	93		*Mur*. He's a Traitor.	6-	282-	682-
	1712	266	94		*Son*. Thou ly'st thou shagge-ear'd Villaine.	5-	281-	681-
	1713	267	95		*Mur*. What you Egge?	4-	280-	680-
	1714	268	96		Yong fry of Treachery?	3-	279-	679-
	1715	269	97		*Son*. He ha's kill'd me Mother,	2-	278-	678-
177°	1716	270	98		Run away I pray you. *Exit crying Murther*.	1-	277-	677-

Scena Tertia.

Enter Malcolme and Macduffe.

Angle	Play	Act	Scene		The Tragedie of Macbeth	Scene	Act	Play
	1717	271	1		*Mal*. Let vs seeke out some desolate shade, & there	276-	276-	676-
	1718	272	2		Weepe our sad bosomes empty.	275-	275-	675-
180°	1719	273	3	A	*Macd*. Let vs rather	274-	274-	674-
	1720	274	4	A	Hold fast the mortall Sword: and like good men,	273-	273-	673-
	1721	275	5		Bestride our downfall Birthdome: each new Morne,	272-	272-	672-
	1722	276	6		New Widdowes howle, new Orphans cry, new sorowes	271-	271-	671-
	1723	277	7		Strike heauen on the face, that it resounds	270-	270-	670-
	1724	278	8		As if it felt with Scotland, and yell'd out	269-	269-	669-
	1725	279	9		Like Syllable of Dolour.	268-	268-	668-
	1726	280	10		*Mal*. What I beleeue, Ile waile;	267-	267-	667-
	1727	281	11		What know, beleeue; and what I can redresse,	266-	266-	666-
189°	1728	282	12		As I shall finde the time to friend: I wil.	265-	265-	665-
	1729	283	13		What you haue spoke, it may be so perchance.	264-	264-	664-
	1730	284	14		This Tyrant, whose sole name blisters our tongues,	263-	263-	663-
	1731	285	15		Was once thought honest: you haue lou'd him well,	262-	262-	662-
	1732	286	16		He hath not touch'd you yet. I am yong, but something	261-	261-	661-
	1733	287	17		You may discerne of him through me, and wisedome	260-	260-	660-
	1734	288	18		To offer vp a weake, poore innocent Lambe	259-	259-	659-
	1735	289	19		T' appease an angry God.	258-	258-	658-
	1736	290	20		*Macd*. I am not treacherous.	257-	257-	657-
198°	1737	291	21		*Malc*. But *Macbeth* is.	256-	256-	656-
	1738	292	22		A good and vertuous Nature may recoyle	255-	255-	655-
	1739	293	23		In an Imperiall charge. But I shall craue your pardon:	254-	254-	654-
	1740	294	24		That which you are, my thoughts cannot transpose;	253-	253-	653-

Angle	Play	Act	Scene	The Tragedie of Macbeth	Scene	Act	Play
	1741	295	25	Angels are bright still, though the brightest fell.	252-	252-	652-
	1742	296	26	Though all things foule, would wear the brows of grace	251-	251-	651-
	1743	297	27	Yet Grace must still looke so.	250-	250-	650-
	1744	298	28	*Macd.* I haue lost my Hopes.	249-	249-	649-
	1745	299	29	*Malc.* Perchance euen there	248-	248-	648-
207 °	1746	300	30	Where I did finde my doubts.	247-	247-	647-
	1747	301	31	Why in that rawnesse left you Wife, and Childe?	246-	246-	646-
	1748	302	32	Those precious Motiues, those strong knots of Loue,	245-	245-	645-
	1749	303	33	Without leaue-taking. I pray you,	244-	244-	644-
	1750	304	34	Let not my Iealousies, be your Dishonors,	243-	243-	643-
	1751	305	35	But mine owne Safeties: you may be rightly iust,	242-	242-	642-
	1752	306	36	What euer I shall thinke.	241-	241-	641-
	1753	307	37	*Macd.* Bleed, bleed poore Country,	240-	240-	640-
	1754	308	38	Great Tyrrany, lay thou thy basis sure,	239-	239-	639-
216 °	1755	309	39	For goodnesse dare not check thee: wear y thy wrongs,	238-	238-	638-
	1756	310	40	The Title, is affear'd. Far thee well Lord,	237-	237-	637-
	1757	311	41	I would not be the Villaine that thou think'st,	236-	236-	636-
	1758	312	42	For the whole Space that's in the Tyrants Graspe,	235-	235-	635-
	1759	313	43	And the rich East to boot.	234-	234-	634-
	1760	314	44	*Mal.* Be not offended:	233-	233-	633-
	1761	315	45	I speake not as in absolute feare of you:	232-	232-	632-
	1762	316	46	I thinke our Country sinkes beneath the yoake,	231-	231-	631-
	1763	317	47	It weepes, it bleeds, and each new day a gash	230-	230-	630-
225 °	1764	318	48	Is added to her wounds. I thinke withall,	229-	229-	629-
	1765	319	49	There would be hands vplifted in my right:	228-	228-	628-
	1766	320	50	And heere from gracious England haue I offer	227-	227-	627-
	1767	321	51	Of goodly thousands. But for all this,	226-	226-	626-
	1768	322	52	When I shall treade vpon the Tyrants head,	225-	225-	625-
	1769	323	53	Or weare it on my Sword; yet my poore Country	224-	224-	624-
	1770	324	54	Shall haue more vices then it had before,	223-	223-	623-
	1771	325	55	More suffer, and more sundry wayes then euer,	222-	222-	622-
	1772	326	56	By him that shall succeede.	221-	221-	621-
234 °	1773	327	57	*Macd.* What should he be?	220-	220-	620-
	1774	328	58	*Mal.* It is my selfe I meane: in whom I know	219-	219-	619-
	1775	329	59	All the particulars of Vice so grafted,	218-	218-	618-
	1776	330	60	That when they shall be open'd, blacke *Macbeth*	217-	217-	617-
	1777	331	61	Will seeme as pure as Snow, and the poore State	216-	216-	616-
	1778	332	62	Esteeme him as a Lambe, being compar'd	215-	215-	615-
	1779	333	63	With my confinelesse harmes.	214-	214-	614-

Angle	Play	Act	Scene	The Tragedie of Macbeth	Scene	Act	Play
	1780	334	64	*Macd.* Not in the Legions	213-	213-	613-
	1781	335	65	Of horrid Hell, can come a Diuell more damn'd	212-	212-	612-
243°	1782	336	66	In euils, to top *Macbeth*.	211-	211-	611-
	1783	337	67	*Mal.* I grant him Bloody,	210-	210-	610-
	1784	338	68	Luxurious, Auaricious, False, Deceitfull,	209-	209-	609-
	1785	339	69	Sodaine, Malicious, smacking of euery sinne	208-	208-	608-
	1786	340	70	That ha's a name. But there's no bottome, none	207-	207-	607-
	1787	341	71	In my Voluptuousnesse: Your Wiues, your Daughters,	206-	206-	606-
	1788	342	72	Your Matrons, and your Maides, could not fill vp	205-	205-	605-
	1789	343	73	The Cesterne of my Lust, and my Desire	204-	204-	604-
	1790	344	74	All continent Impediments would ore-beare	203-	203-	603-
252°	1791	345	75	That did oppose my will. Better *Macbeth*,	202-	202-	602-
	1792	346	76	Then such an one to reigne.	201-	201-	601-
	1793	347	77	*Macd.* Boundlesse intemperance	200-	200-	600-
	1794	348	78	In Nature is a Tyranny: It hath beene	199-	199-	599-
	1795	349	79	Th' vntimely emptying of the happy Throne,	198-	198-	598-
	1796	350	80	And fall of many Kings. But feare not yet	197-	197-	597-
	1797	351	81	To take vpon you what is yours: you may	196-	196-	596-
	1798	352	82	Conuey your pleasures in a spacious plenty,	195-	195-	595-
	1799	353	83	And yet seeme cold. The time you may so hoodwinke:	194-	194-	594-
261°	1800	354	84	We haue willing Dames enough: there cannot be	193-	193-	593-
	1801	355	85	That Vulture in you, to deuoure so many	192-	192-	592-
	1802	356	86	As will to Greatnesse dedicate themselues,	191-	191-	591-
	1803	357	87	Finding it so inclinde.	190-	190-	590-
	1804	358	88	*Mal.* With this, there growes	189-	189-	589-
	1805	359	89	In my most ill-composd Affection, such	188-	188-	588-
	1806	360	90	A stanchlesse Auarice, that were I King,	187-	187-	587-
	1807	361	91	I should cut off the Nobles for their Lands,	186-	186-	586-
	1808	362	92	Desire his Iewels, and this others House,	185-	185-	585-
270°	1809	363	93	And my more-hauing, would be as a Sawce	184-	184-	584-
	1810	364	94	To make me hunger more, that I should forge	183-	183-	583-
	1811	365	95	Quarrels vniust against the Good and Loyall,	182-	182-	582-
	1812	366	96	Destroying them for wealth.	181-	181-	581-
	1813	367	97	*Macd.* This Auarice	180-	180-	580-
	1814	368	98	stickes deeper: growes with more pernicious roote	179-	179-	579-
	1815	369	99	Then Summer-seeming Lust: and it hath bin	178-	178-	578-
	1816	370	100	The Sword of our slaine Kings: yet do not feare,	177-	177-	577-
	1817	371	101	Scotland hath Foysons, to fill vp your will	176-	176-	576-
279°	1818	372	102	Of your meere Owne. All these are portable,	175-	175-	575-

Angle	Play	Act	Scene		The Tragedie of Macbeth	Scene	Act	Play
	1819	373	103		With other Graces weigh'd.	174-	174-	574-
	1820	374	104		*Mal.* But I haue none. The King-becoming Graces,	173-	173-	573-
	1821	375	105		As Iustice, Verity, Temp'rance, Stablenesse,	172-	172-	572-
	1822	376	106		Bounty, Perseuerance, Mercy, Lowlinesse,	171-	171-	571-
	1823	377	107		Deuotion, Patience, Courage, Fortitude,	170-	170-	570-
	1824	378	108		I haue no rellish of them, but abound	169-	169-	569-
	1825	379	109		In the diuision of each seuerall Crime,	168-	168-	568-
	1826	380	110		Acting it many wayes. Nay, had I powre, I should	167-	167-	567-
288 °	1827	381	111		Poure the sweet Milke of Concord, into Hell,	166-	166-	566-
	1828	382	112		Vprore the vniuersall peace, confound	165-	165-	565-
	1829	383	113		All vnity on earth.	164-	164-	564-
	1830	384	114		*Macd.* O Scotland, Scotland.	163-	163-	563-
	1831	385	115		*Mal.* If such a one be fit to gouerne, speake:	162-	162-	562-
	1832	386	116		I am as I haue spoken.	161-	161-	561-
	1833	387	117		*Mac.* Fit to gouern? No not to liue. O Natiõ miserable!	160-	160-	560-
	1834	388	118		With an vntitled Tyrant, bloody Sceptred,	159-	159-	559-
	1835	389	119		When shalt thou see thy wholsome dayes againe?	158-	158-	558-
297 °	1836	390	120		Since that the truest Issue of thy Throne	157-	157-	557-
	1837	391	121		By his owne Interdiction stands accust,	156-	156-	556-
	1838	392	122		And do's blaspheme his breed? Thy Royall Father	155-	155-	555-
	1839	393	123		Was a most Sainted-King: the Queene that bore thee,	154-	154-	554-
	1840	394	124		Oftner vpon her knees, then on her feet,	153-	153-	553-
	1841	395	125		Dy'de euery day she liu'd. Fare thee well,	152-	152-	552-
	1842	396	126		These Euils thou repeat'st vpon thy selfe,	151-	151-	551-
	1843	397	127		Hath banish'd me from Scotland. O my Brest,	150-	150-	550-
	1844	398	128		Thy hope ends heere.	149-	149-	549-
306 °	1845	399	129		*Mal. Macduff,* this Noble passion	148-	148-	548-
	1846	400	130		Childe of integrity, hath from my soule	147-	147-	547-
	1847	401	131		Wip'd the blacke Scruples, reconcil'd my thoughts	146-	146-	546-
	1848	402	132		To thy good Truth, and Honor. Diuellish *Macbeth,*	145-	145-	545-
	1849	403	133		By many of these traines, hath sought to win me	144-	144-	544-
	1850	404	134		Into his power: and modest Wisedome pluckes me	143-	143-	543-
	1851	405	135		From ouer-credulous hast: but God aboue	142-	142-	542-
	1852	406	136		Deale betweene thee and me; For euen now	141-	141-	541-
	1853	407	137		I put my selfe to thy Direction, and	140-	140-	540-
315 °	1854	408	138	S	Vnspeake mine owne detraction. Heere abiure	139-	139-	539-
	1855	409	139	S	The taints, and blames I laide vpon my selfe,	138-	138-	538-
	1856	410	140		For strangers to my Nature. I am yet	137-	137-	537-
	1857	411	141		Vnknowne to Woman, neuer was forsworne,	136-	136-	536-

Angle	Play	Act	Scene	The Tragedie of Macbeth	Scene	Act	Play
	1858	412	142	Scarsely haue coueted what was mine owne.	135-	135-	535-
	1859	413	143	At no time broke my Faith, would not betray	134-	134-	534-
	1860	414	144	The Deuill to his Fellow, and delight	133-	133-	533-
	1861	415	145	No lesse in truth then life. My first false speaking	132-	132-	532-
	1862	416	146	Was this vpon my selfe. What I am truly	131-	131-	531-
324°	1863	417	147	Is thine, and my poore Countries to command:	130-	130-	530-
	1864	418	148	Whither indeed, before they heere approach	129-	129-	529-
	1865	419	149	Old *Seyward* with ten thousand warlike men	128-	128-	528-
	1866	420	150	Already at a point, was setting foorth:	127-	127-	527-
	1867	421	151	Now wee'l together, and the chance of goodnesse	126-	126-	526-
	1868	422	152	Be like our warranted Quarrell. Why are you silent?	125-	125-	525-
	1869	423	153	*Macd.* Such welcome, and vnwelcom things at once	124-	124-	524-
	1870	424	154	'Tis hard to reconcile.	123-	123-	523-
				Enter a Doctor.			
	1871	425	155	*Mal.* Well, more anon. Comes the King forth	122-	122-	522-
333°	1872	426	156	I pray you?	121-	121-	521-
	1873	427	157	*Doct.* I Sir: there are a crew of wretched Soules	120-	120-	520-
	1874	428	158	That stay his Cure: their malady conuinces	119-	119-	519-
	1875	439	159	The great assay of Art. But at his touch,	118-	118-	518-
	1876	430	160	Such sanctity hath Heauen giuen his hand,	117-	117-	517-
	1877	431	161	They presently amend. Exit.	116-	116-	516-
	1878	432	162	*Mal.* I thanke you Doctor.	115-	115-	515-
	1879	433	163	*Macd.* What's the Disease he meanes?	114-	114-	514-
	1880	434	164	*Mal.* Tis call'd the Euill.	113-	113-	513-
342°	1881	435	165	A most myraculous worke in this good King,	112-	112-	512-
	1882	436	166	Which often since my heere remaine in England,	111-	111-	511-
	1883	437	167	I haue seene him do: How he solicites heauen	110-	110-	510-
	1884	438	168	Himselfe best knowes: but strangely visited people	109-	109-	509-
	1885	449	169	All swolne and Vlcerous, pittifull to the eye,	108-	108-	508-
	1886	440	170	The meere dispaire of Surgery, he cures,	107-	107-	507-
	1887	441	171	Hanging a golden stampe about their neckes,	106-	106-	506-
	1888	442	172	Put on with holy Prayers, and 'tis spoken	105-	105-	505-
	1889	443	173	To the succeeding Royalty he leaues	104-	104-	504-
351°	1890	444	174	The healing Benediction. With this strange vertue,	103-	103-	503-
	1891	445	175	He hath a heauenly guift of Prophesie,	102-	102-	502-
	1892	446	176	And sundry Blessings hang about his Throne,	101-	101-	501-
	1893	447	177	That speake him full of Grace.	100-	100-	500-
				Enter Rosse.			
	1894	448	178	*Macd.* See who comes heere.	99-	99-	499-

Angle	Play	Act	Scene	The Tragedie of Macbeth	Scene	Act	Play
	1895	449	179	*Malc.* My Countryman: but yet I know him not.	98-	98-	498-
	1896	450	180	*Macd.* My euer gentle Cozen, welcome hither.	97-	97-	497-
	1897	451	181	*Malc.* I know him now. Good God betimes remoue	96-	96-	496-
	1898	452	182	The meanes that makes vs Strangers.	95-	95-	495-
360°	1899	453	183	*Rosse.* Sir, Amen.	94-	94-	494-
	1900	454	184	*Macd.* Stands Scotland where it did?	93-	93-	493-
282 deg	1901	455	185	*Rosse.* Alas poore Countrey,	92-	92-	492-
	1902	456	186	Almost affraid to know it selfe. It cannot	91-	91-	491-
	1903	457	187	Be call'd our Mother, but our Graue; where nothing	90-	90-	490-
	1904	458	188	But who knowes nothing, is once seene to smile:	89-	89-	489-
	1905	459	189	Where sighes, and groanes, and shrieks that rent the ayre	88-	88-	488-
285 deg	1906	460	190	Are made, not mark'd: Where violent sorrow seemes	87-	87-	487-
	1907	461	191	A Moderne extasie: The Deadmans knell,	86-	86-	486-
	1908	462	192	Is there scarse ask'd for who, and good mens liues	85-	85-	485-
	1909	463	193	Expire before the Flowers in their Caps,	84-	84-	484-
	1910	464	194	Dying, or ere they sicken.	83-	83-	483-
288 deg	1911	465	195	*Macd.* Oh Relation; too nice, and yet too true.	82-	82-	482-
	1912	466	196	*Malc.* What's the newest griefe?	81-	81-	481-
	1913	467	197	*Rosse.* That of an houres age, doth hisse the speaker,	80-	80-	480-
	1914	468	198	Each minute teemes a new one.	79-	79-	479-
	1915	469	199	*Macd.* How do's my Wife?	78-	78-	478-
291 deg	1916	470	200	*Rosse.* Why well.	77-	77-	477-
	1917	471	201	*Macd.* And all my Children?	76-	76-	476-
	1918	472	202	*Rosse.* Well too.	75-	75-	475-
	1919	473	203	*Macd.* The Tyrant ha's not batter'd at their peace?	74-	74-	474-
	1920	474	204	*Rosse.* No, they were wel at peace, when I did leaue 'em	73-	73-	473-
294 deg	1921	475	205	*Macd.* Be not a niggard of your speech: How gos't?	72-	72-	472-
	1922	476	206	*Rosse.* When I came hither to transport the Tydings	71-	71-	471-
	1923	477	207	Which I haue heauily borne, there ran a Rumour	70-	70-	470-
	1924	478	208	Of many worthy Fellowes, that were out,	69-	69-	469-
	1925	479	209	Which was to my beleefe witnest the rather,	68-	68-	468-
297 deg	1926	480	210	For that I saw the Tyrants Power a-foot.	67-	67-	467-
	1927	481	211	Now is the time of helpe: your eye in Scotland	66-	66-	466-
	1928	482	212	Would create Souldiors, make our women fight,	65-	65-	465-
	1929	483	213	To doffe their dire distresses.	64-	64-	464-
	1930	484	214	*Malc.* Bee't their comfort	63-	63-	463-
300 deg	1931	485	215	We are comming thither: Gracious England hath	62-	62-	462-
	1932	486	216	Lent vs good *Seyward*, and ten thousand men,	61-	61-	461-
	1933	487	217	An older, and a better Souldier, none	60-	60-	460-

Angle	Play	Act	Scene	The Tragedie of Macbeth	Scene	Act	Play
	1934	488	218	That Christendome giues out.	59-	59-	459-
	1935	489	219	*Rosse.* Would I could answer	58-	58-	458-
303 deg	1936	490	220	This comfort with the like. But I haue words	57-	57-	457-
	1937	491	221	That would be howl'd out in the desert ayre,	56-	56-	456-
	1938	492	222	Where hearing should not latch them.	55-	55-	455-
	1939	493	223	*Macd.* What concerne they,	54-	54-	454-
	1940	494	224	The generall cause, or is it a Fee-griefe	53-	53-	453-
306 deg	1941	495	225	Due to some single brest?	52-	52-	452-
	1942	496	226	*Rosse.* No minde that's honest	51-	51-	451-
	1943	497	227	But in it shares some woe, though the maine part	50-	50-	450-
	1944	498	228	Pertaines to you alone.	49-	49-	449-
	1945	499	229	*Macd.* If it be mine	48-	48-	448-
30 deg	1946	500	230	Keepe it not from me, quickly let me haue it.	47-	47-	447-
	1947	501	231	*Rosse.* Let not your eares dispise my tongue for euer,	46-	46-	446-
	1948	502	232	Which shall possesse them with the heauiest sound	45-	45-	445-
	1949	503	233	that euer yet they heard.	44-	44-	444-
	1950	504	234	*Macd.* Humh: I guesse at it.	43-	43-	443-
312 deg	1951	505	235	*Rosse.* Your Castle is surpriz'd: your Wife, and Babes	42-	42-	442-
	1952	506	236	Sauagely slaughter'd: To relate the manner	41-	41-	441-
	1953	507	237	Were on the Quarry of these murther'd Deere	40-	40-	440-
	1954	508	238	To adde the death of you.	39-	39-	439-
	1955	509	239	*Malc.* Mercifull Heauen:	38-	38-	438-
315 deg	1956	510	240	What man, ne're pull your hat vpon your browes:	37-	37-	437-
	1957	511	241	Giue sorrow words; the griefe that do's not speake,	36-	36-	436-
	1958	512	242	Whispers the o're-fraught heart, and bids it breake.	35-	35-	435-
	1959	513	243	*Macd.* My Children too?	34-	34-	434-
	1960	514	244	*Ro.* Wife, Children, Seruants, all that could be found.	33-	33-	433-
318 deg	1961	515	245	*Macd.* And I must be from thence? My wife kil'd too?	32-	32-	432-
	1962	516	246	*Rosse.* I haue said.	31-	31-	431-
	1963	517	247	*Malc.* Be comforted.	30-	30-	430-
	1964	518	248	Let's make vs Med'cines of our great Reuenge,	29-	29-	429-
	1965	519	249	To cure this deadly greefe.	28-	28-	428-
321 deg	1966	520	250	*Macd.* He ha's no Children. All my pretty ones?	27-	27-	427-
	1967	521	251	Did you say All? Oh Hell-Kite! All?	26-	26-	426-
	1968	522	252	What, All my pretty Chickens, and their Damme	25-	25-	425-
	1969	523	253	At one fell swoope?	24-	24-	424-
	1970	524	254	*Malc.* Dispute it like a man.	23-	23-	423-
324 deg	1971	525	255	*Macd.* I shall do so:	22-	22-	422-
	1972	526	256	But I must also feele it as a man;	21-	21-	421-

NUMBERED FIRST FOLIO TEXT   325

Angle	Play	Act	Scene	The Tragedie of Macbeth	Scene	Act	Play
	1973	527	257	I cannot but remember such things were	20-	20-	420-
	1974	528	258	That were most precious to me: Did heauen looke on,	19-	19-	419-
	1975	529	259	And would not take their part? Sinfull *Macduff*,	18-	18-	418-
327 deg	1976	530	260	They were all strooke for thee: Naught that I am,	17-	17-	417-
	1977	531	261	Not for their owne demerits, but for mine	16-	16-	416-
	1978	532	262	Fell slaughter on their soules: Heauen rest them now.	15-	15-	415-
	1979	533	263	*Mal*. Be this the Whetstone of your sword, let griefe	14-	14-	414-
	1980	534	264	Conuert to anger: blunt not the heart, enrage it.	13-	13-	413-
330 deg	1981	535	265	*Macd*. O I could play the woman with mine eyes,	12-	12-	412-
	1982	536	266	And Braggart with my tongue. But gentle Heauens,	11-	11-	411-
	1983	537	267	Cut short all intermission: Front to Front,	10-	10-	410-
	1984	538	268	Bring thou this Fiend of Scotland, and my selfe	9-	9-	409-
	1985	539	269	Within my Swords length set him, if he scape	8-	8-	408-
333 deg	1986	540	270	Heauen forgiue him too.	7-	7-	407-
	1987	541	271	*Mal*. This time goes manly:	6-	6-	406-
	1988	542	272	Come go we to the King, our Power is ready,	5-	5-	405-
	1989	543	273	Our lacke is nothing but our leaue. Macbeth	4-	4-	404-
	1990	544	274	Is ripe for shaking, and the Powres aboue	3-	3-	403-
336 deg	1991	545	275	Put on their Instruments: Receiue what cheere you may,	2-	2-	402-
	1992	546	276	The Night is long, that neuer findes the Day. *Exeunt*	1-	1-	401-

---

Actus Quintus.

Enter a Doctor of Physicke, and a Wayting Gentlewoman.

	1993	1	1	*Doct*. I haue too Nights watch'd with you, but can	77-	400-	400-
	1994	2	2	perceiue no truth in your report. When was it shee last	76-	399-	399-
	1995	3	3	walk'd?	75-	398-	398-
339 deg	1996	4	4	*Gent*. Since his Maiesty went into the Field, I haue	74-	397-	397-
	1997	5	5	seene her rise from her bed, throw her Night-Gown vp-	73-	396-	396-
	1998	6	6	pon her, vnlocke her Closset, take foorth paper, folde it,	72-	395-	395-
	1999	7	7	write vpon't, read it, afterwards Seale it, and againe re-	71-	394-	394-
	2000	8	8	turne to bed; yet all this while in a most fast sleepe.	70-	393-	393-
342 deg	2001	9	9	*Doct*. A great perturbation in Nature, to receyue at	69-	392-	392-
	2002	10	10	once the benefit of sleep, and do the effects of watching.	68-	391-	391-
	2003	11	11	In this slumbry agitation, besides her walking, and other	67-	390-	390-

Angle	Play	Act	Scene	The Tragedie of Macbeth	Scene	Act	Play
	2004	12	12	actuall performances, what (at any time) haue you heard	66-	389-	389-
	2005	13	13	her say?	65-	388-	388-
345 deg	2006	14	14	*Gent.* That Sir, which I will not report after her.	64-	387-	387-
	2007	15	15	*Doct.* You may to me, and 'tis most meet you should.	63-	386-	386-
	2008	16	16	*Gent.* Neither to you, nor any one, hauing no witnesse	62-	385-	385-
	2009	17	17	to confirme my speech. *Enter Lady, with a Taper.*	61-	384-	384-
	2010	18	18	Lo you, heere she comes: This is her very guise, and vp-	60-	383-	383-
348 deg	2011	19	19	on my life fast asleepe: obserue her, stand close.	59-	382-	382-
0°	2012	20	20	*Doct.* How came she by that light?	58-	381-	381-
	2013	21	21	*Gent.* Why it stood by her: she ha's light by her con-	57-	380-	380-
	2014	22	22	tinually, 'tis her command.	56-	379-	379-
	2015	23	23	*Doct.* You see her eyes are open.	55-	378-	378-
	2016	24	24	*Gent.* I but their sense are shut.	54-	377-	377-
	2017	25	25	*Doct.* What is it she do's now?	53-	376-	376-
	2018	26	26	Looke how she rubbes her hands.	52-	375-	375-
	2019	27	27	*Gent.* It is an accustom'd action with her, to seeme	51-	374-	374-
	2020	28	28	thus washing her hands: I haue knowne her continue in	50-	373-	373-
9°	2021	29	29	this a quarter of an houre.	49-	372-	372-
	2022	30	30	*Lad.* Yet heere's a spot.	48-	371-	371-
	2023	31	31	*Doct.* Heark, she speaks, I will set downe what comes	47-	370-	370-
	2024	32	32	from her, to satisfie my remembrance the more strongly.	46-	369-	369-
	2025	33	33	*La.* Out damned spot: out I say. One: Two: Why	45-	368-	368-
	2026	34	34	then 'tis time to doo't: Hell is murky. Fye, my Lord, fie,	44-	367-	367-
	2027	35	35	a Souldier, and affear'd? what need we feare? who knowes	43-	366-	366-
	2028	36	36	it, when none can call our powre to accompt: yet who	42-	365-	365-
	2029	37	37	would haue thought the olde man to haue had so much	41-	364-	364-
18°	2030	38	38	blood in him.	40-	363-	363-
	2031	39	39 S	*Doct.* Do you marke that?	39-	362-	362-
	2032	40	40	*Lad.* The Thane of Fife, had a wife: where is she now?	38-	361-	361-
	2033	41	41	What will these hands ne're be cleane? No more o'that	37-	360-	360-
	2034	42	42	my Lord, no more o'that: you marre all with this star-	36-	359-	359-
	2035	43	43	ting.	35-	358-	358-
	2036	44	44	*Doct.* Go too, go too:	34-	357-	357-
	2037	45	45	You haue knowne what you should not.	33-	356-	356-
	2038	46	46	*Gent.* She ha's spoke what shee should not, I am sure	32-	355-	355-
27°	2039	47	47	of that: Heauen knowes what she ha's knowne.	31-	354-	354-
	2040	48	48	*La.* Heere's the smell of the blood still: all the per-	30-	353-	353-
	2041	49	49	fumes of Arabia will not sweeten this little hand.	29-	352-	352-
	2042	50	50	Oh, oh, oh.	28-	351-	351-

Angle	Play	Act	Scene	The Tragedie of Macbeth	Scene	Act	Play
	2043	51	51	*Doct.* What a sigh is there? The hart is sorely charg'd.	27-	350-	350-
	2044	52	52	*Gent.* I would not haue such a heart in my bosome,	26-	349-	349-
	2045	53	53	for the dignity of the whole body.	25-	348-	348-
	2046	54	54	*Doct.* Well, well, well.	24-	347-	347-
	2047	55	55	*Gent.* Pray God it be sir.	23-	346-	346-
36°	2048	56	56	*Doct.* This disease is beyond my practise: yet I haue	22-	345-	345-
	2049	57	57	knowne those which haue walkt in their sleep, who haue	21-	344-	344-
	2050	58	58	dyed holily in their beds.	20-	343-	343-
	2051	59	59	*Lad.* Wash your hands, put on your Night-Gowne,	19-	342-	342-
	2052	60	60	looke not so pale: I tell you yet againe *Banquo's* buried;	18-	341-	341-
	2053	61	61	he cannot come out on's graue.	17-	340-	340-
	2054	62	62	*Doct.* Euen so?	16-	339-	339-
	2055	63	63	*Lady.* To bed, to bed: there's knocking at the gate:	15-	338-	338-
	2056	64	64	Come, come, come, come, giue me your hand: What's	14-	337-	337-
45°	2057	65	65	done, cannot be vndone. To bed, to bed, to bed.	13-	336-	336-
				Exit Lady.			
	2058	66	66	*Doct.* Will she go now to bed?	12-	335-	335-
	2059	67	67	*Gent.* Directly.	11-	334-	334-
	2060	68	68	*Doct.* Foule whisp'rings are abroad: vnnaturall deeds	10-	333-	333-
	2061	69	69	Do breed vnnaturall troubles: infected mindes	9-	332-	332-
	2062	70	70	To their deafe pillowes will discharge their Secrets:	8-	331-	331-
	2063	71	71	More needs she the Diuine, then the Physitian:	7-	330-	330-
	2064	72	72	God, God forgiue vs all. Looke after her,	6-	329-	329-
	2065	73	73	Remoue from her the meanes of all annoyance,	5-	328-	328-
54°	2066	74	74	And still keepe eyes vpon her: So goodnight,	4-	327-	327-
	2067	75	75	My minde she ha's mated, and amaz'd my sight.	3-	326-	326-
	2068	76	76	I thinke, but dare not speake.	2-	325-	325-
67°	2069	77	77	*Gent.* Good night good Doctor. *Exeunt.*	1-	324-	324-

Scena Secunda.

*Drum and Colours. Enter Menteth, Cathnes,
Angus, Lenox, Soldiers.*

	2070	78	1	*Ment.* The English powre is neere, led on by *Malcolm,*	37-	323-	323-
	2071	79	2	His Vnkle *Seyward,* and the good *Macduff.*	36-	322-	322-
	2072	80	3	Reuenges burne in them: for their deere causes	35-	321-	321-

Angle	Play	Act	Scene	The Tragedie of Macbeth	Scene	Act	Play
	2073	81	4	Would to the bleeding, and the grim Alarme	34-	320-	320-
	2074	82	5	Excite the mortified man.	33-	319-	319-
63 °	2075	83	6	*Ang.* Neere Byrnan wood	32-	318-	318-
	2076	84	7	Shall we well meet them, that way are they comming.	31-	317-	317-
	2077	85	8	*Cath.* Who knowes if *Donalbane* be with his brother?	30-	316-	316-
	2078	86	9	*Len.* For certaine Sir, he is not: I haue a File	29-	315-	315-
	2079	87	10	Of all the Gentry; there is *Seywards* Sonne,	28-	314-	314-
	2080	88	11	And many vnruffe youths, that euen now	27-	313-	313-
	2081	89	12	Protest their first of Manhood.	26-	312-	312-
	2082	90	13	*Ment.* What do's the Tyrant.	25-	311-	311-
	2083	91	14	*Cath.* Great Dunsinane he strongly Fortifies	24-	310-	310-
72 °	2084	92	15	Some say hee's mad: Others, that lesser hate him,	23-	309-	309-
	2085	93	16	Do call it valiant Fury, but for certaine	22-	308-	308-
	2086	94	17	He cannot buckle his distemper'd cause	21-	307-	307-
	2087	95	18	Within the belt of Rule.	20-	306-	306-
	2088	96	19 S	*Ang.* Now do's he feele	19-	305-	305-
	2089	97	20	His secret Murthers sticking on his hands,	18-	304-	304-
	2090	98	21	Now minutely Reuolts vpbraid his Faith-breach:	17-	303-	303-
	2091	99	22	Those he commands, moue onely in command,	16-	302-	302-
	2092	100	23	Nothing in loue: Now do's he feele his Title	15-	301-	301-
81 °	2093	101	24	Hang loose about him, like a Giants Robe	14-	300-	300-
	2094	102	25	Vpon a dwarfish Theefe.	13-	299-	299-
	2095	103	26	*Ment.* Who then shall blame	12-	298-	298-
	2096	104	27	His pester'd Senses to recoyle, and start,	11-	297-	297-
	2097	105	28	When all that is within him, do's condemne	10-	296-	296-
	2098	106	29	It selfe, for being there.	9-	295-	295-
	2099	107	30	*Cath.* Well, march we on,	8-	294-	294-
	2100	108	31	To giue Obedience, where 'tis truly ow'd:	7-	293-	293-
	2101	109	32	Meet we the Med'cine of the sickly Weale,	6-	292-	292-
90 °	2102	110	33	And with him poure we in our Countries purge,	5-	291-	291-
	2103	111	34	Each drop of vs.	4-	290-	290-
	2104	112	35	*Lenox.* Or so much as it needes,	3-	289-	289-
	2105	113	36	To dew the Soueraigne Flower, and drowne the Weeds:	2-	288-	288-
94 °	2106	114	37	Make we our March towards Birnan. *Exeunt marching.*	1-	287-	287-

Angle	Play	Act	Scene	The Tragedie of Macbeth	Scene	Act	Play
				Scena Tertia.			
				Enter Macbeth, Doctor, and Attendants.			
	2107	115	1	*Macb.* Bring me no more Reports, let them flye all:	70-	286-	286-
	2108	116	2	Till Byrnane wood remoue to Dunsinane,	69-	285-	285-
	2109	117	3	I cannot taint with Feare. What's the Boy *Malcolme*?	68-	284-	284-
	2110	118	4	Was he not borne of woman? The Spirits that know	67-	283-	283-
99°	2111	119	5	All mortall Consequences, haue pronounc'd me thus:	66-	282-	282-
	2112	120	6	Feare not *Macbeth*, no man that's borne of woman	65-	281-	281-
	2113	121	7	Shall ere haue power vpon thee. Then fly false Thanes,	64-	280-	280-
	2114	122	8	And mingle with the English Epicures,	63-	279-	279-
	2115	123	9	The minde I sway by, and the heart I beare,	62-	278-	278-
	2116	124	10 46²	Shall neuer sagge with doubt, nor shake with feare.	61-	277-	277-
				Enter Seruant.			
	2117	125	11	The diuell damne thee blacke, thou cream-fac'd Loone:	60-	276-	276-
	2118	126	12	Where got'st thou that Goose-looke.	59-	275-	275-
	2119	127	13	*Ser.* There is ten thousand.	58-	274-	274-
108°	2120	128	14	*Macb.* Geese Villaine?	57-	273-	273-
	2121	129	15	*Ser.* Souldiers Sir.	56-	272-	272-
	2122	130	16	*Macb.* Go pricke thy face, and ouer-red thy feare	55-	271-	271-
	2123	131	17	Thou Lilly-liuer'd Boy. What Soldiers, Patch?	54-	270-	270-
	2124	132	18	Death of thy Soule, those Linnen cheekes of thine	53-	269-	269-
	2125	133	19	Are Counsailers to feare. What Soldiers Whay-face?	52-	268-	268-
	2126	134	20	*Ser.* The English Force, so please you.	51-	267-	267-
	2127	135	21	*Macb.* Take thy face hence. *Seyton*, I am sick at hart,	50-	266-	266-
	2128	136	22	When I behold: *Seyton*, I say, this push	49-	265-	265-
117°	2129	137	23	Will cheere me euer, or dis-eate me now.	48-	264-	264-
	2130	138	24	I haue liu'd long enough: my way of life	47-	263-	263-
	2131	139	25	Is falne into the Seare, the yellow Leafe,	46-	262-	262-
	2132	140	26	And that which should accompany Old-Age,	45-	261-	261-
	2133	141	27	As Honor, Loue, Obedience, Troopes of Friends,	44-	260-	260-
	2134	142	28	I must not looke to haue: but in their steed,	43-	259-	259-
	2135	143	29	Curses, not lowd but deepe, Mouth-honor, breath	42-	258-	258-
	2136	144	30	Which the poore heart would faine deny, and dare not.	41-	257-	257-
	2137	145	31	*Seyton*?	40-	256-	256-

Angle	Play	Act	Scene	The Tragedie of Macbeth	Scene	Act	Play
				Enter Seyton.			
126°	2138	146	32	*Sey.* What's your gracious pleasure?	39-	255-	255-
	2139	147	33	*Macb.* What Newes more?	38-	254-	254-
	2140	148	34	*Sey.* All is confirm'd my Lord, which was reported.	37-	253-	253-
	2141	149	35	S	*Macb.* Ile fight, till from my bones, my flesh be hackt.	36-	252-	252-
	2142	150	36	S	Giue me my Armor.	35-	251-	251-
	2143	151	37		*Seyt.* 'Tis not needed yet.	34-	250-	250-
	2144	152	38		*Macb.* Ile put it on:	33-	249-	249-
	2145	153	39	Send out moe Horses, skirre the Country round,	32-	248-	248-
	2146	154	40	Hang those that talke of Feare. Giue me mine Armor:	31-	247-	247-
135°	2147	155	41	How do's your Patient, Doctor?	30-	246-	246-
	2148	156	42	*Doct.* Not so sicke my Lord,	29-	245-	245-
	2149	157	43	As she is troubled with thicke-comming Fancies	28-	244-	244-
	2150	158	44	That keepe her from her rest.	27-	243-	243-
	2151	159	45	*Macb.* Cure of that:	26-	242-	242-
	2152	160	46	Can'st thou not Minister to a minde diseas'd,	25-	241-	241-
	2153	161	47	Plucke from the Memory a rooted Sorrow,	24-	240-	240-
	2154	162	48	Raze out the written troubles of the Braine,	23-	239-	239-
	2155	163	49	And with some sweet Obliuious Antidote	22-	238-	238-
144°	2156	164	50	Cleanse the stufft bosome, of that perillous stuffe	21-	237-	237-
	2157	165	51	Which weighes vpon the heart?	20-	236-	236-
	2158	166	52	*Doct.* Therein the Patient	19-	235-	235-
	2159	167	53	Must minister to himselfe.	18-	234-	234-
	2160	168	54	*Macb.* Throw Physicke to the Dogs, Ile none of it.	17-	233-	233-
	2161	169	55	Come, put mine Armour on: giue me my Staffe:	16-	232-	232-
	2162	170	56	Seyton, send out: Doctor, the Thanes flye from me:	15-	231-	231-
	2163	171	57	Come sir, dispatch. If thou could'st Doctor, cast	14-	230-	230-
	2164	172	58	The Water of my Land, finde her Disease,	13-	229-	229-
153°	2165	173	59	And purge it to a sound and pristine Health,	12-	228-	228-
	2166	174	60	I would applaud thee to the very Eccho,	11-	227-	227-
	2167	175	61	That should applaud againe. Pull't off I say,	10-	226-	226-
	2168	176	62	What Rubarb, Cyme, or what Purgatiue drugge	9-	225-	225-
	2169	177	63	Would scowre these English hence: hear'st y of them?	8-	224-	224-
	2170	178	64	*Doct.* I my good Lord: your Royall Preparation	7-	223-	223-
	2171	179	65	Makes vs heare something.	6-	222-	222-
	2172	180	66	*Macb.* Bring it after me:	5-	221-	221-
	2173	181	67	I will not be affraid of Death and Bane,	4-	220-	220-
162°	2174	182	68	Till Birnane Forrest come to Dunsinane.	3-	219-	219-
	2175	183	69	*Doct.* Were I from Dunsinane away, and cleere,	2-	218-	218-

Angle	Play	Act	Scene	The Tragedie of Macbeth	Scene	Act	Play
164°	2176	184	70	Profit againe should hardly draw me heere. *Exeunt*	1-	217-	217-

Scena Quarta.

Drum and Colours. Enter Malcolme, Seyward, Macduffe, Seywards Sonne, Menteth, Cathnes, Angus, and Soldiers Marching.

	2177	185	1	*Malc.* Cosins, I hope the dayes are neere at hand	27-	216-	216-
	2178	186	2	That Chambers will be safe.	26-	215-	215-
	2179	187	3	*Ment.* We doubt it nothing.	25-	214-	214-
	2180	188	4	*Seyw.* What wood is this before vs?	24-	213-	213-
	2181	189	5	*Ment.* The wood of Birnane.	23-	212-	212-
	2182	190	6	*Malc.* Let euery Souldier hew him downe a Bough,	22-	211-	211-
171°	2183	191	7	And bear't before him, thereby shall we shadow	21-	210-	210-
	2184	192	8	The numbers of our Hoast, and make discouery	20-	209-	209-
	2185	193	9	Erre in report of vs.	19-	208-	208-
	2186	194	10	*Sold.* It shall be done.	18-	207-	207-
	2187	195	11	*Syw.* We learne no other, but the confident Tyrant	17-	206-	206-
	2188	196	12	Keepes still in Dunsinane, and will indure	16-	205-	205-
	2189	197	13	Our setting downe befor't.	15-	204-	204-
	2190	198	14 S	*Malc.* 'Tis his maine hope:	14-	203-	203-
	2191	199	15	For where there is aduantage to be giuen,	13-	202-	202-
180°	2192	200	16 A	Both more and lesse haue giuen him the Reuolt,	12-	201-	201-
	2193	201	17 A	And none serue with him, but constrained things,	11-	200-	200-
	2194	202	18	Whose hearts are absent too.	10-	199-	199-
	2195	203	19	*Macd.* Let our iust Censures	9-	198-	198-
	2196	204	20	Attend the true euent, and put we on	8-	197-	197-
	2197	205	21	Industrious Souldiership.	7-	196-	196-
	2198	206	22	*Sey.* The time approaches,	6-	195-	195-
	2199	207	23	That will with due decision make vs know	5-	194-	194-
	2200	208	24	What we shall say we haue, and what we owe:	4-	193-	193-
189°	2201	209	25	Thoughts speculatiue, their vnsure hopes relate,	3-	192-	192-
	2202	210	26	But certaine issue, stroakes must arbitrate,	2-	191-	191-
191°	2203	211	27	Towards which, aduance the warre. *Exeunt marching*	1-	190-	190-

Angle	Play	Act	Scene	The Tragedie of Macbeth	Scene	Act	Play
				Scena Quinta.			
				Enter Macbeth, Seyton, & Souldiers, with Drum and Colours.			
	2204	212	1	*Macb.* Hang out our Banners on the outward walls,	55-	189-	189-
	2205	213	2	The Cry is still, they come: our Castles strength	54-	188-	188-
	2206	214	3	Will laugh a Siedge to scorne: Heere let them lye,	53-	187-	187-
	2207	215	4	Till Famine and the Ague eate them vp:	52-	186-	186-
	2208	216	5	Were they not forc'd with those that should be ours,	51-	185-	185-
	2209	217	6	We might haue met them darefully, beard to beard,	50-	184-	184-
198°	2210	218	7	And beate them backward home. What is that noyse?	49-	183-	183-
				A Cry within of Women.			
	2211	219	8	*Sey.* It is the cry of women, my good Lord.	48-	182-	182-
	2212	220	9	*Macb.* I haue almost forgot the taste of Feares:	47-	181-	181-
	2213	221	10	The time ha's beene, my sences would haue cool'd	46-	180-	180-
	2214	222	11	To heare a Night-shrieke, and my Fell of haire	45-	179-	179-
	2215	223	12	Would at a dismall Treatise rowze, and stirre	44-	178-	178-
	2216	224	13	As life were in't. I haue supt full with horrors,	43-	177-	177-
	2217	225	14	Direnesse familiar to my slaughterous thoughts	42-	176-	176-
	2218	226	15	Cannot once start me. Wherefore was that cry?	41-	175-	175-
207°	2219	227	16	*Sey.* The Queene (my Lord) is dead.	40-	174-	174-
	2220	228	17	*Macb.* She should haue dy'de heereafter;	39-	173-	173-
	2221	229	18	There would haue beene a time for such a word:	38-	172-	172-
	2222	230	19	To morrow, and to morrow, and to morrow,	37-	171-	171-
	2223	231	20	Creepes in this petty pace from day to day,	36-	170-	170-
	2224	232	21	To the last Syllable of Recorded time:	35-	169-	169-
	2225	233	22	And all our yesterdayes, haue lighted Fooles	34-	168-	168-
	2226	234	23	The way to dusty death. Out, out, breefe Candle,	33-	167-	167-
	2227	235	24	Life's but a walking Shadow, a poore Player,	32-	166-	166-
216°	2228	236	25	That struts and frets his houre vpon the Stage,	31-	165-	165-
	2229	237	26	And then is heard no more. It is a Tale	30-	164-	164-
	2230	238	27	Told by an Ideot, full of sound and fury	29-	163-	163-
	2231	239	28 S	Signifying nothing. *Enter a Messenger.*	28-	162-	162-
	2232	240	29	Thou com'st to vse thy Tongue: thy Story quickly.	27-	161-	161-
	2233	241	30	*Mes.* Gracious my Lord,	26-	160-	160-

Angle	Play	Act	Scene	The Tragedie of Macbeth	Scene	Act	Play
	2234	242	31	I should report that which I say I saw,	25-	159-	159-
	2235	243	32	But know not how to doo't.	24-	158-	158-
	2236	244	33	*Macb*. Well, say sir.	23-	157-	157-
225°	2237	245	34	*Mes*. As I did stand my watch vpon the Hill	22-	156-	156-
	2238	246	35	I look'd toward Byrnane, and anon me thought	21-	155-	155-
	2239	247	36	The Wood began to moue.	20-	154-	154-
	2240	248	37	*Macb*. Lyar, and Slaue.	19-	153-	153-
	2241	249	38	*Mes*. Let me endure your wrath, if't be not so:	18-	152-	152-
	2242	250	39	Within this three Mile may you see it comming.	17-	151-	151-
	2243	251	40	I say, a mouing Groue.	16-	150-	150-
	2244	252	41	*Macb*. If thou speak'st false,	15-	149-	149-
	2245	253	42	Vpon the next Tree shall thou hang aliue	14-	148-	148-
234°	2246	254	43	Till Famine cling thee: If thy speech be sooth,	13-	147-	147-
	2247	255	44	I care not if thou dost for me as much.	12-	146-	146-
	2248	256	45	I pull in Resolution, and begin	11-	145-	145-
	2249	257	46	To doubt th' Equiuocation of the Fiend,	10-	144-	144-
	2250	258	47	That lies like truth. Feare not, till Byrnane Wood	9-	143-	143-
	2251	259	48	Do come to Dunsinane, and now a Wood	8-	142-	142-
	2252	260	49	Comes toward Dunsinane. Arme, Arme, and out,	7-	141-	141-
	2253	261	50	If this which he auouches, do's appeare,	6-	140-	140-
	2254	262	51	There is nor flying hence, nor tarrying here.	5-	139-	139-
243°	2255	263	52	I 'ginne to be a-weary of the Sun,	4-	138-	138-
	2256	264	53	And wish th' estate o'th' world were now vndon.	3-	137-	137-
	2257	265	54	Ring the Alarum Bell, blow Winde, come wracke,	2-	136-	136-
246°	2258	266	55	At least wee'l dye with Harnesse on our backe. *Exeunt*	1-	135-	135-

Scena Sexta.

Drumme and Colours.
Enter Malcolme, Seyward, Macduffe, and their Army,
with Boughes.

	2259	267	1	*Mal*. Now neere enough:	12-	134-	134-
	2260	268	2	Your leauy Skreenes throw downe,	11-	133-	133-
	2261	269	3	And shew like those you are: You (worthy Vnkle)	10-	132-	132-
	2262	270	4	Shall with my Cosin your right Noble Sonne	9-	131-	131-
	2263	271	5	Leade our first Battell. Worthy *Macduffe*, and wee	8-	130-	130-

Angle	Play	Act	Scene	The Tragedie of Macbeth	Scene	Act	Play
252°	2264	272	6 S	Shall take vpon's what else remaines to do,	7-	129-	129-
	2265	273	7 S	According to our order.	6-	128-	128-
	2266	274	8	*Sey.* Fare you well:	5-	127-	127-
	2267	275	9	Do we but finde the Tyrants power to night,	4-	126-	126-
	2268	276	10	Let vs be beaten, if we cannot fight.	3-	125-	125-
	2269	277	11	*Macd.* Make all our Trumpets speak, giue thê all breath	2-	124-	124-
258°	2270	278	12	Those clamorous Harbingers of Blood, & Death. *Exeunt*	1-	123-	123-
				Alarums continued.			
				Scena Septima.			
				Enter Macbeth.			
	2271	279	1	*Macb.* They haue tied me to a stake, I cannot flye,	122-	122-	122-
	2272	280	2	But Beare-like I must fight the course. What's he	121-	121-	121-
261°	2273	281	3	That was not borne of Woman? Such a one	120-	120-	120-
	2274	282	4	Am I to feare, or none.	119-	119-	119-
				Enter young Seyward.			
	2275	283	5	*Y.Sey.* What is thy name?	118-	118-	118-
	2276	284	6	*Macb.* Thou'lt be affraid to heare it.	117-	117-	117-
	2277	285	7	*Y.Sey.* No: though thou call'st thy selfe a hoter name	116-	116-	116-
	2278	286	8	Then any is in hell.	115-	115-	115-
	2279	287	9	*Macb.* My name's *Macbeth.*	114-	114-	114-
	2280	288	10	*Y.Sey.* The diuell himselfe could not pronounce a Title	113-	113-	113-
	2281	289	11	More hatefull to mine eare.	112-	112-	112-
270°	2282	290	12	*Macb.* No: nor more fearefull.	111-	111-	111-
	2283	291	13	*Y.Sey.* Thou lyest abhorred Tyrant, with my Sword	110-	110-	110-
	2284	292	14	Ile proue the lye thou speak'st.	109-	109-	109-
				Fight, and young Seyward slaine.			
	2285	293	15	*Macb.* Thou was't borne of woman;	108-	108-	108-
	2286	294	16	But Swords I smile at, Weapons laugh to scorne,	107-	107-	107-
	2287	295	17	Brandish'd by man that's of a Woman borne. *Exit.*	106-	106-	106-
				Alarums. Enter Macduffe.			
	2288	296	18	*Macd.* That way the noise is: Tyrant shew thy face,	105-	105-	105-
	2289	297	19	If thou beest slaine, and with no stroake of mine,	104-	104-	104-
	2290	298	20	My Wife and Childrens Ghosts will haunt me still:	103-	103-	103-

NUMBERED FIRST FOLIO TEXT 335

Angle	Play	Act	Scene	The Tragedie of Macbeth	Scene	Act	Play
279°	2291	299	21	I cannot strike at wretched Kernes, whose armes	102-	102-	102-
	2292	300	22	Are hyr'd to beare their Staues; either thou *Macbeth*,	101-	101-	101-
	2293	301	23	Or else my Sword with an vnbattered edge	100-	100-	100-
	2294	302	24	I sheath againe vndeeded. There thou should'st be,	99-	99-	99-
	2295	303	25	By this great clatter, one of greatest note	98-	98-	98-
	2296	304	26	Seemes bruited. Let me finde him Fortune,	97-	97-	97-
	2297	305	27	And more I begge not. *Exit. Alarums.*	96-	96-	96-
				Enter Malcolme and Seyward.			
	2298	306	28	*Sey.* This way my Lord, the Castles gently rendred:	95-	95-	95-
	2299	307	29	The Tyrants people, on both sides do fight,	94-	94-	94-
288°	2300	308	30	The Noble Thanes do brauely in the Warre,	93-	93-	93-
	2301	309	31	The day almost it selfe professes yours,	92-	92-	92-
	2302	310	32	And little is to do.	91-	91-	91-
	2303	311	33	*Malc.* We haue met with Foes	90-	90-	90-
	2304	312	34	That strike beside vs.	89-	89-	89-
	2305	313	35	Sey. Enter Sir, the Castle. *Exeunt. Alarum*	88-	88-	88-
				Enter Macbeth.			
	2306	314	36	*Macb.* Why should I play the Roman Foole, and dye	87-	87-	87-
	2307	315	37	On mine owne sword? whiles I see liues, the gashes	86-	86-	86-
	2308	316	38	Do better vpon them.	85-	85-	85-
				Enter Macduffe.			
297°	2309	317	39	*Macd.* Turne Hell-hound, turne.	84-	84-	84-
	2310	318	40	*Macb.* Of all men else I haue auoyded thee:	83-	83-	83-
	2311	319	41	But get thee backe, my soule is too much charg'd	82-	82-	82-
	2312	320	42	With blood of thine already.	81-	81-	81-
	2313	321	43	*Macd.* I haue no words,	80-	80-	80-
	2314	322	44	My voice is in my Sword, thou bloodier Villaine	79-	79-	79-
	2315	323	45	Then tearmes can giue thee out. *Fight: Alarum*	78-	78-	78-
	2316	324	46	*Macb.* Thou loosest labour	77-	77-	77-
	2317	325	47	As easie may'st thou the intrenchant Ayre	76-	76-	76-
306°	2318	326	48	With thy keene Sword impresse, as make me bleed:	75-	75-	75-
	2319	327	49	Let fall thy blade on vulnerable Crests,	74-	74-	74-
	2320	328	50	I beare a charmed Life, which must not yeeld	73-	73-	73-
	2321	329	51	To one of woman borne.	72-	72-	72-
	2322	330	52	*Macd.* Dispaire thy Charme,	71-	71-	71-
	2323	331	53	And let the Angell whom thou still hast seru'd	70-	70-	70-
	2324	332	54	Tell thee, *Macduffe* was from his Mothers womb	69-	69-	69-
	2325	333	55	Vntimely ript.	68-	68-	68-
	2326	334	56	*Macb.* Accursed be that tongue that tels mee so;	67-	67-	67-

Angle	Play	Act	Scene	The Tragedie of Macbeth	Scene	Act	Play
315°	2327	335	57	For it hath Cow'd my better part of man:	66-	66-	66-
	2328	336	58	And be these Iugling Fiends no more beleeu'd,	65-	65-	65-
	2329	337	59	That palter with vs in a double sence,	64-	64-	64-
	2330	338	60	That keepe the word of promise to our eare,	63-	63-	63-
	2331	339	61 S	And breake it to our hope. Ile not fight with thee.	62-	62-	62-
	2332	340	62 S	*Macd.* Then yeeld thee Coward,	61-	61-	61-
	2333	341	63	And liue to be the shew, and gaze o'th' time.	60-	60-	60-
	2334	342	64	Wee'l haue thee, as our rarer Monsters are	59-	59-	59-
	2335	343	65	Painted vpon a pole, and vnder-writ,	58-	58-	58-
324°	2336	344	66	Heere may you see the Tyrant.	57-	57-	57-
	2337	345	67	*Macb.* I will not yeeld	56-	56-	56-
	2338	346	68	To kisse the ground before young *Malcolmes* feet,	55-	55-	55-
	2339	347	69	And to be baited with the Rabbles curse.	54-	54-	54-
	2340	348	70	Though Byrnane wood be come to Dunsinane,	53-	53-	53-
	2341	349	71	And thou oppos'd, being of no woman borne,	52-	52-	52-
	2342	350	72	Yet I will try the last. Before my body,	51-	51-	51-
	2343	351	73	I throw my warlike Shield: Lay on *Macduffe,*	50-	50-	50-
332°	2344	352	74	And damn'd be him, that first cries hold, enough.	49-	49-	49-

Exeunt fighting. Alarums.

Enter Fighting, and Macbeth slaine

Retreat, and Flourish. Enter with Drumme and Colours,
Malcolm, Seyward, Rosse, Thanes, & Soldiers.

333°	2345	353	75	*Mal.* I would the Friends we misse, were safe arriu'd.	48-	48-	48-
	2346	354	76	*Sey.* Some must go off: and yet by these I see,	47-	47-	47-
	2347	355	77	So great a day as this is cheapely bought.	46-	46-	46-
	2348	356	78	*Mal. Macduffe* is missing, and your Noble Sonne.	45-	45-	45-
	2349	357	79	*Rosse.* Your son my Lord, ha's paid a souldiers debt,	44-	44-	44-
	2350	358	80	He onely liu'd but till he was a man,	43-	43-	43-
	2351	359	81	The which no sooner had his Prowesse confirm'd	42-	42-	42-
	2352	360	82	In the vnshrinking station where he fought,	41-	41-	41-
	2353	361	83	But like a man he dy'de.	40-	40-	40-
342°	2354	362	84	*Sey.* Then he is dead?	39-	39-	39-
	2355	363	85	*Rosse.* I, and brought off the field: your cause of sorrow	38-	38-	38-
	2356	364	86	Must not be measur'd by his worth, for then	37-	37-	37-
	2357	365	87	It hath no end.	36-	36-	36-
	2358	366	88	*Sey.* Had he his hurts before?	35-	35-	35-

Angle	Play	Act	Scene	The Tragedie of Macbeth	Scene	Act	Play
	2359	367	89	Rosse. I, on the Front.	34-	34-	34-
	2360	368	90	Sey. Why then, Gods Soldier be he:	33-	33-	33-
	2361	369	91	Had I as many Sonnes, as I haue haires,	32-	32-	32-
	2362	370	92	I would not wish them to a fairer death:	31-	31-	31-
351 °	2363	371	93	And so his Knell is knoll'd.	30-	30-	30-
	2364	372	94	Mal. Hee's worth more sorrow,	29-	29-	29-
	2365	373	95	and that Ile spend for him.	28-	28-	28-
	2366	374	96	Sey. He's worth no more,	27-	27-	27-
	2367	375	97	They say he parted well, and paid his score,	26-	26-	26-
	2368	376	98	And so God be with him. Here comes newer comfort.	25-	25-	25-
				Enter Macduffe, with Macbeths head.			
	2369	377	99	Macd. Haile King, for so thou art.	24-	24-	24-
	2370	378	100	Behold where stands	23-	23-	23-
	2371	379	101	Th' Vsurpers cursed head: the time is free:	22-	22-	22-
360 °	2372	380	102	I see thee compast with thy Kingdomes Pearle,	21-	21-	21-
	2373	381	103	That speake my salutation in their minds:	20-	20-	20-
	2374	382	104	Whose voyces I desire alowd with mine.	19-	19-	19-
	2375	383	105	Haile King of Scotland.	18-	18-	18-
	2376	384	106	All. Haile King of Scotland. Flourish.	17-	17-	17-
351 deg	2377	385	107	Mal. We shall not spend a large expence of time,	16-	16-	16-
	2378	386	108	Before we reckon with your seuerall loues,	15-	15-	15-
	2379	387	109	And make vs euen with you. My Thanes and Kinsmen	14-	14-	14-
	2380	388	110	Henceforth be Earles, the first that euer Scotland	13-	13-	13-
	2381	389	111	In such an Honor nam'd: What's more to do,	12-	12-	12-
354 deg	2382	390	112	Which would be planted newly with the time,	11-	11-	11-
	2383	391	113	As calling home our exil'd Friends abroad,	10-	10-	10-
	2384	392	114	That fled the Snares of watchfull Tyranny,	9-	9-	9-
	2385	393	115	Producing forth the cruell Ministers	8-	8-	8-
	2386	394	116	Of this dead Butcher, and his Fiend-like Queene;	7-	7-	7-
357 deg	2387	395	117	Who (as 'tis thought) by selfe and violent hands,	6-	6-	6-
	2388	396	118	Tooke off her life. This, and what need full else	5-	5-	5-
	2389	397	119	That call's vpon vs, by the Grace of Grace,	4-	4-	4-
	2390	398	120	We will performe in measure, time, and place:	3-	3-	3-
	2391	399	121	So thankes to all at once, and to each one,	2-	2-	2-
360 deg	2392	400	122	Whom we inuite, to see vs Crown'd at Scone.	1-	1-	1-
				Flourish. Exeunt Omnes.			

Endnotes

Chapter 1

1. In the essay, 'Time-Beguiling Sport.' Alastair Fowler, *Shakespeare 1564–1964. A Collection of Modern Essays by Various Hands.* Brown University Press, 1964.
   Alastair Fowler also analyzes the number structure of Shakespeare's Sonnets in *Triumphal Forms*. Cambridge University Press. 1970.
2. *Macbeth, The Merchant of Venice, A Midsummer Night's Dream, King Lear, Romeo and Juliet, The Tempest, Hamlet, A Winter's Tale* and *Cymbeline*.
3. *The Norton Facsimile of The First Folio of Shakespeare,* prepared by Dr. Charlton Hinman, Paul Hamlyn, 1968
4. See Appendix 1.
5. I was aware that Acts are regarded by some as merely decorative devices inserted in the First Folio to give it an aspect of Classical lineage.
6. We may note, in passing, that in Shakespeare's numerology, nothing is rigid; rather it is organic, with the laws of compensation, of balance, always at work.
7. $343 = 7 \times 7 \times 7$.
8. *Exploration in Shakespeare's Language* by Hilda N. Hulme, Longman, 1962.
9. *Macbeth, The Merchant of Venice, A Midsummer Night's Dream, King Lear, Romeo and Juliet, The Tempest, Hamlet, A Winter's Tale* and *Cymbeline*.
10. Perhaps John Dee, who died as Shakespeare ceased to write.
11. See Peter J French, *John Dee,* chapter on John Dee and the Sidney Circle pp.126–59.

Chapter 2

1. To obtain the magical number 2401, see Chapter 1. A.T.
2. The halfway point of the act-loop, sometimes referred to by Sylvia as the 'pit' of the act-loop.
3. It would also mean that instead of entering the small circle at line 80 — that is, at Macbeth's words 'Whose there,' when the servant and two murderers knock at the door — we would enter at line 82½, somewhere in the middle of line 83. Line 82 is 'Was it not yesterday we spoke together?' and line 83, which seems to be spoken by both murderers, is, 'It was, so please your Highness.' In the Folio printing there is one comma after 'was.' Clearly this is not a line which lends itself happily to being divided neatly in two.
4. The use of geometrical 'make-weights' (or 'counter make-weights') is known to have been used by Shakespeare in the geometrical/numerical form of the Sonnet Sequence. See Alastair Fowler's analysis of the Sonnet Sequence in 'Triumphal Forms.' A.T.
5. Most editors regard this as two lines put together and print the second half on the following line so that one gets a neat final couplet:
   > 10   Faire is foule, and foule is faire
   > 11   Houer through the fogge and filthie ayre.
6. This theme is taken up once more in Chapter 10. A.T.

Chapter 3

1. Line 41 is the scene centre and thus the axis on which the scene turns. A.T.
2. The lines being referred to are the following (A.T.)
   scene   52   *La.* What Beast was't then
          53   That made you breake this enterprize to me?
          54   When you durst do it, then you were a man:
          55   And to be more then what you were, you would
          56   Be so much more the man. Nor time, nor place
          57   Did then adhere, and yet you would make both:
3. It also appears in scene line 6 with 'But heere, vpon this *Banke* and *Schoole* of time.' A.T.

Chapter 4

1. See Appendix 3.

Chapter 5

1. In Act 1 of *Macbeth* we find animals, birds, plants and the idea of growths and life, but in Act 5 we see blood, death and despair.
2. See Appendix 3 for full comparison of sections.
3. See *Shakespearean Tragedy* A.C. Bradley, Macmillan, London 1910, lecture 10.
4. In this book, in order to make things as visible as possible, mirrored passages are often shown next to each other. The text on the right should alway be read from bottom to top, for it is in this way that the symmetrical relationships can be seen line by line.

Chapter 7

1. Additional support for this interpretation of the 'sev'nights' as 17 nights can be seen if one investigates further the number symbolism of 17 x 9 x 9. Firstly, it should be noted that the initial calculation — 17 x 9 —brings us to that most significant number 153. This is a number found in the Gospel of John (21:11) as representative of those fish caught in the miraculous catch of fishes.

    So Simon Peter went aboard and hauled the net ashore,
    full of large fish, a hundred fifty-three of them; and though
    they were so many, the net was not torn.

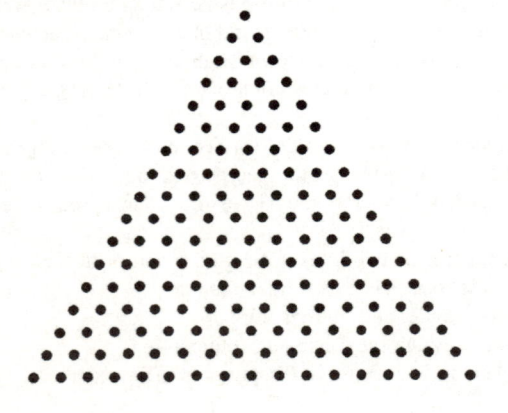

153 is a triangular number based upon the number 17 and traditional sources (especially the chapter on '153' in Pietro Bongo's *Numerorum Mysteria*, 1791) tell us that its symbolism is accepted by all sources to 'Pertain to the resurrection of eternal life' (p 593 *Numerorum Mysteria*). Alastair Fowler, in his essay 'Triumphal Forms (p.185),' speaks of this number: 'It had attracted many interpretations from the Church Fathers and from arithmologists, the dominant theme being symbolism of the Elect. By Shakespeare's time, most commentators understood the distinctive mathematical feature of 153 to reside in its triangularity.'

An enhancement of this number by nine would quite appropriately show us an attempt, on the part of the witches, to assault the 'eternall Iewell' of Macbeth:

    1003   Onely for them, and mine eternall Iewell
    1004   Giuen to the common Enemie of Man,   (3, 1)

This is a theme completely in accord with that proposed by Sylvia.

It should also be noted that Alastair Fowler, again in 'Triumphal Forms' (p.183–197), draws our attention to the fact that Shakespeare had already used the template of 153 (the triangular number based on sides of 17) to form the pyramidal architecture of the Sonnet sequence. (The Sonnets being 154 in number minus Sonnet cxxxvi which asks to be counted as none). A.T.

2. See numbered text for location of 'Wearie sev'nights,' starting at play-line 110.
3. Here is one instance where I would venture an alternative suggestion regarding the starting point of the 'Wearie sev'nights.' It seems more natural to start them on line 126, 'So foule and faire a day I haue not seene,' which is the line following the conclusion of the charm. This alternate starting point still allies us with the steps spoken of by Sylvia in the text, but it also gives us a new finishing point, one 16 lines further on in the text, play-line 1502, and one more potent in meaning and symbolism. Macbeth is now at the very edge of the cauldron and ready to surrender to the witches the remaining control and grounding he has in his own grasp of reality and destiny.

    1502   Though Castles topple on their Warders heads:
             Though Pallaces, and Pyramids do slope
             Their heads to their Foundations: Though the treasure
             Of Natures Germaine, tumble altogether,
             Euen till destruction sicken: Answer me
             To what I aske you.   (4, 1)

The line 'Though Pallaces, and Pyramids do slope' also seems to affirm the relationship the 'Wearie sev'nights' have to the triangular number '153' (see previous comments in Note 1 above) A.T.
4. The word 'Barlet' reminds us of the French word 'Barralet' which refers to the case of a time-piece, or a drum containing a measuring tape; an image perhaps of the *Macbeth* figure.
5. See Note 3 above.
6. Could it be that Shakespeare had a hand in the preparation of the King James Bible? (Adam Nicolson on p. 239 of his book, *God's Secretaries: The Making of the King James Bible,* [Harper Collins 2003] makes the interesting observation: 'Nothing in our culture can match its (King James Bible) breadth, depth and universality, unless, curiously enough, it is something that was written at exactly the same time and in almost exactly the same place: the great tragedies of Shakespeare … That is no chance effect, Shakespeare's great tragedies and the King James Bible are each other's twin mirror. A.T.)

Chapter 8

1. Sometimes altered to 'As thick as Hail / Came post with post.'
2. Oxford English Dictionary under 'saint' is included the following: '1609 Daniel. Civ. Wars I.1iii, And the vnconcieuing vulgar sort, Such an impression of his goodness gave As Sainted him.'
3. The gift of a diamond, traditionally a token of eternal and everlasting love, may only reinforce Sylvia's idea that Duncan has had, and continues to have, a sexual relationship with Lady Macbeth. A.T.
4. Compare *Timon* (looking for gold) 'Thou bright defiler of Hymen's purest bed...'
    Cymbeline II. 3
    She will not stay the seige of loving terms,
    Nor bide th'encounter of assailing eyes,
    Nor ope her lap to saint-seducing gold
5. We give in Appendix 5, the two longer passages that we have related to each other, laid side-by-side, (lines 541 to 620 and lines 620- to 541-).
6. Sylvia is referring to the words 'He ha's no Children' (4, 3. play line 1966) spoken by Macduff on hearing of the slaughter of his whole family by command of Macbeth. Note that this reference to Macbeth is not universally accepted A. C. Bradley for instance, in his book *Shakespearean Tragedy*, suggests that 'He' could also refer to Malcolm. A.T.
7. Girle: young unmarried woman. Second meaning cited in O.E.D. ('child' makes no sense in this context). ;

Chapter 9

1. T*he Library of Greek Mythology by Apollodorus,* Translation by Robin Hard (Oxford World Classics 1997).
2. Book 13. *Ovid's Metamorphoses,* translated by Dryden *et al.*
3. A 'lymbeck' was an old word for an 'alembic;' one of the glass vessels or retorts used in the distillation process. A.T.
    Alembic = An obsolete kind of still consisting of a gourd-shaped vessel and a cap having a long beak for conveying the products to a receiver; the cap of such a still. ME. (Shorter Oxford English Dictionary).
4. Evidence seems to suggest that the location of Macbeth's stronghold was at the eastern extremity of the Crown Hill, Inverness, and not at the present site of Inverness Castle. A.T.

Chapter 10

1. Sylvia was supply teaching at Michael House School, Ilkeston, Derbyshire in the early 1950s.
2. Rygg, Kristin, *Masqued Mysteries Unmasked*: *Early Modern Music theatre and its Pythagorean Subtext,* Pendagon Press, 2000.
3. from *Masqued Mysteries Unmasked,* Kristin Rygg
4. See Chapter 7 regarding the numerical significance of these lines.
5. *Shakespeare, the Invention of the Human,* Harold Bloom, Riverhead Books, New York. 1998. p.517
6. See Bloom, p.534
7. A curiosity in the stage directions of the First Folio shows the entrance of 'King

Malcome' at the beginning of the play (1, 2). Is this simply a punctuation error, or a humorous indication of the beginning of a new cycle?

8 *The Ninth Century and the Holy Grail* by Walter Johannes Stein, Chapter 5. Temple Lodge Press, 1988.

9 It cannot go unnoted that the qualities mentioned by Sylvia are in many respects represented by that great Elizabethan personality, John Dee (1527–1608). As a scientist, mathematician and occultist he was pre-eminent; over and beyond this he was deeply interested in the crafting of new navigational aids (he invented the paradoxal compass and the compass of variation which were to be of great assistance to mariners) so would have had the technical contacts sufficient for the manufacture of the 'figures' in brass. It may also be noted that at some point in his career he had patronage from the Earl of Pembroke, (see Ch. II Charlotte Fell Smith's book, *John Dee,*1909). If there had been a collaboration it would of course have been in the earlier stages, during the period of the forging of the plays themselves.

Chapter 11

1 Chiefly designed by Isaac de Caus and John Webb, but guided and inspired by Inigo Jones.
2 *The Herberts of Wilton,* Tresham Lever, John Murray, London 1967.
3 For example, Christopher Hussey in *Country Life* (May 1963)
4 Not four feet as Christopher Hussey states.
5 '1614. Jackson. Creed III. XI par. 18 marg. Universall absolute obedience unto men is incomparable with true loyalty unto Christ.

   1634. Sir T. Herbert. Trav. 116. Neere mountain Taurus in now a Citie both great and famous, yet incomparable to what she was in Ecbatan's time,' Oxford English Dictionary.
6 Of Penelope Naunton.
7 Of course, it does not prove it — the Golden Section could have been used to make the best of a bad job; but it is worth noting that the very shape of the room directly suggests this ratio, since the simplest way to construct it is within a half-square — that is, a rectangle whose length is twice its breadth.

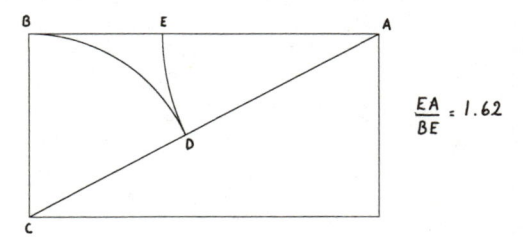

$$\frac{EA}{BE} = 1.62$$

8 In order to make this clear, both pages of the dedication to the Pembroke brothers need to be studied by the reader (see Figures 39 and 40).
9 See *Triumphal Forms* by Alastair Fowler. C.U.P.
10 His written works are known about, but lost.
11 We may guess that this early plan was held by descendants of the same 'grand possessor' who released it finally to Colen Campbell. It may be worth noting that in the same year (1717) modern Masonry was founded. One of the basic symbols is the square.

12 Probably the Single Cube too, for reasons to be discussed at a later date.
13 Sylvia was convinced that a search below the Double Cube room would prove fruitful (A.T.)

Chapter 12

1 Sylvia in fact conceived the solution during the course of a violent thunderstorm. (A.T.)
2 Also 200, 600 and 520 (though giving the awkward ration of 9:13, 13 lines to every 9 degrees).
3 A 'simple ratio' can still include numbers greater than 10.
4 What is true of all the comedies and tragedies in the First Folio that I have studied in detail, may also be true of the Histories. This field awaits exploration.
5 Sylvia sometimes referred to this as the 'pit' of the act-loop. (A.T.)

Bibliography

Aldis, Harry G., *The Printed Book,* Cambridge University Press, 1970.

Apollodorus, *The Library of Greek Mythology*, translation by Robin Hand, Oxford World's Classics, 1997).

Bloom, Harold, *Shakespeare, the Invention of the Human*, Riverhead Books, New York. 1998.

Bongo, Pietro, *Numerorum Mysterium*, Publisher: Bergamo 1599. Reprint: G. Olms 1983.

Bradly, A.C., *Shakespearean Tragedy*, Macmillan, London, 1910.

Fell-Smith, Charlotte, *John Dee*, Constable and Company Ltd. London, 1909.

Flatter, Richard, *Shakespeare's Producing Hand: A study of his marks of Expression to be found in the First Folio,* WW Norton & Co, 1948.

Fowler, Alistair, *Spencer and the Numbers of Time,* Routledge and Kegan Paul Ltd, 1964.

—, 'Time-Beguiling Sport,' in *Shakespeare 1564–1964: A Collection of Modern Essays by Various Hands,* Brown University Press, 1964.

—, *Triumphal Form,* Cambridge University Press, 1970.

French, Peter J., *John Dee. The World of an Elizabethan Magus,* London, Routledge and Kegan Paul, 1972.

Hancox, Joy, *The Byrom Collection: Renaissance thought, the Royal Society and the building of the Globe Theatre*, Johnathan Cape, 1992.

Hard, Robin (Trans.), *Apollodorus Library of Greek Mythology,* Oxford World Classics. 1997.

Hiebel, Friedrich, *Shakespeare and the Awakening of Modern Consciousness.* Anthroposophic Press, 1940.

Hinman, Dr. Charles, *The Norton Facsimile of 'The First Folio of Shakespeare,'* Paul Hamlyn, 1968.

Hulme, Hilda N., *Exploration in Shakespeare's Language,* Longman, 1962.

Huntley, H.E., *The Divine Proportion, A Study in Mathematical Beauty,* Dover Publications 1970.

Hussey, Christopher, Articles on Wilton House in *Country Life,* May 1969.

Kokeritz and Prouty (Eds.), *Shakespeare's Comedies, Histories and Tragedies, Facsimile Edition of the First Folio,* Yale University Press, 1955.

Lawlor, Robert, *Sacred Geometry*, Thames and Hudson, London, 1982.

Lever, Trevor, *The Herberts of Wilton*, John Murray, London, 1967.

Lundy, Miranda, *Sacred Geometry*, Wooden Books, Walker and Co., 1998.

Nicolson, Adam, *God's Secretaries: The Making of the King James Bible*, HarperCollins, 2003.

Ovid's Metamorphoses in Fifteen Books, translation by John Dryden, Alexander Pope *et al,* Heritage Press, 1961.

Rose, Mark, *Shakespeare's Design,* Harvard University Press, 1974.

Rosenberg, Marvin, *The Masks of Macbeth*, University of Delaware Press, 1978.

Rygg, Kristin, *Masqued Mysteries Unmasked, Early Modern Music Theatre and its Pythagorean Subtext*, Pendragon Press, 2000.
Shakespeare, William, *Cymbeline,* Cambridge University Press edition, 1968.
Shakespeare, William, *Troilus and Cressida,* Cambridge University Press edition, 1969.
Stein, Walter Jonannes, *The Ninth Century and the Holy Grail*, Temple Lodge Press, 1988.
Steinberg, S.H., *Five Hundred Year's of Printing,* Pelican, 1955.
Steiner, Rudolf, *Cosmosophy, Vol 1,* Anthroposophic Press, 1985.
Walker, Christopher, (editor), *Astronomy Before the Telescope,* British Museum Press, 1996.
Walters, David, *The Art of Navigation in England in Elizabethan and Stuart Times,* Hollis and Carter, London, 1958.
Wilson, John Dover (Ed), *Macbeth*, Cambridge University Press, 1951.
Wittkower, Rudolf, *Architectural Principles in the Age of Humanism,* W.W. Norton and Co., 1971.
Yates. Frances A., *Shakespeare's Last Plays,* Routledge and Kegan Paul, 1975.